SEX AND CLASS
IN LATIN AMERICA

Women's Perspectives on Politics,
Economics and the Family in the Third World

SEX AND CLASS IN LATIN AMERICA

Women's Perspectives on Politics,
Economics and the Family in the Third World

Edited by

JUNE NASH

HELEN ICKEN SAFA

J.F. Bergin Publishers, Inc.

Library of Congress Cataloging in Publication Data
Main entry under title:

Sex and class in Latin America.

Includes bibliographies and index.
1. Women—Latin America. 2. Sex discrimination
against women—Latin America. 3. Social classes—
Latin America. I. Nash, June C., 1927 — II. Safa,
Helen Icken.
HQ1460.5.S49   1980   305.4'098
        80-13644
ISBN 0-89789-004-3
ISBN 0-89789-003-5 (pbk.)

Published in 1980 by J.F. Bergin Publishers, Inc.
One Hanson Place, Brooklyn, New York 11243 USA

0 089789 987654321

Printed in the United States of America

Photographs: Pp. 23 & 215, Nancy Clark; p. 103 Marcie Jacobson.

ACKNOWLEDGEMENTS

The Joint Committee on Latin American Studies of the Social Science Research Council made possible the conference which brought together scholars from Latin America and North America. In the many months of planning for the conference, the organizers called upon the special knowledge of members of the committee. In particular, we would like to thank Bryce Woods, who facilitated communication with other scholars in the wide network of contacts he has made in Latin America. In addition, we would like to single out Michael Potashnik, Joseph Somers, and Oswaldo Sunkel for their particular interest and encouragement of the proposed conference. Until her departure from the Committee, Ms. Jean Swansen ably assisted us in supplying information and help in the Social Science Research Council Office. Lucy Gertner followed through with the final arrangements facilitating translations and publication. The Ford Foundation provided us with a supplemental fund to bring additional scholars to the Buenos Aires meeting. Robert Myers was exceptionally cooperative, not only in administering the fund, but in promoting a fellowship for the production of a bibliography by Mery Knaster, who has published a preliminary statement in the "Latin American Research Review."

In Argentina, Esther Hermitte took charge of making all of the local arrangements at the Torcuato di Tello Institute. Roberto Cortez Conde extended the hospitality of the Institute and welcomed the participants. We want to thank the staff, as well, for the able and patient handling of emergencies, facilitating communication among participants, and with the many Argentinians and other visitors who joined in the sessions.

We also wish to express our appreciation for the assistance we received from Betsie Hollant, then director of CIDAL, and other members of her staff who made many useful suggestions that helped us in our search for participants.

Finally, we would like to thank the other participants who made contributions to the conference: Hilda Araujo, Aurelia Guadalupe, Sanchez Morales, Virginia Gutierrez, Nora Scott Kinzer, Verena Martinez Alier, Irma Mazelis, Marysa Navarro, and Gabriela Videla Plankey. With editorial limitations and narrowing of the themes to the central ones of sex role and class, we were unable to include all of their papers.

CONTENTS

LIST OF TABLES

INTRODUCTION

The basic difference in viewpoints between women's movements in highly industrialized nations such as the United States, France, and Australia and those in Third World countries of Asia, Africa, and Latin America surfaced at the 1975 conference in Mexico sponsored by the United Nations in celebration of the Year of Women. While the U.S. delegation set a priority on women's issues exclusively defined, many of the women from Third World countries emphasized the problems of uneven development and the global political issues resulting from this. In the U.S. press, this difference was interpreted as an attempt to divert the aims of the conference from strictly defined feminist concerns.

Most of the women's movements in highly industrialized nations fail to realize—or even reject—the significance of these global political concerns for equality among the sexes. Since they are less concerned with the level of economic development than with women's share in the fruits of this development, they press for such reforms as better educational and job opportunities and greater participation in the political process. Although these are rights denied women in many Third World countries, their implementation—given the present class structure—would benefit primarily a small segment of middle- and upper-class women who are in a position to take advantage of these new educational and occupational opportunities and to participate in the political process. For these reasons, many women, particularly in the Third World, reject the demand for equality within a given structure of inequality.

Rather than treating the view of Third World women as a diversionary political tactic, we might well phrase the problem of inequality toward women as an aspect of the uneven development seen throughout the world. The "widening gap" (Ward 1962: Myrdal 1968) between the development of Third World countries and the highly industrialized capitalist centers is a corollary of a world market that has geared the economies of dependent countries to the needs of the advanced centers. In an earlier period these needs were primarily for raw materials such as oil, minerals, and foodstuffs; but now, through the growth of multinational corporations, Third World countries increasingly serve as the source of cheap labor and as a market for manufactured goods formerly produced and sold almost exclusively in highly industrialized nations.

The process of "uneven development," whereby economic growth in Third World countries benefits primarily the developed centers, also sharpens the inequalities within these countries by favoring a small segment of the modernizing elite while the mass of the people continue living in abject poverty. In this context it makes little sense to talk of raising women's status unless, of course, one is referring to a small segment of elite women who have been barred from the political and economic process solely because of their sex. In Third World countries, therefore, class inequalities take priority over sexual inequality, since only a basic structural change aiming at a more equitable distribution of wealth and income, coupled with the recognition of the needs for sexual equality, will benefit working-class women as well as their more privileged sisters. Even in the United States, the failure of the women's movement to take into account the persistent inequalities based on class has limited its appeal to working-class women.

The ideology of male dominance stems from a sexual division of labor in which there is unequal access to the means and rewards of production. In the change from a domestic mode of production, in which women shared the tasks of production, to a capitalist mode, the differential spheres of male and female activity have led to increased inequality, reflected in the attendant ideology. As several of the chapters in this volume point out, the relegation of women to unpaid labor in the home is the primary determinant of their subordinate status in modern capitalist society. It is not men who keep women at home—though they may appear to be the most direct oppressors— but the structure of the capitalist system, which benefits from the unpaid labor of housewives or, in wartime, draws upon this reserve labor supply.

The chapters in this volume were presented at one of the first conferences on women in Latin America organized by the editors and sponsored by the Social Science Research Council, held at the Torcuato di Tella Institute in Buenos Aires. Scholars from Argentina, Brazil, Chile, Colombia, the Dominican Republic, Mexico, Panama, Peru, Puerto Rico, the United States, and Venezuela participated, and represented a variety of social science disciplines. The papers presented at this conference have also been published in Spanish by Sepsetenta, Mexico.

Among the major themes that developed in the course of the conference were the interrelationship of exploitation by class and sex, the ideological reinforcements of sexual subordination, and the impact of modernization and development on women's roles and status in Latin America. These issues cannot be isolated, since, for example, any discussion of the impact of development on women's roles should examine the differential impact on women of various classes. Women's participation in public and private spheres breaks down the arbitrary boundaries patterned on political, economic, and social institutions, and calls for a new strategy in social research that relates the personal and the political, the family and the polity, for both women and men. For example, several of the chapters point out the failure of conventional social science literature to consider domestic production and reproduction in relation to total social production. The way in which woman's domestic image is projected onto her public role as a means of maintaining her subordination was brought to light by several authors exploring sex-defined roles in the family, in the community, and in industry.

As June Nash notes in her essay, a focus on women permits one to critique existing social science models of Latin American society and to question the established framework for analyzing modernization and development, class structure, and other contemporary issues of concern to students of Latin America. The dominant social science models often ignore the participation of women in economic, political, and social change, or interpret it merely as an extension of stereotyped domestic roles. This is true not only of liberal social science theory—such as Parsonian pattern variables or interest group analysis—but also of the Marxist emphasis on the exploitation in the marketplace while ignoring the exploitation of women in the home. Dependency theory, with its emphasis on the international power structure, has thus far failed to relate external dependency to that cultivated in the home, which reinforces patterns of subordination and superordination found at all levels of the society. Developmentalists concentrate on market indexes of progress contained in the GNP (gross national product), ignoring both domestic production within the home and decreasing participation of women in capital-intensive industry. Marginality theory often relegates women to the marginal sector of society, thereby obscuring the fact that women are integrated in the process of production as both producers and consumers of goods and services.

As a consequence of faulty analytic models and inadequate social indicators, the solutions posed by developmentalists often serve to reinforce stereotyped roles. Ester Boserup (1970) and others have shown how UN programs for change tend to send men into areas where they develop activities destined to improve the opportunities for men, often usurping roles carried out by women. Both private and public enterprises promote training programs that favor men, with the assumption that women's domestic roles make them less productive. Programs for women are often cast in volunteer activities that fail to change their dependency relations in the wider society. Cooperatives and self-management schemes designed to increase popular participation in decision-making often serve to relegate women to inferior roles. Stereotyped models of development and modernization prove to be ideologies instead of analyses of change, thereby reinforcing social structures that maintain sex and class inequalities.

It is not only in these areas that women have been relegated to subordinate roles. In intellectual and academic circles, and particularly in social research, women have long been regarded as the objects of social research, or occasionally employed as research assistants (but seldom as theoretical analysts). The responses to questionnaires sent recently to researchers in Latin America reveal that women are more aware than men of exclusion from some spheres of observation and participation, and have developed means of overcoming this exclusion by role redefinition. This seems to sensitize them to subjective factors in analysis and interpretation of data that are not taken into account as often by men. The woman researcher has, as a consequence, a double consciousness, similar to that of blacks or other minorities that suffer discrimination—an awareness of the motives and strategies of the oppressor as well as the inner view of the oppressed, who must respond constantly to the demands made upon them. This awareness is distinct from that of the "stranger" found in the sociological literature of the 1920s and 1930s. It is the view of the insider, aware of the subtleties of discrimination against a second-class participant in the arenas where they are dramatized, ideologized, and reinforced.

Women, as outsiders in the men's house of social science, are in a liminal state. The kind of perspective they develop in this state is not exclusively feminine; it is the response of any group that has been objectified in social discourse without having an opportunity to define propositions dealng with its own being. Anthropologists have become aware of the need for the critical perspective coming from an "emic" or insider's view as people from former colonies have entered the discipline or have criticized it from outside. The critique formulated from such an internal view helps to counterbalance the ideological bias in our models of society and provides a vantage point for viewing the limitations of social science disciplines.

A focus on women does not, therefore, imply an exclusive concern with women, but a new kind of perspective from which to view a variety of social science issues. The essays in this volume document the subordination and exploitation of Latin American women in three main areas: in the family, where a patriarchal structure and ideology stress the woman's primary role as wife and mother, catering to the needs of her husband and children; at work, where lower-class women are confined to low-paid, unskilled jobs as domestic servants, petty vendors, or unskilled factory labor; and in politics, where even the limited role played by women has been restricted largely to the elite, who promote programs such as voting rights, which often are restricted to literate women of the privileged classes.

In this brief introduction, we have suggested some of the areas where a focus on women helps to correct some misconceptions and distortions of reality: in clarifying the relationship between class and sexual inequality, in examining the ideological determinants of women's roles and behavior, and in critically questioning the assumptions about progress implicit in the paradigms of analyzing modernization and development. If this book serves only to clarify and focus some of these issues, it will provide a fertile field for further investigation.

REFERENCES

Boserup, Ester. 1970. "Women's Role in Economic Development". London: Allen and Unwin.

Larguia, Isabel, and John Dumoulin. 1975. "Women's Labor." NACLA, "Latin America & Empire Report" 9, no. 6.

Myrdal, Gunnar. 1968. "Asian Drama: An Inquiry into the Poverty of Nations". New York: Pantheon.

Ward, Barbara E. 1962. "The Rich Nations and the Poor Nations". New York: Norton.

———; Runnalls, J.; and D'Anjou, L., eds. 1971. "The Widening Gap". New York: Columbia University Press.

SEX AND CLASS
IN LATIN AMERICA

Women's Perspectives on Politics,
Economics and the Family in the Third World

1

A CRITIQUE OF
SOCIAL SCIENCE ROLES
IN LATIN AMERICA
June Nash

Social sciences disseminate understanding through models or constructs of the segments of social life they study. These constructs may
serve as analytic charts or as ideology. As new segments of the population enter the discourse, there is a tendency to open discussion on
the models that have served as tools of the trade. Such a critique began when colonized people entered the professional social sciences
formerly dominated by the colonizer. Now, with the advance in research
done by women, another critical approach is beginning. This essay tries
to assess the importance of the models in shaping public policy in development programs and the way in which the feminine critique of the
stereotypes reveals the ideological content of the models.

Recent investigations have revealed the extent of the distortion in
our understanding that results from omission of the female population
or from accepting stereotypes as fact. Political scientists and historians note the absence of commentary on women's political activities but
pay attention to women only when they fall into accepted stereotypes,
such as camp followers or housewives clamoring for more consumption
goods (Chaney 1973; Gueiler 1959; Jaquette 1973; Nash n.d.; Turner
1967). Literary critics, analysts of popular culture, and experts on the
family show how female protagonists are distorted to fit male stereotypes (Butler 1971; Pescatello 1973). Anthropologists have begun to focus on female culture heretofore treated as the infrastructure servicing
and maintaining male culture (Chinas 1973; Hellbom 1967; Murphy and
Murphy, 1974; Rosaldo and Lamphere 1974; Shapiro 1972), although they
have earlier studies in the discipline that have set the pace (Evans-
Pritchard 1963; Kayberry 1939). Economists and sociologists are beginning to take into account women's economic activity, much of which has
not been calculated in the GNP because it never enters the market; their
work reveals the consequent distortion in economic indexes (Aguiar
1976; Boserup 1970; Harkess 1973; Ribeiro and Barbiere 1973; Saffioti
1969; Smith 1973).

These studies suggest that the major conceptual formulations applied in the analysis of Latin America are similarly skewed by having
ignored half of the population. Some Marxist analyses have forgotten
Marx and Engels' dictum that the status of women is the measure of progress, and have treated exploitation only within the production setting
in industry. The fact that the women who service the work force and
render it available to industry do not receive a wage signifies that they
are outside the arena of exploitation by capital and consequently do not
have a socially recognized role in protest movements, as Dalla Costa
and James (1972) point out. Dependency analyses neglect the paradigm
of behavior appropriate to the relations of subordination in a world market that is reinforced in the nuclear family, where patron-client, male-
female, and child-parent relations provide the models for subservience
and acceptance of an inferior lot in life (Nash 1975). Development models are primarily concerned with women insofar as their reproductive and
consumption functions affect savings in the phases of capital accumulation. They have failed to devise a measure of the nonmarket contributions made by women, and as a consequence they have consistently
undervalued women's contribution to the productive process. Modernization theory assumes that man's status is the universal measure of
change and ignores the uneven progress for women in developing countries (Inkeles 1969; Kahl 1968).
        In short, social scientists have until recently accepted stereotypes
that have blinded them to the changing reality of women's participation
in the economic, political, and social life of Latin American societies.
This failure is especially dangerous when social scientists are called
upon to formulate public policy. Crippled by archaic views inherited
from colonial and early independence periods, the development programs
are designed with the male population taken as the activist sector and
the females as the passive bystanders. Even worse, men's view of
women's roles is imposed in Indian areas, where women have shared
the basic productive functions of the society with men.
        Social scientists have played the role of ideologues, sustaining
the notion of progress implied in modernization and development, and
perpetuating social structures constrictive to women's participation in
economic, social, and political life. Their "objective" analyses in fact
reinforce stereotypes of women as wives, mothers, and lovers, even
when these roles are acted on a stage where the props—the male as pro-
tector and breadwinner—are gone. Women socialized with male models
of how to perceive the world have contributed to the errors and fantasies
in the persisting mythology of sex roles and social structures. They
have proved their ability by conforming to the models of reality structured by established figures in the field and on the basis of criteria set
by men. These include making objective statements of social reality,
divorcing the personal perspective from the subject of discourse; elimi-
nating empathetic understanding from observation; and accepting the
terms of universal discourse without recognizing the particularistic

elements that influence the field of observation. By accepting these ritual rules, women became honorary members in the men's house of social science discourse.

As their numbers have increased and as the consciousness of kind has underwritten their sense of self, women social scientists have begun to question what anthropologists call the male models imposed on their discipline (Ardner 1973; La Fontaine 1972; Leavitt et al. 1975), or what sociologists call the failure of paradigms (Bernard 1973). They have called for a reassessment of the research methods in the choice of samples and conclusions, bringing into question the male bias in choice of problems, the pretense of universality in studies that often consider only half or less of the population, and the models predicated on one-sided perspectives. Current studies that bring women into focus are cultivating the binary view, neglected in the past, that most women share with members of oppressed groups, and that comes from what W. E. B. Dubois conceived of as "double consciousness," or seeing both sides because of the need to submit to the will of the dominant (see Leavitt et al. 1975). In order to correct our vision of reality, we must make sex perspective an objective part of our analysis.

MODELS OF SOCIAL REALITY IN LATIN AMERICA

Modernization

Latin American studies in the 1950s and 1960s were dominated by Weberian and neocolonial models of modernization and development exported along with the consumer products of North American firms. Progress was measured by indexes of energy consumption, of GNP, crude birth and death rates, and of some gross measures of cultural levels: illiteracy, educational attainment, percentage of radio sets, and so on (Vekemans and Segundo 1960, p. 88). Figures failed to reveal the distribution of income, the purchasing power of wages, or the domestic consumption and interfamilial distribution of wage returns. Even worse, there were large poverty-blighted areas and even entire countries that did not have even these crude statistics.

Development was the goal, a development predicated on industrialization and modeled on the Western drive to produce more and more useful goods in highly capitalized industries, even at the expense of a byproduct of useless people. Modernization linked to a philosophical assumption that progress is measurable in terms of a rising GNP and increasing consumption of energy resources has negative aspects in the depletion and destruction of natural resources and the wasteful exploitation of human labor. Value is assessed only in relation to those goods and services that enter into a market and consequently are assessed by narrow economic constructs.

The emphasis on market factors as an index of progress leads to a devaluation of goods and services that do not enter a market. In the process of modernization, women's products and services have been ignored, and in some cases eliminated from the market as their handicrafts yield to the competition of factory-made goods. Their services have been confined to domestic spheres that no longer are centers of productivity, as they were during the household stages of production. Excluded from the modernizing sectors of the society because of persisting domestic responsibilities and exclusion from higher-paying jobs, women's range of economic and political activities has been narrowed rather than expanded in the process of modernization. The putative widening of horizons assumed to be the correlate of modernizing societies when only men are taken into consideration, becomes its opposite with the increasing privatization of women's activities (Leacock 1972). Unmeasured by indexes of modernization, women's work is consequently devalued by those concerned with progress.

Comparative statements about modernization and the gains attributed to industrialization often take as their base line earlier stages in mature economies. Assertions of progress based on such comparisons ignore the fact that in the initial phases of industrialization, there was a process of debasement of labor in comparison with pre-industrial stages. Industrialization was not progress for the artisan left without employment and forced into proletarian dependency. Women, who were an important part of the pre-industrial artisan work force, lost a market for their products and were excluded from some of the new opportunities, ill-paid though they were, in the industrial sector. Thus the conclusions of Bernard Rosen and Anita La Raia (1972) that women in industrial communities have a greater sense of personal efficacy, enjoy more egalitarian relations with their husbands, place a greater emphasis on independence and achievement in the socialization of children, and perceive the world in a more activist perspective ignore an earlier period in history in which women fulfilled a vital function in agriculture, in gathering forest products, or in fishing, as well as in contemporary societies where household economies persist. As Wertheim (1964, p. 7) points out, "The subordinate position of women is, therefore, rather an urban phenomenon and widespread in oriental commercial districts. For rural societies, this subordination of women certainly cannot be taken as an omniprevalent characteristic."

The mystique of modernization begins with the Weberian assumption that the past must be replaced with the new, that the rational must supersede the irrational (equated with the traditional order). Karl Deutsch (1961) sums up this view of modernization as "the process in which major clusters of old social, economic and psychological commitments are eroded and broken and the people become available for new patterns of socialization and behavior." The key to modernization, he continues, is exposure to aspects of modern life through demonstrations of machinery, buildings, the availability of consumer goods in response to their being advertised in the mass media, changes of residence, urbanization, change from agricultural occupations, literacy, and the growth of per capita income.

S. N. Eisenstadt (1966) is an even stronger advocate of progress implied by industrialization along lines of Western capitalism. In his view of modernization as a breakdown of traditional ascriptive criteria of status, he ignores the sex ascription that continues to operate in most modern societies. Praising the advance in highly differentiated political structures, he forgets that women have less chance to influence decision-making than when more political activities stemmed from the household base. Extolling the spread of potential political power to wider groups, he fails to mention that these wider groups are associations of men that explicitly or implicitly exclude women from unions, political parties, and even cooperatives and collectives designed to gain greater participation of the masses in productive processes.

When we bring the oppressed sectors of society into this picture, we threaten the social structuring of reality perceived from a dominant elite viewpoint. Modernization cannot be equated with liberalization, universalistic criteria, greater rationality, and recognition of achievement so long as over half of the population is reduced in its spheres of action, participation, and rewards. We cannot assume progress and rationality in a system that must generate more propaganda and more appeals to archaic sensibilities in order to maintain over half the population in subordination. The Parsonian pattern variables of modernization are revealed as an ideology validating modernization predicated on private capitalist exploitation.

The differential impact of modernization on women and men has not been noted until recently because women have not been part of the interviewing sample, nor have they been senior investigators of the problem. Marjorie Gans et al. (1970) point out that Alex Inkeles interviewed 5,500 people in Argentina, Chile, India, Pakistan, Israel, and Nigeria, none of whom were women, yet their ON scale purported to be a comparative sociopsychological measure of individual modernization. Joseph Kahl (1968) perpetuated this error when he and his assistant interviewed 1,300 men in Brazil and Mexico, then titled his book The Measurement of Modernization: A Study of Values in Brazil and Mexico. M. Weiner's anthology on modernization (1966) includes only male contributors who deal with the male segment of the population. The only author to mention the "non-participants" (Wood 1966) includes "hardcore minority of marginal men, displaced workers and increasingly old people," but fails to mention women.

Unlike other segments of the population, women are consistently neglected in samples because of an assumed universalistic criterion that has men central to the system. It is not an oversight to exclude women from the sample, but a fundamental premise of a social science in which men are the measurement of change. When we take women into account in studying modernization, as Gans et al. (1970) did in their

interviews of 322 wives and 623 men, we become aware that women do
not exhibit the expected correlates of modernization. They lag behind
men in socioeconomic status, education, mobility, and occupational
choice (Gans et al. 1970). Excluded from managerial and productive
work in the modernizing sectors, they are likely to resist changes that
are interpreted as threatening. Since the objective conditions that make
for the conservative attitudes attributed to women are not analyzed,
these characteristics are attributed to the feminine nature, a mystique
of timidity and passivity. We must go further, however, questioning
the model of modernity itself and its failure to reveal the selective discrimination of the process in which segments of the population are favored or rejected in advanced capitalist industrialization.

There is one arena in which women are permitted and even encouraged to participate in modernization: as consumers in an ever more
elaborated scale of preferences and products. The consumer ideology
of modernization gives an illusion of progress and movement within a
technologically defined superstructure of revolution that is nevertheless
antithetical to adaptive social change, as Juliet Mitchell (1971, pp.
30-31) and Michele Mattelart (1971, p. 157) show. Women are the tar-
get of the consumer economics of modern business. By their constant
consumption of changing styles and trends, they maintain the rising demands required to sustain sales and profits. Women are, as Mattelart
shows, the consumers of the gadgets and styles that make them seem
the manipulators rather than the victims of modernity (Mattelart 1970,
p. 162). Even their liberation drives are absorbed with a consumer cult
in which the right to smoke Virginia Slims or redecorate a living room
in the latest mode marks the pinnacle of success. Women's function in
maintaining high consumption levels validates the productive infrastructure based on exploitation and denial of a productive role for them in
the modernizing sector. Male advertisers have finessed the threat of
real liberation of women by imposing their ideas upon the movement:
freer sex and greater consumption through ever more faddish clothing
to make women themselves a more desirable object of consumption. It
is no coincidence that a rising hemline was associated with rising demands by women for greater independence, nor that women's liberation
movements in the United States and Latin America expressed their first
protest against the use of women as sexual objects in the communications industry (Mitchell 1971, p. 37).

Modernity, or entry into the expanding consumer market of man-
made goods, is predicated on a development in which the goals are defined by the markets of the capitalist producing centers. Their films,
magazines, and television programs provide the models for stimulating
consumer interest on the periphery, creating needs where there were
undefined wants and unsatisfied aspirations, exacerbating the economic
dependency by means of an ever-increasing debt structure mediated
through the balance-of-trade deficits. Developmentalist solutions called for import substitution to check the flow of receipts from primary

goods back to the consumer markets of the center, but the markets they served catered to the luxury-consuming upper classes and put added burdens on the trade imbalance by calling for sophisticated machinery made in the industrial centers as well as imported raw materials unavailable in the new production centers. Even the lower classes became consumers of products unavailable or produced at great social cost in their countries: cosmetics, dentifrices, patent medicines, crockery, cooking ware—items that replaced indigenous products available at little or no cost before the invasion of foreign goods. The rising demand for foreign goods—ranked higher because they were foreign—minimized the market for local goods. Since they were often the products of household-based crafts, fitted in with domestic and child-rearing tasks, the loss of these low-cost productive centers increased the dependency of local producers on the mass-production market. The multipurpose, highly adaptive household productive system is the victim of development that concentrates on industrial settings in both rural and urban areas.

Women's work, which supplemented and sustained the family income and gave stability and a modicum of independence to the primary breadwinner, was devalued and, in many cases, eliminated. Nonetheless, the kind of indexes used to prove the greater rationality of the industrial system supported the development sense of progress. Because more goods entered the market, as household-based crafts were eliminated, the GNP grew and confirmed the choices made. When reformist pressures led to land reform or other measures that tipped the scale toward self-sufficiency, the falling GNP "proved" the inefficiency of the change. When, for example, the Mexican government in the 1930s yielded to demands of the peasantry to implement the revolutionary laws of 1927 on land reform, agricultural production fell—not because there was a lower crop return, as some concluded, but because subsistence agriculture satisfied the immediate needs of the producer and, as a consequence, was not tallied in the GNP.

Dependency

Dependency, cultivated on the world market as well as on the internal market, is a by-product of the shift from artisan and household production to industrialization controlled from metropolitan centers of production. The shift is particularly marked in its effect on women. Relying on the uncertain earnings of a dependent wage earner, their subservience is even more marked than that of the industrial worker. Dependency theory rarely links this relationship to the chain of dependencies forged in the international capital market. When the status of women in society is viewed only as an aspect of the domestic setting, their subordination to a male breadwinner appears to be a factor of personal oppression, not of capitalist exploitation. However, women commentators have demanded that the extension of exploitation by private capitalists be recognized in the domestic sphere. Flora Tristan (Desanti 1972, preface) summed up the exploitation of both working-class and bourgeois women as the kept servants of men of all classes thus: "The most oppressed man can oppress another human being, who is his wife. She is the proletarian of the very proletariat." When she broke free from French petit bourgeois family life in the early nineteenth century, she began to voice the suffering and needs of the working class. Her sympathy extended to the prostitutes, the beggars, the imprisoned women of London and France, left out of the formal Marxist analyses (Tristan 1959).

The dependent victims of industrial progress are still largely ignored by both radical and conservative male analysts. Mariarosa Dalla Costa and Selma James (1972), Isabel Largia and John Demoulin (1972), Selma James (1973), and Elizabeth Jelin (1976) reveal how women's unpaid labor in production and reproduction extends the exploitation of industry into the privacy of the home. The unpaid work of women runs up to 99.6 hours a week (Chase National Bank, quoted in Mitchell 1971, p. 102). More studies are needed of the costs to industry of dining halls and dormitories, and the time lost because of unstructured leisure, in order to assess the relative costs of servicing and maintaining a work force in the nexus of the family in comparison with commercial services. The family is implicitly recognized as a cheaper solution, as revealed by industrial relations managers' attempts to foster the nuclear family by subsidizing reproductive costs and direct payment to workers for family dependents (Nash 1975). At the same time, we must recognize that until there is a valid, socially recognized basis for domestic services, the contribution women make will not be assessed even by constructing market indexes of their input, because of its elusive quality. More important than the domestic services they provide, women serve as instruments of social control, as Julia and Herman Schwendingers point out (1971, p. 796), socializing the present and future members of the labor force to accept their roles in industry. They quote the early liberal ideologists of the family, L. I. Ward (1883) and W. I. Thomas (1907), who perceived women as a factor in social production whose management of the working-class men in their off hours decreased social expenses and improved the efficiency and functioning of industry.

The dependency status of women in the political and social life of the community and the nation reinforces the dependency relations at higher levels of integration. This stems from the material conditions imposed on women within the domestic unit and the social relations that result from them. On the one hand, there is the pressure on women to bear the major responsibility for life and death processes. Cut off from a social network where they can share these burdens, especially after their "liberation" from the extended kin group, women often turn to religious and political institutions to share these burdens. This factor, rather than an inherent conservatism, causes them to support the very institutions in which they are oppressed.

On the other hand, the workingman has less latitude to act politically, given the domestic dependents he must support. His vulnerability, multiplied by that of his family, reduces his ability to react to exploitation even when he is fully conscious of his class interests. The low margin of subsistence and the high debts deriving from consumer dependency reduce his chances for planning ahead, a feature often ascribed to personality or cultural factors (Lewis 1966) rather than to economic conditions. Despite vulnerability as the only breadwinner, I have seen workers in the tin mining communities of Bolivia resist their wives' entry into employment. Many of the technologically advanced sectors of the society as well as from governmental decision-making seems to justify this kind of analysis. However, if we accept the structural base of marginality as developed by Jose Nunn (1969, p. 201) and Rodolfo Stavenhagen (1970), we see the move toward permanent displacement by technology of large segments of the population from productive work that is intrinsic in the nature of capital-intensive industry penetrating economies that do not have the expansion potential to absorb displaced manual labor in any but low-paid service capacities. To include women as a category in this segment minimizes the impact of the theoretical advance they make in discussing the implications of monopoly capital over competitive forms of labor exploitation.

Further, to classify women's role in production and reproduction as marginal means that one accepts the distortion, implied in consumer advertising, that their fundamental activities as providers of food, health, and welfare are frivolous and the woman in her domestic role is a plaything (Mitchell 1971, p. 42). So long as these functions were socially supported and figured as the main goal of production in a household economy, women's activities in the home were centrally important to the total productive sphere (Camarano 1971; Oleson 1971).

The jobs that women perform in the modern sectors of the economy to which they gain entry—as secretaries, research assistants, communications supervisors, educators—have a kind of "reproductive" function, as Mitchell (1971, p. 37) shows. They mediate between men in the nerve centers of complex societies, seen but rarely heard, stimulating production over which they have no control, becoming consumers of the products they inspire but do not produce, and finally becoming "consumed"—petted, admired, and seduced—by the men who produce for them.

DEVELOPMENTAL SOLUTIONS AND FEMININE STEREOTYPES

Contradictory statements about women in development, some emphasizing their adaptability to change and others showing them as a force of stability disciplining men, reveal the inadequacy of our constructs for explaining personality, culture, and society. The contradictions stem from a mystique that attributes attitudes to an eternally

feminine character and ignores social class conditions and economic
factors. The United Nations Commission on the Status of Women report
on women in community development (1972, p. 11) clarifies some of
these factors:

> Experts in social development and change have noted that
> where women's organizations are active, changes are intro-
> duced quickly and maintained easily. Women are, on the
> whole, receptive to change for one explicable reason: they
> have usually more to gain by changes brought about by com-
> munity development than by clinging to the status quo. It
> has been observed, however, that rural women, who have
> frequently shown more desire for innovation and change in
> this respect than men, often lack the organizations through
> which to express this desire effectively. In fact, village
> women's associations, voluntarily set up for social devel-
> opment and welfare, are a rare phenomenon in developing
> countries.

The report indicates that in many countries, the role of women in
community development was not recognized until recently. Developers
continue to defeat the interest and enthusiasm women have shown by
casting them in stereotyped roles imported from the developed countries.
Many programs, such as the Better Family Living projects sponsored by
the Food and Agricultural Organization, have as their objective "the
maintenance of values and functions of home and family living and planning of a happy family life" (United Nations 1972). Even when let out
of the home, women are channeled into stereotyped roles, such as
stenographers and typists in urban African development projects (United
Nations 1972, p. 22), nurses and midwives in New Zealand (United Nations 1972, p. 32), or mothercraft and homecraft through UNICEF (United
Nations 1972, p. 31). Despite the valuable contribution the UN report
makes in revealing the status of women in development projects, woven
throughout the document are the contradictions implicit in Western
thought about women's place. Viewing their fundamental responsibility
as centered in the home and related to such areas as nutrition and sewing, it advocates a program that in effect permits women to enter other
activities only after they have completed these basic functions, much
as a cow is let out to pasture after being milked.
Frequently women are directed toward volunteer work, whereas men
are channeled into paying jobs in the development projects, thus reinforcing the sense that their work is, and should be, unpaid. Thus while
the United Nations (1970, p. 3) points to the blocks to women's participation—lack of educational training, vocational guidance, and counsel-
ing; traditional attitudes of both men and women toward roles; and the
division of labor in the market—its projects often reinforce rather than
do away with the inequality. Ester Boserup has shown (1970) how tech-

nicians sent in by development agencies are concerned with cash crops where men predominate in the labor force, while women's subsistence crops are rarely considered an important basis for improvement. Co-operatives, whose stated aim is to improve the general human welfare, succeeded in defeating an economically successful crop in East Africa because men received the money from the crops their wives produced through their control of the cooperative (Apthorpe 1970, p. 70). Anna Rubbo (1975) has shown how the Colombian ICA succeeded in decreasing subsistence crops farmed by women in commercial agriculture by urging peasants to cut down the perennial coffee and cocoa trees and to replace them with "green revolution crops: corn, soya, beans and tomatoes. The new agriculture, which was more technified and required the use of fertilizers and machinery, upset the ecology and contributed to single-crop cultivation, in which the risks are higher. Alberti (n. d.) states that in Peruvian cooperatives, a married woman is subordinate to her husband; but unmarried women occupy positions of importance. Orlando Fals Borda (1972) shows, in his review of cooperatives, that subsistence crops that are mainly women's work rarely are included in the purview of cooperatives.

The failure to take account of women's positive contribution as housewives is evident in Yugoslavia, where the government announced on International Woman's Day (New York Times, March 9, 1974) that under the new constitution promulgated in February 1974, housewives will not be eligible to participate in the political process at the national level, either by choosing federal leaders or by serving in such posts themselves. This was brought about by the provision of organizations of associated labor in which productive bases provide representation at each level. In response to criticism, Dr. Antun Vratusa, vice-president of the federal Executive Council, defended the system, stating: "You must understand that under our socialist system the object is not to have a traditional parliament in which each sector of society is represented. Our parliament has been designed to give the working class specifically direct control over government of the country." By implication, this means that women are not members of the working class and that their services are not a contribution to the society.

By separating out the differential impact of industrialization on men and women, we can learn about the system as a whole. Assumptions about progress must be assessed along with the economic vulnerabilities, and the political and social dependencies cultivated in government, the United Nations, and private industry. We learn to question progress that continues to widen income differentials and crystallizes internal dependencies.

STRUCTURAL MODELS IN LATIN AMERICA

The Family

The ideology of the nuclear family as the universal mode of sexual reproduction and socialization of offspring (Murdock 1949) and of the nuclear, patriarchal, male-dominated form as the norm in Latin America persist despite the rising frequency of female-headed households. When they do occur, they are characterized as matrifocal or even matriarchal, a distortion of the role of women in such circumstances, who bear the economic and social burdens of the reproductive nuclei with none of the rewards of social esteem and economic support given to the males who undertake such responsibilities. Persistence of the stereotype of male-headed families, despite the evidence to the contrary, makes women's entry into the labor force a contradiction to their definition of social being, even when they are forced by economic necessity to do so, as Gloria Gonzalez Salazar (1976) shows.

Goode (1963, p. 19) underwrites the ideology of the nuclear family as the bearer of liberation in industrial society, acclaiming the freedom it provides to the individual to choose a spouse, freedom from extended kinship constraints, and egalitarianism. He ignores the fundamental constraints imposed on a woman when she loses the support of her kin and is confined to the narrow social sphere of the connubial pair. Lacking the independence that homecrafts or extended kin ties provided in the past, a woman is forced to choose a spouse not for love, but in consideration of his earning power, and is irrevocably tied to him as increasing offspring limit her ability to enter the labor market. Gross assumptions that class position is equal for husbands and for wives, and that mobility is assumed to aid both partners, overlook the fact that the woman's movement is in fact dependent on her remaining tied to a male. Mobility for the male, particularly in periods of dynamic economic and political change, is often predicated on abandoning the wife who was the mate of an impoverished youth as he rises in national leadership and enters a new social class. In periods of rising inflation, men may gain increases in their pay that are not passed on to their wives in the form of housekeeping allowances, as a recent study of the British workers shows (New York Times, September 21, 1975).

Demographic Structure

The politics of demography in relation to rising numbers in the labor market, falling employment, and a declining death rate have overshadowed the basic human rights involved. Because birth control has been promoted by the United States through the Peace Corps, AID and private business, in many Third World countries it has been associated with reactionary attempts to subvert people's revolutionary movements. The argument is often made that underdeveloped countries of Latin America are not overpopulated but, on the contrary, have vast undeveloped areas where rising populations can be absorbed. Since these populations are posed as a threat to the aims of control by foreign powers, the control over births is cast as another expression of dominance. Contradicting the logic of this position, the conservative institutions of the church and state support the same negative position with regard to birth control.

What is not taken into account in either position is the right that women should have to control reproduction in the interest of their own liberation. Large families inhibit the political effectiveness of the lower classes, particularly of women, thus maintaining conservative and reactionary regimes. Rising population puts an additional burden on Third World countries, which serve, as Selma James points out (1973), as "massive repositories [reproducing] the industrial reserve armies from Port of Spain, Calcutta, Algeria, the Mexican towns of the United States border to the kitchens and bedrooms of the metropolis." At the point when young people become economically active, they are forced to migrate to centers of production, often to the metropolitan centers themselves to find work. The poor populations of the world reproduce and maintain the active labor force until it becomes exploitable to serve in low-paid production or service jobs.

Women experience in their own flesh the tragic consequences of what planners call "overpopulation," and what Third World people see as a systematic deprivation of their share of gross international products. When I was doing research in the mining community of Oruro, Bolivia, I saw that women deprived themselves of protein in the distribution of food, which they gave preferentially to the male breadwinner and to male children, and less to female children and themselves. A miner explained to me that women were in the forefront of the labor struggles in the mines because it was they who had to face the children and tell them that there was nothing to eat, and it was they who had to bear the pain of death from malnourishment or neglect when they were forced to enter the work force to help support a large family.

Education and Occupational Level

In all Latin American countries women have lower literacy ratings than men. In all countries they represent less than half of the population in third-level educational institutions (I. L. O. 1975); the proportion of female illiterates is on the increase and now constitutes two-thirds of the world's 800 million illiterate adults (New York Times, September 4, 1975). However, we cannot conclude that improvement of educational

opportunities for women will improve their ability to enter higher occupational ranges. Lower educational levels are a symptom, not a cause,
of systematic discrimination. In the United States, for example, where
a higher percentage of women enter upper-level educational institutions,
their professional ratings do not match those of men (Oppenheimer 1972).
Cynthia Epstein (1970) shows that with the enormous increase in higher
education from 1910 to 1960, women's participation in professions remained the same or increased only slightly. Academicians remained
constant at 19 percent of the total employed in colleges and universities; women lawyers have increased from 1 percent to 3.5 percent of
the profession; and doctors have risen from 6 to 6.8 percent. U.S. data
on comparable income and education for men and women indicate that
at each educational level, women earn from less than half to no more
than three-quarters of what men of comparable education earn, and the
overall proportion is 60 percent of what men earn.

The plea for greater educational opportunities is a quasi solution
for a structural situation that maintains women in subordination to the
male sector of the work force at every level. To give lack of education
as the reason for discriminatory status is to confuse agency with agent.
Limitation of entry into education is a means of excluding women from
higher statuses; the reason for their exclusion lies in the total social
construction of roles. In the lower classes, boys are favored education-
ally over girls, on the assumption that they are more likely to succeed.
Even when able to enter universities, women may not do so because they
realize they will have little chance to put their professional training into practice. However, although education cannot be posed as a solution,
it serves to increase dissatisfaction and thus to promote pressure for
structural change.

WOMEN'S PERSPECTIVES IN THE SOCIAL SCIENCES

Women social scientists are more willing than men to admit the influence of their personal perceptions and empathy with their subjects
on their choice of problems and analysis of data. Flora Tristan (1959),
one of the few women commentators of the past century whose words
survive in print, reveals the introspection that guided her narrative:

> In the course of my narration, I often speak of myself. I re-
> flect on my sufferings, my thoughts, my affections; all result
> from the orientation that God has given me, from the educa-
> tion I have received and from the position that the laws and
> prejudices have made me.

The products of male social commentators are characterized by mastery,
ego separation, and enhancement of self, as Jessie Bernard (1973, p.
782) suggests, in contrast with the work of feminine observers. Their

assumed universality is underwritten by the identification of humankind with "men" (Lenero 1976). Their questions are posed universalistically, even when their sample is exclusively male. Histories serve to crystallize values that are played out at selective points of reference for thinking about contemporary events. Heroic figures are those who carry out the exploits valued by men and recounted in their history. The histories we are taught in grade school provide us with the selective perception to comment on contemporary events.

We are now in a liminal state in the art of the social sciences. The values on which our selective criteria are premised are being questioned by people who were never before a significant enough part of the profession to challenge them. These include women and natives of the cultures scrutinized. Not only do they find the old paradigms wanting, but the very construction of social reality appears to be based on preconceptions that do not yield to a changing reality.

The search for new paradigms is now in vogue in Latin American studies. With the burgeoning of research focusing on women, one can hope that they will include both male and female perspectives in a stereoscopic view of Latin American social reality. The essays in this book are a step in this direction.

REFERENCES

Acker, Joan. 1973. "Women and Social Stratification, a Case of Intellectual Sexism, " American Journal of Sociology 78, no. 4: 936-45.

Aguiar, Neuma. 1976. "The Impact of Industrialization on Women's Work Roles in the Northeast of Brazil. " This volume.

Apthorpe, Raymond J. 1970. "Some Problems of Evaluation. " In Cooperatives and Rural Development in East Africa, ed. C. G. Widstrand, pp. 209-29. New York: Africana Publishing Corp.

Ardner, Shirley. 1973. "Sexual Insult and Female Militancy. " Man 8, no. 3: 422-40.

Baetjer, Anna Medora. 1946. Women in Industry, Their Health and Efficiency. Philadelphia: W. B. Sauvers Co.

Bart, Pauline B. 1971. "Sexism and Social Science: From the Gilded Cage to the Iron Cage, or the Perils of Pauline. " Journal of Marriage and the Family 33: 734-45.

Bernard, Jessie. 1973. "My Four Revolutions: An Autobiographical History of the American Sociological Association. " American Journal of Sociology 78, no. 5: 739-91.

Blachman, Morris. n. d. "Eve in Adamocracy: Women and Politics in Brazil." Paper read at the American Political Science Association, 1972.

Boserup, Ester. 1970. Women's Role in Economic Development. London: Allen and Unwin.

Butler, Cornelia Flora. 1971. "The Passive Female: Her Comparative Image by Class and Culture in Women's Magazine Fiction." Journal of Marriage and the Family 33.

Camarano, Chris. 1971. "On Cuban Women." In Liberation Now, pp. 364-76. New York: Dell Publishing Co.

Carlos, Manuel L., and Lois Sellers. 1972. "Family, Kinship Structure and Modernization in Latin America." Latin American Research Review 7, no. 2: 95-124.

Chaney, Elsa. 1973. "Old and New Feminists in Latin America: The Case of Peru and Chile." Journal of Marriage and the Family 35, no. 2: 331-43.

Chinas, Betty. 1973. The Zapotec Women. New York: Holt, Rhinehart and Winston.

Dalla Costa, Mariarosa, and Selma James. 1972. "Women and the Subversion of the Community." In The Power of Women and the Subversion of the Community. Bristol: Falling Wall Press.

Desanti, Dominique. 1972. Flora Tristán, la femme révolté. Paris: Hachette.

Deutsch, Karl. 1961. "Social Mobilization and Political Development." American Political Science.

De Vries, Egbert, and Jose Medina Echavarria. 1960. Social Aspects of Economic Development in Latin America. Vol. I. New York: UNESCO.

Eisenstadt, S. N. 1966. "Modernization, Growth and Diversity." America Latina 9, no. 1: 34-58.

Elmendorf, Mary. 1972. "The Mayan Woman and Change." Ph. D. dissertation, Union Graduate School.

Epstein, Cynthia Fuchs. 1970. Woman's Place: Options and Limits in Professional Careers. Berkeley: University of California Press.

Evans-Pritchard, E. E. 1963. The Position of Women in Primitive Societies and Other Essays in Social Anthropology. New York.

Fals Borda, Orlando. 1972. El reformismo por dentro en América Latina. Mexico City: Siglo XXI.

Gans, Margorie, Jose Pastore, and Eugene A. Wilkening. 1970. "A mulher e a modernizacao da familia brasileira." Pesquish o planejamento 12: 97-139.

Gissi Bustos, Jorge. 1976. "Mythology About Women with Special Reference to Chile." This volume.

Gonzalez Salazar, Gloria. 1976. "The Participation of Women in the Mexican Labor Force." This volume.

Goodale, Jane C. 1971. Tiwi Wives: A Study of Women of Melville Island, North Australia. Seattle: University of Washington Press.

Goode, William J. 1963. World Revolution and Family Patterns. New York: Free Press.

Gueiler Tejada, Lydia. 1959. La mujer y la revolucion. La Paz.

Harkess, Shirley J. 1973. "The Pursuit of an Ideal: Migration, Social Class and Women's Roles in Bogota, Colombia." In Female and Male in Latin America, ed. A. Pescatello. Pittsburgh: University of Pittsburgh Press.

Hellbom, Anna-Britta. 1967. La participacion cultural de las mujeres: Indias y mestizas en el Mexico precortesiano y postrevolucionario. Stockholm: Etnografiska Museet.

Inkeles, Alex. 1969. "Making Men Modern: On the Causes and Consequences of Individual Change in Six Developing Countries." American Journal of Sociology 75, Sept.: 208-25.

International Labour Office. 1975. Equality of Opportunity and Treatment for Women Workers. International Labour Conference, 60th Session, Report 8. Geneva.

James, Selma. 1973. "Sex, Race and Working Class Power." Race Today. January.

Jaquette, Jane. 1973. Women in Politics. New York: John Wiley.

Jelin, Elizabeth. 1976. "The Bahiana in the Labor Force in Salvador, Brazil." This volume.

Jusenius, Carol, and Michael Finn. n. d. "The Position of Women in the Ecuadorian Economy." Estudios Andinos. In press.

Kahl, Joseph. 1968. The Measurement of Modernization: A Study of Values in Brazil and Mexico. Austin: University of Texas Press.

Kayberry, Phyllis M. 1939. Aboriginal Woman, Sacred and Profane. London: George Routledge and Sons.

Kinzer, Nora Scott. 1973. "Women in Latin America, Introduction." Journal of Marriage and the Family 35: 299-312.

La Fontaine, Jean. 1972. "Ritualization of Women's Life Crisis in Bugisu." In The Interpretation of Ritual; Essays in Honour of A. I. Richards. London: Tavistock.

Larguia, Isabel, and John Demoulin. 1972. "Toward a Science of Women's Liberation." NACLA, Latin America and Empire Report 6.

Leacock, Eleanor. 1972. "Introduction." The Origin of the Family, Private Property and the State in the Light of the Researches of Lewis H. Morgan, by Frederick Engels. New York: International Publishers.

Leavitt, Ruby Rohrlich, Barbara Sykes, and Elizabeth Weatherford. 1975. "Aboriginal Woman: Male and Female Anthropological Perspectives." In Towards an Anthropology of Women, ed. Reina Reitter. New York: Monthly Review Press.

Lenero, Marina del Carmen Elu. 1976. "Women's Work and Fertility: Mexico." This volume.

Lerner, Daniel. 1964. The Passing of Traditional Society; Modernizing the Middle East. New York: Free Press.

Lewis, Oscar. 1966. "The Culture of Poverty." Scientific American 215, no. 41: 19-25.

Lundberg, Ferdinand, and Marynia F. Farnham. 1947. Modern Woman: The Lost Sex.

Mattelart, Michele. 1970. "El nivel mitico en la prensa seudoamorosa." Cuadernos de la realidad nacional 3: 221-34.

Mintz, Sidney. 1971. "Men, Women and Trade." Comparative Studies in Society and History 13, no. 3: 247-69.

Mitchell, Juliet. 1971. Woman's Estate. New York: Pantheon.

Murdock, George P. 1949. Social Structure. New York: Macmillan.

Murphy, Yolanda, and Robert F. Murphy. 1974. Women of the Forest. New York: Columbia University Press.

Nash, June. 1975. "Dependency and the Failure of Feedback: The Case of Bolivian Mining Communities." In Atti del XL Congresso internazionale degli Americanisti, Roma, Genova, 3-10 sep. 1972. Genoa: Tilgher.

———. n. d. "Women in Resistance Movements in Bolivia." In Women Cross-Culturally: Change and Challenge, ed. R. Rohrlich Leavitt. The Hague: Mouton.

Nunn, Jose. 1969. "Superpoblacion relativa al ejercito industrial de reserva y masa marginal." Revista Latinoamericana de ciencias sociales.

Oleson, Virginia. 1971. "Context and Posture: Notes on Socio-cultural Aspects of Women's Roles and Family Policy in Contemporary Cuba." Journal of Marriage and the Family 33: 548-60.

Oppenheimer, Valeria K. 1972. "Rising Educational Attainment, Declining Fertility and the Inadequacies of the Female Labor Market." In Commission on Population Growth and the American Future.

Pescatello, Ann. 1973. Female and Male in Latin America; Essays. Pittsburgh: University of Pittsburgh Press.

Ribeiro, Lucia, and M. Teresita de Barbiere. 1973. "La mujer obrera chilena; una aproximacion a su estudio." Cuadernos de la realidad nacional 16: 167-202.

Rosaldo, Michele Zimbalist, and Louise Lamphere. 1974. Women, Culture and Society. Stanford, Calif.: Stanford University Press.

Rosen, Bernard C., and Anita L. La Raia. 1972. "Modernity in Women and tan Index of Social Change in Brazil." Journal of Marriage and the Family 34: 353-60.

Rosen, Ruth. 1971. "Sexism in History, or Writing Women's History Is a Tricky Business." Journal of Marriage and the Family 33: 541-46.

Rubbo, Anna. 1975. "The Impact of the Spread of Capitalism in Rural
    Columbia." In Towards an Anthropology of Women, ed. Reina
    Reitter. New York: Monthly Review Press.

Saffioti, Heleieth Iara B. 1969. A mulher na sociedade de classe: mito
    e realidade. Sao Paulo: Quatro Artes.

Schwendingers, Julia, and Herman Schwendingers. 1971. "Sociology's
    Founding Fathers: Sexists to a Man." Journal of Marriage and the
    Family 33: 783-99.

Shapiro, Judith. 1972. "Sex Roles and Social Structure Among the
    Yanomama Indians of Northern Brazil." Ph.D. dissertation, Co-
    lumbia University.

Smith, Margo. 1973. "Domestic Service as a Channel for Upward Mo-
    bility: The Lima Case." In Female and Male in Latin America, ed.
    A. Pescatello, pp. 197-201. Pittsburgh: University of Pittsburgh
    Press.

Stavenhagen, Rodolfo. 1970. "Social Aspects of Agrarian Structure in
    Mexico." In Agrarian Problems and Peasant Movements in Latin
    America, ed. R. Stavenhagen, pp. 125-70. New York: Doubleday
    Anchor.

Steinmann, Anne, and David J. Fox. 1969. "Specific Areas of Agree-
    ment and Conflict in Women's Self-Perception and Their Perception
    of Men's Ideal Woman in Two South American Communities and an
    Urban Community in the United States." Journal of Marriage and
    the Family 31, no. 2: 281-89.

Thomas, W. I. 1907. Sex and Society. Boston: Gorham Press.

Tristan y Moscozo, Flora. 1959. Peregrinaciones de una paria; selec-
    cion portico y notas de Catalina Recavarren de Zizold. Lima: Tierra
    Nueva.

Turner, Frederick C. 1967. "Los efectos de la participacion feminina
    en la revolucion de 1910." Historia Mexicana 16: 602-20.

United Nations Commission on the Status of Women. 1970. Participa-
    tion of Women in the Economic and Social Development of Their
    Countries. New York.

_____. 1972. Participation of Women in Community Development. New
    York.

United Nations Economic Commission for Latin America (ECLA). 1970. Development Problems in Latin America. Austin: University of Texas Press.

Vekemans, Roger, and J. L. Segundo. 1963. "Essay on a Socio-economic Typology of the Latin American Countries." In Social Aspects of Economic Development in Latin America. E. de Vries and J. Medina Echevarria, eds. UNESCO.

Ward, L. I. 1883. Dynamic Sociology. New York: Appleton and Co.

Weiner, M., ed. 1966. Modernization, the Dynamics of Growth. New York: Basic Books.

Wood, R. 1966. "The Future of Modernization." In Modernization, the Dynamics of Growth, ed. M. Weiner, pp. 40-54. New York: Basic Books.

THE FAMILY
AND IDEOLOGICAL
REINFORCEMENT OF
SEXUAL SUBORDINATION

The family, though a much-studied phenomenon in Latin America, has seldom been analyzed as a primary agent for the ideological and structural subordination of women. At all class levels the Latin American family is marked by a patriarchal structure that maintains that woman's place is in the home and that she must defer to her husband in all matters relating to the world outside the home. At the same time, women are often forced to assume major responsibility for children born out of wedlock or from a broken marriage, so that the actual family structure in Latin America often contradicts the formal patterns of male dominance.

As several of the essays in this volume point out (Jorge Gissi, Maria Lenero, Heleieth Saffioti, Helen Safa), both men and women subscribe to this rigid definition of sex roles and accept it as "natural." Thus, by internalizing these values, women become agents of their own subordination and also serve to transmit these values to future generations. The family is seen as a refuge from the hostile world outside; and women are afraid to leave the protection of the home for the competitive and impersonal worlds of business, politics, and industry, which are considered the domain of men. Women are socialized to believe that they are privileged to remain within this restricted sphere provided by their husbands, and must in return obey men and cater to all their needs and wishes.

While this rigid definition of sex roles severely restricts the woman's authority outside the home, it does give her considerable control within the private domain of the family. She is primarily responsible for raising the children, particularly in daily matters of attention and discipline; and sons as well as daughters often feel closer to their mothers than to their fathers, who are seen as distant authority figures. The husband will not help her with household chores; but neither will he intervene in domestic affairs, where a woman is considered to have greater expertise. Thus, as Helen Safa points out, in the domestic domain, however restricted, women do have an area in which their knowledge and authority is respected.

While women enjoy a limited degree of autonomy in the domestic sphere, this authority is not translatable into social power or position in the larger society. The only valid status recognized by the larger society is that gained through participation in the public world or work; and occupation becomes the primary determinant of a family's social standing, especially in the new and mobility-oriented middle class. However, since men are considered the principal wage earners, it is the man's occupational status that generally determines the family's social rank. In the lower class, the lack of differentiation among largely unskilled occupations, coupled with the massive trend toward wage labor (largely poorly paid and unstable), weakens the man's role as provider and leads to a loss of his status both in the family and in the larger society.

This helps to explain, as Jorge Gissi notes, why the manifestations of machismo, or male dominance, are even more pronounced in the lower-class family. Since the family remains the single domain in which the rural or urban poor have any authority, however limited, the man is threatened by any attempt by his wife to exercise greater freedom and authority. Paradoxically, proletariat women have generally been gain-fully employed at a higher rate than elite women and often make a sub-stantial contribution to family income. The high incidence of female-based households, particularly in the lower class, reflects the growing number of Latin American women who are called upon to support their families entirely. Whether the man abandons his family, fathers chil-dren outside of marriage, or the couple agrees to separate, the woman is generally left with the complete responsibility for the children. Often it is the man's difficulty in finding a job and adequately supporting his family that drives him from the household. Thus, while the lower-class women are, at an ideological level, still dominated by men, at a struc-tural level they are often more independent than their middle-class sis-ters.

The continued impact of ideology on women's definition of sex roles can be seen in their attitudes toward work. As several of the essays point out, most women see work only as a temporary necessity from which they hope to be relieved as soon as they can find a man to as-sume financial responsibility. They still conceive of men as primary providers. Safa notes, however, that in female-based households, women are much more likely to develop a commitment to work, since a job is no longer a temporary expedient but a permanent necessity.

It is only among elite women that work can become a source of self-fulfillment, since they can afford the preparation necessary for a professional career. However, Gissi and Lenero note that even pro-fessional women tend to choose occupations that are extensions of their domestic roles—social work, teaching, nursing—thus minimizing com-petition with men in traditionally male occupations. The expansion of education for women and the growth of urban white-collar and profes-sional occupations, chiefly in the last fifty years, has led to a con-siderable increase in paid employment for women of elite status. This has not been matched by a parallel increase in employment opportunity or status for lower-class women, who are still confined to menial work as domestic servants, petty vendors, or unskilled factory workers.

Until the present population boom, it was sufficient to treat wom-en as a reserve labor force, to be called upon in times of need, such as war or economic boom. Women, particularly if they were married and had children, could never really be considered "unemployed" because they could always fall back on their reproductive role as wives and mothers. Now, however, women are being told to have fewer children,

which further negates their domestic role. Lenero describes the difficulty in trying to change the orientation of women who have so long been
conditioned to the value of their reproductive role, and criticizes population control programs that treat women as reproductive machines requiring only the development of a more refined technology (such as the
IUD). While working women appear to have fewer children, the data are
thus far inconclusive. In any case, countries such as Mexico, with a
labor surplus, are unable to absorb massive numbers of women into the
labor force. Thus, while more jobs and education for women are important, they are unlikely to have a marked impact on population increase
at this time, since the number of women able to take advantage of new
opportunities is still relatively small. At the same time, Lenero cautions
against population programs that emphasize solely the material advantages of fewer children.

In her essay Safa attempts to demonstrate how women's traditional
roles as wife and mother can be used as an avenue for their mobilization
and not simply rejected as reactionary. In the Puerto Rican shantytown
that Safa studied, there is a strong sense of solidarity among women,
based on mutual aid between kin and neighbors, that could be mobilized
around such domestic issues as child care, living conditions in the community, better education and consumer issues, thus drawing women into
greater involvement into the public domain. Given the limitations on
female employment noted above, Safa feels it would be a mistake to rely
exclusively on work for raising the class consciousness of working-
class women, who tend to regard their roles as wives and mothers as
primary.

While Judith Shapiro's essay differs from the others in this section
in its concern with indigenous Yanomamo women, it enables us to sort
out some of the features of male/female relationships that occur in nonmarket societies. Shapiro traces the subordination of Yanomamo women
to their structural position in the community, in which men, especially
brothers-in-law, have greater opportunity to develop cooperative activities (such as hunting) and ritual exchanges, thereby reinforcing male
values in religious and ceremonial life. In sharp contrast with the
shantytown women described by Safa, Yanomamo women lack a solidarity base for extending cooperative ties, since they are often separated from their kin groups at marriage and participate only minimally
in religious and ceremonial life. Thus, the women's social world is less
differentiated and offers less scope than that of men. All relations with
the outside world, which in the case of the Yanomamo are limited to
neighboring villages and the supernatural, are handled by men. This
presents interesting parallels with our own modern urban society, where
religious, political, and economic institutions have long been controlled by men, thereby reinforcing their dominance in the family. Thus,
while the structural basis for male dominance among the Yanomamo is
rooted in a kinship idiom, it results in an ordering of priorities similar
to that in complex societies.

A study of preclass societies such as the Yanomamo reveals more
clearly the structural basis of male dominance in our own society. It
is interesting to compare, for example, the isolation of Yanomamo wom-
en, working alone in their root-crop gardens, with that of the modern
suburban housewives, who also lack a natural basis of solidarity in
their communities and are forced to define their role in relation to men
as husbands or fathers. One could also compare the highly structured
world of Yanomamo men with that of the business world of the corporate
elite, who share their own form of ritual and ceremonial exchange (Domhoff 1974). Shapiro's analysis demonstrates above all that the subordination of women at any level of development is not to be attributed to
the female personality, as some other studies have suggested, but to
the structural features outlined here.

While Shapiro's data suggest that the sexual subordination of woman antedates the advent of class society, this does not negate the decisive impact of modern industrial capitalism in restricting the woman's
sphere of activity still further. By removing production from the home
and transferring it to the factory and other public workplaces, industrial
capitalism changed the function of the family from a productive unit, in
which family members shared the work as well as the fruits of their labor, into a consumption unit where the woman became largely dependent
upon the man as the principal wage earner. Except for a limited number
of poorly paid wage earners, woman's productive capacity was reduced
to a domestic role of housewife, whose contribution in terms of maintaining and reproducing the labor force remains largely unrecognized
and undervalued.

The present ideology of sex roles in Latin America supports the
modern capitalist class system, which benefits from continued female
subordination, particularly outside the home. Women serve primarily
as a reserve labor force, which can be called upon when needed at very
low wages, or used within the home to sustain a present and future generation of workers. They presumably are compensated for their isolation
and dependency by their primary role as wives and mothers, which both
church and state seek to mystify so that women do not become aware
of their subordination and exploitation. Patriarchal domination in the
home is supported by male control of the institutions in the larger society, with mutual reinforcement of roles and the values associated
with them in the public and private sphere. Viewed in this light, it is
difficult to regard the family as simply a private institution. Rather,
as Gissi notes, it serves as a primary transmitter and support of the
values and ideology of the larger society and the state.

The mythology of the passive female, who enjoys her dependence
and is afraid to achieve or compete in traditionally male areas of activity, serves primarily to legitimize the existing patriarchal class
structure and to obscure the structural factors underlying female subordination, such as the lack of opportunity for cooperative and solidary
groupings among women, their limited access to resources outside the

home, and their inability to control these resources to their own advantage. Dependency and passivity in women are the result of these factors rather than inherent characteristics. Changes in female personality require changes in societal conditions molding these personalities, including patriarchal domination in the home and class oppression mediated largely through males in the larger society.

REFERENCE

Domhoff, G. William. 1974. Bohemian Grove and Other Retreats: Study in Ruling-Class Cohesiveness. New York: Harper and Row.

2

MYTHOLOGY ABOUT WOMEN, WITH SPECIAL REFERENCE TO CHILE

Jorge Gissi Bustos

The social sciences long ago demonstrated the interrelationship among economic, cultural, ideological, juridical, and political phenomena. Consideration of these interrelationships is essential in order to understand the "feminine problem." Today, as yesterday—although to a lesser degree—there is discrimination and degradation of women in all the above-mentioned areas. This essay will be directed to the ideological-cultural aspects, since the socioeconomic situation is treated elsewhere (Gissi n. d.). However, the analysis of the ideological-cultural aspects would be incomprehensible without reference to the radically different conditions of life of each sex. To a great extent this situation is due to the division of labor, which has two related aspects. First, man's work is performed outside the home and remunerated, while women's work is the reverse. Second, when both sexes work outside the home and collect a salary, they perform different kinds of work and their functions are given different statuses and payments. The second aspect of the division of labor is derived from the first. The dividing lines have become subtler and have prompted many to speak of the "emancipation" of women as something already achieved. However, this second aspect of the division of labor also indicates the lack of emancipation for three fundamental reasons:

1. The majority of women in the world do not work outside the home, nor do they receive any remuneration.
2. Those who work are discriminated against in every way.
3. Ideological-cultural aspects are maintained by both sexes and derive from the first and more radical aspect of the division of labor, thus obscuring a critical view of the condition of women (and of (men).

This article is part of an unpublished, more comprehensive work that tries to show the relationship between theory and empirical studies.

I will concentrate on this third aspect. How and why do men and women hold and practice myths about women (and men)? The dominant view held in the world, and most particularly in Latin America, is the masculine one. The ideological-cultural dominance of the male is closely tied to his economic, legislative, and political control. The male idea of himself as superior to women I shall call "machismo." This ideology does not pertain only to ideas, but also to habits and a daily life regulated by it. In this sense ideology implies a certain culture; and that culture, as a way of life, implies ideas—a certain world view. That is why frequently I will use ideological-cultural as a single concept. Although the term "ideological" may be used alone, it should be interpreted in the cultural context; ideologies about the sexes are the particular expression of a vision of society and of the world that transcends both sexes. This is a fundamental outlook that should not be forgotten.

Many women are "machistas," consciously or unconsciously. This ideology of woman with regard to herself keeps her oppressed or dominated because she honors the habits and beliefs that are opposed to her self-realization, thus confining the expression of her potential within the narrow limits imposed by the dominant machista ideology. There are similarities between male and female ideologies, but similarity does not mean equality. Indeed, although both sexes believe that men are better at abstract thought, or make better leaders, this belief is lived differently by each sex. Different life situations condition important differences in outlook and justify our speaking of tight dialectic relationships between the female and male machista ideologies, both of which are related to the life situations of the sexes in all other aspects.

THE IDEOLOGICAL-CULTURAL SITUATION

The sexes are divided in all aspects, including the ideological-cultural, as a result of the original division of labor. The male legislates and controls political and economic power, as well as presenting (as a general rule, unconsciously) his dominant ideology as "the truth." Like other social groups, the male sex is "forced, in order to secure his aims, to state his interests as the common interest of society. In other words, to present his ideas in universal form and state them as the only rational and universally valid ones." (Bottomore-Rubel 1967, p. 101). This situation makes it "normal" for men and women to believe that "a woman should not work," "that she should obey," and so on.

In most of Western society there is an economic, juridical, and ideological displacement of women and the family with respect to other institutions. Because of this displacement she does not collect a salary and is not legally equal, and ideologically both sexes are not considered to be equally "apt" (be this view explicit and conscious or subtle and unconscious).

Within this framework the family, and particularly woman, constitute an active and efficient force against change in women and the family. Family, as a "private" world is a shelter from man's "public" problems. Similarly, religion, considered as something "spiritual," was and is—in its alienated form—a shelter from material problems (Lahve, no date available).

However, a family is not a "private" institution; on the contrary, it is one of society's fundamental ideological-cultural transmitters. Besides, "whether the institutions that transmit are public or private is not important, what is important is how they function. 'Private' institutions may perfectly 'function' as the ideological apparatus of the state" (Althusser 1970). Thus, what is considered "private, intimate and spiritual" is functional in maintaining given social relations, since oppressive ideologies accept the status as "natural" and reproduce it.

The primary agent in this ideological-cultural transmission is the family, for it has charge of the child at the most malleable age. As David Cooper (1972, p. 10) points out:

> In any exploiting society the family reinforces the effective power of the ruling class, providing a paradigmatic tool easily controlled by all social institutions. Thus, we find the family structure duplicated in the social structure of the factory, the union, the school (grade and high school), the university, big business, the church, political parties and the government machinery, mental and general hospitals, etc.

My hypothesis is that there exists a dialectic between woman, the family, and society. The cultural repression of women has particular economic, political, intellectual, emotional, and sexual implications. The problem is transformed into a vicious circle when the repressed woman also becomes a repressor. Carlos Castilla del Pino (1971, p. 71) states this proposition as follows:

> Woman is repressed and she assimilates, to a lesser or higher degree, her apprenticeships so that her "sublime" function of motherhood with all the attributes, including those of the "ideal woman" (with which we are presented annually) becomes the establishment's primary tool of repression.

In this manner, the domination of the family is transmitted in particular ways to the sexes and the different social classes. Cooper (1972, p. 31) makes explicit that process by which women and family exert repression:

> Characteristically the family indoctrinates children to become a certain kind of son or daughter (later on husband,

wife, father, mother), giving them a totally imposed liberty
minutely circumscribed, allowing them to move through the
narrow interstices of a rigid net of relationships.

Although the family has always been recognized as a socializing
agent, and for the past century recognized as having the greatest psychological influence, it has been almost totally unresearched as an
authoritarian institution, with the exception of a few clinical studies
operating within a psychological framework. There are more critical
studies with a social perspective about mass media, school, and religion than about the family. This is not accidental, but the result of a
logic inherent in the dominant culture. The closer we are to it, the less
clear it becomes. Louis Althusser (1970, p. 123) has said, "Ideology
never says, 'I am ideological'"; but T. Adorno and N. Horkheimer
(1969, pp. 131, 138) saw it clearly:

> As one of the most important educational powers, the family
> assumes the task of reproducing the characteristics demanded
> by social life, investing it with the indispensable capacity
> of behaving in accordance to the specific authoritarianism
> upon which depends in great measure the survival of the bour-
> geois civil order. . . . In this manner, the child bases his
> own moral attitudes, and therefore his own conscience, on
> the dominant father figure and finally learns to live from the
> parent he perceives as effectively existent, learning also the
> bourgeois relationship to authority not only within the partial
> sphere of the family. The family has turned into an entity
> through which the society operates, aside from providing
> education for proper social behavior. Thus it shaped men the
> way they had to be to undertake the tasks prescribed by the
> social system.

In this manner, the authoritarian family creates the "authoritarian
personality" (Adorno and Horkheimer 1969, Chapter 11) and vice versa;
both are functions of and reproduce an authoritarian social system.
Freud demonstrated that the superego is primarily the external authority,
which is later internalized but always heteronomous, and that the family is central to its creation. In this manner, he stated, the superego
"becomes the 'carrier of tradition.'" (quoted in Fromm 1972, p. 190).
Later Fromm writes (1972, pp. 237-38): "Another factor must be added
to this, based on society's patriarchal authoritarian structure. Women
are always the weaker in this society and as the sadist normally hates
and despises the weak, his attitude toward women becomes hostile and
cruel." In machismo, as will be shown, aggressivity is frequent. Dia-
lectically, women "conform." "In any event we see that dependency
and obedience are looked upon by some men as purely positive attributes (and by some women, I will add) even within their conscience,

while for others this dependency is one of the most disgusting and un-
pleasant existent" (Fromm 1972, p. 234).

Thus, these dynamics have been applied, and are being applied,
for the domination of the sexes and races. The superego mediates the
dominating ideologies. Freud emphasized sex because it was the most
repressed factor within the Victorian culture. We only have to think
about sex's relationship with religion, as one of its most important
agents, and the remains of feudal ideology during Victorian times (and
even today). Sexual repression also continues today, even when heavily
disguised, having an effect on domination of women and of other groups.
Yet if sexual repression appeared to be only a psychological and sexual
problem, further reflection has invested it with another dimension. Freud
blamed parents and culture in the abstract, but later Reich (1969, p. 96)
was more sociological and dialectical, asking himself, "What interest
does society have in sexual repression?"

Interest focused on socialization in and for frustration, limiting the
"pleasure principle" in favor of the "reality principle": the adaptation
to pain, to masochism. I will return later to this "reality principle," to
the general and sexual frustration of women vis-a-vis men.

I believe we should revise some of these theories in the light of
empirical research, especially as they refer to the Chilean situation.

CULTURE AND IDEOLOGY ABOUT WOMEN IN CHILE

The Machista Ideology in Men

As I have extensively written elsewhere (Gissi n. d.), the division
of the sexes evolved into the division of labor, which relegated women
to work at home and men to work outside, thus creating a complex ideological and legal superstructure that legitimized this division and the
discrimination it implies. This superstructure is perpetuated by presenting as natural many characteristics pertaining to both sexes, which
are real but basically result from the division of labor and its deriva-
tives. These characteristics are not a principal cause of the division
of labor, as both men and women believe. As a result of this division,
man granted himself more rights than duties and to woman, who in general consents, he gave more duties than rights. One of the classical
forms of Western machismo was the "patria potestad." Its definition in
Fairchild's Sociological Dictionary reads as follows: "Expression of
Roman origin which refers to the father's rights upon the members of his
family . . . including his slaves. These rights were recognized by the
Law of the Twelve Tablets (450 B. C.) and they were almost absolute,
including life and death. The power of the pater familias over the sons
was limited only in one aspect: before condemning an offspring to

slavery or death a family council formed by the adult members of the clan (or 'the extended family') had to be convened. The son remained under the patria potestad as long as his father was alive . . ." (FCE 1966, p. 212). Doubtless this is not the general situation today, but some of its aspects remain.

Let us examine some of the current ideological manifestations of machismo in Chile.

Housework

Says a factory worker, "My husband does not even rinse a cup. If he drinks coffee, when I come home I find the dirty cup; if he gets breakfast, takes out another cup and it also stays dirty" (Ribeiro and Barbieri 1973, p. 185). When the journalist Maria Elena Richard (Cenfa 1973) asked slum dweller Edelmira Sanchez if the woman is helped at home, she answered, "In my particular case yes. . . . But this happens rarely among working families . . . there are very few husbands like mine . . . man lacks conscience in this respect. . . ."

Yet the results of Michele and Armand Mattelart's research involving men from diverse social levels are even clearer (1970, pp. 131-33). When men are asked to describe the "ideal woman," a college student says, "should be devoted to the home", "I wish she were a loving mother"; a clerk, "a housewife concerned with the welfare of husband and children"; a factory worker, "home-loving and concerned only with her home"; a peasant, "concerned only with home and children, good housemaker, dinner should be ready when I get home." The Mattelarts conclude (1970, p. 159): "In short, as far as young men's concepts of the relationships inside the home, woman's traditional role of wife and mother dominates all social levels. However, it would seem to be retreating among students and white collar employees."

This decrease in the traditional role of women as seen by the young is very weak, though, as we can see when they continue: "Aside from a very reduced proportion of university students (4%) the awareness about the eventual need women might have of professional achievement, or at least of working outside home, is absolutely absent from the sample. . . ."

Male Superiority

Male superiority presents itself under intellectual, physical, and characterological aspects. For example, women are considered less able to undertake responsible chores. This idea is expressed below by a businessman, although he begins by apparently disagreeing with the dominant ideology, as is often the case with the disguised "modern" machismo: "I think women are as capable or more than men in handling certain chores, especially when refering to guidance and planning; but I am not so sure regarding personnel management . . ." (Ribeiro and

Barbieri 1973, p. 188). Another opinion follows the same style: "Naturally, women would not be accepted in those positions involving the management of great numbers of masculine personnel under them. I don't know if this would be due to prejudice or lack of experience" (Ribeiro and Barbieri 1973, p. 189). In any event, the answers from the different social classes to another investigation by the Mattelarts (1968, p. 124) are unmistakable:

Lower class: "Women are inferior."
Lower class: "They cannot be as independent as men."
Upper class: "Unable to perform executive duties."
Upper class: "Due to psychological conditions they are just not capable."
Upper middle class: "Man's character is more compatible with an executive position."
Lower middle class: "Women, due to their feminine condition, to their shyness, cannot face up to difficult situations."

These quotes, gathered through empirical research, demonstrate the clear definition of the machista ideology of the Chilean man, regardless of his social class.

Authoritarianism

The dominant ideology of men is that nature has given authority to them and they act accordingly: Even to attend the school mothers' meeting or the community meetings, a wife must have her husband's permission. They are not allowed to go out without their husbands' consent. In our social class it is like that," comments a slum dweller. She continues, "Women are mistreated. Men think they are, how can I say it, almost kings, that they have to be waited on and pampered in everything. Even to the point of demanding more attention than the children" (Cenfa 1973, pp. 63-64). Parallel to this male authoritarianism practiced by men is a feeling of submission on the part of many women. For example, in another study (Rojas et al. 1973) it was found that the women slum dwellers of Santiago, Chile, accept that "men have the right to punish corporally the disobedience of their wife and children." The authors comment, "Women seem to feel a certain degree of pride and pleasure regarding this situation" (p. 58).

Returning to men's ideology, the Mattelarts (1970, p. 149) state:

The fundamental differences between the sexes are the main argument used by the young workers of both sexes to justify the existence and maintenance of a drastically separated status of men and women and to deny women access to the same rights enjoyed by men . . . The attachment to the tra-

ditional image of women reflected in an implicit model of relationships between the sexes which could be upset in the
event of equal rights to both sexes, has a higher importance
in the office workers and factory workers categories. Especially among the former, this preoccupation with the effects of moral degeneration is related to the apprehension of
losing the advantages of feminine submission given in exchange for masculine protection.

A factory worker says, "They get uppity." Another factory worker adds, "If men and women have equal rights,
women will abuse men which will bring about trouble."

These quotations clearly reveal the relationship among the feelings
of discrimination, authoritarianism, insecurity, and fear held by the
"macho" man. The previously quoted slum dweller expresses it clearly,
explaining man's opposition to work and study for women: "Most men
do not like the idea. They believe that the woman who goes to work
does it because she is cheating on her husband." And talking about
schooling: "They disagree completely on that. I can see it in my own
husband. . . . Why? Because men are afraid that if a woman learns
she may turn out to be better than they are and become superior, which
they dislike profoundly" (Cenfa 1973, p. 65).

According to another study, men have denied working positions to
women in France, Yugoslavia, and Chile (Covarrubias and Munoz 1972,
p. 15). Man's fear, linked to authoritarianism, was also expressed to
the Mattelarts (1968, p. 120). If the woman works, one man stated,
"a rivalry between man and woman results." Another asserted, "Wom-
en become independent and they lost respect for their husband." Both
are statements of middle-class respondents. In all social classes more
negative developments are anticipated if the woman works outside the
home (Mattelart 1968, p. 118; Rojas et al. 1973, p. 66). In Quebec,
Gerald Fortin (1971, p. 237) found the same attitudes:

The great majority of husbands are opposed to the wife's
work, regardless of whether or not they have children, and
the children's ages . . . the only way to maintain a woman's
fidelity is through economic dependence. . . . to allow a
wife to work is to confess publicly to not being a man. . . .
Work removes women from the husband's authority (she becomes independent) and at the same time deprives him of the
most important proof of his masculinity. . . . He cannot
expect to awake admiration or love in his wife. . . .

This shows clearly the superimposition of the economic over the psychological sexual variables. It also demonstrates plainly that male potency
in these areas is dependent on the guaranteed impotence of women in
the same areas.

Thus, machismo appears to be both a defense and a compensation. It would be very interesting to know to what measure it is a refuge for the man's insecurity outside the home, especially for lower-class men. In such cases, one also wonders how and when it relates to a global social view, also of an authoritarian type (Gissi n. d.), inasmuch as machismo expresses a fear to lose (or not to have) sexual potency ("if she goes out, she will cheat on her husband"), economic potency (she becomes "uppity"), and/or intellectual potency ("may become superior to men . . ."). If this were the case, machismo would be an essential compensation for men of the lower class and, therefore, necessary for current social stability. The verticality in the family will have a dialectical relationship with the verticality of society. This should be researched further. Meanwhile, the above quotations should not surprise us: Proudhon (Cuvillier 1939, p. 66) had also fears and prejudices: "How fortunate he is, his wife is not such a fool that she cannot prepare a good stew, neither is she so intelligent that she can discuss his writings."

Machismo and the Church

We know that St. Peter said, "The husband is the head of the wife, just as Christ is the head of the Church" (Epistle to the Ephesians), "Man is the image of God and the mirror of his glory whereas woman reflects the glory of man" (Epistle to the Corinthians), and "Women should not be allowed to obtain education or instruction, she should obey, serve and keep silent." Pope Pius XI in 1930 stated, in his encyclical Casti connubis, that if woman "descended from the exalted position bestowed upon her by the Gospel, she will fall again into servitude and would become, as in the past, just an instrument of men." St. Thomas stated, centuries before that, "Woman is a frustrated man, an occasional being." To these quotations and to a summary of the history of women's problems from the viewpoint of the Church we will only add that, as an institution, the Church discriminates without any subtlety. To the question posed to the nun-educator Carmen Perez as to whether machismo exists within the Church, she replied (Cenfa 1973, pp. 69-70):

> Of course it exists! I believe this is a condition in which
> the Church is not backing a theory or a voluntary desire from
> within. I think it is a consequence of the historical-cultural
> repressed situation of women through the ages. . . . wom-
> en in Roman society were second class citizens and lived
> secluded within an inside courtyard of the house. Undoubt-
> edly St. Peter could not refer to them in any other way: she
> should cover her head, be subservient to man and should not
> be allowed to speak in the assembly. . . . the Church has
> always assimilated whatever society's opinion of women has

been. . . . Now, when the time comes to make decisions
within the Parochial Councils in most parishes only men are
consulted, regardless of the fact that the membership of the
Church is composed of a higher proportion of women. Nevertheless, the decisions are made by men. That is the problem!

This attitude of the Church is interesting because it is an important
agent of ideological-cultural transmission. The present influence of the
Church in the popular and general ideology should be researched further,
especially as far as the sexes and the family are concerned.

Sexuality

Both sexes consider it normal that man be "polygamous" and woman
"monogamous". For example, says a group of men, "Man's infidelity
is 'natural' but not woman's" (Rojas et al. 1973, p. 6). Men demand
virginity of women; and in spite of (or because of) a more pronounced
machismo among the lower social classes, the frequency of sexual relations is low (Quijada 1973, p. 202). This poses some questions regarding sexual manifestations in both sexes, especially in the lower
social classes, and their relationship to authoritarianism, repressive
socialization, and ideological-cultural aspects.

The Oppressive Machismo Ideology in Women

As we know, the ideological-cultural aspect is conditioned partly
by daily life, by "existence that determines conscience," and by the
most important transmitting agents: family, school, religion, mass
media, and work.

As far as woman's situation, daily living, family, and work are almost identical. This fact permits us to hypothesize a strong repressed
ideological cohesion. The other agents—mass media, religion, and
school—are largely controlled by men. Therefore, there will be a majority of women with oppressive ideologies. They should, of course,
be differentiated according to social class, country of origin, membership in other institutions, and work inside or outside the home.

The Mattelarts (1970, p. 147) write: "80% of the boys and 68% of
the girls declared themselves wholly in favor of sexual equality. The
surprising finding is the discrepancy between the answers from boys
and girls. The latter, even more pronounced among white collar workers
(62% against 46%) appear to be accomplices, at least in its character
or principle, to a situation that does not favor them . . . the imbalance
between the answers of both sexes is not repeated among the factory
workers or the peasants where more or less half of the boys and girls
are openly opposed to the 'equality principle.' "

These percentages give the "emancipation" of women a bad outlook that increases if one takes into consideration that women, including those belonging to the privileged and "modern" (university student) sectors, are even more conservative than men. Also, in private life conscious answers usually are followed by an attitude more traditional than that verbalized.

Housework

This is considered fundamental for women. Those who try to find work outside the home are compelled by economic considerations, according to the known investigations undertaken in Chile. According to Lucia Ribeiro and Teresa de Barbieri (1973, p. 195):

> To the factory worker, her basic role is that of wife and mother; work's function is either to assist in the children's education or help the husband. Woman, by the act of being incorporated into the productive process, is forced to break the traditional role of wife and mother which continues to be the fundamental one. Thus she justifies her largely unfavorable feelings to outside work when she has small children: "Of course, when a woman has small children, it is nicer that she stays at home taking care of them."

Angelica Ducci et al. (1972, p. 125) found that a great percentage of women with technical skills do not work outside the home but use their skills in domestic work. The majority had studied dressmaking (44. 93 percent); those trained as nurse's aides, or with skills in arts and crafts totaled 27. 53 percent. In other words, the selection of fields of study and the interest of women are immersed in the myth that "woman belongs at home." On the other hand, the selection of university careers is also linked to domestic tasks and necessities at home. Ducci et al. (1972, p. 72) found that 36. 36 percent of college graduates do not work outside the home. Paz Covarrubias (1972, p. 3) says that 25. 9 percent of the total number of women who have completed university studies and received their credentials do not work outside the home; the same is true of 44. 4 percent of women capable of average professional work.

Women with a university education who are working outside the home "have no great commitment to society" (Ducci et al. 1972, p. 123). They demonstrate the same level of individualism found among the factory workers cited earlier. These women choose "social" professions—careers that represent women's traditional ideology about the universities and about their usefulness at home.

The percentage of women in the schools at the University of Chile in 1966 was as follows (Mattelart 1968, p. 224):

School	Percent
Medicine	17. 3
Nursing	100. 0
Obstetrics and pediatrics	100. 0
Medical technology	92. 1
Dentistry, chemistry, and pharmacy	46. 1
Architecture	38. 8
Art	70. 2
Education	59. 6
Social work	90. 9
Journalism	56. 0
Psychology and sociology	61. 0

Following the patterns of these women in school, mothers oppressed by the same ideology express the same aspirations for their daughters: "Psychology, 'because it is useful at home'; dentistry, 'because she could use it at home'; medicine and psychology, 'because she knows how to take care of her children and family'; social work, 'because it is appropriate for her sex, '" (Mattelart 1968, pp. 184-85).

Besides tradition and the role of victim-accomplice played by women, there is an individualism in young and middle-aged women regarding the selection and use of a university career or a training course that is easily understood in view of their physically and ideologically cloistered life style. In view of these considerations, special care should be taken regarding the creation of institutions and programs oriented to the socialization of domestic work. Do they really want it? Which one do they want? Under what conditions? Only prudently planned projects based on valid diagnoses would prevent the creation of institutions only because they could be economically useful. This prudence is recommended because of the reduced percentage of women taking advantage of the facilities of the child care centers (Ducci et al. 1972) and other data: "We like the idea of public laundries as long as they do a good job, because even though we are working class women we are also demanding, and if the clothes are not cleaned properly, we would refuse them" (Ribeiro and Barbieri 1973, p. 199).

Further research by Rojas et al. (1973, p. 62) shows: "With respect to the possibility of collective organization of chores traditionally defined as the exclusive responsibility of the mother and which she has always undertaken autonomously, such as child care centers, communal laundries, communal dining places close to towns or camps, there exists strong resistance because of attitudes such as: 'nobody takes care of my children as I do'; 'I refuse to eat a meal when I don't know how it was prepared'; 'nobody washes clothes as carefully as I do'; etc. "

These expressions are related to other findings concerning the individualism and the "naturalness" of work at home. These conditions help us to understand attitudes of "resistance to world change, " deriving from the objective-subjective condition of oppression. Once again, all questioning should be considered in relation to the social vision that these attitudes imply—and reinforce with their transmission to the new generation. Women perpetuate the distribution of roles and the authoritarianism they imply with such attitudes as "The boy must be taught what it means to be a man, and the girl what it means to be a woman" (Rojas et al. 1973, p. 60). This transmitted and legitimated division leads us to the "authoritarian personality" and to the domination and mythology of the sexes, classes, and other oppressed strata.

Inferiority of Women

The legitimation of economic and intellectual dependence, implicit or not in the division of work, assigns to woman a particular role that places her in a position of inferiority. The internalization of such a view is demonstrated even in the university careers selected, in which the traditional role coexists with the least possible intellectual demand. But let us consider woman's "self-image" (in psychological terms), which is the female ideology regarding the woman's place in society (in sociological terms) by examining the expressed attitudes of respondents to questionnaires administered by the Mattelarts (1970, pp. 149, 151):

> Factory worker: "Women have always been inferior to men."
> White collar worker: "She should work, yes . . . as long as
>   she keeps her woman's place, not high-
>   er than men's."

Such feelings of inferiority and incapability are combined with feelings of resignation, as respondents to Ribeiro and Barbieri's questionnaire (1973, p. 191) show:

> . . . for men yes, because if they are mechanics they are promoted to office workers, but for women no. I think that, because of age and also because of lack of education; therefore we are not offered positions of responsibility. I think that we are not able to fulfill a higher position.

The components of oppressive ideology and low self-image are thus related to the real economic, occupational, and educational segregation in Chile; and this segregation is maintained in part because of the same oppressive ideology in women. Given such conditions, Ribeiro and Barbieri point out (1973, p. 200):

> The exploitation becomes "natural" and the problems generated by the working situation itself are not discussed even when they are common to all the workers of a company. They

do not participate actively in unions and they accept the decisions made by the male employees.

Sexuality

It has been observed that sexual relations are less frequent among lower-class males than among males of the middle and upper classes. Conflicts stemming from this area cause a high percentage of frigidity in women, reported as close to 60 percent overall and to 70 percent among the lower classes (Taibo 1971). On the other hand, only 13 percent of women in the lower social classes married "for love" (Quijada 1973)—another manifestation of authoritarianism, the cultural and sexual repression of women, and their dependence upon men. Related research in Peru and Mexico has demonstrated that women from lower social classes usually have children without planning or wanting them (Aduriz 1972).

Similar problems have been found in Buenos Aires, Argentina. Alfredo Bauer (1970, p. 174) reports the following:

> R. Kertesz and his collaborators conducted a revealing survey in the maternity ward of the Ranson Hospital among mothers from extremely underprivileged social classes, unskilled workers, most of them illiterate, mostly unmarried and slum dwellers, those who were not domestic servants. Lack of any kind of sexual education was, according to the authors, almost absolute. No contraceptive device at all had been used by two-thirds of them, and among those that had used one it had been the crudest one, coitus interruptus. Only exceptionally did we find a real desire for motherhood.

In Chile as well there is, among lower-class persons, "an imbalance between the ideal and real size of a family" (Gonzalez 1969, p. 440). In the marginal urban populations of Santiago, women have an average of 5.4 children and an average of seven pregnancies; two of every five women regret having had more children than they would have wanted. In this respect there is also the problem of abortion: during 1961 it was estimated that in Santiago there was one abortion for every three births, and in 1965 almost twenty abortions for every hundred live births (Gonzalez 1969, p. 440).

This clearly shows that the sexual situation is deplorable: frequently women from low social groups marry without wanting to; have sexual relations, and have children, without wanting them; and often confront the medical problems of abortion. However, there is a resignation in the relationship with the "macho," a very conflictive relationship. There is need for research on the relationship between women's "destiny to suffer" and the "destiny of the poor," as well as the multiple ideological-cultural and social implications that this relationship might have.

FINAL NOTE

In addition to the analyses presented here, further empirical research is needed on all myths concerning men and women, and their empirical and theoretical significance. This would require viewing the ideological-cultural domain as both influenced by and influencing economy, law, and politics. (The economic situation has been covered elsewhere.) I have also studied the Chilean empirical material on this variable, particularly in reference to work, and on the political variable. We still lack comparison and a synthesis of ideological and cultural differences guided by a theory that avoids idealistic reductionism. I trust that some of these aspects will be undertaken by others and that from this common work there will stem a precise and detailed analysis together with a cultural program that will lead us toward the real liberation of women, and thus of men, children, and society. I do not think that the ills of society will be remedied through women's liberation; neither do I agree with the traditional thinking of the left that, by remedying society, women will be liberated. I think I have demonstrated that this is impossible. It is only another version of machismo, in which women are placed outside of society while society is changing to better itself and in which they will be included "when everything is ready."

REFERENCES

Adorno, T., and N. Horkheimer. 1969. La sociedad. Buenos Aires: Proteo.

Aduriz, Joaquin. 1972. "Asi viven y asi nacen." Revista eure 5 (July).

Althusser, Louis. 1970. "Ideologia y aparatos ideologicos de estado." In Psicologia social, ed. Ricardo Zuniga. Valaparaiso: Universidad Catolica.

Bauer, Alfredo. 1970. La mujer: Ser social y conciencia. Buenos Aires: Ediciones Silaba.

Bottomore-Rubel. 1967. Sociologia y filosofia social. Barcelona: Peninsula.

Castilla del Pino, Carlos. 1971. Cuatro ensayos sobre la mujer. Madrid: Alianza editorial.

Cenfa. 1973. "Familia, educacion, sociedad." Cenfa no. 2 (March).

Cooper, David. 1972. La muerte de la familia. Buenos Aires: Paidos.

Covarrubias, Paz, and Monica Munoz. 1972. Algunos factores que inciden en la participacion laboral de las mujeres de estratos bajos. Santiago: Instituto de Sociologia, Universidad Catolica de Chile.

Ducci, Angelica, et al. 1972. El trabajo: Un nuevo destino para la mujer chilena? Santiago: Instituto Laboral.

Fortin, Geraldo. 1971. "Aspectos sociologicos del trabajo femenino." Boletín documental sobre la mujer 1: doc. 71/1.

Fromm, Eric. 1972. Psicoanalisis y sexpol. Buenos Aires: Granica.

Gissi, Jorge. n. d. "Un marco teorico-dialectico para la comprensión de la situacion de la mujer." Unpublished ms.

Gonzalez, Gerardo. 1969. "La regulacion de la natalidad: Algunos antecedentes objectivos." Revista mensaje 182 (September).

Lahve, Christian. El refugio de la masas. Santiago: Editorial del Pacifico.

Mattelart, Michele, and Armand Mattelart. 1968. La mujer chilena en una nueva sociedad. Santiago: Editorial del Pacifico.

_____. 1970. Juventud chilena: Rebeldia y conformismo. Santiago: Editorial Universitaria.

Quijada, Rodrigo. 1973. "Sexo y conducta sexual en Chile." Cuadernos de la realidad nacional nos. 6-9.

Reich. 1969. "Irrupcion de la moral sexual." In Sexualidad y represion, ed. Carlos Perez. Buenos Aires.

Ribeiro, Lucia, and Teresa de Barbieri. 1973. "La mujer obrera chilena." Cuadernos de la realidad nacional 161.

Rojas, M. Luisa, Teresa Rodriguez, Rosa Larrain, and M. Teresa Chadwick. 1973. Analisis ideologico de la familia. Santiago: Instituto de Sociologia, Universidad Catolica de Chile.

Taibo, Eduardo. 1971. Conduct sexual de los chilenos. Santiago: Imprenta Sanziva.

3

WOMEN'S WORK
AND FERTILITY
Maria del Carmen Elu de Lenero

Most Latin American countries are experiencing an accelerated population growth. Fertility rates remain high because of a number of inter-
related factors. This situation has led social scientists and policy-
makers to become interested in the variables affecting women's
reproductive behavior. Of special interest are those related to social
mechanisms that could induce, develop, and accelerate a decline in
fertility, thus perhaps leading to a return to the equilibrium that existed
before the reduction of the mortality rates.

Among the factors that are frequently related to fertility is women's
work. This phenomenon is both quantitatively and qualitatively important. On the one hand is the undeniable increase in women's participation in economic activity. On the other hand is the also undeniable
fact that women's work is strategically located between the sociofamilial
system and the socioeconomic structure of society. It can thus constitute an excellent yardstick to measure how the two are related, the
values upon which the relationships are based, and the norms that direct them.

In the same way, women's work appears to have the capacity to
act as an element to generate change in both attitudes and behavior.
Among these changes, those that might have a direct bearing on reproductive behavior, especially those tending toward a decrease in fertility, would acquire a special importance. Hypothetically, the relationship can be presented in the following manner: the more important a
woman's labor, the lower her fecundity.

What has been described in recent empirical investigations is an
ambivalent and ambiguous situation that neither confirms nor denies a
causal relationship between female labor and fertility. This indicates
the complexity of the problem and the need to base fertility phenomena
in the context of the society, culture, polity, and economy in which
they occur.

Interrelationships between women's work and fertility in a given
society cannot be studied in isolation. They must be untangled and

discovered within the complexities of the social reality in which they
occur, and which provides both the factors that condition them and that
are derived from them. Any study planned, undertaken, or analyzed that
does not recognize, or ignores, the social context of the phenomena to
be studied probably will not be successful.

Therefore, the primary objective of this essay is to present a series
of sociological premises that will serve as frames of reference for understanding the information on fertility collected by past studies. It will
also lay the groundwork for the formulation and the implementation of
future investigations. This work refers principally to Mexico, but many
of the considerations are valid for other Latin American countries, especially those in the Andes, which have had similar sociocultural tra-
jectories and similar processes of acculturation, and are in other ways
similar to present-day Mexico.

The study will be developed in three stages: in the first I shall try
to place female labor in the sociofamilial context in which it developed.
In the second I will present the numerical data on fertility in Mexico
and suggest their principal implications at both the social level and the
familial level. The third stage is the analysis of the existing data and
the proposal of hypotheses on the interrelationship between women's
work and fertility, beginning with the formulations established in each
of the preceding sections.

THE GENERAL CONDITIONS OF WOMEN'S WORK

Mexican women have shared the problems of all working women,
which are basically connected to their conditions as women and to the
lack of social recognition they have received; on the other hand, Mexican women are concerned with the problems of their relevance to a complex and ambiguous society that is in a continuous process of unequal
acculturation and development. The result is the product of three con-
ditioning factors: the sex role as a woman; her place in the economic
structure as a worker; and the sociocultural historical context of Mexico.

Women have worked throughout human history. Only in isolated
cases have women belonging to the upper-middle and upper classes of
the social hierarchy given themselves—and continue to give themselves—the luxury of not working because it would reflect negatively
on their status.

Women have worked in all kinds of occupations; their work is not
characterized by specialization. They have worked the land, cared for
cattle, suffered slavery, and lived in servitude. Women have been artisans, and factory workers. They have seen the rural economy replaced
by spinning and weaving machines, and they have witnessed the technological change from the plow to the tractor. In addition, they have
gone to war, when it was necessary. Women have also joined the liberal

professions. It is paradoxical that in view of all of this female activity, women's work has not been considered central to the social process, as men's has been. Labor history is written about the working man, not the working woman.

Evelyn Sullerot (1970, Chapter 1) tells us of her difficulties in finding sources that would permit her to follow the history of women's work, since the philosophers and historians, while assuming that they are making universal analyses, base their generalizations on the male subject. Thus they give the impression not so much of trying to exclude women but, what is worse, of forgetting them entirely in their observations on the social relations of labor.

In addition, the same linguistic term, "man," is used to designate the human being as well as the male of the species, thus giving the impression of identifying a given sex with the whole species. This is not unimportant, for it underscores even more the idea that the history of humanity is written as the history of the male.

It seems that there has always been a lack of equality between the labor assigned to women and the prestige or social status accorded that labor. The work reserved exclusively for females has never received social recognition. Neither the rough occupations that required strength and physical resistance, such as, according to Sullerot (1970, Chapter 1) "the rock crushers of Antiquity, or the mill turners," nor the delicate occupations that required skill and patience, such as "the weavers of gold and silk of the Middle Ages," received social recognition.

It can be said, therefore, that the valuation given women's work has been adverse to women. When manual labor was not accorded social value, women participated in it. Similarly, in an age when women dedicated themselves to the production of children, clothing, and food, this work was undervalued and despised. In Greece, for example, manual labor was considered almost a subhuman activity, not consonant with the true essence of the free man, whose abilities, it was felt, should develop in philosophy, art, politics, and war—areas to which women could never aspire, let alone reach. Plato said, "If nature had not needed women or slaves, she would have given the shuttles the ability to thread themselves": a doubly meaningful phrase, because women are defined in terms of a despised occupation.

At present, we tend to measure a person's value by the work he does. When we meet someone, we ask, "Who are you" to receive an answer about his occupation. Consequently, when one is dealing with a woman and she answers, "I don't do anything" or "I stay at home," she establishes the absence of her personal social status.

The devaluation of the occupations assigned to women has reached such an extreme, and the notion of "women's work" has degenerated to such a degree, that what women do inside their houses is not considered work at all, to the point of making much female activity socially invisible. Today a woman is considered as really working only if she has a paid job, generally outside the home.

Consequently, in a situation where productive work is considered as the source of a person's real social status, women are practically marginalized from such work: if they do participate, they do it in a timid way and at a disadvantage, both in terms of the jobs taken and in terms of the money received, which is dedicated to consumption.

The history of the undervaluation and/or the concealment of female labor as far as social recognition is concerned, reveals a human society where men have always been the dominant class, and as such have generated their own ideology, which tends to keep women on a secondary level. Women have thus spent their capacities and energies as a function of the requirements of established systems, in a society in which they have not participated in the exercise of power. Women have always been on the sidelines.

Not even when they have participated in the revolutionary struggles that were strategic for the liberation of humanity, and that has as their theme "Liberty, Equality, and Fraternity" have women received the rights for which they fought in exchange for their efforts.

In France, during the Enlightenment and after the Revolution, the determining influence of Rousseau was clear and well-defined. In his Emilio the position is explicitly stated: all education for women should lead them to be servants to men. Similarly, Robespierre banned women from political activity, insisting that the "natural organization of women" made them incapable of it. Chamuette, supporting the law that forbade women to unite in assemblies, said, "Nature says to women: be women. Your work is in the tender cares of childhood and in the sweet discomforts of maternity. . . . do you wish a reward? You shall have it. . . . You shall be the divinity of the domestic sanctuary, there you shall reign . . ." (Sullerot 1970, pp. 77 ff.). This is the oft-repeated deception of woman in which she is exalted in the abstract, but denied her rights in fact. Later, in the nineteenth century, work became practically a religion, through which one could supposedly achieve justice and success in life.

In the eighteenth century, Europe had prepared itself for this view. Luther and Calvin were the first to define work as a service to God, and laid the foundations for what was later called the Protestant ethic (and subsequent secularization). Philosophers and social scientists supported the new mystique: "Everything will be worked, including the air, which needs to be heated," said Hegel. Bergson was even more definite: "Man celebrates his divinity to the extent that he is a worker." Homo faber is given all honors; with Homo sapiens he will lead to the development of the new man.

And woman? In what developmental stage was she living? Once again the lack of correlation between her position and society was absurd. The ideology that created the conceptions of Homo sapiens and Homo faber is, paradoxically, the same that denied women education and kept them at home. To achieve this, the nineteenth century created a new image for her, that of "educating mother." This strategy was not used for the first time, nor would it be used for the last. As we shall see below, the exaltation of the importance of the family and of the "natural" functions of women within it has been used by society to keep women away from other matters in which they might manifest interest, and in which they might become competitive with those in power.

The industrial revolution altered the labor system profoundly. The movement from the home to the factory had grave consequences for female labor, which became displaced. It was proved once again that the social valuation of work depends on the sex of the person who performs it. The same manual activities that women had performed inside their houses, with little recognition, were now done in a factory, by men. For example, the production of preserved and bottled foods acquired "importance" with its move to a factory.

Despite all vicissitudes, European and American women began a hard fight for their right to work at the dawn of the twentieth century. Paradoxically, it was two international catastrophes that brought women their best work opportunities: World War I and World War II. Men had to fight, and women were called upon to take their positions in industry. Hundreds and thousands of women managed to maintain the most important industries of the warring countries: metallurgy, chemistry, and especially armaments.

Of course, at the end of each war, after the men's military demobilization, the situation became tense. Women who had enjoyed social recognition and valuation, in addition to the satisfaction of earning a salary, did not want to return to the seclusion of their homes and take a step "backward." The men, who could hardly recognize their women with their short hair and independent airs, tried to regain their familial and occupational leadership; and to a great extent they succeeded. Many women stopped working. Those whose husbands or fathers had died, tried to continue working; but they were generally transferred to occupations that men did not want, especially office work and sales.

At this point in history, the conditions that had dogged the social development of women reappeared: attributes "interior" (in the home) and "inferior" to characterize their labor. Male-dominated society created a series of mechanisms to maintain women in a marginal and dependent position. To succeed, it used many kinds of arguments, generally with the common theme of "It is only natural."

The biological circumstance that human beings are sexually differentiated, and that one of the sexes desires and nurtures the young, has been managed by society in an arbitrary and contradictory manner. One of the frequent arguments used throughout the ages to keep the woman at home is that she must be "protected" from the dangers of the outside world: "The working woman exposes her virtue." Prostitution in one form or another has always lurked in arguments against female labor, and its dangers a good pretext that disallows women their right to work. It could have been quite otherwise: the encouragement of female labor could have served to prevent prostitution, which often is practiced because women do not know, or cannot find, any other means to earn a living. If one tries to relate female labor to prostitution, it is very clear that the first has never led to the second.

In summary, we may say that women's work has always been conditioned by social discrimination against the female sex. Women's activities have been, and continue to be, characterized by undervaluation implicit in "at home" and "inferior." Whenever possible, women are kept inside the family home; and when that is not possible or convenient, they are placed at the lower end of the occupational scale. And, what is worse, women have been accomplices in this situation.

WOMEN'S WORK IN MEXICO: SOCIOCULTURAL CHARACTERISTICS

The Mexican working woman shares the unequal and inferior conditions that have characterized the history of female labor in the West. In addition, she is placed within the complex sociocultural system of contemporary Mexico, which, like many other Latin American countries, is a difficult unit to identify when referring to its culture and value systems. Mexican culture and value systems can help us design logical models to explain the relationship between women's work and fertility in that society.

In Mexico, as in other Latin American countries, it is overly simple to speak of "a culture." It is better to speak of a superposition of cultures in a continuous but unfinished process of acculturation, in which all elements have not yet merged into one.

The Conquest marked the first great cultural shock, with the meeting of indigenous culture and the Western culture brought by Spain. The process continued through the following centuries through contacts with other European countries, especially with France. In this century the culture that arose from the revolution is confronted with the new civilization of industrial capitalism. Significantly, this is occurring without the disappearance of any of Mexico's earlier cultures. As a result of these survivals, we can recognize three stratified subcultures in the present social system of Mexico. They are easily distinguishable in their broad characteristics, but in reality they intertwine themselves in a number of combinations (Lenero Otero n. d.).

There is a value complex corresponding to each of these subcultures. Values are understood here as "the elements of a compartmentalized symbolic system which provide criteria for the selection of guiding alternatives for choices which are intrinsically open in any situation" (Parsons 1966, p. 31).

Before describing the different subcultures it is appropriate to repeat that the traits characterizing them do not necessarily constitute a description of what the entire populations included in each believe and act upon. Rather, the subcultures are described as ideal types. These general traits, once identified and abstracted, serve as instruments of sociological analysis to help us discover the congruence and explanations of particular social behaviors (Weber 1944, pp. 16 ff.).

The three subcultures to which we refer can be theoretically isolated and distinguished as the folk or indigenous subculture, the traditional rural or urban subculture, and the modern and distinctively urban subculture.

The ideal values of the folk or indigenous subculture are basically those derived from a sacred, fatalistic syncretism in which man depends on his environment and on forces that are alien and beyond his control. Magic and taboo merge; everything leads to a prohibition ethic. The search for values is focused on the past, and social prestige depends on ascriptive status. Social structure is based on a family, clan, or tribe, which assumes global responsibilities. The roles of men and women are "naturally" defined.

In this subculture, women's work is a function of the community and forms part of the subsistence economy. The physical domain of women's labor may transcend the walls of a domestic unit, but the quality of women's work remains "within the walls." Because mortality is high, a paternalistic attitude predominates, for this is the only way in which the species can be preserved. Fertility is not a private or personal matter that concerns the woman, or even the couple. It concerns the family and the community, which practically merge into one. In a recent analysis it has been calculated that 12 to 15 percent of the Mexican population live under values similar to those of this subculture (the numbers depend on the inclusiveness of the criteria) (Lenero Otero n. d.).

The traditional subculture, while it is usually considered a rural subculture, also exists and persists in urban areas. In it, social control is based on "what they will say." The authority figures are the Church and the state, which sometimes agree and sometimes are in conflict. Life is seen as static, and the ideal is that each generation should repeat the activities of the previous one, thus maintaining and duplicating values, norms, and conduct. Social status is ascriptive and is revalidated by a feeling of loyalty to the predetermined ascription. The name of the family into which one is born is extremely important. Kinship is a basic element of the system.

Male and female roles are perfectly differentiated. The semi-extended family constitutes the productive unit, generally dedicated to cattle-raising and agriculture. Women's work is defined as a function of the family unit, and it goes without saying that it is done in "the interior" of the home. The social values relating to fertility are pronatalist for expansionist effects. Factors of human adjustment and regulation are ultimately left to Providence. More than 50 percent—perhaps 60 percent—of the Mexican population (and the figure might be correct for other Latin American countries) are currently living in societies whose predominant characteristics fall within the value system of this subculture.

The modern subculture is informed by a complex of values that explains the behavior of a constantly increasing percentage of the population. Among its broadest characteristics are a secularized conception of life oriented toward the future, an ethic of freedom of conscience based on self responsibility, and science and technology as the replacement for Providence as ultimate arbiter of human affairs. Institutions proliferate to satisfy needs previously taken care of by the family. The nuclear conjugal family becomes the unit of consumption.

Social status is based on achievement and not on ascription; this generates a strong sense of competence among individuals in which belonging to a particular sex does not determine any basic differentiation. Women's work responds to personal vocation. In the face of the population explosion, this subculture is anti-natalist, and individual fertility responds to qualitative rather than quantitative needs.

These three subcultures correspond to three key stages that Western societies have in general followed. What is especially complex, in the case of Mexico, is that this process has occurred only in the last 500 years; and the values of the folk or indigenous subculture persist with the values of traditional society and the modern society.

To further complicate the contexts that determine women's work and fertility, the Mexican family institution, while it has followed a process qualitatively similar to that undergone by the society, has not done so at the same pace. Thus the same developmental process has brought society to a different stage from that of the family.

An index of this can be observed in the process of secularization. Society passes from a stage of fatalism to faith in a clerical Providence, and finally to secularization and the development of individual values. Primitive syncretism and clerical paternalism have developed into the institutionalized Church, which maintains the sacred in society. Secularism has led to the development of the state, which holds temporal power. With the advance of modernization, secondary institutions have proliferated; and as the process of secularization advances, the state and its derived or parallel organs acquire more power.

But as society becomes secularized, the family also changes while remaining connected to the Church. The family is considered sacred; and even as the process of secularization advances, the family remains one of the last bastions of holiness in the folk and traditional subcultures.

Moreover, the difference between the whole society's rate of change from folk to traditional to modern values, and the slower rate of change that occurs in the family institution corresponds to differences in the process of social development among men and women. Men achieve secular values more rapidly, while women retain sacred and traditional cultural traits.

This difference in rates of development is repeatedly found in contemporary Mexico, and of course it conditions women's work and their fertility. There is a lack of synchronization in personal development,

and women's work is characterized as done "at home" and "inferior."
Even the treatment accorded women is a function of what is considered
"natural" to their sex. All of these phenomena represent a persistence
of sacred and traditional values.

Contemporary Mexico, with its confluence of subcultures, presents
a panorama in which women work in all of the ways they have throughout history. We find woman working in the most primitive way, carrying
very heavy loads on her shoulders; we see her working the land and caring for cattle; we see her living in servitude; she works as an artisan
and as an industrial laborer. She, too, has witnessed the technological
progress that substituted the tractor for the plow; and with difficulty,
and only after overcoming many obstacles, she has also become a professional. In addition, we have also seen her, in this century, fighting
in the revolution.

Given the superposition of subcultures and the juxtaposition of different, and even opposed, values, anomic situations arise in which behaviors occur that are barely within the norms, and that are incongruent
with the values upon which they are based. The result is the classic
society in transition. It is only within the context of this multivalent
value system that we can hope to explain some of the attitudes and circumstances that surround the paid work of the Mexican woman, as well
as her fertility. Otherwise, these phenomena are completely indecipher-
able.

The Mexican woman who works outside the home, especially if she
is married, does so with a guilt complex. She believes that "women's
place is in the home" and that "her natural mission is to be a wife and
mother." These opinions were given by young women about to marry, as
explanations of why they did not plan to continue working after marriage
(Elu de Lenero 1969, p. 128). We found these attitudes, with variations,
not only among girls with middle-level education, but also among university students. It is clear that they correspond to typical valuations
of the traditional subculture.

Among married women, the internal conflict is notably more serious.
The proportion of women who work after marriage decreases considerably. In a recent study in which 2,500 women were interviewed, 58.6
percent had worked before their marriage but only 13.7 percent did so
after marriage (Elu de Lenero 1970) because their work became the reason
for all the negative things that could happen in their homes. It is not
that other people say this; the women themselves believe it.

Despite the frequency of this type of opinion, the proportion of
working women is constantly increasing. This is justified by claiming
economic necessity, making it appear that working does not depend on
the woman's own decision, but that it is the result of circumstances
beyond her control. In this way, women try to "defend themselves"
against the conflict created by the divergence between their norms and
their conduct.

Society, as well as the family, adds to women's guilt with the argument that "she is taking away the opportunity to work from soneone (a
man) who really needs it, because he has a wife and children who depend on him." In a society where the labor supply is far above the demand, this is a strong argument, even when statistics show that there
are many families where women are the "head of household" (12 percent,
according to the census), and even when the working man is often single.

Women's work, whether they are married or single, tends to be
temporary. Women work until they marry, or until their husbands get
work or a raise in salary. This circumstantial character is a real ob-
stacle to progress that, with other factors, maintains women in "inferior" positions in the occupational hierarchy.

For this reason, the Mexican woman who works does so under traditional values, in the light of which she "ought to be at home"; and
her earnings benefit the family. Moreover, the decision whether to work
does not belong to her. In the study surveying more than 2,500 couples
(Elu de Lenero 1970), 57 percent of the women and 74 percent of the
men felt that it was up to the man to decide "whether or not the woman
should work." Only 3.2 percent of the men conceded that women had
the right to make this decision (Elu de Lenero 1970). On the other hand
22.4 percent of the men and 43 percent of the women agreed that a woman's working for pay outside the home was acceptable only when the
man "needed" economic help.

Women's occupations are dependent on the same cultural structure
that determines women's behavior and norms. Therefore, women cannot
justify their work in terms of their personal interest. For this reason,
if we are to understand the situation, women's occupations must be
placed in the cultural context to which women are subordinated.

In an attempt to respond as much as possible to the "imperatives"
of the traditional subculture, and partly to control their feelings of
guilt, women, when they work, try "not to go beyond their positions,"
and thus bring their second-class citizenship from their homes to the
office. This leads to an ambiguous situation: their work relationships
they try to maintain in the traditional stereotypes of masculine and feminine behavior as they appear in the family structure. A woman's supervisor or (male) working partner takes on the authority and male superiority of father or husband. Rarely will she dare to protest when the man
is paid more for the same work—often simply because he is male. And
if they are equally qualified, and a male is chosen for an opportunity to
excel or to be promoted, she remains quiet because she knows that to
speak out would hardly be compatible with the permanent role she has
at home, a role that must be safeguarded at all costs if she does not
wish to succumb to her own conflicts. Moreover, her promotion at work
would imply an attempt to compete with her male colleagues, who would
accept this with difficulty.

This can be illustrated with empirical data obtained from an investigation undertaken among young women about to be married (Elu de Lenero

1969). Most of the girls were working in lower-middle-class occupations (office workers, sales girls, beauticians, and so on). Three-fourths of them had educations below the equivalent of the third year of high school. To the question "Would you like to continue working after you are married?" 71 percent said yes. To "Do you intend to do it?," only 40 percent gave an affirmative answer. Of these, 76 percent indicated that they would work to "help with the household expenses and to have more money to send the children through school." Twelve percent said that they would like to work after being married in order to escape a bit from the routine of housework, and only 6 percent considered work as an important opportunity to learn new things. The rest did not know what their reasons were.

On the other hand, the 60 percent who did not plan to work divided their reasons in the following manner: 40 percent thought it was a woman's obligation to "stay at home;" 34 percent said that "their husbands would not permit it;" 8 percent said that "they liked housework very much, and . . . wished to dedicate themselves entirely to it;" and 5 percent thought "it would be too hard to dedicate themselves to two activities, housework and work outside the home." Thus, only a minority even of young women dared to give reasons related to their personal inclinations. The majority rationalized their motivations as a function of familial needs.

If the above is correct, so is the fact that when women do work, they are exposing themselves to the values of the modern subculture, where they will learn of liberty, justice, responsibility, democracy, competence, commitment: values contradictory to those of the traditional subculture they have been taught. The same does not occur to men, because their entry into the labor market is a logical step in their personal development; women's entry into the labor market puts them in conflict with their work relationships, with their families, and—what is worse—with themselves.

As was pointed out earlier, Mexican society is in transition between two value systems that are often contradictory. The result is a society where ambiguity is the only logical explanation of behavior. In a process of transition, Gino Germani points out (1971, pp. 26 ff.), there are inequalities; that is, not all of society's sectors are at the same level. There are areas that can be considered "advanced" and areas that, because of "the persistence of value orientations" that are not modern, are more "backwards," with a relationship to the others that is not always one of coexistence, but one of hegemony.

These considerations are perfectly applicable to the condition of the working woman and her relations to the masculine labor world. In this process, which is already one of conflicting values in transition, Mexican women's labor is in a condition of maximum confusion. They suffer the disadvantages of no longer having what they wanted to leave, but cannot reach the advantages they wished to achieve (Castellanos 1970, p. 20).

This transitional situation can lead as easily to the reinforcement of the traditional situation as it can become the occasion for breaking the vicious circle and, as Germani says, act as a "decision point"— that is, be an element that can produce a reorientation. Whether it does or not depends heavily on the global circumstances of society, but basically it depends on the constancy and strength of the working women and their determination to reorient and to force the evolution of the sociocultural institutions that have held women in such bondage. One of the most important institutions in which women are entwined is, without doubt, the family.

In societies like Mexico's and those of other Latin American countries that share this transitional condition, women's work is not in itself a factor that can occasion a profound change in the sociocultural position of women; we often find it supporting a traditional situation in which the woman is treated as an object, for her work is not the product of a decision that she deliberately made. Nor is it the result of a liberalized family structure. Moreover, this work is grounded in the context of a capitalist society where "having more" is synonymous with success, so that the woman who achieves a greater economic capacity becomes an easy prey to publicity that is especially directed to her and that makes her an object of consumption. Such publicity raises a woman's economic demands, tells her how to dress, how to become more beautiful, how to resemble the "woman of the year"— in short, it caricatures her and makes her one more article of consumption.

But women's work also contains a seed of liberation, even if it was not sown for that reason. The fact that women work puts them in contact with values that can make them agents of change, first in themselves and later in the structures that enclose and delimit them, so that women can create a new image for themselves and a new family. The new woman will be able to demand rights and to act responsibly; the new family will, instead of forcing the woman into a double alienation and turning her into a double proletarian, be the basis for the formation of freer individuals. The new family cannot be the result of mass production, as though it were a shirt or shoes: it must be the result of craftsmanship, made with care—with technology at the service of creativity.

FERTILITY IN MEXICO: GENERAL DATA

The ambiguous and ambivalent context we have described can help us understand fertility in a country like Mexico; to understand how high rates of birth are sustained both among sectors of the population that live under subhuman conditions and among those at the highest levels of social stratification.

In 1970 there were 48. 3 million inhabitants in Mexico, and by March 1974 there probably were about 54 million. In 1981, it is estimated that the population will be 71. 9 million (Benitez and Cabrera 1966); the projection for the year 2000 is 135 million inhabitants (Lenero Otero, in press). This demographic growth is attributable to the maintenance of high birth rates (49. 9 percent in 1930, 44. 3 percent in 1940, 45. 5 percent in 1950, 44. 6 percent in 1960, and 43. 0 percent in 1970), in conjunction with falling mortality rates (25. 6 percent, 22. 0 percent, 15. 1 percent, 10. 4 percent, and 10. 0 percent, respectively). As a result this has led to an annual growth rate of more than 3. 0 percent in the past three decades. At present it is 3. 5 percent yearly (Colegio de Mexico 1970, pp. 14, 47). Foreign immigrations have played an insignificant role in this growth, given the restrictive policies of Mexican governments.

This continuous growth has resulted in a younger population. The graphic representation of this phenomenon would be a pyramid with a very broad base (the young population) and a very narrow top (the adult and older population). In 1970, 71. 8 percent of the population was less than 30 years old and 46. 2 percent was less than 15 years old (Secretariat of Industry and Commerce 1970, p. xvii). By 1980 the population under 15 years of age will have reached 35 million (Benitez and Cabrera 1966, pp. 49 ff.). We will not consider here the effects this might have on health, education, and life styles; but we do not want to ignore the repercussions that it might have on women's work, if we consider it as a dependent variable and fertility as the independent variable.

A population growth of this magnitude, in confunction with the displacement of populations and inequalities entailed by economic growth, is leading to higher unemployment rates in Mexico. It is calculated that in 1980 the labor force will be approximately 21 million. To avoid unemployment in that year—to eradicate that which already exists and to control it in future years—it will be necessary to create 14 million positions of high productivity (Trejo Reyes 1973, p. 167) by that data. This goal is completely impossible to reach, because it would require a rate of investment that the country cannot afford. (It has been calculated that each job requires 50, 000 pesos in investment.) This is without taking into account the female labor force, which is increasingly incorporated into the economically active population. It is important, moreover, to note that the rate of growth of women's participation in the economically active population is greater than that of the whole labor force and that of the whole population (Navarrete 1969, p. 35).

In a society with no discrimination between men and women, the available jobs would be occupied by the most qualified persons, regardless of their sex. But given the conditions existing in Mexico, where the values of the traditional subculture persist, it is possible that a cultural mechanism may be generated to prevent women from entering the labor force, as has been done in the past. Of course, this will not be easily compatible with the present policy of lowering the birth rate.

Mexico's population growth was produced by the alteration of one element in the system (mortality rate) by means that the system did not generate, but that were imported, and that did not form part of a balanced process of change in values, attitudes, and conduct. However, once the equilibrium is upset, there is little to do but to try to reestablish it. But it is not easy.

Women's high fertility rates and men's reproductive conduct are strongly rooted and maintained by the value system that supports the traditional subculture. The lack of ideological congruence in the whole society is continually visible. Thus, infant mortality rates are reduced as a result of intensive health campaigns that coexist with sanitary codes prohibiting contraceptives; similarly, a recently initiated family planning program is overshadowed by a change in the laws permitting youths to contract marriage at an earlier age.

This differs from the developed countries, where a reduction in the death rate was part of the technical advance reached by a given society at a certain moment in its history, and where the reduction of the birth rate occurred in a manner that can be said to have been logical and spontaneous, and part of the same process.

POSSIBLE INTERRELATIONS BETWEEN WOMEN'S WORK AND FERTILITY: ANALYSIS OF THE DATA

The information made available by the investigations on fertility undertaken by the Latin American Center for Demography (Rothman 1969, pp. 11 ff.) reveals a difference in the average number of live children born to working women and unemployed women in Mexico City. Among working women (who work at home or outside their homes) the rate is 3.77, and among unemployed women the rate is 4.08. The difference is greater if we compare only those who work outside the home, and who have a live birth rate of 3.42, with those who work at home and who have almost the same rate as those who don't work at all.

A similar situation was found by the IMES investigation on the Mexican family, in which the average number of live children were 5.1 for women working at home, 4.1 for those who work outside the home, and 4.7 for those who didn't work at all (Lenero Otero 1966-67).

Nevertheless, in another study by IMES, it was found that those who worked had more children than those who didn't work (Zetina 1972, p. 59). This is understandable, given that with a greater number of children, there will be greater economic need; and we have already seen that economic need is the most often cited reason to work. It is possible that work was begun after the birth of several children, so that the correlation changes its significance.

In order for these correlations to have a causal significance, it will be necessary to design experimental research problems in which it will be possible to control the initial periods of fertility and work, and to follow individual case histories.

In general, the information obtained by most investigations support the hypothesis raised earlier with respect to an inverse relationship between women's work and fertility, because work can influence certain variables that in turn act on fertility. These variables include very broad and general ones, such as the social and economic structure to which individuals belong, as well as factors more directly related to the number of children a woman may have. We will call the latter "intermediary" variables.

If we take fertility as the dependent variable and attempt to order the independent variables, beginning with the most immediate variables and ending with the most distant ones, it is possible to formulate a sociological model of analysis that in general considers the following:

1. The first block of variables consists of the means of fertility control, or intermediary variables. These can be classified in three groups: factors that can affect copulation (including the age which sexual relations are begun, permanent celibacy, unutilized intervals during the fertile period, voluntary abstinence, and frequency of coitus); factors that determine whether or not the coital act is a reproductive act, or "conception variables": involuntary sterility, the use or nonuse of contraceptive methods, and voluntary sterility; and the variables of gestation, which determine whether the product of conception reaches birth (involuntary fetal death and voluntary fetal death).

2. The second block of variables includes those related to the values and social norms that can so greatly influence family size, as can each of the intermediary variables.

3. The remaining blocks of variables consist of those related to personality, family structure, and social structure.

The number of resulting children, or the level of fertility, can depend on multiple combinations of these variables; and the explanation of how women's work affects fertility will have to be sought in the cultural context. Available information permits us to relate women's work to some of the intermediary variables; for the others, we can only construct hypotheses that will provide paths for future investigations.

Considering the relation between the use of contraceptives or contraceptive methods and women's work, there is a percentage difference in favor of those who work outside the home (30. 2 percent) as opposed to those who do not work (25. 1 percent). We have no information on the behavior of those who work at home; but it is possible that their behavior is, as we have seen on other occasions, more similar to that of women who don't work. In view of this possibility, the differing percentages of use of contraceptives among working and unemployed women would diminish.

We found that 44. 8 percent of working women had had seven or more children, while only 32. 3 percent of the women who did not work had had that many children. Abortion frequencies were higher—62. 6 percent—among women who have never worked than among those who have (50. 0 percent). It must be pointed out that these figures underestimate the number of abortions among Mexican women (it has been estimated at 700, 000 per year); but one must remember that abortion is illegal, so that the data are easily hidden.

It would be interesting to know when women begin to use contraceptives, and whether there is any relationship with the women's occupational level. Also, it would be helpful to discover at what point women's work creates opportunities to discover contraceptive methods. It is clear that, among working women and unemployed women, misinformation predominates; but it is slightly greater among those who do not work (Trejo Reyes 1973).

We also tried to establish a relationship between family planning— including knowledge, acceptance, and use of contraceptive methods— and women's work, but the results did not yield significant differences (Lenero Otero 1966-67).

Another interesting relationship is that between women's work and the age of marriage. If marriage is late, logically the period of coital exposure is limited. It is a fact that Mexican women, whether they work or not, marry early (approximately 65 percent marry at 21 years or younger) (Rothman 1969; Lenero Otero 1966-67). This is congruent with the persistence of values from the traditional subculture, where marriage is a goal and the woman who does not marry is an object of contempt.

When the two variables are correlated, a slight difference appears: Those who were not working at the time they were interviewed were, on the average, younger when they married. We cannot, however, know whether their occupational status at the time they married was the same as that when they were interviewed. Nonetheless, while we have emphasized that women work principally until they find someone to depend on, it is very possible that the feeling of being economically capable may make working women more demanding in their requirements for a husband than those who have no other recourse.

This is fairly evident when the "ideal age" for marriage is asked about. The "ideal age" for marriage is not itself an intermediary variable, but it is a factor that can affect a number of them. Among working women the ideal age to contract matrimony is higher, especially among those who work outside their homes (32. 5 percent of these consider that 25 years or older is the ideal age to marry). This opinion is shared by 22. 2 percent of those who do not work. Among those who felt that women should marry before 22 years of age, there is a difference of 13. 5 percent in favor of those who do not work (Rothman 1969), which is fairly significant.

As for the other intermediary variables, we do not have sufficient information to answer our many questions. How does women's work affect her exposure to coitus? How does it affect sporadic sexual unions? How does it affect fetal mortality, voluntary or not? The answers will doubtless depend on other intervening variables. We must therefore design research proposals that stipulate multivariate analysis and control over the sequence of these variables.

About the second block of variables, those including values and relative norms concerning both the level of fertility and the intermediary variables, we have the following information. It is well known that the average ideal number of children is very high in Mexico. This is the case among women who work as well as among those who don't. In both cases the number is close to four children, and is slightly higher among those who do not work (Elu de Lenero 1969).

Among women who work outside the home, 60 percent considered four or less the ideal number of children. Forty percent of the women who work at home agreed, as did 38.3 percent of those without paid employment. The three categories of women show similar percentages concerning the ideal number of five children. Among those who have six or more children as an ideal are 27.6 percent of those who work outside the home, 43.5 percent of those who work at home, and 45.8 percent of those who have no paid occupations (Elu de Lenero 1969).

Another important index is the desired number of children: we always found that this number was smaller than the number of children actually borne. This provides evidence for the existence of "unwanted children," a situation that occurs more often among working women. These births presumably could have been avoided if the elements that negatively affect the variables of exposure to coitus and gestation had been present. In one of the studies, the presence of unwanted children was apparent: 40 percent of the women answered that the number of children they had was higher than they would have wished to have (Elu de Lenero 1969). But there were no significant differences between working and unemployed women. Nor were there notable differences among the two groups' responses to the questions "Do you plan to have more children?" and "How many children do you think are convenient to have?," nor differences in approval or disapproval of family planning. Other indexes from this block of variables are necessary to explain their influence.

In the intricate cultural transition in which the Mexican woman lives, it is logical that her greater or lesser acceptance of the values from the modern subculture would influence the intermediary variables that affect fertility. The data suggest a greater tendency toward the indexes of modernism among women who work than among those who do not. Various value indexes of the traditional and modern subcultures were used to construct a test of conservatism and progressivism. As we sorted the interviewed women into categories, we found that 13.1 percent of those who worked outside the home, 24 percent of those who worked at home, and 19.8 percent of those who did not work were classified as "very conservative"; 12.4 percent, 5.2 percent, and 8.9 percent, respectively, were classified as "very progressive" (Lenero Otero 1966-67). Curiously, it appeared that those who worked at home were more conservative than those who had no paid employment.

It is very important, nonetheless, to point out that the differences that we have found between Mexican women who work and Mexican

women who don't work are much less significant than those between the
Mexican working woman and the working woman in, say, Buenos Aires
(Rothman 1969), where the process of cultural transition has reached a
different stage and there is a much more marked tendency toward the
ideal values of the modern subculture; in Buenos Aires, the process of
acculturation may be considered more complete, and other social processes are operating (see Elu de Lenero 1975).

FAMILY STRUCTURE, WORK, AND FERTILITY
AMONG MEXICAN WOMEN

When family planning programs are spoken of, there is always an
insistence that the couple should act as the decision-making unit. It
is thought that the development of all of those factors that indicate a
greater integration of the couple—such as communication, accord, companionship, and conjugal satisfaction—will lead to a more efficacious
planning of births, and consequently to a decrease in fertility (Lenero
Otero 1966-67).

Thus, the way in which women's work relates to these indexes can
tell us the kinds of influences we can expect from them on fertility.
Nonetheless, we find ourselves again on the ambiguous and shaky
ground that characterizes the Mexican transitional process.

Both in the study undertaken by Celade (Rothman 1969) and in the
investigations by IMES, it was found that the work of women coincided
with high indexes of personal and conjugal dissatisfaction, a fairly
logical situation in the social and familial context that we have been
describing. In this context, women's work can most assuredly be considered as a dependent variable to the dissatisfaction.

This dissatisfaction can also lead women, and in fact does, to
control their fertility, but not following the model of the integrated
couple. Rather, they follow the other, much more frequent model, in
which the woman decides on her own not to have more children. This
decision does not arise from conjugal communication, but from the situation of a woman who simply "can't handle" the children she already
has, and decides not to have even one more, whether her "lord" agrees
or not. This is the same type of woman who points out the fallacies in
the generalization that a family in which the man and woman plan hap-
pily and together for their children is a lovely picture.

It is important to emphasize that in these cases, which are in the
majority, there has been no real planning of fertility, but a desire to
stop all births. Until now, the great majority of women attending family planning clinics have done so in order to avoid having more children
(Elu de Lenero 1969).

But does this mean that the couple could be the decision-making
unit after all? No. If this were the case, the situation would not be

as complex. It does exist, and we have found it among couples of higher income and levels of education. There, indeed, the harmonic relation
between conjugal satisfaction and women's work appears to work better
(Lenero Otero 1966-67).

In these families, women are accorded a different treatment in their
homes; there is greater collaboration on the part of the men in domestic
activities; and women participate more in the family system of authority-
even though, among this same group, the men continue to believe that
it is they who should decide whether women work. Again, this situation
would be incomprehensible if we did not ground it in a Mexican society
at an intermediary stage of transition, where ideal values are not mono-
lithic. Ambivalence permits a situation in which one can be and not be
at the same time; the results and the social dynamic depend on the dialectical capacity of individuals and institutions. In the present case,
it will depend on whether working women will take advantage of the opportunity that this ambiguity accords them, so that the social dynamic
will move in their favor.

THE ARTICULATION OF BIRTH CONTROL, WORK, AND THE DEVELOPMENT OF WOMEN

This opportunity arises now because we are at a critical stage in
the history of the world and of women, which has created a convergence
of interests. The history of the social development of women is, as we
have seen, related to catastrophes. At present it is related to a world
emergency, and the catastrophe is called the population explosion.

The disequilibrium between the growth of the population and the
productive capacity needed to satisfy it preoccupies the world. No one
would dream of stopping scientific research on how to continue lowering mortality rates. Demographic policies focus on fertility, and countries multiply programs that lead women to have fewer children. It is
difficult to achieve this, however, because humanity has spent all of
its history making women believe that their reason for existence is to
have lots of children—and women believe it. Maybe the problem of population growth that now confronts the world can in part be attributed to
having marginalized women from a more active social participation, and
having confined them to a reproductive role.

It is difficult to change what has been developed over centuries,
and society knows it. There are two possibilities. One is to treat wom-
en as though they were reproductive machines programmed to have children, and now to attempt to reprogram them not to have children. But
this alternative doesn't work, because, mysteriously, many resistances
arise. The second option is to develop women so that they may become
whole persons.

This can only be achieved when women are no longer "objects"—
if the decision to have fewer children, or none at all, is accompanied

by self-responsibility, by freedom to consider the possible choices, and by rupture of the alienating ties of dependence.

Women will not grow as persons simply by having fewer children if this is not accompanied by greater opportunities for development as social beings. That is, opportunities must be open to women, so that they may participate broadly in the construction of a better world. Here is precisely the opportunity. Society and women need a new image of women. We must take advantage of the resources that one can provide to construct the other. Access to education and greater participation in the labor force can heavily favor this change, but alone they are not enough; they must be accompanied by a revaluation of the image of women and human beings.

Women's work can be a liberating medium when it helps her to awaken her critical spirit, to take decisions on her own, and to abandon preestablished dogmas. If not, it can mean a greater alienation, the acceptance of new roles to play and new stereotypes to respond to, perhaps even more dangerous and enslaving because the mask covering them may be more attractively painted.

FINDING THE MEANING OF THE INVESTIGATION

Social science research needs in Latin America are almost limitless. Until now very little has been done. Rather than present a list of possible topics, I want to ask the question "Research for what?" It is well-known that research forms part of a political view, and that these views are sustained by given philosophies. It is also known that women do not yet have access to the organizations that generate population policies, because these institutions have not responded to the process of democratic participation, but have reacted to the same norms that control the institutional functioning of social structures.

Women began to suffer population growth before they knew it was a problem that preoccupied the whole world. They had felt it in their flesh when they could not feed their children, when some died in the waiting room of a first aid station, when they stood in line from five in the morning to be able to enroll their children in schools. But in order to be heard, they had to wait for those "above" to become frightened by the population explosion. Now there is concern about the population explosion on the national and international levels.

How can one guarantee that a decline in the birth rate will really bring greater opportunities for human development in the neediest sectors of the population? Greater access to resources is a question of life or death for large parts of the population, but what is the frame of reference in which these resources are controlled when a society presents its birth control propaganda as the choice between a child and a refrigerator?

To what point will women become accomplices of a civilization that has confused being more with having more, in which everything is a function of "man the consumer?" What can women do to prevent this from happening? This is what must be investigated. We need research to determine more humane ways of population control, research to discover the values of the different sectors of the population. We need research as a communication channel between those for whom decisions are made and those who make the decisions. We need research to implement educational programs at all levels, that can become the repository for the voices of many Indian villages, where the inhabitants live in subhuman conditions and are not interested in contraception because it means the end of their race. We need research that will echo the anguish of women who cannot feed their children and don't know what to do; research that shows which values are transcendent, and which are obstacles for greater human development. We need research that opens new perspectives, warns of dangers, illustrates the search for solutions for different kinds of needs. We need interdisciplinary research to help us discover mankind's true aspirations and that puts scientific advances at the service of these aspirations. We need research, in short, that liberates and does not serve as one more instrument of greater alienation.

It is very possible that working women will have to reduce their biological fertility, but their social responsibility does not lie in merely being less fertile. To the contrary. At this critical moment, women themselves find themselves in a strategic position because they have succeeded in entering the system, and they must develop their procreative abilities to a level that may have been impossible to achieve previously. Women have in their hands the possibility of procreating a new culture, a new family, and—what is more important—a new woman. All this can be accomplished through the discovery of what it is "to be a woman" in the modern world. If they don't do it, no one else will; and women will continue to be objects, out of step with humanity's development.

With 1974 as the Year of Population, and 1975 as the Year of Women, the system is giving us opportunities that we have never had before, and are unlikely to have again. How shall we take advantage of them? There are only two possibilities. Either we arm ourselves with valor, and accept our responsibility to the world, to the family, and to ourselves, or we continue to complain without accepting the challenge to stop being "objects."

And if the working woman takes this path in the field of the social sciences, the responsibility becomes gigantic. She must outdo herself and prepare for professional, methodologically sound work that is valuable but, beyond that, constitutes an adequate scientific implementation of programs of true women's liberation that will surely develop more just forms of coexistence and offer greater opportunities for the development of the human being.

REFERENCES

Benitez, Raul, and Gustavo Cabrera. 1966. Proyecciones de la poblacion de Mexico, 1960-1980. Mexico City: Banco de Mexico, De-
   partamento de Investigaciones Industriales.

Castellanos, Rosario. 1970. "La participacion de la mujer en la edu-
   cacion formal." Presented at the Forum on the Role of the Mexican
   Woman in the Movement of National Productivity. Mexico City:
   Ed. Mundo Grafico, Centro Nacional de la Productividad.

Colegio de Mexico. 1970. Dinamica de la poblacion. Mexico City:
   Ed. Colmex.

Elu de Lenero, Maria del Carmen. 1969a. Efectos psicosociales de la
   planeacion familiar en el Distrito Federal. Mexico City: Instituto
   Mexicano de Estudios Sociales.

_____. 1969b. Hacía donde va la mujer mexicana? Mexico City: Ed.
   IMES.

_____. 1970. Investigacion sobre el noviasgo en Mexico. Mexico
   City: Ed. IMES.

_____. 1975. El trabajo de la mujer en Mexico: Alternativa para el
   cambio. Mexico City: Ed. IMES.

√Freedman, Ronald, David Kingsley, and Judith Blake. 1967. Factores
   sociologicos de la fecundidad. Mexico City: Ed. Colegio de Mexico and Centro Latino-americano de Demografía.

Germani, Gino. 1971. Sociologia de la modernizacion. Buenos Aires:
   Ed. Paidos.

Lenero Otero, Luis. 1966-67. Investigacion de la familia en Mexico.
   Mexico City: Instituto Mexicano de Estudios Sociales.

_____. n. d. "Social Implications of Demographic Growth and Birth of
   a Population Policy: The Case of Mexico" (provisional title). Population Bulletin. (In press.)

Navarrete, Ifigenia M. de. 1969. La mujer y los derechos sociales.
   Mexico City: Ed. Oasis.

Parsons, Talcott. 1966. El sistema social. Madrid: Ed. Revista de
   Occidente.

Rothman, Ana Maria. 1969. La participacion femenina en actividades economicas en su relacion con el nivel de fecundidad en Buenos Aires y Mexico. Santiago, Chile: Ed. Celade.

Secretariat of Industry and Commerce. 1970. General Census of the Population. Mexico City: Direccion General de Estadistica.

Sullerot, Evelyne. 1970. Historia y sociologia del trabajo femenino. Barcelona: Ed. Peninsula.

Trejo Reyes, Saul. 1973. Industrializacion y empleo en Mexico. Mexico City: FCE.

Weber, Max. 1944. Economia y sociedad. Mexico City: FCE.

Zetina, Guadalupe. 1972. "El trabajo de la mujer casada y su vida familiar ante el cambio social." B.A. thesis in social sciences, Ibero-American University, Mexico City.

4

CLASS CONSCIOUSNESS
AMONG WORKING-CLASS WOMEN
IN LATIN AMERICA:
PUERTO RICO
Helen Icken Safa

Conventional Marxist analysis of class consciousness in advanced capitalist or dependent underdeveloped societies has concentrated upon men and their participation in the labor force as primary factors. Women have generally been regarded as a secondary labor reserve, primarily responsible for "unproductive" domestic labor, and therefore not crucial to the development of proletarian consciousness in either developing or underdeveloped societies.

Recently this downgrading of female labor and participation in class struggle has been seriously criticized, particularly by writers with a feminine perspective (such as Lamphere 1973; Leacock 1972; Vogel 1971). These writers point out that woman's increasing participation in the urban labor force in both advanced industrial and Third World societies is overlooked, and her role in peasant agricultural production has generally been ignored. There has also been a failure to recognize woman's domestic role in maintaining and reproducing the labor force as essential to the stability of the capitalist system (Larguia and Dumoulin 1972). The wages earned by male workers in effect also subsidize the unpaid labor of the housewives, which is automatically devalued because it is outside the money economy. However, as Margaret Benston notes, while woman's domestic labor may not produce exchange value (wages), it does have use value that is consumed within the family (Benston 1969, p. 15).

The distinction between exchange value and use value, Benston (1969, pp. 15-16) notes, occurs primarily with the advent of capitalism, which takes commodity production outside of the home and into the factory and marketplace. In pre-industrial peasant economies, women worked alongside men as an integral family unit in agricultural production. Ester Boserup's (1970) analysis of woman's role in economic development in Third World countries supports Engels' notion that woman's status declined with the advent of class society, industrial capitalism, and the sharp distinction between the private world of the family and the public world of work. Women were no longer partners with men in a joint economic enterprise, but dependent upon a man's wages for their survival and that of their families.

Thus, under capitalism, household labor remains in the premarket stage (Benston 1969, p. 15). Even if housework can be considered useful labor, it still leaves the woman dependent upon the man and isolates her from other women and men, since housework is carried out independently within each private household. Dependency upon the male and isolation from other workers, particularly women, are crucial factors inhibiting the development of class consciousness in women of all class sectors.

Engels felt that women's entry into the labor force would raise their consciousness and status. However, while wage work outside the home may bring the woman more independence and freedom, it has also created a dual burden for most women, who are still held responsible for the care of the home and children. Several studies suggest that this burden may lead to severe stress and alienation, particularly among working-class women who cannot afford to hire outside domestic help (Piho 1973; Lamphere 1973; Rapoport 1971). Thus, even when women work, they are incompletely proletarianized. They tend to regard their family roles as primary, and to see their jobs as another way of aiding their families.

In this essay, it will be argued that because of the centrality of women's family roles, particularly in Latin America, they cannot be ignored in the formation of female class consciousness. Class consciousness in women involves not only oppression in the workplace, as members of the working class, but sexual subordination in the home, resulting from a strongly patriarchal family structure. Sexual subordination affects women at all levels of society; but elite women are endowed with certain privileges, accruing from this class position, that makes their sexual subordination less visible and onerous. Sexual subordination in Latin America is also masked by a female mystique, often called Marianismo, by which the ideal female role is compared to the Virgin Mary, long-suffering but never complaining, sheltered and protected from evil worldly influences (see Stevens 1973). This ideal continues to be operative among working-class women, and is used to justify class as well as sexual oppression (see Gissi 1974). However, working-class women enjoy none of the privileges of elite class position, and thus are forced to bear the dual burden of sexual subordination at home and class oppression outside.

Women themselves clearly are not a class, but members of another class, depending on their socioeconomic position in society. All too often, the class position of women is defined not by women themselves, even when they are working, but by their husbands or fathers, whose status they assume. While this is another clear reflection of women's dependency on men, it does not mean that women cannot acquire class consciousness independently. It does suggest that the process by which women acquire class consciousness will be different and more difficult than it is for men.

Participation in the labor force may be a sufficient condition for the formation of class consciousness in men, but I would argue it is not sufficient for women, who suffer from sexual subordination as well as class oppression. Class consciousness is here defined as a cumulative process by which women recognize that they are exploited and oppressed, recognize the source of their exploitation and oppression, and are willing and able to organize and mobilize in their own class interests. We thus distinguish between what John Leggett, basing himself on Marx, has termed the cognitive and evaluative aspects of class consciousness. According to Leggett, "The cognitive aspect refers to whether workers utilize class terms, identify with this class, and display an awareness of the allocation of wealth within the community or society. The evaluative aspect refers to the extent to which workers think in terms of class struggle in order to achieve class goals" (Leggett 1967, p. 39). Thus, only through class struggle is full consciousness achieved.

While this essay is limited to an analysis of class consciousness among working-class women in Latin America, it has obvious implications for working-class women in any capitalist society. Class consciousness always takes place within a particular cultural setting, so it is necessary to explore both specific cultural features and class factors in the formation of class consciousness. In this essay the data are drawn largely from my own study of shantytown families in San Juan, Puerto Rico, including a broad survey sample conducted in 1959 and an intensive restudy of selected families in 1969, after their relocation to various parts of the San Juan metropolitan area. Since the data were not collected for the purpose of examining class consciousness, we have had to reinterpret a great deal in an attempt to shed light on this subject. We have also tried to suggest some of the changes taking place in women's family and occupational roles during this critical time period in Puerto Rican history and their impact on class consciousness, particularly in the younger generation.

OPERATION BOOTSTRAP AND FEMALE EMPLOYMENT

In the early 1940s Puerto Rico embarked upon an ambitious development program, popularly known as Operation Bootstrap, designed to transform the island from a stagnant rural economy, dependent largely on the export of sugarcane to American markets, to an industrialized society with higher standards of living through more employment; higher wages, better health, housing, and education; and other social welfare measures.

The results of Operation Bootstrap are shown in the shift from agricultural to nonagricultural employment, particularly in manufacturing, trade, and services. After 1952, industry became the dominant mode of economic activity on the island, with manufacturing generating $999 million of net income in 1971 (Informe Estadistico 1971, Table 8). Economic

growth and high government expenditures for public health, housing, and
education have brought improved standards of living and sharp declines
in mortality rates, illiteracy, and other indexes of social well-being.
However, increased employment has been unable to absorb dramatic
population increases (resulting from improved living standards), with
the result that unemployment has continued to hover around 12 percent.
With the recent recession, felt much more acutely in Puerto Rico, unemployment has increased dramatically.

Industrialization and economic growth in Puerto Rico have resulted
in increasing participation of women in the labor force.* In 1970, wom-
en constituted 27.1 percent of the total labor force, up from 22.0 percent in 1962, an increase due totally to nonagricultural employment
(Comision de Derechos Civiles 1972, p. 132). This difference would
appear to be due to the fact that, at least in this early phase of industrialization in Puerto Rico, which emphasized light manufacturing, wom-
en were employed at a rate nearly equal to men. Thus, in 1970, women
constituted 48.6 percent of the labor force in manufacturing (Comision
de Derechos Civiles 1972, p. 133). They also constituted 44.8 percent
of the persons employed in public administration and 47.2 percent of
those in service jobs (Pico 1974, p. 133), two other fast-growing employment sectors.

Women provided a cheap labor force for the start of industrialization in Puerto Rico. In the industries established through the Office of
Economic Development, the salary differential was as high as 30.3 percent in industries where women predominated, as compared to those employing mostly men (Pico 1974, pp. 138-39). This reflected the fact
that women are concentrated in the manufacture of nondurable consumer
goods, such as textiles, clothing, leather goods, and tobacco, where
pay is considerably lower than in such durable goods as metal, stone,
or glass products, where men predominate (Pico 1974, p. 136). The
average salary for all women working full-time in 1970 was $3,006,
compared with $3,382 for men. However, women were concentrated in
the lower-paid jobs, with 42.2 percent receiving less than $2,000 a
year, compared with 26.7 percent of the men (Pico and Hernandez 1974,
p. 5).

---

*Although the number of women workers has increased steadily in
this century, the percentage of all women 14 years and over who are
actually employed has declined from 26.1 percent in 1930 to 22.9 percent in 1970. (Pico 1974, Table 1). The percentage of men employed
decreased even more dramatically, from 81.0 percent in 1930 to 54.72
in 1970 (Pico 1974, Table 1). These decreases would appear to be due
to such factors as overall population increase, increased life expectancy, and, most important, outmigration, particularly for men and wom-
en of working age.   + ed!

The recent concentration upon heavy capital-intensive industry in Puerto Rico and in other developing areas also threatens female employment. In these capital-intensive industries, labor tends to be reduced to a minimum and to be highly skilled, favoring the creation of a labor aristocracy in which men predominate. Recent case studies of three large petrochemical industries in Puerto Rico reveal a total absence of women in the production line and a very meager representation at official and managerial levels (Pico 1974b, p. 4).

FEMALE OCCUPATIONAL ROLES IN THE SHANTYTOWN

In the survey conducted in 1959 in Los Peloteros, a shantytown in the heart of the San Juan metropolitan area, 22 percent of the women were currently employed and an additional 45 percent had been previously employed. Thus, the great majority of women in the shantytown had worked at some point in their lives, which completely contradicts the Latin American ideal of la mujer en su casa ("the woman in her home"). This ideal is also being questioned by women of the elite, who are seeking professional and other prestige forms of employment in increasing numbers. It was never practiced among women of the working class, who in both the rural and the urban areas were always forced to work to add to the family income.

Paulita, now a young mother of seven children, recalls how she came to San Juan as a child with her mother, two sisters, and a brother. Her mother worked as a domestic and only one child could live with her; the others lived in foster homes. Speaking of the difficulties women faced then, Paulita notes:

> . . . At that time women who had a problem, who had left their husbands, the majority became prostitutes (paganas), right? Because they had no choice. If they were very young, they didn't want them working in families because they fell in love with the husband. And since they couldn't find work, those women went to sin because they didn't have any schooling. . . .

Many women in Los Peloteros continued to work as domestic servants, or in other service occupations, while the more fortunate had factory jobs, considered the most desirable occupations. The salary differential was substantial, with factory workers in 1970 earning an average annual income of $2,571, compared with $874 for domestic servants (Pico and Quintero 1974, p. 6). In addition, domestic service was considered very demeaning, and placed the woman in a completely dependent patron-client relationship, in which it is difficult to develop any class consciousness or collective solidarity (see Smith 1973). The

domestic servant is one of the chief instruments by which elite women
maintain their privileged status in capitalist society. She is as isolated
as the housewife, and more exploited.

Though opportunities for women in the working class have been concentrated in low-paid, unskilled jobs, the rapid expansion of occupational opportunities in the last two decades has created in women a near
universal desire for upward mobility. Most working-class women are
optimistic about the future for themselves and other women; they feel it
is each individual's responsibility to progress as much as possible.
Lydia, one of our younger informants who has been particularly successful, compares herself with other girls in the shantytown where she grew
up, and notes:

> In general terms we had the same opportunities. . . . That
> is, we came from poor homes and at home we had more or
> less the same education in the moral and material sense.
> Nevertheless, many of them today are married, they have no
> further preparation. I even know of some girls who would
> like, if they could, to return and start their life over again.
> . . . The desire to excel (superarse) has not been as great
> in them as in others. The desire to excel of each individual,
> it doesn't matter where he is or where he lives, that helps
> a great deal to enable him to move forward.

This drive toward upward mobility has tended to mitigate the development of class consciousness among working-class women, since the
emphasis is on individual initiative and competition rather than on collective class solidarity.

Expanding occupational opportunities have also placed a new value
on education for women. Among the adult generation surveyed in the
shantytown in 1959, despite generally low educational levels, women
fared even worse than men; 22.3 percent of the women had never gone
to school at all, and 39.4 percent had never gone beyond the fourth
grade (Safa 1974, p. 23). Most of these women were migrants who grew
up in the rural area, where there were few schools beyond the fourth
grade. Now, however, as jobs and educational opportunities for wom-
en have increased in the urban area, the value of education for girls has
been recognized; and among the adolescent generation in the shantytown,
the educational level of girls is on a par with that of boys (Safa 1974,
p. 23).

Flor reflects the new ideology of equality of opportunity for the
sexes when she states:

> Women can do everything as well as men. They can become
> presidents, they can become everything, they can rise to all
> man's jobs. Today there is no longer any difference between
> men and women.

   Flor gained much of her drive and initiative from her mother, who
managed to raise a family of eight children on the sale of canita (illegal
rum). Flor's father was a chronic alcoholic who often beat his wife and
children, and even turned his wife over to the police out of sheer re-
sentment of her economic independence. Even when he worked, most
of his salary went for drink for himself and his friends.

   Women such as Raquel, who cannot rely on a husband to support
them, are often forced to become the principal breadwinners for their
families. In 1970, 47.6 percent of divorced women worked, compared
with 22 percent of married women living with their husbands (Pico and
Quintero 1974, p. 1). Men who are separated from their wives cannot
be relied upon for child support, and often migrate to the mainland to
avoid family responsibilities. Welfare payments are generally too low
for families to survive, though they have increased substantially since
the original study was conducted in 1959. At that time, for example,
Carmen, a young widow with five small children, received $50 a month
from public welfare, which she supplemented with part-time work as a
laundress. Now she receives $82 a month for herself and one minor
child, in addition to what her oldest children give her. Welfare, however, creates another form of dependency, not on the husband but on
the state. Thus it is another factor inhibiting the development of class
consciousness, particularly important in advanced capitalist societies,
where welfare policies are more developed. Puerto Rico certainly has a
more elaborate welfare program than most Latin American countries, and
it is heavily subsidized by the U.S. federal government.

   The growing number of female-headed households among the working
class in Latin America is an extremely important development for the
formation of class consciousness among women. Women who are heads
of households are more prone to develop a stronger commitment to their
work role because they become the principal breadwinners for the family
(see Piho 1973). They cannot afford to regard their work roles as temporary or secondary, as do most of the married women in the shantytown.
This lack of commitment to a work role plays a crucial role in the absence of class consciousness among women in the shantytown, since
they never identify with their work role or stay on one job long enough
to develop a relationship with their peers. Thus, in the survey conducted in 1959, the great majority of women in the shantytown who had
worked never saw their fellow employees after work or participated in
union activities. The reason is clear: women must rush home after work
to care for children and do household chores, whereas men are free to
join their friends and, as the survey demonstrated, often meet their best
friends through work. Women in the shantytown tend to work sporadi-
cally, as the need arises, for which such menial occupations as domestic service and other service jobs are ideally suited.

   Women who are the sole support of their families are more likely to
develop class consciousness than women who are still primarily dependent on men to support them. However, as a study of female

textile workers in Mexico demonstrated, the pressure of family responsibilities and the fear of losing their job may also prevent these women from expressing open dissatisfaction with the long hours, low pay, and miserable working conditions (Piho 1973). Thus, female household heads are still restrained by the other factors that hamper the development of class consciousness among Latin American working-class women generally: the concentration in unskilled labor, the role of welfare, and the burden of family and household responsibilities. Although younger women have growing confidence in their ability to find work and to compete with men for better jobs, their family roles remain central.

FAMILY ROLES AND SEXUAL SUBORDINATION

In order to understand the impact of the family on the class consciousness of women in Latin America, it is necessary to analyze the structure of the shantytown household and the sharp segregation of roles. The man's authority is based largely on his role as economic provider, which is weakened by the high rate of unemployment, poor wages, low skill and educational levels, and minimal possibilities for upward mobility. Even the traditional kinship and religious roles that may confer status on men in primitive or peasant societies are taken from him in an urban industrial society. The woman's domestic role, on the other hand, is left relatively intact. She has primary responsibility for the care of the home and children, and derives her authority from her close relationship with her children and female kin. The strong emotional bond between a woman, her children, and her female kin group results in a pronounced matrifocal emphasis in shantytown families.

Matrifocality, as used here, is not limited to families where the woman assumes the actual role as head of household, but is also found in families with a stable male head, where his role is marginal to the primary sphere of mother-child relationships. Though half of the households sampled in Los Peloteros were of the nuclear family type, household composition becomes more complex among older women who were married twenty years or more; among them, there is a larger percentage of extended families and households headed by females, reflecting not only the greater life expectancy of women but also the increasing autonomy of women as they grow older. One-fourth of the women sampled report being married in consensual union, which often tends to be more unstable than civil or church marriages; more than half of these women have been married more than once.

Two-thirds of the adult women sampled were first married between the ages of 15 and 19, a tendency that does not appear to be on the decline in the younger generation, except among the most upwardly mobile. Several of the daughters of our informants, born and raised in the urban area, have entered into marriage or consensual union at 14 or 15, usually

conceiving a child within the first year. They have little knowledge of
the world outside the home, and pass from dependence on their parents
to dependence on their husbands. Clearly this is another factor inhibiting the development of class consciousness in working-class women.

Many girls marry young in order to escape the confinement of a pa-
rental home, only to face worse tyranny with their husbands. A woman
may not be able to leave the house without her husband's permission,
and generally confines her social life to family gatherings and informal
visits with neighbors. Husbands and wives seldom go out together except as a family. She is required to wait on her husband, to have supper
ready when he arrives from work, and to take care of all the housework
and the children without his help. A common pattern is for the husband
to give his wife a weekly allowance for household expenses; and she
may not know, beyond this, how much money he makes or spends on
himself. Many men prohibit their wives from working, even when they
could use the extra income, because it casts doubt on their own ability
as provider and gives the women too much independence. Even the limited authority women unjoy in the domestic sphere is not translatable
into social power or position in the larger society (see Sachs 1974: 219).
In the shantytown, there is a sharp division between the public world of
work and the private world of the family; and men try, so far as possible,
to confine their wives to the latter. The man acts as spokesman for his
family in all dealings with the outside world: on barrio committees, in
the local housing cooperative; in political parties, for example, the
membership is almost exclusively male. Responsibility for social control in the shantytown also rests largely with the man. For example,
men may attempt to end a fight between neighbors or tell a drunkard to
do his drinking elsewhere, while women are hesitant to intervene in
nonfamily affairs. This lack of experience and authority in the public
sphere also limits the development of class consciousness in women.

Economic instability is the most frequent cause of marital breakdown. There is no strong conjugal bond in the shantytown household
to hold a man and wife together in the face of economic adversity. There
is no investment in property, no status to uphold, no deep emotional
tie. The younger generation of women are less likely to accept the abuse
their mothers stood for, including beatings, infidelity, and lack of financial support. Flor, Raquel's daughter, recalls how her father used
to enter their house in the middle of the night in a drunken rage and begin to beat them all and chase them from the house. She said she would
not stand for the same behavior from her husband: "Absolutely, and if
he hits me, I won't stand for it, not even once. Here at this time there
are so many ways of solving problems, that he doesn't lay a finger on
me." The younger generation of working-class women clearly feel they
have greater legal support and protection from male abuse. Nearly all
our respondents, male and female, felt that women today enjoy more
freedom and independence than previously.

Nevertheless, the abuse suffered by many women at the hands of
their husbands makes them feel far more oppressed by men and marriage

than by their class position. Nearly three-fourths of the women interviewed in 1959 felt that most marriages are unhappy, and blamed this largely on the man and his vices. It is hard for women to realize that men may be taking out their frustration and hostility toward tedious, unrewarding jobs and lives on women and their children, who are the working-class man's only subordinates. What women feel most directly is man as the oppressor, and therefore much of their own hostility is directed against men rather than against the class system. This deflection of discontent onto men also limits the development of class consciousness, since the issue becomes individual liberation from men, rather than class struggle with men to overcome mutual exploitation.

Marital problems are handled in highly individualized ways, and women seldom confront their husbands openly with their dissatisfaction. Instead of protesting, women attempt to manipulate men into doing what they want, and into believing that men are the real boss in the household while they are quietly running things (see Stevens 1973). Much of the public deference to male authority is based on this premise. This manipulative strategy is very similar to that employed by both men and women toward all persons in higher authority, employers, government officials, doctors, storekeepers, and so on. "I obey but I do not comply" is an old Puerto Rican peasant saying. In the attempt to avoid open conflict, manipulation employs a highly individualistic mode of gaining the advantage over one's adversary. It emphasizes the subordinate nature of the client vis-a-vis the dominant patron by stressing the client's helplessness and dependency, and the need for the patron's (husband's) protection and guidance. This is seen most clearly during pregnancy, when women bear living proof of their husband's virility, but also make demands on their husbands that would be totally rejected at another time. These demands, known in Puerto Rico as entojos, are usually in the form of cravings for special food or drink, which if denied, according to folk belief, might harm the unborn fetus. Thus, even when pregnant, the woman is not representing her own interest, but the child's.

The way in which patron-client relationships limit the development of class consciousness and collective solidarity among the Latin American proletariat generally is widely recognized (see Mintz 1967); patron-client relationships promote the development of dyadic, vertical relationships that hinder the formation of horizontal and collective peer group relationships necessary to class consciousness. However, as June Nash (n. d., p. 23) has pointed out, the way in which these mechanisms of dependency permeate the entire social structure, including the family, helps to explain how they are perpetuated from generation to generation. Women learn to be dependent at an early age, and to use manipulative strategy with men. This mitigates the possibility of collective solidarity among women, who see each household as a private battleground.

SOURCES OF FEMALE SOLIDARITY AND STATUS

Despite these divisive tendencies, however, there is far more female solidarity in the shantytown than in middle-class neighborhoods characterized by isolated nuclear families. Much of the solidarity is expressed through the kin group, which, despite the norm of bilaterality, tends to be mediated through women. Children generally maintain close contact with their parents after marriage, and the mother-daughter tie is particularly strong. The first child is often born in the grandmother's home and retains a close tie to her throughout life. One of our younger informants repeatedly returned home when her children were born, so that the grandmother could take care of her children while she was in the hospital and help her during her convalescence. She also leaves her children with her (adopted) mother daily while she and her husband work.

There is also extensive mutual aid among families in the shantytown, particularly the women. They borrow from each other, not only cups of sugar or electric irons, but even water and electricity or the use of a refrigerator. They also share in child-rearing. In the evening, children may gather in a neighbor's house to watch television. If they are hungry, they are fed. Neighbors will rush to comfort crying children, or try to entice them out of a temper tantrum with a bright new penny or a flavored ice cube. At the same time, they do not hesitate to scold a naughty child or ask a neighbor's child to run an errand for them. In this way, shantytown families avoid the intense and often strained relationships of the isolated nuclear family, where the woman has none of these sources of aid or friendship. In this sense, the domestic role of the woman in the Puerto Rican shantytown is less isolating or alienating than that of the middle-class housewife. It may also be less tedious and exploitative than the occupational roles of many shantytown men.

Most women in the shantytown, working or not, would argue that their primary rewards lie within the domestic sphere of their children and family. A woman feels that her own validation and status as a woman rests with her children, for whom she feels primary responsibility. One woman who could not bear children adopted three of her brother's children (after he was imprisoned for killing his adulterous wife). Several women whose husbands had died or left them continued to have children with other men. Sometimes it led to a stable relationship with the man, but more often it did not. Though clearly they were being exploited by the men, these women knew no other means of gaining self-identity or social recognition. The ideal role of wife and mother was for them still paramount.

The domestic role of the women in the shantytown can be compared to that of the black woman under slavery. Angela Davis (1971, pp. 6-7) has argued:

It was only in domestic life—away from the eyes and whip
of the overseer—that the slaves could attempt to assert the
modicum of freedom they still retained. . . . In the infinite
anguish of ministering to the needs of the men and children
around her (who were not necessarily members of her immediate family), she was performing the only labor of the
slave community which could not be directly and immediately
claimed by the oppressor. . . . She was therefore essential
to the survival of the community.

The woman in the shantytown, by being the mainstay of the family
and the wider kin group, also provides this function for the oppressed
urban proletariat. Though men and women are alienated in their work
roles, they have a domestic sphere to which they can retreat and which
capitalism has as yet been unable to destroy. Though the family has
been destroyed as an economically productive unit, social relationships
within the family and between neighbors and kin remain highly viable.
This is particularly important to the working class, who have no other
source of status and identity, and who are subjected to extreme exploitation in their relationships with other classes in the metropolis, which
are governed by status and market relationships (see Safa 1974, pp.
66-68).
The family and interpersonal relationships in the shantytown can
be compared with those in public housing, a planned community created
by the government to house the urban poor. In public housing, the cohesion, built up over many years in the shantytown, breaks down; mutual
aid is weakened, and families become more suspicious of each other.
Housing management begins to intervene in the internal affairs of the
family, checking on income, furnishings, household composition, and
other private matters; and the family no longer provides the refuge it
could in the shantytown. The public housing family is alienated, not
only because of its low socioeconomic status, which it shares with the
shantytown, but because family and community life has been disrupted
by the agencies of the state. Public and private domains are blurred as
the government begins to control the personal lives of public housing
residents.

CONCLUSIONS

Sexual subordination must be taken into account, along with class
oppression, in assessing the potential for the development of class
consciousness among working-class women in Latin America. The traditional subordination of the woman in the patriarchal family, found at
all class levels in Latin American society, limits her autonomy, freedom, and self-confidence. It restricts her to a narrow domestic sphere

where, however, she has been able to maintain considerable authority vis-a-vis the children and where extended kin and neighborly relations have prevented the alienation experienced by the woman in the isolated nuclear family.

Calls for the dissolution of the family and an end of child-bearing as a liability are clearly no solution. We cannot simply dismiss the family as a reactionary instrument of capitalist society, particularly in the working class, where it fulfills so important a function as the last refuge from capitalist exploitation. Were the family to be weakened, as is already happening in some working-class sectors of Puerto Rico, women would become as alienated as most men, who already are marginal to the domestic sphere and totally exposed to exploitative relationships on the job and in other public sectors.

I am not arguing for a reinstitution of the bourgeois nuclear family, which has proved extremely alienating and isolating to women. Unfortunately, many working-class families, as they move out of the shantytown and into middle class urbanizaciones, are already following this pattern and acquiring the competitive, individualistic, and consumer-oriented values that often accompany upward mobility in a capitalist society. Nor am I arguing against the entry of more women into the labor force, though I agree with Vogel (1971, p. 2) and others that as long as women constitute primarily a source of cheap labor for capitalism, as is abundantly evident in Latin America today, they are not promoting their own liberation or class consciousness. Rather, I am arguing that women's family roles should be considered a potential source of revolutionary strength in the working class.

Mariarosa Dalla Costa (1972) and others suggest that women be paid for domestic work, which would end their dependency on men and give housework exchange value. However, it might also give the state (which would probably be required to pay) the means to control the woman's domestic labor the way capitalism now controls all exchange value. Welfare payments for female-based households have certainly led to greater control and have merely shifted the dependency of women from their husbands to the state. Payment of women for domestic labor would redistribute income, as Margaret Benston (1969, p. 23) suggests, but would not necessarily lead to greater class consciousness.

Any movement for mobilization or class consciousness must take advantage of the natural basis of solidarity that already exists in the community. In the shantytown, we have identified a strong sense of solidarity among female kin and neighbors, expressed through mutual aid and close friendship. These ties could be strengthened through public support, and channeled into cooperative day care centers, health centers, and food distribution centers, like those in Chile created under the Allende government. This would be one way to break through the isolation of the nuclear family and to stimulate the development of more communal forms of child care and other household tasks, which could serve as the basis for the creation of a socialist society.

At this point, we may say that shantytown women have not passed beyond the very initial stages of class consciousness—that is, they may feel a sense of oppression, both within the family and within the larger society, but they are very unclear as to the source of this oppression, or how to deal with it. To use John Leggett's terminology, they have not passed beyond the cognitive stage of class consciousness, and are far from collectively representing their interests in the larger society.

However, it is clear that shantytown tomen share a greater sense of sexual subordination than of class oppression. It is men who abuse them, who fail to support them, and who confine them to the home and burden them with family responsibilities. As long as working-class women see their primary opponents as men, and as long as men regard them as subordinates in the class struggle, there is little hope for a shared struggle against common exploitation.

According to Isabel Pico (1974), working-class women did demonstrate greater class consciousness in the earlier stages of industrialization in Puerto Rico. Pico has shown how, prior to 1930, working-class women, employed chiefly in tobacco, home needlework, canning, and other early manufacturing industries, were active in the union movement as well as in the Socialist Party. The relative decline of these industries and the resulting dispersion of the female labor force into service and other marginal jobs apparently helped to deflect this growth in class consciousness, as did the demise and eventual incorporation of the Socialist Party into the reformist Popular Party. The leadership of the women's movement was then taken over by petit bourgeois women, who found a growing source of employment in public education, and who were chiefly interested in legal and social equality (women's suffrage and more education for women). Though pretending to speak for all women (as in the United States), the women's suffrage movement promoted primarily the class interests of elite women, to the point where illiterate women were initially denied the vote. The historic class split in the women's movement, both in the United States and in Puerto Rico, points to the virtual impossibility of building a women's movement across class lines. Historically, as well as in the present, the class interests of elite and working-class women are too diverse, and this cannot overcome a common sense of sexual subordination.

The primary obstacles to the development of class consciousness among working-class women in Latin America lie in the strict sexual division of labor, at home and on the job, their subordination within a patriarchal family structure, and their restriction to the private sphere of domestic labor. No simple solution will eradicate all of these obstacles. Rather, any attempt to develop class consciousness among working-class women must attack all three areas where women are subordinate: work, the family, and the community. It must not only promote entry of women into the labor force but end the sexual division of labor, which keeps women in poorly paid, low status jobs, and forces them to take on the dual burden of domestic responsibilities and employ-

ment. It must make men share in household responsibilities and socialize housework by creating public institutions that lighten the domestic
role, such as free day care centers, laundromats, and communal eating
places with "take-home" foods. It must also encourage women to take
a greater role in community affairs, on barrio committees, and in political parties, so that their needs and interests will also be represented.

Viewing class consciousness from a feminist perspective permits
one to question whether the narrow focus on work roles is even appropriate for men in the Latin American working class. As the marginal labor force in the cities grows larger, due to capital-intensive industrialization and continued rural-urban migration, it also becomes harder for
men to find stable employment or to identify with their work role. Unskilled men find jobs when and where they can, and have no particular
occupation. Under these circumstances, it also becomes difficult to
develop class consciousness among men in the workplace, and it may
become necessary to explore men's family and community roles as an
alternative (see Leggett 1967, pp. 6-7). We have seen that in the Puerto
Rican shantytown, some men participate actively in barrio committees,
political parties, and other community activities. In Chile the campa-
mentos served as an important basis for the development of political
activity and consciousness. The community may serve as a more appropriate locale than the factory for the development of class consciousness
among the Latin American working class.

The analysis of class consciousness among working-class women
in Latin America points up the need to revise traditional Marxist theory
in the light of new conditions in Third World as well as advanced capitalist societies. We cannot wait for all women to enter the labor force
while jobs in the low-income sector are diminishing, nor can we expect
women to carry the dual burden of family and job responsibilities any
longer. Their class interests as women clearly rest both in promoting
greater job opportunities for women at all class levels and in eliminat-
ing patriarchal family structures and sexual ideologies that relegate
women to an inferior and dependent role. Such changes are unlikely to
come about, in capitalist or socialist society, until working-class
women unite and demand attention to their needs within the large society. As Sheila Rowbotham (1973, p. 124) has written:

> The predicament of working-class women is the most poten-
> tially subversive to capitalism because it spans production
> and reproduction, class exploitation and sex oppression.
> The movement of working-class women is thus essential for
> the emergence of socialist feminism because the necessary
> connections are forced upon women who are working-class
> when they take action. . . . They need each other, they
> need the support of male workers, and their fight at work
> connects immediately to their situation at home. Their or-
> ganization and militancy is vital not only for women's liber-
> ation but for the whole socialist and working-class movement.

REFERENCES

Benston, Margaret. 1969. "The Political Economy of Women's Libera-
    tion." Monthly Review 21: 13-27.

Boserup, Ester. 1970. Woman's Role in Economic Development. New
    York: St. Martin's Press.

Comision de Derechos Civiles. 1972. La igualdad de derechos y opor-
    tunidades de la mujer puertorriquena. San Juan: Estado Libre Aso-
    ciado de Puerto Rico.

Dalla Costa, Mariarosa. 1972. "Women and the Subversion of the Com-
    munity." Radical America 6: 67-102.

Davis, Angela. 1971. "Reflections on the Black Women's Role in the
    Community of Slaves." Black Scholar 3.

Gissi Bustos, Jorge. 1974. "Mitologia sobre la mujer." Paper pre-
    sented at SSRC Conference on Feminine Perspectives in Social Sci-
    ences, Buenos Aires.

Informe Estadistico al Gobernador. 1971. San Juan: Oficina del Gober-
    nador, Junta de Planificacion, Estado Libre Asociado de Puerto Rico.

Lamphere, Louise. 1973. "Women's Work, Alienation and Class Con-
    sciousness." Paper presented at 72nd annual meeting of the Ameri-
    can Anthropological Association, New Orleans.

Larguia, Isabel, and John Dumoulin. 1972. "Toward a Science of Wom-
    en's Liberation." In Women in Struggle NACLA.

Leacock, Eleanor Burke, ed. 1972. The Origin of the Family, Private
    Property and the State. By Frederick Engels. Introduction by Lea-
    cock. New York: International Publishers.

Leggett, John. 1967. Class, Race and Labor: Working Class Con-
    sciousness in Detroit. New York: Oxford University Press.

Lewis, Oscar. 1966. La Vida: A Puerto Rican Family in the Culture of
    Poverty. New York: Random House.

Mintz, Sidney. 1967. "Caribbean Nationhood in Anthropological Per-
    spective." In Caribbean Integration. S. Lewis and T. C. Mathews,
    eds. San Juan: Institute of Caribbean Studies, University of Puerto
    Rico.

Nash, June. n. d. "Dependency and the Failure of Feedback: The Case of Bolivian Mining Communities." Mimeo.

Pico, Isabel. 1974a. "Apuntes preliminares para el estudio de la mujer puertorriquena y su participacion en las luchas sociales de principios del siglo XX." Paper presented at SSRC Conference on Feminine Perspectives in Social Sciences, Buenos Aires.

_____. 1974b. "The Quest for Race, Sex, and Ethnic Equality in Puerto Rico." Paper presented at meeting of Latin American Studies Assn., San Francisco.

Pico, Isabel, and Marcia Quintero. 1974. "Datos basicos de la mujer en la fuerza trabajadora en Puerto Rico." Appendix to paper presented at Buenos Aires conference. (See Pico 1974a.)

Piho, Virve. 1973. "Life and Labor of the Female Textile Worker in Mexico City." In Cross-Cultural Perspectives On the Woman's Movement and Women's Status. Ruby R. Leavitt, ed. The Hague: Mouton Press.

Rapoport, Rhona, and Robert Rapoport. 1971. Dual Career Families. Penguin Books.

√ Rowbotham, Sheila. 1973. Woman's Consciousness and Man's World. Penguin Books.

√ Rubbo, Anna. n. d. "The Spread of Rural Capitalism—Its Effects on Black Women in the Cauca Valley, Western Colombia." Mimeo.

√ Sachs, Karen. 1974. "Engels Revisited." In Women, Culture & Society. M. Rosaldo and J. Lamphere, eds. Stanford, California: Stanford University Press.

Safa, Helen Icken. 1974. The Urban Poor of Puerto Rico: A Study in Development and Inequality. New York: Holt, Rinehart and Winston.

√ Smith, Margo. 1973. "Domestic Service as a Channel of Upward Mobility for the Lower Class Woman: The Lima Case." In Female and Male in Latin America, ed. Ann Pescatello. Pittsburgh: University of Pittsburgh Press.

Stevens, Evelyn. 1973. "Machismo and Marianismo." Society 10.

Vogel, Lise. 1971. "The Earthly Family." Radical America 7: 9-50.

5

SEXUAL HIERARCHY
AMONG THE YANOMAMA
Judith Shapiro

Many of the essays in this volume focus on the author's own country; the others deal with societies that are foreign, yet in many respects
fundamentally similar to the authors' own. What I propose to discuss is
the position of women in a society that is very different from my own,
one that can certainly be called exotic. This interest in the exotic might
be seen as a natural and obvious result of the fact that I am an anthropologist. I happen to see it that way myself. Many of my colleagues,
however, would disagree. They are concerned with bringing anthropology
home, and maintain that the essential features of the anthropological
enterprise, however this may be defined, still obtain in the study of
one's own culture.

There is, in fact, a current interest on the part of anthropologists
in combining the roles of analyst and "native." This development is in
some measure a logical outcome of the anthropological concern for
studying human groups from the perspective of their members. The anthropologist, realizing that he can never really become an insider in
another society, may turn to the study of his own and welcome the production by other societies of their own anthropologists.

The position of the trained "native," as opposed to the foreign anthropologist, has been particularly enhanced by two recent trends. The
first is an attempt to decolonialize the profession, to do away with the
hierarchical and exploitative aspects of the relationship between anthropologist and subject. One way of doing this is to transform these roles
so that the outsider/insider relationship becomes a symmetrical col-
leagueship and the investigator/subject relationship ceases to carry the
weight of cultural difference and political inequality. (Inequality in the
form of class difference may continue to characterize the investigative
situation, but let's leave that aside for the moment.)

The second trend is the degree of attention anthropologists have
recently been directing toward systems of meaning. The study of ide-
ational aspects of culture—as opposed, for example, to cultural ecology

or behavioral sociology—has, for obvious reasons, a particular potential for identification between investigator and "native" informant.

The respective advantages of viewing a society from the "inside" and from the "outside" have already been much discussed and are, for the most part, too obvious to require belaboring here. Suffice it to say that the inside view draws upon a wealth of subtle understandings available to the outsider only after much time, if at all. The outside view reveals those aspects of a society that the initiated take for granted or of which they are totally unaware; such a view is also the basis for any comparative work. It seems to me that the distinctive contribution of anthropology lies in its attempt to deal with both perspectives and, indeed, with the tensions between them. Furthermore, such an approach is, in my opinion, tied to the experience of cultural otherness.

This, then, is the context in which I shall place my discussion of the position of women in Yanomama society.

Many writers in the field of women's studies, notably those with feminist concerns, have encountered the problem of relating an "objective" analysis of women's social roles and life experiences to the manner in which women themselves perceive these things. The double-focus quality of anthropological fieldwork led me to see this issue as a particularly central one. On the one hand, I wanted to open my mind to a world of very different meanings, to understand as much as I could of the life experiences of Yanomama women, and to see the social universe as it appears through their eyes. On the other hand, I wanted to find an appropriate framework for going beyond these women's own perspectives on their society and on the events of their everyday lives. The second aspect of the task presented particular difficulties, since I was attempting to work with notions of inequality and hierarchy. In seeking to apply these concepts to another society (as opposed to dealing with the appearance of such notions in another society's system of ideas), I found myself being led to make cross-cultural value judgments.

Those who have studied women in their own societies have faced a similar problem insofar as they have tried to make significant statements about the lives of women whose social class or background differs from their own. The issue here is usually seen in terms of elitism: social scientists tend to apply their own bourgeois notions as if these were absolute rather than relative values, thereby committing the double sin of intellectual naiveté and arrogance. The possibility of avoiding elitism—or its cross-cultural equivalent, ethnocentrism—is generally associated either with the ability to develop a profound sympathy and admiration for the group under study or with the limitation of one's investigations to matters that are unproblematically objectifiable.

Do we decide, then, that the social scientist, especially when dealing with another society, has no business talking of such things as injustice, exploitation, and oppression? If we do not so decide, are we justified—as Marx maintained when he pointed out that it is not the slave who can teach us about slavery—in going beyond people's own

views of their situation? And if we are so justified—if such concepts
as "false consciousness," for example, are valuable and even necessary
in sociocultural analysis—how do we make evaluative statements in a
responsible and cross-culturally relevant manner?

It is not my intention to propose that anthropology become an essentially judgmental enterprise. I am merely suggesting that our moral
faculties and ethical sensibilities may serve us better (and, in turn, be
better served) in cross-cultural research than most anthropologists have
hitherto assumed. I would also suggest that the ability to be a responsible critic may be the mark not only of a more profound and detailed
knowledge of another society, but also of the willingness to take that
society as seriously as we take our own.

I did not go to Yanomamaland with the express purpose of studying
women. In fact, I did not even go to South America with the express
purpose of studying the Yanomama. I wound up among them as the result
of a series of logistic problems and unexpected opportunities, an experience that will be understood by those who have done fieldwork in
the tropical forest area. It was only after my return from the field that
I came to focus my interests on the contrasting positions of the sexes
in Yanomama society. And it has only been in the last couple of years
that I have begun to think more explicitly about the comparative study
of women's social roles. I cannot, then, present to you the results of
a planned research project carried out in the field. What I can do at
present is to outline the main topics that would, in my opinion, have
to be included in a satisfactory study of women's place in Yanomama
society, and then discuss how material already gathered contributes to
such a study.

The project that I would now wish to carry out would include an investigation of the culture of sex. What are the essential attributes of
maleness and femaleness? What meanings are associated with sexual
symbolism? What kinds of criteria are used to evaluate proper sex identity?* What is the ideology associated with the sexual division of activities? What is the relationship between ideas about sexual difference
and other modes of differentiating among persons? To what degree is
this relationship overt and to what degree covert? What is the connection between qualities that are thought to be sex-linked and those that

---

*In our own society, for example, the notion of innate temperament
is basic to the conceptualization of sexual differences, and emotional
style is an important ingredient of appropriate sex role performance. As
Margaret Mead pointed out (Mead 1935), there are societies in which
this seems not to be the case. The sexual division of labor—the kinds
of tasks a person performs—may be the crucial differentiating factor,
and need not involve questions of temperament and character. Mead's
inquiry into the consequences of such divergent approaches to sex identity should be taken up again and pursued further.

are the basis for the allocation of prestige? How does differential prestige accruing to various activities relate to the sexual division of labor?
To what degree do the sexes form separate subcultures? Are there characteristic differences between the world views of men and women? How
are such differences revealed in their definitions of particular situations?
(A particularly interesting example of the way in which men and women
may define situations differently and of the sort of "reality bargaining"
that may ensue is found in Rosen n. d.)

What are the behavioral attributes of roles and activities characteristic of the respective sexes? What general differences does one observe between the activity patterns of men and women? Are communal
activities more characteristic of one sex than of the other? What kinds
of tasks are allocated by sex? How can the intrinsic properties of such
tasks be described?* How does the structuring of women's relationships
compare with the patterning of social bonds between and among men?
What are the characteristic forms of male/female relationship? What
types of control are evidenced in interactions between men and women?

The foregoing set of questions may contribute to a sort of "notes
and queries" for the comparative study of sex roles. They can help to
guide research and can, in turn, be elaborated upon and further refined
as such research is carried out. I should add that, in dividing the questions into two categories, I do not intend to establish a distinction between kinds of phenomena but, rather, to maintain the analytic distinction between an actor's and an observer's perspective.

Let us now turn to the Yanomama. † In studying the position of
women in this South American society, I have attempted to analyze the
following aspects of sex role structuring and of what I feel can be called
sexual hierarchy among the Yanomama: the degree of control that men

---

*By "intrinsic properties" I mean the kind of description an observ-
er might make and that would not depend on the actor's own attitudes.
I assume that it is both possible and necessary to be able to speak about
the quality of an activity in objective terms, though I recognize the difficulties involved.

†The Yanomama, who inhabit a territory extending from southeastern
Venezuela into adjacent areas of northwestern Brazil, constitute the
largest group of relatively uncontacted Indians in South America. The
estimate of their total population was close to 10, 000 at the time of my
fieldwork in 1967-68 and has been revised upward since then. Their
villages generally consist of a single circular dwelling. Individual nuclear or polygynous family units are ranged around the periphery of the
communal dwelling, which, in larger villages, takes the form of a lean-
to surrounding a spacious, open plaza. The central area of the house,
or village plaza, serves as the scene for intervillage feasts, ceremonies,

exercise over women and the way in which the latter are used to express
relationships among the former; the relative atomization and diffuseness
of the female social universe, as compared with the more highly structured world of male relationships; and the extremely unequal participation of the respective sexes in those activities that form the sphere of
ceremony and ritual (Shapiro 1970, 1972). It is the second point that
will provide the focus for the present discussion; the other two subjects
will be touched upon insofar as they relate to this basic structural difference between the social roles of men and women.

In terms of the considerations set out above, I will deal primarily
with the behavioral attributes of social roles from an observer's point
of view. Dyadic and group relationships are here described in terms of
the kinds of activity and association they imply, as revealed in the observation of the daily round of Yanomama life. I am, unfortunately, unable to describe the "culture of sex" among the Yanomama and, as a
consequence, also am unable to deal with the relationship between ideology—or social knowledge in the broader sense—and praxis. What I
have done thus far, then, should be seen as a contribution to one aspect
of the study of the respective position of the sexes in Yanomama society.

One subject about which an ethnographer is able to obtain reliable
information during the early stages of fieldwork is the organization of
daily activities. One can keep track of the comings and goings of village members, see which tasks are performed by which persons, and
who associates with whom. The ethnographer living among the Yanomama soon realizes that the activities that make up the daily round of
life are for the most part carried out in a highly individualized manner.
This is true of both men's work and women's work. Men usually go out
singly to hunt, work in their respective garden plots, or pay informal
visits to neighboring villages. Inside the communal house, a man tends
to sit in his own dwelling area, either working on an artifact or lounging
in his hammock. If he is hungry and his wife is not there, he will prepare some food for himself and eat alone.

Activities performed by women are similarly individualized. Meal
preparation is carried out by each woman in her own section of the
house. Even when co-wives are cooking simultaneously for the same
husband, each will prepare the food that she herself has gathered or
harvested. Two or more women may go out together to harvest garden
crops, to collect wild foods, or to cut firewood; but once out, each

---

and ritual events. A small village may have as few as 30 members; populations of larger villages may exceed 200 individuals.

The major source of subsistence among the Yanomama is provided
by slash-and-burn horticulture. Unlike the "classical" tropical forest
societies, however, for them plantains and bananas are more important
cultigens than manioc. Arboriculture provides an important seasonal
supply of food in the form of peach palm fruit. Fishing is of only secondary importance throughout most of the area, the Yanomama being essentially a nonriverine people.

woman goes about her own business. If they go in a group, this is in part because women avoid being alone at any distance from the house.

Over and above this general pattern of individualization, however, the sphere of male activities differs from that of women in that it provides more opportunities for regularized cooperation between pairs of men, as well as group endeavors involving a division of labor among participants. The most important form of regularized cooperation between men involves those who are potential or actual brothers-in-law. (More will be said about this relationship below.) Men related to one another in this manner commonly hunt together, help one another in various tasks, and spend a considerable amount of time socializing. Group endeavors include tasks such as canoe-building and certain stages in the construction of houses. The raiding party is a particularly important form of male group activity, especially in those areas of Yanomamaland where warfare is most intense. Ceremonial events involve a good deal of association among men, both in the preparation for these events and in the ceremonial activities themselves. In some areas of Yanomamaland, it is common for groups of men to gather at the end of the day, at which time hallucinogenic drugs are taken and representatives of the spirit world are contacted. Though there is no formal men's house among the Yanomama, the central plaza of the village functions as an arena for male activities, particularly on ceremonial occasions. Men also hold conversations from their hammocks, speaking loudly enough to be heard in other sections of the house—a pattern not characteristic of women.

Fundamental differences between the social worlds of men and women can also be analyzed by considering their respective roles in the context of the kin classificatory system. It has been common in traditional ethnographic monographs to consider the kinship terminology as the major blueprint for the differentiation of social roles and to present an account of social organization in terms of an inventory of the dyadic bonds specified thereby. While most anthropologists have come to take a more subtle approach both to kin classification itself and to the kinds of relations that obtain between such categorizations and social action, it remains true that basic categories specified in the terminological system provide a fundamental guide to the ordering of social relations. What is of interest in the Yanomama case, in the context of the present discussion, is how a terminological system that is symmetrical for males and females corresponds to a very asymmetrical ordering of dyadic relationships. The asymmetry is seen both in terms of the content of particular paired roles and in the degree of structural differentiation among them.

Yanomama kinship terminology is of the type generally designated as "bifurcate-merging." Parents' siblings of the same sex as the parent are classified with the respective parents, and children of these relatives are classified with siblings. Parents' siblings of the opposite sex are set off by separate terms, as are their children. A congruent bifurcation and merging operate on the first descending generational level.

In the case of the Yanomama, the bifurcation that appears on each of these three generational levels can be thought of as a division between classificatory consanguines and classificatory affines. In other words, all members of a person's own generation who are not classified as siblings will be classified as potential spouses or siblings-in-law; relatives of adjacent generations who are not classified with parents and children are classified as potential parents-in-law and children-in-law.

Let us now take a closer look at categories of relationship between males. Relationship categories that fall into what I have, for the sake of convenience, called the class of "consanguines" include one set of terms for relatives of the same generation (relative age being recognized) and one set of terms for relatives of adjacent generations. In the case of males, such terms designate relationships between men who are in the same "patrilineage."* On the local level, membership in such a group involves certain common rights and responsibilities, for the most part with regard to the allocation of female relatives in marriage. The wider reckoning of lineage ties has not yet been revealed as involving significant forms of social action, but seems to be a part of Yanomama ideology (Chagnon 1968; Ramos 1972).

Terms used between males who are "affines" to one another mark relationships that are clearly patterned and of considerable structural significance. The relationship between men who call one another "brother-in-law"—men of the same generation who are either potential or actual affines—may, in many respects, be considered the most highly elaborated bond in Yanomama society. This relationship, more than any other, is explicitly associated with an expectation of balanced and enduring reciprocity. The man one calls "brother-in-law" is the man from whom one expects to receive things and to whom one expects to give in return. More specifically, the central exchange in question, and that around which all others revolve, is an exchange of women. The men placed in this category are thus, above all, potential sources of wives. The bond is a highly solidarist one, characterized by a considerable degree of physical affection in the case of young men; such affection frequently has a sexual component and may include homosexual activities. Men of different generations, in the chronological sense, who are related to one another in this way will also engage in displays

---

*The use of the term "patriliny" in the analysis of Yanomama society raises certain problems. I think that in this case the social opposition between men and women is itself more central for the understanding of "patriliny" than is the case among societies like those in Africa, for example, in which descent constructs are clearly more significant. I have developed this argument in a paper entitled "Lineality and Sexual Hierarchy: The Yanomama Case," presented in a special symposium on the Yanomama at the American Anthropological Association meeting in 1974.

of physical affection; I have seen men in their thirties lying in hammocks embracing young boys who are their "brothers-in-law." Married men whose "brother-in-law" tie has been actualized tend not to be as physically expressive in their interactions with one another. Their relationship takes the form of cooperating in work endeavors and spending a good deal of time in one another's company.

The "brother-in-law" tie provides the idiom for the creation of new relationships with previously unrelated groups. (Lévi-Strauss [1943] has described a similar phenomenon for the Nambikwara of central Brazil.) It is also used for outsiders such as male missionaries and anthropologists, with the goal of defining these relationships in terms of cooperation and exchange. It is of interest to note that when a Yanomama shaman calls upon his spirit familiars for help, he addresses them as "brother-in-law." The moral meanings associated with this type of relationship between men are clearly of fundamental importance in Yanomama society. (My use of the phrase "moral meaning," as applied to kinship terms, is taken from Bloch [1971].) One might also say that certain features characterizing human relationships in general (reciprocity, solidarity) are, in Yanomama society, associated with the "brother-in-law" tie in a particularly explicit manner.

The set of reciprocal terms that mark the relationship between male classificatory affines of adjacent generations can be translated in a number of ways. Following the pattern of the previous discussion, we might translate them as "potential or actual father-in-law"/"potential or actual son-in-law." The relationship is one that, in most accounts of kinship terminologies, is generally rendered into English as "mother's brother"/"sister's son." My own inclination, in considering through what links the relationship is reckoned, would be to follow those anthropologists who have concentrated on the phenomenon of affinal inheritance, thus deriving it from "father"/"son" ties, on the one hand, and "brother-in-law" ties, on the other. Adjacent generation classificatory affines, thus, are to be thought of as "father's brother-in-law," "brother-in-law's father," and so on. In choosing one translation over another, no claim is made that any simple English rendering will do justice to the Yanomama term; the point is that an emphasis on patrilateral-affinal linkages seems to be more appropriate than one on matrilateral-sibling linkages. The issue may also be stated in terms of a tendency to emphasize relationships as traced through males.

The relationship between classificatory male affines of adjacent generations differs from the "brother-in-law" tie by virtue of its asymmetry. This may be expressed either in protectiveness, as when the younger partner in the relationship is still a boy, or through the exercise of authority, as in the case of actual father-in-law/son-in-law relationships. These moral meanings would seem to be revealed in the fact that this relationship provides the idiom by which the Yanomama conceive of the tie between a pet and its owner.

A man performs a considerable amount of work for his wife's parents as part of his bride service. Such labor takes a different form from that which he carries out for his "brother-in-law." A man works for, rather than with, his father-in-law; such transactions take place in a context of respectful distance rather than camaraderie. The father-in-law is not subject to as stringent a pattern of avoidance as is the mother-in-law and, in cases of village endogamous marriage, where the father-in-law is a person known since childhood, the relationship will usually lack much of the tension that would otherwise characterize it. However, even in these situations, marital arrangements are accompanied by a marked change in behavior, toward the expression of a greater degree of constraint and respect.

Let us now turn to the ordering of relationships between women. The point that I shall try to demonstrate is that while kin terminology has the same structure regardless of the sex of the speaker, the terms used by a woman do not correspond to the same kind of differentiated social world that has just been described for men.

Looking first at a woman's relationships with those she terms "mother" and "sister," we may say that a woman's tie to her own mother is indeed a close one, this being generally less the case for her relationship to a sister. A woman cannot, however, expect to go on living in close proximity to her female relatives unless she marries endogamously or into a neighboring village. Because of Yanomama marriage patterns, especially in their relation to political life—the use of marriages to establish alliances, the incidence of wife capture as a result of raiding, shifts in alliance patterns that leave women isolated behind "enemy lines"—it is common for Yanomama women to find themselves separated from those with whom they have had the closest bonds. Such a separation may come quite early in a girl's life, since marriages are contracted and coresidence established while the wife is still very young. (Some women are living with their husbands before puberty.)

It was said above that "father"/"son" and "brother"/"brother" relationships among men involve the dimension of common lineage membership. There is no such significant dimension to a woman's relationship to her "sisters." I am not even sure that it makes much sense to speak of women as members of lineages at all.

Turning now to classificatory affinal relationships between women, we find in the female relational scheme no parallel to the highly significant "brother-in-law" relationship. There is no easily discernible difference in the quality of behavior between "sisters" and "sisters-in-law," as there is between "brothers" and "brothers-in-law". The relatively minor social importance of affinal ties between women, as compared with those between men, follows from the male-dominated nature of alliance and exchange in Yanomama society. There is no structure of reciprocity at the root of the "sister-in-law" tie, no transfer of human and material wealth through which members of such a dyad define their mutual positions. Co-wife relationships may involve either classificatory "sisters" or "sisters-in-law." In either case, relation-

ships between the women tend toward separateness rather than cooperation. Each woman has her own cooking fire at which she prepares food
for herself, her husband, and her children. There is no structure of
authority between older and younger wives. The kinds of norms that
equilibrate and regulate relations among co-wives and responsibilities
of the husband to each of them in certain other polygynous societies
are relatively undeveloped among the Yanomama. A newer and younger
wife tends to monopolize the Yanomama husband's attention, and is not
likely to be a source of cooperation and companionship to the older wife.

The relationship of mother-in-law to daughter-in-law, a channel
for the expression of female domestic authority in some patriarchal
societies, is not particularly prominent among the Yanomama. There is
no pattern of deference and avoidance comparable with that between
father-in-law and son-in-law.

A comparison of intra-male and intra-female relationship patterns
reveals a social world that is less differentiated and more restricted in
scope for women than for men. Women's roles have a tendency to be
more diffuse, their relationships with one another less explicitly defined than is the case for men. Another interesting contrast emerges if
we compare the two relationships on which we placed particular emphasis in our discussion of the respective sexes: the "brother-in-law"
bond between men and the "mother"/"daughter" bond between women.
The male bond is the one that involves affines of the same generation;
the female bond is one that involves consanguines of different generations. It is the former relationship that is associated with the creation
of new relationships, with the outward movement of exchange and alliance. In Yanomama society, such intra-generational bonds provide a
more important mode of social integration than do any relations based
on genealogical continuity. The mother/daughter bond, in this context,
does not function to link two social units; it is more properly thought
of in terms of the restricted family group, working, as it were, at right
angles to the system of affinal exchange that is dominated by men.

The subject of male-female relationships is not being treated
directly in this essay. I will merely note that relationships between
men and women generally involve clear patterns of control of the former
over the latter. A woman's "brothers" and "fathers" are those who have
the power to decide how she will be disposed in marriage. The marital
relationship itself shows a considerable degree of male dominance, by
South American tropical forest standards. A woman is accorded deference and owed certain obligations by her son-in-law, but this relationship is basically characterized by avoidance. The males over whom a
woman directly exercises authority are children. In sum, the organization of power along sexual lines leads, on the one hand, to the subordination of women in male-female relationships and, on the other, to
a low development of relations of either solidarity or authority among
women themselves.

The general points that have come out in the foregoing discussion of the social position of men and women among the Yanomama are dramatically illustrated when we turn to a description of ritual and ceremonial events.

The two features that most clearly mark activities set aside from the rest of the daily round by the degree of interest, energy, preparation, and excitement devoted to them, and that I would place under the rubric of "ritual and ceremony," are the facts that they take place in the central plaza of the village house and/or involve the use of hallucinogenic drugs. The first point relates to the communal nature of these activities and the second to their association with a transcendental sphere. In considering what kinds of persons, relationships, and groups are particularly salient in the course of ritual and ceremonial activities, I would like to stress both the reflective and the creative aspects of these events. On the one hand, they accord a heightened recognition to certain parts of the social order; on the other, they are an important source of the higher valuation of those statuses, roles, and collectivities involved in their performance.

Yanomama ceremonial life centers around a pattern of inter-village feasting. The cycle of activities associated with these events is roughly as follows: Once the date of the feast has been set and invitations sent out, large quantities of food crops and game must be amassed. Hunting in preparation for a feast generally is not carried out in the usual individualized manner, but involves a communal expedition by the men. Cooking for a feast is also carried out in a special manner: whereas daily meals are prepared by women at their own cooking fires in individual family dwelling areas, food for feasts is cooked by men on large fires built in the central plaza.

When the guests arrive, initial interactions between hosts and visitors usually take the form of formal dialogues between one or more pairs of men in which news of various kinds is exchanged. Trade matters may also be broached and general declarations made concerning the state of relations between the groups and the significance of the feast. At this point, the visiting group is still camped outside the village and only representatives have entered into contact with the hosts. The formal entry of the visiting group consists of the dramatic entrance of the male guests one by one. Each man, who is painted and wearing body ornaments, makes a full tour of the plaza circumference, brandishing his weapons. When each man has made his entrance, the group clusters in the center of the village, standing silently until they are invited by their hosts to take their places in the various dwelling areas in the house. The male guests then recline in hammocks while the male hosts put on a similarly martial display. Women guests filter inconspicuously into the village, remaining in the peripheral area of the house.

The first night of the visit marks the opening of a series of ceremonial dialogues between the men of the respective villages. These dialogues, which serve the various functions of news exchange, trade negotiations, and the arrangement of marital and political alliances, take a variety of forms, each with its characteristic rhythm and postural style. The interaction itself involves a high degree of mutual coordination and a great expenditure of physical and emotional energy. In some dialogues, the two men stand or sit several feet apart, chanting alternately at one another. A more intense form of ritualized conversation involves the partners' being seated together on the ground, locked in a tight embrace, a typical position being chest-to-chest with one man's legs encircling the body of the other. The men will shout directly into one another's ears, and the rate of speech alternation is so rapid that the two are often exchanging monosyllabic utterances. Ceremonial dialogues sometimes proceed in the manner of relay races—a man who has previously been on the sidelines will come forward to take the place of his village mate; some time thereafter, the other participant will similarly be replaced by one of his fellow villagers. It is also common for several dialogues to go on at once; at such times, the village plaza will be filled with pairs of men simultaneously engaged in ritual conversations.

These dialogues are usually conducted under the influence of hallucinogenic drugs. The particular form of energy provided by the drugs both contributes to and is associated with the fact that these conversations tend to be marathon affairs. The participants work themselves into extraordinary states of excitation that are sustained for long periods of time—a man may, for example, converse without interruption for hours—until total exhaustion sets in. Though women may contribute to the subjects under discussion from the sidelines, they never participate directly in these activities.

In addition to these dialogues, there are also more aggressive confrontations that commonly occur between men during the course of a feast. These are the formal duels for which the Yanomama are famous (Chagnon 1968) and which take a variety of forms, including chest-pounding, back-scraping, and head-beating. This form of fighting is highly stylized, entailing an alternation of blows, and is accompanied by the taking of drugs. Duels of this type often involve groups of men acting as teams, and are thus an occasion for the males of one village to unite in aggressive confrontation against the males of another.

Women may, in the course of a festival, perform songs and dances of their own. In such cases, they arrange themselves loosely in a circle. One woman will initiate the song and the others will join in, more or less in unison; the accompanying dance consists of small steps back and forth. Men have similar songs of their own. Such singing is not invested with the same degree of interest and importance as the other activities. The relatively relaxed and uncoordinated quality of the women's dancing contrasts with the highly formalized and energetic quality of the men's events.

Women also participate in the mortuary observances that may occur in the course of a feast. The Yanomama cremate their dead and save the ashes in gourds; at a later date, the gourds are broken open and the ashes either are consumed with a drink made of mashed bananas or are poured over a fire. Women play a prominent role as mourners, chanting and dancing while holding objects that belonged to the deceased. At one mortuary rite that I observed, an old woman—the maternal grandmother of the child who was being mourned—poured the bone ash upon the fire.

Another activity involving women that occasionally occurs in the course of a feast is one in which men and women link arms and dance together; this dance, which I did not observe but was told about, does not appear to involve husbands and wives but is, rather, connected with more or less institutionalized extramarital liaisons between members of different villages.

The concluding events of a festival cycle include final trading arrangements and a large-scale food distribution. This food, which has been prepared communally by the men of the host village, is given to the male household heads of the visiting group.

It will be seen from this rather sketchy overview of the cycle of events that make up a Yanomama feast that such ceremonial occasions are predominantly male affairs. The two kinds of social units that are most salient during such activities are the group of adult males of a village and the pairs of men involved in relations of exchange and alliance. The first unit is defined largely in aggressive terms, as can be seen from the entry of the guests, the formalized confrontations between groups of male co-villagers, and in the war games that may occur in the course of a feast and that prefigure actual raids. The celebration of a community of males among the Yanomama is connected with an active warfare pattern.

As for the pairs of men engaged in ceremonial dialogue, we may see in their close conversational embrace a physical representation of the integrative significance of the kinds of intra-generational dyadic bonds discussed above. Partners in exchange and alliance, they illustrate the point made by those anthropologists who view marriage in terms of the relationships it establishes between men. The duels can be seen as representing the reverse side of men's relationships to one another—the tensions and instabilities associated with an emphasis on male agressivity—and submitting this too to formalization and ritual.

The place of women during inter-village feasts is, for the most part, on the sidelines. We cannot even say that they form the audience, as may be the case when ceremonial activities are performed by males, since the behavior of Yanomama men on such occasions seems to be directed primarily toward one another. To the degree that women do participate, their actions are relatively unorganized and not associated with any clearly defined groups or relationships.

One other aspect of Yanomama ritual life that I would like to mention briefly is shamanism. The functions of the Yanomama shaman are essentially the same as those described for shamans in other societies: curing sick individuals and protecting the group as a whole from external threats, both of these activities being carried out through contacts with spirit beings. Among the Yanomama, such contacts are established with the aid of hallucinogenic drugs.

Yanomama shamans are always men. Shamanistic collaboration, moreover provides a significant form of male association. Though a shaman often works alone, it is not uncommon for two or more shamans to cooperate in curing, especially when illness or some other misfortune has affected several village members simultaneously; shamans from different local groups may come together for such purposes. Shamans who are working together not only conceive of themselves as united in a common enterprise, but also serve as a professional audience for one another's activities. Shamans may also mobilize a larger group of men to aid them in some endeavor, a striking illustration of which is provided in an excellent film by Napoleon Chagnon, entitled "Magical Death." (The filmed episode is an attempt by men from two allied villages to kill, through magical means, the children of an enemy village by stealing and devouring their souls.) In his guise as representative and even personification of the local group, the shaman conducts monumental spiritual struggles in which he attracts danger directed at the village to himself and in turn directs the psychic message of his own village outward to others. The world of spirits in which the shaman moves is, to some degree, open to all men. Through the ingestion of hallucinogenic substances, they too can cause their eyes to become "sharp" enough to see the spirits. It is only women who remain mohoti, or "ignorant," in this regard.

The predominance of men in ritual and ceremonial activities, which amounts to their predominance in the most important sphere of communal life and to a virtual male monopoly of sacred knowledge, both expresses and reinforces the sexual hierarchy of Yanomama society in general.

I have emphasized that the world of women differs from the world of men in terms of its relative lack of internal differentiation and in the greater restrictedness of its social networks. The lesser degree of formalization in the relationships and activities of women and the differential distribution of certain kinds of social knowledge were commented upon. In considering the significance of such factors, I am reminded of the way in which W. L. Warner expressed the difference between men and women in the society he had studied, the Murngin of northern Australia. He noted that the male life cycle was characterized by a significant widening of social ties, a number of important passages from one status to another during the period of adulthood, and an increasing command over a body of sacred knowledge. The fact that women's lives lacked such dimensions was seen to result in a female social personality that was less developed and complex than that of a male (see Warner 1937).

Some may consider this sort of formulation to be objectionable. Defining the position of women in a negative and derivative manner might be expected in the case of a male anthropologist whose access to the world of women is likely to be limited and who tends to absorb the attitudes of his male informants; that such an approach should be taken by a female investigator seems to require a greater degree of justification.

I think it is relevant in this connection to point out what I see as a major ambivalence in the current wave of writings on the position of women in society. Many female investigators working in this area seem torn between the desire to present systems of sex role differentiation as unjust and exploitative and the wish to see women's roles as equal in importance to those of males. The latter attempt to "balance the books" sometimes takes the form of maintaining that the existing inequality pertains not so much to the roles themselves as to the degree of recognition accorded to them. Thus, to take an example from our own society, the negative aspects of the housewife role are seen in terms of its low prestige, which in turn stems from the fact that it is not associated with material reward or recognized in the occupational hierarchy on which comparative status is based.

While the attempt to evolve a more positive approach to the study of women clearly has had a salutary effect on anthropological investigations, we are still left with the problem of whether or not we wish to deal with the issue of sexual hierarchy and, if so, how. It seems to me that the issue of inequality should be faced, and that it is to be considered with regard both to how the roles played by the respective sexes are culturally evaluated and to fundamental properties of the roles themselves. In point of fact, one might expect these two factors to have some sort of relation to one another. Social roles, moreover, may be considered in a negative as well as in a positive light; they may be defined not only in terms of the behaviors they entail but also in terms of those that they preclude.

The difficulties of dealing with sexual inequality in cross-cultural perspective were touched upon at the beginning of this essay. Such an endeavor involves drawing upon the moral judgments we are accustomed to make as members of a particular society, exposing ourselves to moral universes different from our own, and attempting to set up some sort of objectifiable criteria for the description of social roles. Such an attempt to combine elements of cultural relativism, positivist methodology, and the richness of our own "common sense" knowledge may appear as either hopeless naiveté or uninspired eclecticism. But it is, at present, the only approach to the study of women that I find satisfactory.

REFERENCES

Biocca, Ettore. 1970. Yanoama, the Narrative of a White Girl Kidnapped by Amazonian Indians. New York: Dutton. Translation of Yanoama dal racconto di una donna rapita dagli Indi. Bari: Leonardo da Vinci, 1965.

Bloch, Maurice. 1971. "The Moral and Tactical Meaning of Kinship Terms." Man 6: 79-87.

Chagnon, Napoleon. 1968. Yanomamo, The Fierce People. New York: Holt, Rinehart and Winston.

Lévi-Strauss, Claude. 1943. "The Social Use of Kinship Terms Among Brazilian Indians." American Anthropologist 45: 398-409.

Mead, Margaret. 1935. Sex and Temperament in Three Primitive Societies. New York: William Morrow and Co.

Ramos, Alcida. 1972. "The Social System of the Sanuma of Northern Brazil." Ph.D. dissertation, University of Wisconsin.

Rosen, Lawrence. n.d. "Bargaining for Reality: A Study of Male-Female Relations in Morocco."

Shapiro, Judith. 1970. "Yanomama Women: How the Other Half Lives." Paper delivered at the American Anthropological Association meeting, San Diego.

_____. 1971. "Male Bonds and Female Bonds: An Illustrative Comparison." Paper presented in a symposium on anthropological perspectives on sexual antagonism, at the American Anthropological Association meeting, New York.

_____. 1972. "Sex Roles and Social Structure Among the Yanomama Indians of Northern Brazil." Ph.D. dissertation, Columbia University.

Warner, W. Lloyd. 1937. A Black Civilization.

Women's participation in the labor market in Latin America is conditioned by their class status, their primary identification as wives and mothers, and the occupations available to them in the changing economy. As the economy of Latin America has shifted from an agrarian to an urban-industrial base, women have lost their production functions as members of a peasant family labor force and are forced to depend on men as providers or to seek independent wage employment. The chief sources of urban employment for uneducated lower-class women have been in such low-paid and unskilled jobs as domestic servants, petty vendors, and factory jobs, though these have also tended to diminish with the trend toward capital-intensive industrialization. At the same time, urbanization and industrialization have opened up more jobs for women in white-collar and professional occupations, many of which are filled by educated women of the elite who can now find jobs commensurate with their status.

Though their increasing employment in "respectable" white-collar and professional occupations has made wage labor for women more acceptable in Latin American society, women's entry into the labor market at every class level is conditioned by their primary identification as wives and mothers. Working-class women seek jobs principally to supplement the family income, and are often forced to assume the role of primary breadwinner if their husbands are unemployed or have abandoned the family. Even professional women tend to be concentrated in teaching, social work, nursing, and other jobs that are extensions of their domestic activities.

The labor of women in the home is devalued because it is unpaid and hence is considered "unproductive," since it does not enter into the calculation of the gross national product. The crucial role that women play in maintaining and reproducing the labor force is largely neglected, with some notable exceptions from feminist writers (for instance, James and Dalla Costa 1972; Larguia and Dumoulin 1972; Leacock 1972; Mitchell 1973; Sullerot 1971). The way in which the unpaid productivity of women within the family permits the depression of wages of the male breadwinner, especially in the lower class, is also ignored. In effect, the man's wages are supposed to sustain the entire family; but without the unpaid services of his wife, how own productivity and the family's general welfare would be seriously undermined.

The subordinate position of women in the occupational structure is another example of the uneven penetration of capital that is manifest in regional and national differences of levels of development. As Samir Amin (1974), Andrew Frank (1967, and Arghiri Emmanuel (1972)

105

have postulated, this unevenness of development reinforces the trend
toward concentration and accumulation of capital by enhancing the per
capita productivity of certain sectors at the same time that it creates
reserves of low productivity in the marginal labor force. Essays in
this section by Elizabeth Jelin and Heleieth Saffioti provide case
material for assessing some of the implications of uneven development
for women as a subordinate or reserve labor force.

In pointing out the low status and return of the jobs that women
perform, we should not forget the extraordinary capacity women have
demonstrated to sustain life—their own and that of their dependents—
in carrying out the work to which they have been relegated. Women
often accept low-status jobs because their primary concern is not with
the job itself, but with the family's survival. As several of the essays
in this volume point out, work outside the home is justified as an extension of the woman's nurturing role and is seldom sought for individual gain or status. Petty vendors risk their entire capital every day,
buying goods and peddling them at small margins of profit (Arizpe 1974).
Female factory workers spend twenty years of their lives working in
miserable conditions at abysmal salaries, for without this income their
families would starve (Piho 1973). Even at higher levels of employment,
women have learned to cope with childbearing and child-rearing while
occupying full-time jobs in occupational situations defined in relation
to male employees who are relatively free of such obligations.

Some of the predictions about the demise of the nuclear family
because of the industrial occupation of women have not been realized.
On the contrary, patterns of male dominance and paternal authority
established in the family have persisted as women have been squeezed
out of productive activities they occupied in the early days of labor-
intensive industrialization. Neuma Aguiar demonstrates, with data from
her research in the mixed economy of Bahia, Brazil, how the distribution of rewards linked to the skills and capacities of the human labor
force that exists in rural commercial crop production is reproduced in
industrial work. In agricultural production organized by family units,
the physical capacity of the male worker is assumed to provide the
greatest value and he is accorded the highest wage return. This differential persists in the case of the farinha and tile factories, where
discriminatory pay scales, social benefits, and status were applied to
women in the industrial context as an extension of their subordinate
production role in the rural family. Aguiar's work challenges the conventional model of social change, which opposes traditional agricultural systems of work to factory production, since it shows the persistence of characteristic relations carried over from the preindustrial
days.

The central problems in women's entry into productive spheres in
Brazil are posed by Jelin as the effect of low-paid domestic services
on the demand for goods and services in the managerial class, competition between simple production of goods in the domestic setting and

that in the capital enterprises, and the effect of unpaid domestic activity in the working-class family. She makes the point that the low wages for domestic services paid by the bourgeoisie permits them to reinvest the money saved in capital enterprises. In addition, it enables the middle-class woman to enter into employment, a point made by Gloria Gonzalez Salazar and Maria del Carmen Elu de Lenero. This serves to underline the opposing class interests reflected in middle-class women's phrasing of liberation in terms of occupational and professional alternatives to domestic roles, while lower-class women seek escape from unrewarding paid labor.

In the capital-intensive stage of industrial production, the participation of women in industry is often reduced below that of the early stages of industrialization. Saffioti demonstrates the downward curve in the industrial employment of women in Brazil and relates it to similar changes in other countries. The partial participation of women in the labor force is a special technique for maintaining a reserve supply of workers who are not demoralized by employment, since they can always fall back on their domestic role. Mobilized in time of war or in the upswings of the business cycle, they are released when men return to take their jobs or when production slows down. Saffioti emphasizes that this is not a unique characteristic of the Third World countries; it also occurs in the centers of industrial production.

Because women are typically assigned the major responsibility for the care of the family, and because they are assumed to have limited physical stamina, they are considered less desirable employees. With the assumption that they will not remain in the labor market because of the priority given to family, they are not given the training for more advanced and more meaningful jobs. Elsa Chaney and Marianne Schmink document the restrictions placed on women's participation in production with technological advance.

While the bulk of the evidence supports their thesis that women are progressively cut off from machine production that has a higher per capita productivity, it could be argued that technological advance is not in itself, nor is it always, a deterrent to women's employment. Some innovations make possible a breaking down of the task structure and, hence, weakening of the control of the skilled trades over jobs, thus opening the door to women. For example, women's entry into textiles was made possible by the power looms, and later improvements led to their displacement of men in the textile mills throughout the nineteenth century. However, women's jobs in cutting cloth were lost to men when an improved cutting machine that cut more thicknesses required the greater force of male cutters, who displaced them in the silk trade in 1860 (Baker 1964, p. 52). Shoemaking was man's work in the early decades of the nineteenth century, when a skilled man served a seven-year apprenticeship and learned the whole trade; but when machine production was set up, women began to be employed more widely after 1852 (Campbell 1893, p. 55). The data Chaney and

Schmink assemble must be viewed from the broader perspective of a complex interaction of cultural and economic factors that condition the employment of women.

Puerto Rico provides a good example of the pattern of reducing the number of women employed in industry. As articles of consumption were manufactured in industry instead of the home, women followed their jobs into the factories. This process was reversed in Puerto Rico after 1930, when employment of women reached a peak. Isabel Pico notes the marked difference in working-class and middle-class women's attitudes in the early decades of the twentieth century industrialization: while working-class women felt oppression in class terms and organized in trade unions as early as 1904, women of the petite bourgeoisie emphasized legal and social restrictions, and worked for legal and political reform. The way in which these reforms benefited largely these same elite women is illustrated by the vote, which was restricted to literate (hence educated) women.

The impact of women's entry into productive roles is minimized by their being cut off from entry into unions and political parties dominated by men, as well as by competing responsibilities in the home. The lack of child care facilities for working women is a direct corollary of the low priority given to women's productive activities both within and outside the home. As Chaney and Schmink point out, even in socialist countries, where the child care facilities and maternity provisions enable far more women to work outside the home, the input into these and into labor-saving devices for the home are contingent on the need for women in the labor force rather than being a continuous social responsibility.

Protective labor legislation, which raises the costs of hiring women, minimizes the marginal utility of women in production and leads to employer discrimination. Gloria Gonzalez Salazar concludes in her essay that juridical parity in education, civil rights, occupations, and political life is belied by the real discrimination against women based on the persistence of old patterns. Even in professional occupations, women tend to enter those professions that are an extension of domestic roles, where discrimination is less marked.

Since women's participation in production is limited to that of a reserve labor force or in occupations that project aspects of domestic roles in a public setting, and since the fields where they have penetrated are peripheral to policy-making centers, their participation in the labor force has had less impact on the consciousness of employers than the actual contribution they make to the economy would suggest. The tendency to equate nonremunerative tasks performed in the home with nonproductive tasks requires a reconceptualization of the socio-demographic categories related to employment and productive activity. As Morris Blachman commented, the GNP of almost any nation could be doubled only by including the uncounted and nonremunerated hours of women's work.

REFERENCES

Amin, Samir. 1974. Accumulation on a World Scale: A Critique of the
    Theory of Underdevelopment. New York: Monthly Review Press.

Arizpe, Lourdes. 1974. "Las Marias" y la migracion indigena a la
    ciudad de Mexico. Mexico City: Instituto Nacional de Antropo-
    logia e Historia.

Emmanuel, Arghiri. 1972. Unequal Exchange: A Study of the Imperialism
    of Trade. New York: Monthly Review Press.

Frank, Andrew G. 1967. Capitalism and Underdevelopment in Latin
    America: Historical Studies in Chile and Brazil. New York:
    Monthly Review Press.

Gueiler Tejada, Lydia. 1959. La mujer y la revolucion. La Paz:

James, Selma, and Mariarosa Dalla Costa. 1972. The Power of Women
    and the Subversion of Community. Bristol: Falling Wall Press.

Jaquette, Jane. 1974. Women in Politics. New York: John Wiley.

Larguia, Anabel, and John Dumoulin. 1972. "Toward a Science of
    Women's Liberation." Latin America and Empire Report 6, no. 10.

Leacock, Eleanor Burke. 1972. "Introduction" to Frederick Engels,
    The Origin of the Family Private Property and the State. New York:
    International Publishers.

Mitchell, Juliet. 1973. Woman's Estate. New York: Vintage Books.

Piho, Virve. 1973. "Life and Labor of the Female Textile Worker in
    Mexico City." In Cross-Cultural Perspectives on the Women's
    Movement and Women's Status, ed. Ruby R. Leavitt. The Hague:
    Mouton.

Sullerot, Evelyne. 1971. Woman, Society and Change. New York:
    McGraw-Hill.

6

THE IMPACT OF
INDUSTRIALIZATION
ON WOMEN'S WORK ROLES
IN NORTHEAST BRAZIL
Neuma Aguiar

The main assumption of this essay is that industrialization can be made to fit several forms of social organization of production, including hybrid industrial and rural systems such as certain types of plantations and haciendas.* My proposition, therefore, is that some systems of production show a complementary relationship between industrial and rural activities. This proposition demands a reformulation of our way of thinking about the impact of industrialization upon the rural areas. I hold that certain characteristics of the social organization so far taken as rural can also adjust to industry.

Industries may organize themselves according to a family structure. I am not referring here to the frequent occurrence of a family's ownership of capital. I am referring to the family organization of labor in industry, where the woman holds the same position at work that she holds within the family organization of rural labor. To demonstrate this proposition about the social organization of industrial production and the system of masculine and feminine roles which it involves, I shall first analyze the sociological literature that starts from an opposite point of view—that industrialization revolutionizes the rural forms of social organization, such as the role of the family and the social position of the woman at work. I shall then proceed to discuss the data of

---

*The classification of rural properties in the area of Ceara and of the types of plantation and hacienda (large landholding), with characteristics similar to the ones we are studying, has been made by Allen W. Johnson (1971). For a typology of plantations applicable to Latin America, see George Beckford (1972, esp. ch. 1 and app. 1; 1973, pp. 243-63).

The research funds for this paper were provided by the Brazilian National Research Council and the Ford Foundation.

research I carried out in one area of southern Ceara in northeastern Brazil, on the division of labor in systems of production that use technology of different complexity, and on the system of social stratification that ensues. These data permit us to demonstrate the existing shortcomings of some aspects of the theories about the industrial revolution and to suggest alternative explanations (Aguiar 1970).

INDUSTRIALIZATION AND SOCIAL CHANGE

A common model generally used in theories of social development takes two ideal types as its theoretical point of departure: one rural traditional, at times also called feudal, and another, at a more advanced stage of evolution, called capitalist or modern industrial. The more evolved one is in a position of relative autonomy, the other in one of relative dependence. The developed system imposes technical innovations on the underdeveloped one, creating imbalances that upset it in its original stage. Such disturbances may force the underdeveloped system to another stage of integration, however, can occur only in the long run. *

An example of the application of this model in relation to the family is offered by Neil Smelser, who analyzes industry and the family as social systems. He holds that industrialization induces changes in the family system when it gives rise to dissatisfactions in the family economy. He suggests that when these dissatisfactions occur, new adjustments are made in order to channel the agitation into a structure more in harmony with the new industrial society. He also asserts that these dissatisfactions arise only when there is a breakdown of community ties that existed in the factory and when these are replaced by a system of social anonymity. The growth of factory units leads to a decrease of community feelings that prevailed before (Smelser 1959).

Among other authors who discuss the relationship between the family and industrialization, William Goode throws doubts on some assumptions of the theory by showing that other forms of family organization, such as the communal one, are compatible with industrialization (Goode 1960). Sidney Greenfield (1961) makes a similar criticism when he shows that the nuclear family may precede industrialization, suggesting also the compatibility that the extended family may have

---

*These effects of industrialization were put forward by Bert Hoselitz and Wilbert Moore (1960, esp. Moore, "Industrialization and Social Change"). Also see Clark Kerr et al. (1960). For a criticism see Manning Nash (1967), Eric Hobsbawm (1971), and Neuma Aguiar (1969, 1970).

with an urban-industrial structure. Extending the criticism to the
systemic model even further, I consider its approach to the interrelation
between industrial and agricultural activities to be limited. The propositions that industrialization modifies patterns of family structure
and that, consequently, industrialization modifies the role of the woman,
granting her a higher social position, are questionable in the light of
my research.

Marxist theory also refers to the impact of technological change
on the role of the woman. In Pre-Capitalist Economic Formations and
Capital, Marx (1906; 1966) proposes that, parallel to the growth of
capital and the worker's alienation from his conditions of production
and reproduction, transformations arise in the social organization of
production that are the result of technology. I shall not, at this point,
discuss the theory that Marx developed on the transformation of modes
of production up to the capitalist system. It will be sufficient to refer
to his propositions about the transition from handicrafts to manufacture
and, then, to industry, in which transformations within the system of
cooperation occurred. Individual work was replaced by collective work,
introducing a technical division of labor. At this stage of evolutionary
change the role of human force in propelling the instruments of production continued to be of great importance; manufacture still prevailed,
since the machine had not yet been introduced. The specialization of
activities resulting from the system of cooperation created a hierarchy
of labor according to the degree of technical specialization. Marx also
held that, with the introduction of the machine as a force external to
man, the role played by human labor would diminish. This important
change in the organization of production was seen as favoring the employment of women and children as a substitute for or in addition to
male labor. The introduction of the machine would reduce the need for
specialized labor and therefore would diminish the distance between
the social strata generated by manufacture (Marx 1906; 1966).

My objection to these propositions of Marxist theory is based on
the system of stratification within industry. Rather than abolishing the
use of human force, it maintains and often extends the social stratification system. Instead of equalizing the social position of women in
relation to men, machine technology crystallizes the differential status
of the sexes.

If we take, as a point of departure, industries in the rural areas,
we may observe that, directly or indirectly, the workers remain tied to
the field. Seventy-six percent of the women and 63 percent of the men
in our sample grew up in the rural area. I have described these kinds
of ties between industrial and agricultural work in a previous work
(Aguiar 1973). One of the cases that were part of the research I developed in Cariri was a factory located on a farm. In the other factories
the ties with agriculture existed but were not as sharply delineated as
the ones in the farm-factory. They became clear, however, to the
attentive observer: 34 percent of the industrial workers in the sample

cultivated plots of land. I also showed the articulation between industrial work, handicrafts, and domestic enterprises, as well as the role
of family labor in these activities of transformation.

The relationship between these modes of production that are my
object of study coincides with some of the conclusions that Brazilian
social scientists have reached about plantations and peasantry
(Palmeira 1972). Not only does the plantation possess, besides agriculture, a system of transformation; it also has a peasantry with whom
it shares a stratified market of consumer goods (Velho 1973). Furthermore, the structure of exploitation of the labor force maintained by the
plantation in relation to its tenants is reproduced by the peasantry in
the form of family exploitation. In the same way in which the plantations allocate small plots of land to the families for cultivation, the
head of a peasant family, or patrao, allocates small plots of land to
his workers for cultivation by their relatives (Garcia and Heredia 1971).
Sons and daughters work some days for themselves (Garcia and Heredia
1971; Velho 1969). The heavier work load is reserved for the men
(Velho 1969; Mendes Chavez 1972). These conditions are reproduced
in the transformation of the products of the land. The peasant family,
like the worker's family on the plantation, distributes work and rewards
among its family members according to the use of human force. The
distribution of rewards is linked to the skills and capacities of the
human body insofar as they contribute to the family subsistence. Among
the peasantry, as in the domestic enterprises, the use of physical labor
has a special place in the control of the production of the means of
subsistence.

The conditions of this sexual division of labor are reproduced,
although in different form, in industrial work. My research can be
used to verify some of these assumptions.

THE RESEARCH

The research was carried out in Cariri, an area of Ceara where a
rural structure dominates, made up mainly of small landholdings
(minifundios) and some large landholdings (latifundios). This region
suffered two stages of industrialization: an earlier one, in which sugar
mills and cotton gins prevailed, and a recent one, with a structure of
corporations, in which the most modern machinery was introduced for
the production of tiles, bricks, flour, shoes, and sweets. A growing
urban nucleus has become a commercial center within the region and
possesses a diversified system of handicrafts. Some of these industries, the old as well as the new, produce articles similar to those
manufactured by hand. In my research I tried to take advantage of the
process of internal differentiation of handicrafts, domestic enterprises
and small and medium-size industries engaged in the transformation of
the same products, made of clay, corn, and manioc.

The work started with six months of participant observation in those enterprises chosen for the research. I studied two ceramics and two corn flour factories. I also collected data on a fifth industry (manioc starch) that had closed. In the first four industries we obtained responses to 192 questionnaires. The other 58 were obtained in 11 casas de farinha (houses or buildings in which the peasant family, or the family of the tenant living on the plantation, makes its flour, with the help of simple tools) and six brickyards; among these, one casa de farinha and one brickyard were very carefully observed. Additional data on these last two activities were subsequently obtained with the help of two graduate students who returned to the area under my supervision.

The style of observation I adopted was as a participant because I had family ties in the area. This, however, put me in a peculiar situation, since people knew my origin, yet my behavior as someone who had grown up in Rio de Janeiro was strange to them. There was further confusion because, although I had the status of a married woman, I interacted with the men in their workplaces, which went entirely against the rules of the community concerning the behavior of married women. The position that the community finally ascribed to me was that of a teacher. *

My behavior was the object of surprise and curiosity. I was asked about women, work, and family relations in the city where I lived. This type of questioning occurred mainly in the factories, and was quite independent of the sex and social class of the inquirer. The ambiguity of my position stimulated the women in the factory to speak about the difficulties they had in relation to their work, which stemmed from their sex. Their complaints awakened in me, apart from the partisanship I already had and that was ascribed to me, a desire to intervene personally; I pointed out to the owner that the fact that the married women were dismissed and not allowed to work in the factory generated discontent among them.

After the period of observation we drew up a questionnaire using the local language, and interviewed respondents with the help of local interviewers. Not all enterprises selected for the research employed women. Handicrafts and small brick and tile factories had only a male labor force. I shall concentrate in this essay on two types of activities: casas de farinha and a relatively large factory making ceramic products that will be called Large Ceramics. Although they manufacture different products, they permit a comparison of the sexual division of labor and the effects of industrialization. In the factory we shall discuss mainly

---

*For the position of the teacher in relation to her sex status and work, see Klaas Woortman (1965). For the opportunities that these structural openings give rise to in relation to the woman in society, see Joan Acker (1973).

the situation in the section concerned with pressing the tiles. Since the process of transforming manioc into flour used in the domestic enterprise (the process not used in the factories) also has a stage of pressing, this choice can improve our comparison. However, I am not looking for the similarity between the activities, but for an analogy between different forms of the social organization of production (see Bourdieu 1966).

IDEOLOGY AND ACTIVITY OF THE WOMAN AT WORK

The ideology of the woman's role in relation to the family and to work is made explicit in folk literature. Part of this literature, which deals with family morals and the religious taboos arising from family relationships, has been analyzed elsewhere (Aguiar 1973). Using the structuralist method in the analysis of this ideology, I have demonstrated the existence of a strong taboo that separates the familial and public domains. When women leave the local setting where family relationships prevail and seek contact in remote places where they meet men face-to-face interaction, violent collective sanctions are imposed. These are of a symbolic nature and serve to depersonalize the woman, who is treated as chattel or as a domesticated animal. When a person rebels against the norms of the community, the penalty for breaking the taboos, especially those of an incestuous nature, is severe, whether it involves men or women.

The ideology that predominates is similar to the code of honor that prevails in the Mediterranean Kabyle society described by Bourdieu (1970). Analyzing the concentric circles of privacy, beginning with the home as the innermost circle, he shows how the woman, the center of the familial domain, is controlled by her image as a good housewife, and how the man must protect the intimacy of his home. The most important area of secrecy is that of the wife, since it is linked to the man's honor. The other concentric circles of intimacy radiate into the community and extra-communal areas. Just as the home maintains relations of secrecy with the village, so the village maintains relations of secrecy with other villages and with society at large (Garcia and Heredia 1971).

In Cariri, the segregation of married women from public places, such as the factory, becomes obvious from our data. While 83 percent of the women in the sample were single, only 43 percent of the men, among our 250 interviewees, were married. If, however, we sort the data according to type of activity, we can observe that in the casas de farinha there is a higher proportion of married women than in the other production units in our sample.

The ideology of the rural community fits well with the national ideology concerning women's labor in industry. This is underwritten

TABLE 6. 1

Marital Status and Sex Ratio in the Studied Activities

Marital Status	All Activities*		Casas de Farinha		Large Ceramics	
	Men (%)	Women (%)	Men (%)	Women (%)	Men (%)	Women (%)
Single	43	83	40	57	43	98
Married	54	13	60	33	54	2
Separated	1	2		7	1	—
Widow(er)	1	2		3	2	—
Unspecified	1	—	—	—	—	—
Total	160	90	15	30	104	57

*Includes the 250 questionnaire responses for all the activities, and is not the sum only of those obtained in the casas de farinha and Large Ceramics.

Source: Compiled by the author.

by labor legislation granting women a series of privileges that the enterprises see as additional costs of production.

In the casas de farinha, however, there is no labor legislation, since such laws are just beginning to be systematically extended to the rural area. The proportion of married women workers is large, for work is organized by the owner of the product, who, as head of the family, recruits relatives, neighbors, and friends. We shall describe below the tasks assigned to males and females in the processing of manioc flour. Before that, however, I should like to examine the relationship of single and married women in the factory. Recruitment for work is not carried out by the father or husband. People of the same community work together in the factory, yet they are not necessarily bound by close relationships.

In one of the sections of the enterprise, the respondents discussed their role as women in relation to the family, to the community, and to the factory. They said that they had difficulties in persuading their families that they should work in the factory. One of them said that her father had given her a sound beating when he found out that she and her sister wanted to work there; the sister escaped beating by hiding. Nowadays, while the fathers may approve of their working in the factory, husbands and fiances often disapprove. One woman who was engaged to be married said that her fiance did not want her to continue working after marriage: "The people in the place where he works think that I should continue working. I would prefer to stay but he says that he does not want me to. I think that two people earning makes life easier."

The ideology of appropriate roles and behavior in the family and
the community serves to restrict the work opportunities of the women,
whereas the family economy legitimizes their work aspirations.

One of the women observed that the women workers think that it
is bad to get married and to leave the firm, and that it would be good
if one of them established a precedent by returning to work after getting
married. She also said that she had never discussed this in meetings
or with the supervisors, or even with the directors. She accepted the
policy of the factory, justifying it on the ground that a woman had been
found petting with a married man, and therefore the directors had decided not to accept any more married women. Another woman said that
the neighbors had raised a huge campaign against the single girls who
were going to work in the factory. She pointed out, however, that some
of those neighbors were now working there. Still another asserted that
the men did not want them to work because they wanted the women all
to themselves. Furthermore, the men were suspicious of other men because they thought that they were making sex jokes with the women and
were not respecting them. The macho morality legitimizes the restrictions to female work.

Imposing respect toward the women is delegated to the men. When
I asked the directors about the policy of recruiting women, they said,
after some hesitation, that they did not hire married women. During the
midnight shift some rather disagreeable incidents might occur. He cited
the case of one of the supervisors of the ovens, who was denounced for
his behavior toward women workers. The directors appointed several
people to observe him, and he was found to be pinching the girls. The
directors then arranged another job for him in another factory.

The directors asserted their desire to maintain a sense of moral
respect and community feeling in the factory, taking on part of the
father role. They also emphasized their preference for employing girls
who had relatives in the firm, hiring them for work on the same shift
as their brothers. They also added that the policy of the factory favored
the raising of the standard of living of the local families, thus stimulating the recruitment of relatives so that the additional wages earned
could lead to an improved life style. They thought, however, that the
presence of married women on the same shifts as the husbands would
be a greater source of conflict than single women working side by side
with their fathers and brothers. They said that the problem of the married women was generally taken care of by the husbands who would not
let them work, citing the case of a married woman who had recently
separated from her husband and who was working in the factory.

On a recent visit to the area, one of the directors told me that the
factory had opened its doors to women so that they could continue
working after being married and even when they were pregnant. I was
not able to observe, however, how widely this new policy was being
implemented.

The position of the labor force that lives in the communities near
the factories, and maintains a relationship both with industry and

agriculture, raises the question of the future of the families' main
source of income. Rural life depends on large families. The married
women bear the labor force and find it difficult or impossible to realize
their work aspirations in industry. The true source of the conflict lies
in the contradiction between the demand for a large family in the rural
areas and the industrial constraints on married women.

In the factory environment there exists a system of kinship analogous to that of the casas de farinha. The table below will permit us
to draw comparisons between the two types of activity.

The men show a greater propensity to work in places where they
have no relatives than women, although both sexes have very strong
kinship relations in the context of their work. In Large Ceramics this
tendency is sharpened by the factory policy. It may also be noted that
among the women who have kinship relations with the other workers,
41 percent have relatives in the same section, 17 percent have all their
relatives in another section. The figures for the men, in the same
order, are 15, 25, and 60 percent.

The system of family control is transferred to the factories, although in this case it has a more impersonal characteristic. The role
of head of the family is shared, within factory, between the father of
the family and the director of the factory.

TABLE 6. 2

Kinship and Sex Ratio in Studied Activities

Number of Relatives in Factory	All Activities*		Casas de Farinha		Large Ceramics	
	Men (%)	Women (%)	Men (%)	Women (%)	Men (%)	Women (%)
None	40	31	47	47	36	19
1—2	32	37	29	43	35	35
3—4	19	12	24	10	18	18
5 or more	9	20	—	—	11	28
Total	160	90	17	30	104	57

*Includes the 250 questionnaire responses for all activities and
is not the sum only of those obtained in the casas de farinha and
Large Ceramics.

Source: Compiled by the author.

TABLE 6. 3

Place of Residence and Sex Ratio in Industry and
in Domestic Enterprises

	Casas de Farinha		Large Ceramics	
Lives With	Men (%)	Women (%)	Men (%)	Women (%)
Father or mother	29	50	41	85
Husband or wife	65	23	53	2
Alone	—	—	1	—
Relatives or friends	6	23	5	13
Patron	—	4	—	—
Total	17	30	104	55

Source: Compiled by the author.

Residence and kinship relations are presented in Table 6. 3 by sex
and according to the type of activity. It may be noted that whereas
22 percent of the women declared that they did not help their parents
with money, 50 percent of the men declared the same thing.

I can now introduce information from my research of a more detailed
and standardized nature on social stratification in industries and domestic enterprises.

SEXUAL STRATIFICATION IN DOMESTIC ENTERPRISE AND IN INDUSTRY

The restructuring of a rural way of life in industry is also denoted
by objective variables which indicate the relatively inferior role the   ?
woman plays, receiving lower wages and social benefits than men, in
industry as much as in domestic enterprises.

Difficulties due to the various kinds of labor payment prevent us
from making a global comparison between the activities of transformation we have studied, since only in some types of factories are wages
used as a system of reward. The sample included 68 percent of persons
who declared that they were earning wages. The distribution of wages,
in the form of monthly payments, demonstrates that 51 percent of the
salaried women in the sample received less than 80 cruzeiros, whereas
only 20 percent of the men received this wage. Forty-one percent of the
women received between 80 and 109 cruzeiros, with 55 percent of the
men receiving the same sum. Eight percent of the women received more
than 110 cruzeiros (2 percent received between 170 and 199 cruzeiros,

but no woman was found in the higher scale of 200 cruzeiros or more).
As for the men, 25 percent earned more than 110 cruzeiros (3 percent
received 200 cruzeiros and above). If we take the daily wage as a criterion of income, we can take into account part of the activities of
transformation that are associated with rural work. Since there are no
formal working contracts in this situation, the day of work or the production of a given amount is taken as the basis for issuing rewards in
kind. In our sample, of the 14 percent who declared that they received
their wages daily, 38 percent were women and 62 percent men. Of the
women, 46 percent received 0.60 centavos daily and 54 percent 0.80
centavos. Not one of the men fell into this bracket: 86 percent received
between 2.00 and 2.90 cruzeiros per day; 10 percent between 3.00 and
3.90 cruzeiros; and 5 percent above 3.90 cruzeiros.

In short, whatever the mode of payment, the women are on a lower
scale than the men. The same discrimination exists in terms of social
benefits: 66 percent of the women in our sample did not enjoy one such
benefit, with 46 percent of the men in the same position. In the casas
de farinha no benefits at all were granted, whatever the sex. In Large
Ceramics, 47 percent of the women interviewed did not have social benefits, in comparison with 24 percent of the men.

While it is not my intention to deny the differences between the
activities of transformation linked to agriculture and those linked to industry, many factors remain unaltered. Some of the factories in the
study received government incentives in order to develop, on the assumption that industrialization leads to an improvement of life through
an increase in the number of jobs. It is also assumed that the upward
mobility of workers is stimulated, in part through the granting of social
security benefits. One of the primary features that remains unaltered
is the lower status of women in relation to that of the men in the factory, as far as income and social benefits are concerned.

With regard to education, however, the situation is different. The
woman worker has, on average, a higher level of aducation than her
male partners of the same class, with the sole exception of what I considered to be the upper educational stratum and that referred to the echelons concerned with the control of production (see Blachman 1973).

Using one's head instead of arms is not seen as something very
important among the workers, for reading has little worth for those who
earn their living by using physical force. We can understand now why
the status of teacher is acceptable as a female occupation. Intellectual
work is considered light and easy. The ideology of force is cited by
other authors within the context of work, and frequently related to the
activities of the casas de farinha, where the kind of work considered
heavy—grinding the manioc, which is powered by hand, or roasting the
flour in the oven—is restricted to the men, whereas the lighter tasks
are reserved for the women. This ideology is one of the components of
the machismo morality. In reality, however, the woman also does heavy
work, since subsistence occupations demand that such tasks be performed (Garcia and Heredia 1971).

TABLE 6.4

Years of Schooling and Sex Ratio in Industry and Domestic Enterprises

| Schooling | Casa de Farinha | | Large Ceramics | |
	Men (%)	Women (%)	Men (%)	Women (%)
No schooling	47	40	10	2
1st-2nd primary	47	57	48	38
3rd-5th primary	6	3	25	42
Secondary	—	—	17	18
Total	17	30	104	57

Source: Compiled by the author.

The analysis of the work in the casas de farinha shows that although force and physical exertion are important, they are not the only values taken into account when considering the performance of tasks that spring from the division of labor. If production is a good, the body technique establishes the value (Mauss 1968). It is not only the capacity to exert bodily strength which counts, but also the way in which it is utilized. The use of one's skill is one criterion taken into consideration by the workers when evaluating the tasks of men and women. The research showed that there are several possible criteria, and that the evaluations varied in accordance with the type of criterion employed, whether it referred to the difficulty of the task or to its importance, or to the degree of knowledge required. The variations, however, were small.

The processing of manioc is an activity closely linked to rural work. Land is divided and rented in sharecropping contracts and has, in general, a casa de farinha in its main quarter, where the workers process the manioc. In virtue of the sharecropping contract, those who rent a plot of land owe the proprietor one-tenth of the manioc flour produced. Two partners are involved here, the owner of the instruments of production and the owner of the means of production, who has command over the labor force. The owner of the product recruits the labor force.

The hard manual labor of the workers who dig up the manioc with a hoe and transport the roots to the casa de farinha with the help of donkeys is done by men who are paid on a daily basis. The women peel the roots with knives. This work is paid on a per day basis or else rewarded with payments in the form of meals. The peeled product is ground by the grinder, whose work is made easier by the presence of a machine. One can still find, in some places, manioc grinders run by human power; this, however, tends to occur less now in Cariri. This type of work is usually performed by men, who are generally rewarded according to the amount they produce; there are, however, occasions on which it is done by women. The dough is compressed with wooden presses, which are moved by the physical effort of a man; this work is paid according to production. The product is then taken for the extraction of gum by women whose skill is essential for a good production. The gum is placed in troughs and put out to dry in the sun. This work, often performed by the women, does not require skill but constitutes a complementary activity. The dough is then put through a sieve, this work being performed by either men or women. As with the drying of the gum, this is extra work that is not specifically rewarded; it can be paid in cash or in kind (manioc flour, gum, or tapioca). The dough is then roasted in the oven; roasting requires stamina, since it means working day and night, standing upright near the heat, holding an immense wooden rake with which the manioc flour is stirred until it is finally ready (Fontenele 1969).

The occupations of the casas de farinha were evaluated by those who worked there. This is important, since it allows us to relate the division of labor and ideology in a more systematic manner. Carrying the manioc from the land to the casa de farinha was taken as the standard occupation, with a value of 10; this was done so as to be able to rate the other occupations according to a technique developed by Robert Hamblin (1971). The median for all the evaluations was then obtained. The results given here refer to the three criteria that were presented to the workers for judgment.

The men's occupations with the greatest value are rated almost double the value of the women's occupations with the smallest rating. However, at least one feminine occupation had a high rate (washing the gum). As far as the criterion of knowledge is concerned, the washer has more skill than the carrier of the manioc, for when it comes to difficulty or importance of the work, skill is equal to force. It should be noted that the washer also uses force to extract the gum from the dough.

Roasting and pressing require skill and strength, but the occupations involved in the production of manioc flour are not classified exclusively in terms of force. Women have some chances, although much less than the men, who are at an advantage because of their physical strength and practical knowledge.

There are also economic reasons, for although the price offered for gum is greater than that for flour, a measure of manioc furnishes more flour than gum. Faced with insufficient criteria to explain the higher rates for the masculine occupations than for the feminine ones, we believe that the most important factor is that the men have command over the production in the casas de farinha.

In the factory taken as a case study, the number of occupations is much greater than in the casa de farinha. I shall describe only the ones related to the section in charge of the pressing of the product. The factory produced, among other things, ceramic tiles; this was done by pressing the clay that had been previously ground and sieved. The tiles were then packed in boxes that also were produced in the factory and

TABLE 6.5

Median Values of Activities in a Casa de Farinha

Activity	Sex by Which Performed	Knowledge	Importance	Difficulty
Peeling	Woman	6	8	8
Sieving	Woman Man	6	8	7
Drying	Woman	6	9	7
Placing gum in the sun	Woman	8	7	7
Taking water from the well	Man	8	8	10
Digging manioc	Man	9	10	9
Washing	Woman	10	10	10
Grinding	Woman Man	10	10	10
Pressing	Man	10	10	10
Roasting	Man	16	15	15

Note: The occupation taken as a standard for evaluation was transporting manioc from the land to the casa de farinha, which was given the value of 10.

Source: Compiled by the author.

that were lined with small ceramic bricks highly resistant to heat, so that they would not be damaged by baking. After use, the small bricks were checked in the section for repairs and prepared for new use. The filling of the boxes was done by packers. In the same section there were also carriers, cleaners, and a section supervisor, as well as the workers involved in the process described above. During different parts of the day other people responsible for the supervision and control of the work moved around the section, such as the laboratory assistant, the production supervisor, and the industrial director.

The pressing team consisted of a presser, a woman who caught the ceramic tiles as they came out of the machine, a woman packer, a carrier who brought the ground clay from the section where it had been sieved, and a cleaner. The presses varied in quality, some being faster than others. A premium was given to anyone whose production passed the average of 8.5 square meters of material pressed per hour. The financial rewards, worked out monthly, came to 50 percent of the wage. As a reward for the women, the directors presented pieces of cloth for dressmaking. Just as in the casa de farinha, the women received part of their earning in kind. The directors of the factory had discovered that a rise in productivity did not depend solely on the pressers; their female helpers were also involved.

TABLE 6.6

Median Values of Activities in the Pressing Section
of Large Ceramics

Activity	Sex by Which Performed	Importance	Deviation Typical of the Woman	Deviation Typical of the Man
Siever	Man	8	30	15
Brick classifier	Woman	8	15	15
Repairman	Man	8	20	10
Cleaner	Man	9.5	30	15
Assistant repairman	Man	10	25	12
Carrier of clay	Man	10	10	20
Packer	Woman	10	20	12
Tile catcher	Woman	10	50	100
Presser of press 5	Man	10	15	12
Presser of press 8	Man	10	30	20
Presser of press 11	Man	10	40	20
Box presser	Man	12.5	35	20
Laboratory assistant	Man	12.5	30	15
Section supervisor	Man	13.5	30	12
Production dept. supervisor	Man	15	35	10
Industrial director	Man	17	35	10

Note: The occupation presented as the standard for judgment was
mechanic's assistant, with a value of 10.
Source: Compiled by the author.

The occupations were evaluated by taking the work of the mechanic's assistant as having the value of 10; this was the standard used for
measuring the other activities. The evaluations were obtained by using
the same criteria as in the casa de farinha. However, in order to evaluate the difficulty of the tasks, a longer list was presented to the workers, including occupations from all over the factory and not only from
the pressing section. I presented a shorter list to the pressing workers
dealing only with the occupations of their particular section and employing the criteria of importance of occupation and know-how.

Table 6.6 contains not only the median occupational evaluations
but also two deviations that I consider to be typical of a minority group,
but nevertheless important. I thought it valuable to include them for
comparison and interpretation of the data. The important occupations
are linked to the control of the factory. Of the three female occupations,
one had the lowest rate and the other two had the same rate as the clay
carrier.

In order to minimize the number of errors, our strategy for measuring
the occupations required their random presentation to the workers and
removing the median from all the values assigned to a given occupation
(Hamblin 1971). This last operation, however, hides variations that
form part of the error. Apart from the norm we shall take the deviation—
some of the hidden variations—and examine the individual evaluations
in order to achieve a better understanding of the nature of the values
assigned to each activity. Some of these inferences had already been
suggested by the qualitative data. According to an industrial worker who
had previously been a cowboy and who was now working as a carrier, the
most important job in the factory was his, which involved carrying heavy
loads; he asserted that it was his work that got the factory in operation.
He also said that anyone could do the light work but that no one wanted
to know about the heavy work. Among the 46 interviewed in the pressing
section, ten evaluated the work of the carrier as having equal or greater
importance than that of industrial director. The data, however, take us
further. Six of these were men and four women.

One woman's occupation also presents a deviation of the same nature. The occupation of catching the tiles registered 18 values (11 given
by women and 7 by men) that rated equal to or above that of industrial
director. The ratio varied from 1:1 to 10:1. This was not because this
was a woman's job, for another occupation performed only by women
(packer) presented only seven evaluations that rated it equal or superior
to that of industrial director. The explanation lies in the fact that the
occupation presents a high risk of bodily injury. Several tile catchers
had lost their thumbs in the presses, their fingers caught while taking
the tiles out of the machine. These accidents decreased in scale, but
were not entirely rooted out with the security precautions taken by the
factory. I have here touched upon another side of the cult of the body,
but this time I shall present it in relation to women. Although the value
given to the control of the product is an ideology of the factory that
reaches down to the workers, those who struggle for their subsistence
value their bodies (see Sigaud 1971). Whoever risks his body receives
high marks from his companions, who know what is at stake.

The risk and value of using one's body are differentiated by sex.
The women who share this ideology are more sensitive to the risks to
their own bodies than the men are. Another component of this ideology
is maternity (Stevens 1973, p. 63). We shall, however, not study this
aspect in the research. The men assert mainly the value of their physical strength.

CONCLUSION

We have tried to show the similarity of position occupied by women in activities linked directly to the land and in industrial activities. We have pointed out the importance of the family in the industrial setting and the role that results for the woman, which stems from the strong presence of the family in her work environment. We have shown how the situation on the land repeats itself in industry: the relatively inferior position that the industrial woman occupies as far as wages and social benefits are concerned. There is the exception of education, a possible road toward greater mobility, as long as there are educational resources in the area that might permit the continuation of schooling.

Finally, the values issuing from the division of labor in the manufacture of manioc and in one section of the ceramics factory were demonstrated. The role of control over the production, implicit in the casas de farinha and explicit in Large Ceramics, was linked to the importance of the exertion of the human body by the man, who is seen not only as supplying physical strength but also as a provider of subsistence. This value is a component of both the masculine and the feminine ethic.

The possibility of exploring the similarities between domestic and industrial enterprises arose as a result of substituting the model of the industrial revolution, which contrasts and opposes the activities linked to agriculture and to industry, for a model that reasserts the complementarity between the two types of production and their ideologies, which contain both differences and also structural similarities.

REFERENCES

Acker, Joan. 1973. "Women and Social Stratification: A Case of Intellectual Sexism." In Changing Women in a Changing Society, ed. Joan Huber. Chicago: University of Chicago Press.

Aguiar, Neuma. 1969. "O modelo de mudanca por detras das teorias de anomia e mobilizacao." América Latina 3:

_____. 1970. "Condicionamentos socio-culturais do desenvolvimento industrial do Ceara." Revista de ciencias sociais 1, no. 1: 96-109.

_____. 1973. Totem e tabu no Nordeste. Rio de Janeiro: IUPERJ.

Beckford, George L. 1972. Persistent Poverty. New York: Oxford University Press. Especially Chapter 1 and Appendix 1.

_____. 1973. "Economic Organization of Plantations of the Third World." Studies in Comparative International Development 7, no. 3: 243-63.

Blachman, Morris J. 1973. "Eve in Adamocracy." New York University Occasional Papers no. 5.

Bordieu, Pierre. 1966. "Condition de classe et position de classe." Archives européenes de sociologie 7: 201-23.

_____. 1970. "The Sentiment of Honour in Kabyle Society." In Honour and Shame, the Values of Mediterranean Society. Ed. J. G. Peristiany. Chicago: University of Chicago Press.

Fontenele, Raposo. 1969. Rotina e fome em uma regiao cearense. Fortaleza: Imprensa Universitaria do Ceara. Pp. 51-62.

Garcia, Afranio R., Jr., and Beatriz Alasia de Heredia. 1971. "Trabalho familiar e campesinato." America Latina 14, nos. 1 and 2 (January-June): 10-19.

Goode, William J. 1960. "Industrialization and Family Change." In Industrialization and Society, ed. Bert F. Hoselitz and Wilbert Moore. The Hague: Mouton-UNESCO.

Greenfield, Sidney. 1961. "Industrialization and the Family in Sociological Theory." American Journal of Sociology 67 (November): 312-22.

Hamblin, Robert. 1971. "Mathematical Experimentation and Sociological Theory: A Critical Analysis." Sociometry 34: 423-52.

Hamblin, Robert, and Carole Smith. 1966. "Values, Status and Professors." Sociometry 23 (September): 183-96.

Hobsbawm, Eric. 1971. Industry and Empire. London: Penguin.

Holter, Harriet. 1972. "Sex Roles and Social Change," in Family, Marriage and the Struggle of the Sexes. Recent Sociology, no. 4, ed. Hans Peter Dreitzel, pp. 153-72. New York: Macmillan.

Hoselitz, Bert F., and Wilbert E. Moore, eds. 1960. Industrialization and Society. The Hague: Mouton-UNESCO.

Johnson, Allen W. 1971. Sharecroppers of the Sertao. Stanford: Stanford University Press.

Kerr, Clark, J. T. Dunlop, F. H. Harbinson, and C. A. Myers. 1960.
Industrialism and Industrial Man.

Leite Lopes, Jose Sergio. 1971. "Os salarios das mulheres e sua re-
percussao sobre a situacao da familia da classe trabalhadora." Unpublished ms.

Marx, Karl. 1906. Capital. I, especially Chapters 13-15. New York:
Modern Library.

_____. 1966. Pre-Capitalist Economic Formations. New York: Inter-
national Publishers.

Mauss, Marcel. 1968. "Les techniques du corps." In Sociologie et
anthropologie. 4th ed. Paris: P.U.F.

Mendes Chaves, Luiz de Gonzaga. 1972. "Aspecto da estructura ocupacional de uma regiao pesqueira do Ceara." Revista ciencias sociais 3: 68-69.

Moore, Wilbert. 1960. "Industrialization and Social Change." In Industrialization and Society, ed. Bert Hoselitz and Wilbert E. Moore.
The Hague: Mouton-UNESCO.

Nash, Manning. 1967. Machine Age Maya. Chicago: University of
Chicago Press.

Palmeira, Moacir. 1972. "Latifundium et capitalisme." Unpublished
ms.

Sigaud, Lygia. 1971. "A nacao dos homens." Unpublished ms., Rio de
Janeiro, Museu Nacional.

Smelser, Neil J. 1959. Social Change in the Industrial Revolution. Chicago: University of Chicago Press.

Stevens, Evelyn P. 1973. "Machismo and Marianismo." Society 10
(September-October):

Velho, Otavio. 1969. "O conceito de campones e sua aplicacao a
analise de meio rural brasileiro." America Latina 12, no. 1.

Woortman, Klaas. 1965. "A mulher em situacao de classe." America
Latina 8 (July-September).

7

THE BAHIANA IN
THE LABOR FORCE
IN SALVADOR, BRAZIL
Elizabeth Jelin

The process of economic development and the increasing specialization and division of labor bring about a continuous and growing differentiation between the productive unit and the residence and consumption
unit. However, even in societies where this differentiation process is
highly advanced, domestic activities geared to consumption in residential or family units may include some extraction of raw materials for consumption (food preparation, weaving and dressmaking, house-building)
as well as certain personal services (cleaning house, doing laundry, caring for children and the sick). Traditionally, housekeeping is done by the
women living in each family unit. These activities are carried out as
household production for family consumption, and therefore their product
does not pass through the market and does not enter the monetary circuit
of social production. Registered participation of women in the labor force
is necessarily small because household activities are not included as
part of social production. Here lies part of the reason why the role of
women in society is more often seen as the consumer than as producer.
    The aim of this essay is to analyze the participation of women in
the labor force of Salvador, a city in northeastern Brazil, including
household production as one type of productive organization that is in-
timately related to other types of economic organizations—in this case,
simple production of merchandise, capitalist organization, and state
public administration. *

---

*The analytical scheme that includes these four types of organiza-
tion is discussed in more detail by Elizabeth Jelin (1974). The present
essay is an application of that analytical scheme to female participation
in the labor force, and further develops the discussion of the role of
household activities.
    This essay is part of the study "Labor Force, Employment and So-
cial Participation in Salvador, Brazil," carried out by CEBRAP in collaboration with the Instituto de Recursos Humanos of the University of
Bahia. A preliminary version of it was presented at the conference
"Feminine Perspectives in the Social Sciences in Latin America," Buenos
Aires, March 1974.

In rural areas with a peasant economy, most of the productive activities are geared to family consumption, even if part of the production is commercialized. Such family production for subsistence has no clear and easily calculable monetary value. Therefore, the national accounts are almost always distorted to a degree that varies according to the weight of the peasant economy in the national production.* Nevertheless, it is possible to visualize and take into account food production for household consumption, and in many countries this is estimated and included in the national product. It is more difficult to register in the accounts the production for self-consumption of a large variety of goods and services, such as weaving and making clothes, building and repairing houses, grinding and storing grains and other foodstuffs, carrying water and wood, preparing meals, rearing children, cleaning clothes, and providing medical and religious services.†

The variety of household products and services found in urban areas where a commercialized economy prevails is much smaller than in peasant economies. The long-range historical trend has been an increasing commercialization of productive activities and declining importance of household production. However, household activities are carried out even in highly developed societies with a complex social division of labor. Their importance shows up in a more dramatic way if, instead of taking the peasant family as a comparative framework, the market value of goods and services usually produced in households is estimated. ‡ Hence the frequent paradox found in developed countries with relatively high minimum wages: housewives cannot "afford" looking for a paid job because the market prices of the goods and services produced at home are beyond the income they could get for their work. Thus, if they want to have a paid job, they have to be ready to keep their household duties as well.

In short, when analyzing the economic activity of women, household production has to be included, given its importance in the total social production and the predominance of female labor, both within their

---

*The distortions that result from this fact greatly affect the most common index of development, per capita income. This has been analyzed by Dudley Seers.

†Some estimate of nonmonetary income derived from subsistence activities for family consumption in peasant economies is presented by Ester Boserup (1970, Chapter 9).

‡The discussion presented here places much more emphasis than does Boserup (1970) on the value of urban household activities. The difference is due to the fact that Boserup uses the peasant family as a comparative base, while here more importance is assigned to the monetary cost of the same activities.

own families and in paid domestic service.* The analysis of female participation in the household economy and in other productive activities
is the first step in the analysis of the participation of women in the other
three types of productive organization of the market economy. This essay will also discuss how women's role in the family structure and
household production conditions their employment in the market sectors.

PRODUCTIVE ORGANIZATION AND EMPLOYMENT IN SALVADOR

    The data presented here are part of a research project carried out
in Salvador, Bahia, Brazil. The fieldwork was conducted between 1970
and 1971, and consisted of a survey of 1,115 cases drawn from a random sample of the adult population (over eighteen years old) of the city
(see Berquo 1973). One of the central goals of the project was to study
labor force structure and participation in paid occupations. Hence, data
presented here on unpaid household activities are based on inferences
and not on individual answers to specific questions on the subject.
    Salvador is an almost ideal place for the study of urban organiza-
tion of economic activities. Extremely diverse productive organizations
have been introduced during the four centuries of the region's history.
At present, they continue to exist and are integrated in complex ways.
Salvador developed before, and independently from, any process of industrialization. Until the mid-eighteenth century, when it lost its position as Brazil's capital, its population grew with its role as an agricultural export and import center. Salvador was the center of a relatively
rich and populous rural zone, which during long periods of its history
produced an enormous surplus and gave the city its character as a consumption center for the rural landowning class.
    The decline of agricultural exports led to the decline of the city,
which began to recover slowly only after 1930. Its recovery was due
first to the expansion of the state bureaucracy that accompanied the
growing centralization and power of the national state. Later, the discovery of petroleum in the region created a focus of economic dynamism,
which though weak at first, grew in importance as refineries and the
petrochemical industry were installed. Since 1960 the national government's

------

    *Male domestic servants exist in very few places. Generally they
are found in societies where the tradition of secluding women is combined with an organization of agricultural production based on the extended family, thus freeing the young men, who can then search for
salaried urban work. If the level of urban unemployment is high, paid
domestic service is seen as a viable occupation by the young men.

development policies have promoted private capitalist investments, especially in industry, production, and tourist services. In addition to these factors, which operated directly on the city (although most of them in response to decisions and considerations external to it), the city also received strong in-migratory flows caused by droughts and other factors leading to rural exodus. At present the metropolitan area of Salvador has more than 1.5 million inhabitants. While the city has increasingly integrated communications, transportation, commercial, and service networks, which radiate from the south-central area of the country, such integration entails a loss of regional autonomy.

At present, private capitalism dominates the organization of industry, banking, and tourism: these are the dynamic foci of investment and production, and the rest of the city's economic activity is subordinate to them. Nevertheless, private capitalist organization is not the dominant form in terms of employment, since the expansion of capitalist production did not entail the displacement of other forms of productive activity but, rather, their subordination and adaptation. A large number of productive units are organized as units of simple production of merchandise (this is true both for traditional crafts and for the "new craftsmanship") by independent producers who sell the product of their labors to clients. In addition, there is also the public bureaucracy, which employs many people; its organization and dynamics do not respond (or do so only indirectly) to the laws of capitalist expansion. Finally, there is the household economy, with its unpaid workers and paid domestic service, whose volume of production is considerably greater than is usually supposed.

Table 7.1 presents an estimate of the distribution of the adult population of the city in these four types of productive organizations. The percentages of "unpaid household activities" are estimates reached by subtracting from the total number of women who were not gainfully employed, all the women who lived with their spouses and half of those who did not (widows, single women, or women separated from their husbands); this total was considered as an approximate estimate of the women doing only household work. Men were not included, on the assumption that there are no men who do only unpaid household work.

As can be seen in the table, men and women differ in their participation in the various types of organization. Domestic production is almost exclusively a woman's field. Women also predominate in the simple production of merchandise. Men predominate in capitalist organization, and the difference between men and women employed by the public bureaucracies (among those persons with paid employment) is small. Since the focus of this essay is on female economic activity, we will analyze the participation of women in the four types of economic organization.

Women in the Urban Household Economy

Table 7.1 shows that 63.3 percent of women over 18 years of age are not gainfully employed. Among these a certain number are unemployed

TABLE 7.1

Types of Productive Organization in Salvador

Type of Organization	Percent of Population with Paid Employment			Percent of Total Population over Eighteen		
	Men	Women	Total*	Men	Women	Total*
Paid domestic service	4.0	16.8	8.5	3.3	6.2	4.9
Simple production of merchandise	17.1	39.6	25.0	14.1	14.5	14.3
Private capitalist economy	50.7	19.4	39.7	41.7	7.1	22.7
Public administration	28.2	24.2	26.8	23.2	8.9	15.3
Unpaid household activities	—	—	—	—	53.9	29.6
Unemployed (do not participate in production)	—	—	—	17.7	9.4	13.2
Total	100.0	100.0	100.0	100.0	100.0	100.0
(N)	(298)	(273)	(571)	(362)	(744)	(1,106)

*The percentages in the "Total" columns are based on a weighting of the original data to compensate for the overrepresentation of women in the sample. For information on the characteristics of the sample and the weighting factors according to sex, see Berquo (1973).

Source: Compiled by the author.

but looking for work, a few are incapacitated by illness, and some are students; but most of them are housewives or relatives whose main task is household activities. Furthermore, 6. 2 percent of women—representing 16. 8 percent of those who have paid employment—work in paid domestic service. Since we do not have specific information of the performance of household activities of the women who are not gainfully employed, to analyze this theme we shall have to infer conclusions based on the total number of women not gainfully employed.

Female participation in the labor force depends on age and position in the family structure. Table 7. 2 shows that the rate of employment varies according to the age and marital status of women (as measured by the presence or absence of a spouse in the household at the time of the interview). * The rate of participation in the labor force is higher in the group between 25 and 35 years of age. This is the case both among women who live with their spouses and among those who do not. In this age group seven of every ten unmarried women have gainful employment. Surprisingly, the rate of participation in the labor force is lower among younger women. Possibly many single women between 18 and 24 years of age are students, or unemployed and looking for work. In the older age groups, the proportion of working women decreases, indicating progressive concentration on household labor and incapacity with the onset of old age.

The results presented in Table 7. 2 do not reflect only the effect of the family life cycle on women's active participation in the economy, or on their performance of unpaid household work. The differences between age groups at any given moment are also the result of historical changes that are revealed in the labor market as differences between age groups or cohorts. In a society undergoing change, each new cohort entering the labor market does not repeat the employment pattern of the previous ones. Today's young women entered the labor market at a different moment and with a different training than the older ones, and will certainly show a different pattern of economic participation when they age (Jelin 1972). The Salvador project will permit a deeper exploration of this theme through the complete life histories that were collected and that are now in the process of tabulation and analysis.

As was pointed out above, paid domestic service occupied 16. 8 percent of the gainfully employed women. Domestic service, then,

---

*For studying rates of female participation by age, it is preferable to use as a base the sample of all residents in the selected households, instead of the sample of individuals chosen in each household to be interviewed personally. In the latter sample, the rates of participation by age of the women show some biases, and thus it would be necessary to introduce differential weighting factors according to the occupational status of each age and sex category. The other data presented in this paper, though they are taken from the sample of individuals, do not require such weighting.

TABLE 7.2

Female Participation in the Labor Force, by Age and Marital Status
(all women residents in sampled households)

Age	Lives with Spouse			Does not Live with Spouse*			Total		
	Works	Does not Work	Total	Works	Does not Work	Total	Works	Does not Work	Total
18-24	15.4	84.6	100.0 (117)	46.9	53.1	100.0 (450)	40.4	59.6	100.0 (567)
25-34	26.8	73.4	100.0 (272)	70.5	29.5	100.0 (200)	45.3	54.7	100.0 (472)
35-44	19.0	81.0	100.0 (247)	55.3	44.7	100.0 (114)	30.5	69.5	100.0 (361)
45-54	21.0	79.0	100.0 (128)	52.5	47.5	100.0 (101)	34.9	65.1	100.0 (229)
55 and over	13.3	86.7	100.0 (60)	19.8	80.2	100.0 (111)	17.5	63.3	100.0 (171)
Total (N)	21.0	79.0	100.0 (824)	50.2	49.8	100.0 (976)	36.7	63.3	100.0 (180)

*Includes single, widowed, separated, and divorced women.

Notes: Information on marital status was not available at the time this essay was written. I am therefore using the information on whether there was a spouse living in the same household at the time of the interview.

For a description of this sample of residents, see Berquo (1973).

Source: Compiled by the author.

135

represents an important source of female employment in the city. The women who do this work are usually young (see Table 7. 3), and live in the homes of their employers. Domestic service is numerically very important as an occupational alternative for women in Latin America, especially in urban areas, where it often exceeds 20 percent of total female employment. Despite the numerical importance of domestic service and the complexity of the social relations between the employer and the paid worker, who in some ways is also a member of the family, very few studies have analyzed this type of occupation and the work relations it generates (Hewett n. d.).

In sum, women are overwhelmingly concentrated in domestic work: more than half the women are housekeepers, and their activities are centered in the household (either with or without the help of paid domestic servants). To these we may add those women who do household work only part-time—those who have paid employment outside their homes but are also in charge of household chores for their families. Finally, there are women who work in paid domestic service. We have noted that 6. 2 percent of women did this type of work exclusively, and a considerable number of women combine household work for their own families with paid domestic work as a part-time occupation. Work organization in this case is closer to the pattern of simple production of merchandise, which will be considered next.

Independent Female Producers

Going back to Table 7. 1, it can be seen that 14. 5 percent of the women (39. 6 percent of gainfully employed women) work in simple production of merchandise as independent producers. Table 7. 4 shows the predominant occupational categories: traditional crafts, which include making clothes, cooking, embroidering and weaving, and domestic service, which includes mainly people devoted to such specialized tasks as washing and ironing. As might be expected (Table 7. 3), these independent producers are usually older than the women occupied in the other forms of productive organization, since these include a number of traditional occupations for which formal education is not required. When many of the older women entered the labor force, the alternative of bureaucratic work, which is available to the younger women, did not exist.

Almost 40 percent of the women in simple production of merchandise work less than four hours a day—indicating only a partial dedication to paying jobs—often in activities similar to those performed at home. This shows the fluidity of the labor market that allows a wide range of variations between the exclusive dedication to household work and the extension of similar tasks performed for payment, a pay that supplements the family income. Sewing, repairing and washing clothes, preparing food and occasionally going out to sell it are domestic jobs that can be

TABLE 7.3

Female Employment in Productive Organization, by Age

Age	Paid Domestic Service	Simple Production of Merchandise	Capitalist Sector and Public Administration	Total
18-24	54.4	11.1	21.8	23.1
25-34	26.1	25.0	42.0	32.8
35-44	10.8	27.8	19.3	21.2
45-54	8.7	23.1	12.6	16.1
55 and over	—	13.0	4.2	17.0
Total (N)	100.0 (46)	100.0 (108)	100.0 (119)	100.0 (273)

Source: Compiled by the author.

TABLE 7.4

Female Occupations in Productive Organization

Occupational Category	Paid Domestic Service	Simple Production of Merchandise	Capitalist Organization	Public Administration	Total
Domestic service	100.0	36.1	—	—	31.1
Street vendor	—	8.3	—	—	3.3
Traditional craftswoman	—	45.5	5.7	—	19.0
Unskilled worker	—	0.9	28.3	6.1	7.3
Skilled worker	—	0.9	3.8	3.0	1.8
Professional/ technical worker	—	4.6	24.5	48.5	18.3
Bureaucrat	—	—	20.8	42.4	14.3
Saleswoman	—	—	11.3	—	2.2
Owner/adminis-trator	—	3.7	5.7	—	2.6
Total	100.0	99.9	100.1	100.0	99.9
(N)	(46)	(108)	(53)	(66)	(273)

Source: Compiled by the author.

138

done for third parties without breaking the family routine. These wom-
en's production activities can be compared with those of the subsistence
peasant who sells the surplus of what he has produced for his own consumption—a surplus which often results from family underconsumption,
and is commercialized only because of the need for cash to acquire
goods indispensable for family survival.

The degree of commercialization of household activities in a given
family depends on the level of the family's income and on the woman's
occupational alternatives. The number of hours that a woman is willing
to work for third parties depends on the urgency of the need for cash
(that is, it is inversely related to the level of family income). On the
other hand, married women with children have less time to work for third
parties and may prefer to work in their own houses or under informal arrangements that can be broken when the family situation so requires.
That is, for a large number of independent producers, the central activity is the care of their own households; and paid work remains subordinate to this, depending on family pressures and obligations. The
urban family cannot survive without a minimum cash income. If there
are no other sources of income, the woman has the possibility of com-
mercializing her domestic work to obtain some cash.

Female Employment in the Capitalist Sector
and in the State Bureaucracy

Female participation in these two types of productive organization
is easier to analyze within existing models. Few women work in private
capitalist enterprises: only 7.1 percent of the total, and 19.4 percent
of gainfully employed women do so in Salvador. In these enterprises,
the women are concentrated in a few occupational categories, as can
be seen in Table 7.4: one out of every five women has a bureaucratic
position (almost always as an office worker or secretary): one-fourth
are teachers or nurses in schools and private hospitals, another fourth
hold jobs as unskilled manual workers not directly connected to the
productive process, such as cleaning or preparing food or coffee in offices and factories. The rest hold various occupations, including saleswomen or seamstresses who alter clothes in shops, and a few are owners
of commercial establishments.

The concentration of women in a few occupations is even more marked in the public bureaucracy, which employs 8.9 percent of women (24.6
percent of gainfully employed women). Teachers and nurses constitute
90 percent of the women employed in the public sector. Moreover, in
comparison with private capitalist enterprises, the state employs more
women, not only absolutely but also in relation to the number of men.
While 24.6 percent of the gainfully employed women work in the public
sector, only 28.2 percent of employed men do so. In contrast, the

capitalist enterprises employ 19. 4 percent of the employed women and
50. 7 percent of the employed men (Table 7. 1).

As one would expect because of the educational requirements of
these two sectors, women under thirty-five predominate (see Table 7.3).
Many of these women will become housewives and leave their jobs when
they marry and have children. Nonetheless, a good number will not do
so, especially the teachers, who can adapt the relatively short working
hours of the profession to the needs of a housewife. This indicates a
geniune process of change in the occupational patterns of female employment in Salvador, toward a growing integration into the dynamic and
"modern" sectors of the productive structure. To the degree that these
sectors expand their employment and maintain the pattern of preferring
women for certain occupations, the demand for women in the public bureaucracy and in the capitalist sector will increase (Madeira and Singer
1973).

The private and public sectors are the areas of the economy where
bureaucratic process and the formalization of work relations is most advanced. These are, in fact, the "modern world" of which many authors
speak. In these sectors, female occupations are clearly typed: middle-
level professions (teachers and nurses) and office workers, especially
secretaries. In Salvador, as in many other places (Boserup 1970, Chapters 6 and 7), women rarely have administrative responsibilities or
workers' occupations in industrial production. A great number of cultural norms support this pattern of division of labor between the sexes.
Behind the cultural norms, however, powerful control mechanisms of
the supply and demand of labor, and of the exploitation of female labor
in household activities, operate in cities such as Salvador.

THE HOUSEHOLD ECONOMY IN A CAPITALIST SOCIETY

What is the relationship between the predominance of female labor
in households and in simple production of merchandise, and the mechanisms of exploitation in the capitalist sector? Is there some organic
link and complementarity between the two, or are we faced with a case
of superposition of organizational layers, in which the older patterns
tend to disappear as the new ones expand? The general hypothesis of
this paper is that there is an intimate relation between the various parts
of the social structure. Specifically, the household economy and simple
production are integrated in a subordinate position to the dominant capitalist sector, which exploits them. This probably will result in the am-
plification and continuation of the household and simple production types
of organization rather than their disappearance.

From the point of view of the large enterprises interested in maintaining low wages and in being able to count on a large supply of labor,
the existence of the simple production of merchandise may be profitable.

Often the relations between capitalist enterprise and simple producers of goods and services imply the disguised purchase of the labor force or the exploitation of simple productive units (Jelin 1974). Nonetheless, this is seldom the case of female producers, since it is rare to find independent female producers who work for enterprises and not for individual clients, such as women sewing for factories, cake or confection makers for stores or restaurants, and laundrywomen for business enterprises. Furthermore, given the highly segmented and competitive character of the market for these goods and services, the buying enterprise acts as just one more client.

The relations between the capitalist economy and women working in household activities and in simple production must be analyzed on another level. There are three important aspects in these relations: the effect of the existence of paid domestic service on the demand for goods and services to be consumed by the entrepreneurial class; the possible competition between the simple producers of merchandise and capitalist enterprise dedicated to the production of similar merchandise; and the effect of the household activities performed by the working-class women for their families on the wage level of industrial labor.

The existence of relatively cheap and abundant domestic service affects the quality of life of the bourgeois family, since these cheap personal services allow alternative uses of income. As a source of savings for productive investment, the effect of domestic service is certainly negligible, since the money saved on personal services is surely destined for alternative consumption and not for savings and investment. Thus its existence may increase the demand for luxury goods and services that generally are not produced locally. Finally, the existence of abundant and cheap domestic service deters the capitalization of personal services, thus permitting alternative investments in sectors that yield higher returns.

Let us now consider the supposedly competitive relation between independent female producers and capitalist enterprises dedicated to producing similar goods. First, it is well known that when capitalist organization enters certain areas of production, it displaces the small, independent producer. On the other hand, a given economic activity does not change its organization until it becomes insufficient or unprofitable. In Salvador and in Brazil in general, capitalist investments tend to concentrate in industrial activities and related services, and leave personal services to uncapitalized simple producers using cheap and unskilled labor. This allows a greater concentration of resources for investment in the capitalist industrial sector. Only a growth of consumer demand for capitalized services (either through raising the level of living among the working class or through an increasing shortage of labor) could produce a change in the scale of production of services and consumer goods, which presently is satisfied by simple production.

Dressmaking can provide a good example of this process. For most of the population, their clothes are either sewn at home or are made by dressmakers who work as a supplement to their own household activities, and who charge relatively little for their services. This situation could change if this type of labor becomes scarce, or if the level of income of vast sectors of the population increases, and patterns of mass consumption change. Then dressmaking could become organized in capitalist, industrial enterprises. Only under these circumstances would capitalist investment in this field become profitable and generalized. In fact, the production of some specific goods and services at home, or by independent producers, can continue even after capitalist organization has penetrated and dominated most productive industrial activity, as long as it is possible to maintain the cultural definition of domestic work as the privileged domain of women.

Finally, the relation between household activity and the levels of income of the working class is well known. The performance of numerous tasks at home is the working-class response to low levels of cash income. Given the levels of working-class income, production of clothes, care of children, cleaning and repairing the house, food preparation, and medical and paramedical services performed at home allow a considerably higher life standard than would be possible if all these services had to be purchased in the market, at market prices. At the same time, however, the existence of such ample and multifaceted domestic activity permits the maintenance of low salary levels, since the subsistence salary does not include the monetary cost of these domestic activities. The relationship between low salaries and building one's own home has been pointed out (Oliveira 1970). Many tasks performed at home by the working-class housewife, whether as her principal activity or in addition to paid employment, also serve this function. In summary, the variety of household activities indicates both an adaptation to low salary levels and a means of exploiting the working-class family, since it implies the performance of productive labor, necessary for the families' survival, during the "leisure" time of the workers and their families. In all countries—and Brazil is no exception—there is a wide gap between the cost of living calculated at market prices and the level of the minimum, or even average, wages of industrial workers. The breach is filled with underconsumption or household production.

CONCLUSIONS

The objective of this essay has been to offer some ideas on the productive participation of women based on a reevaluation of the household economy. No doubt the implications of such a reconceptualization are yet to be discovered and compared with alternative approaches in order to understand the significance of household activities. Until this is done, let me make a few comments in the form of conclusions, more as notes for a debate than as established truths.

The first comment has to do with the academic and census definitions of "economic activities," "economically active population," and "participation in the labor force." The arbitrariness of definitions is inevitable. The problem lies in the reification of the categories—that is, the analytical use of originally arbitrary categories as valid descriptions of reality. For some peculiar reason, which would be interesting to investigate, both from the point of view of the sociology of knowledge and from the point of view of the role of public bureaucracies in the definition of the categories of intellectual discussion, household activities within the family are not categorized as productive work, and persons in charge of household activities are classified as "dependents."* This is done without any clear and explicit criteria. Lack of payment is not used as a criterion, since people helping their families without payment in other economic activities are included in the labor force; neither is the final destination of the product used as a criterion, since subsistence peasants are included in the economically active population, as are paid domestic servants who work in a family unit. There can be no doubt of the need to reconceptualize the sociodemographic categories related to employment and productive activity, but starting from a new conceptual scheme that will permit the classification of the diverse modalities of work and nonwork. This reconceptualization must account for domestic work, and must reelaborate the categories of unemployment and of inclusion in or exclusion from the labor force.†

Turning to another theme, practical solutions to the problems of women's work have been suggested from various points of view and ideologies. Feminist movements have demanded "equal pay for equal work," equal opportunities for employment in certain positions (generally high positions), a system of quotas to guarantee female representation in certain occupational circles, and even payment for household work. The justifications for these demands are generally weak, based on simplistic principles that take as their focus a single, isolated aspect of social reality. Doubtless, financial independence and the equality of opportunity are important, and their absence could be a strong basis for mobilization and struggle. Nonetheless, as the Soviet experience has shown, these are no more than symptoms; and little is achieved by changing them. A high proportion of paid women does not automatically

---

*The role of the bureaucratic agencies in charge of collecting data is discussed by Aaron Cicourel (1964). The discussion on what is and what is not a productive activity is as old as the social sciences themselves.

† Paul Singer (1971) suggests a means to eliminate the voluntarism involved in the definition of unemployment. Nonetheless, he does not offer a satisfactory approach to the inclusion of production for family consumption and household production, and he does not consider these as part of social production.

mean equality of rights and duties. Soviet women complain, and not
without justification, that they are working much harder than their husbands, since the whole responsibility for household activities continues
in female hands, above and beyond their paid work.

On the other hand, the alternative suggestion by some feminists
that domestic work be paid, is in most cases (where the payment would
be made by social organizations, and not by the husband) no more than
a mechanism for the redistribution of income. If there is a difference
between social strata in the volume of the household work, it is in favor
of the lower strata. Consequently, women of lower strata would receive
a greater income than the women of higher strata for their housework.
But this would not change the social role of women, nor would it give
them their desired "liberation."*

In fact, the problem of household activities and the central role of
women in it is part of a complex social reality, and cannot be dealt with
in isolation. Theoretically, the problem of women's role in the household and in society is still unsolved. Its solution will require a complex
analysis that should include in the same perspective not only the two
sexes but also the family, as the basic social institution where male
and female come together. By studying the relations between family
structure and the social organization of production—that is, the relation between the social division of labor and the familial and sexual
division of labor—we may be able to understand and explain the types
of productive participation of women (and men), as well as their determinants. We have advanced little in this field since Engels' classical
essay.

Finally, it is important to remember that the relations between the
sexes are not independent of class relations. This is implicit in the
preceding paragraph, which emphasized the need to study the family in
relation to the productive organization and the resulting social classes.
To what degree, in capitalist societies, does the "liberation" that
upper-strata women attain through getting jobs also entail the exploi-

---

*A "solution" to the problem, which is absurd in its confusion of
the activity of the sociologists and social reality, appears in an article
by Joan Acker (1973). She suggests that to solve the problem in studies
of social mobility, one should investigate the prestige level of the
"housewife" occupation. In this way, by assigning a prestige score,
one could eliminate the "horrible" problem of defining the social status
of women by that of their husbands. She thus confuses the stereotypes
and prejudices in prestige evaluations made by the members of the society with the indicators used by social scientists. From there on, she
commits the incredible error of assuming (implicitly) that an operational
handling of prestige indicators would solve the theoretical problem of
placing women in the social structure, as well as the social problems
of women, by giving them an identity and their own "score."

tation of lower-strata women? The use of paid domestic service to liberate professional women from their domestic chores is a common occurrence, especially in Latin American countries, where the supply of domestic labor is abundant and where there are many educated women who can choose whether to participate actively in their professional or occupational life. For these women, paid work is a "liberating" option. For others, paid work, be it domestic or any other type, is an ineluctable necessity for survival. This example is cited only to indicate the futility of posing the feminine "problem" in abstract and universal terms, or of the possibility of women's "liberation." On the contrary, we think that the real world is one of relations between social classes (which vary according to the organization of production), relations of domination and class exploitation, that affect women differently according to the social class and family structure in which they live.

REFERENCES

Acker, Joan. 1973. "Women and Social Stratification; a Case of intellectual Sexism." American Journal of Sociology 79 (January).

Berquo, Elza. 1973. "Pesquisa sobre forca de trabalho, emprego e participacao social em Salvador." CEBRAP.

Boserup, Ester. 1970. Woman's Role in Economic Development. London: George Allen.

Cicourel, Aaron. 1964. Method and Measurement in Sociology. New York: Free Press.

Hewett, Valerie. n.d. "Migrant Female Labor in Colombia: An Analysis of Urban Employment in Domestic Service." Interim report on research in progress. Mimeo.

Jelin, Elizabeth. 1972. "Estructura ocupacional, cohortes y ciclo vital." Actas II Conferencia regional latinoamericana de poblacion. Mexico City: Colegio de Mexico.

_____. 1974. "Formas de organizacion de la actividad economica y estructura ocupacional; el caso de Salvador, Brasil." Desarrollo economico 53 (April-June).

Madeira, Felicia R., and Paul I. Singer. 1973. Estructura do emprego a trabalho feminino no Brasil, 1920-1970. Sao Paulo: Cuaderno CEBRAP 13.

Oliveira, Francisco de. 1970. "A economia brasileira: Critica a razao
    dualista." Estudos CEBRAP 2.

Seers, Dudley.

Singer, Paul I. 1971. Forca de trabalho e emprego no Brasil: 1920-
    1969. Sao Paulo: Cuaderno CEBRAP 3.

8

RELATIONSHIPS OF SEX
AND SOCIAL CLASS
IN BRAZIL

Heleieth Iara Bongiovani Saffioti

The partial socialization of women into the working class constitutes an efficient mechanism whereby the capitalistic society is able
to mobilize an enormous reserve of female labor. Women's socialization in capitalist countries is similar in terms of the dual aspects of
their social roles. This is true for both developed and underdeveloped
nations. In both types of historical capitalistic structures, the social
function of the feminine mystique is the same and its content is similar.
A rationally elaborated image of woman has been disseminated that
seeks to alienate her from the occupational structure. Such an image
was built up in the dominant center of international capitalism, and
from there it has spread—especially through popular scientific works,
movies, television, and fiction—to the economic, social, and cultural
satellite countries, where it has been fused with different cultural traditions. This is part of a process of modernization that is exported
from the center to the peripheral satellites. Through this process, the
imported image becomes a national mystique. Within the peripheral nations, under the strong influence of such ideas, it has not been difficult to reduce a labor force that, in the long run, has less chance within the occupational structure, although there are some fluctuations of
minor importance.

However, it is worth noting that there are crucial differences between the social situation of women in highly industrialized nations and
that of women in underdeveloped ones. As a result of their mode of integration into the capitalist system, the satellite countries do not have
the conditions that would enable them to use the mechanisms for reducing social tensions that have been used by the hegemonic countries
since World War II. There are some exceptions. In some peripheral
countries it has been possible, through austere economic policies, to
promote short- and medium-term periods of economic growth. Also, depending on the appearance of new historical conditions, the redefinition
of the ways in which peripheral countries are integrated within the capitalist world is always a possibility. In this way, the achievement of

a certain degree of growth and/or the establishment of a process of development would increase female participation over the short and medium term. Nevertheless, such an achievement would create economic deterioration in other peripheral areas and, consequently, the amount of change in the situation of the female labor force inside the capitalist system as a whole would be minimal.

On the other hand, we must take into account the machismo cultural complex throughout the underdeveloped world. It exists with particular strength in Latin America, where, as a result, the inferior conditions of women are more dramatically exposed. This does not mean that macho behavior is solely responsible for the reduced participation of women in the job market; rather, with machismo the techniques of dominating women and the rationales that keep them out of the job market are less sophisticated in Latin America than in the central areas of the capitalist system.

Perhaps discrimination is not strong enough to prohibit women from all economic activity. When the family is in a situation of economic need, the woman with a job opportunity and some kind of child care—institutional or a personal arrangement—will work. (This is a possibility only if the sole reason that keeps women in the household is child care.)

Discrimination produces a severe ambivalence in the female personality. It is common to see the woman torn between household and working patterns. This typical female ambivalence is produced through socialization in accordance with the economic exigencies of a highly unstable system subject to cycles of growth and recession; as a result, women become a special kind of worker different from men, whose personalities are developed following the worker pattern alone.

Moreover, in countries with a Latin background, legislation frequently represents a ratification of this ambivalence. Here, under a protectionistic guise, many of the regulations establishing job rules and providing special exemptions for women serve to prohibit certain tasks or to impose certain financial obligations toward female workers on the employer. Although countries with a non-Latin background also support laws that, under the pretext of protection, discriminate against women, it seems that the tendency to legal sanction of discrimination is more frequent in countries where the macho stereotype has stronger social value.

Besides these obsolete arrangements that supposedly protect women but thrust them out of some economic tasks, Brazilian labor legislation grants women a leave of six weeks before and six weeks after child delivery (a period that can be extended in special circumstances). During this time women receive a sum based on the average monthly wage received during their last six months of work. Other requirements, more burdensome for the employer, are found in labor legislation concerning women who have young children.

This kind of legislation makes sense only if the society as a whole assumes the burden of maternity. From the point of view of the capitalist

employer, it is both a legitimate and a common practice to evade this
legislation: first, because he pursues the meximization of profits and,
second, because he assumes that a man's wage is sufficient to produce
and reproduce his own labor force. The capitalist system is flexible
enough in dealing with such questions as the socialization of the burden
of maternity, for the same governmental action that takes the responsibility of building the economic infrastructure that creates the environment for the high profits of private enterprises could also take the responsibility of maintaining the reproduction of the labor force. Besides
the fact that such a measure would immediately give married women the
possibility of work and put more pressure on an already narrow job market, such a hypothesis presents one main difficulty: it goes against the
birth control strategy that has been used in several countries with some
success.

It appears that capitalistic society is not interested either in the
complete destruction of traditional discrimination against women's work
or in any changes in protectionist legislation that legitimize such discriminatory attitudes. Capitalistic society does not want to lose the
capacity to have power over the mobilization of the female labor force.
This is the reason why such a society must preserve the traditional female pattern of ambivalence: its control is made possible by the ambivalence.

There is no systematic study on the participation of Brazilian wom-
en in the job market. Although it is possible to see changes in this
situation, the two basic data sources for such information—the Census
and the National Sample Based on Family-Home Units (Pesquisa Nacional de Amostras por Domicilio)—present different data. The Census
is the more important source for comparative data analysis, although
its data collection is based on changing standards.

According to the first Brazilian Census of 1872, women represented
45.5 percent of the national labor force. They were concentrated in
agriculture (35.0 percent) and domestic work (33.0 percent), with about
20.0 percent working as seamstresses, 5.3 percent in the textile industry, and 6.7 percent in other activities. If we exclude those in domestic work, women still constituted an important percentage of the
national labor force (37.4 percent). This high proportion was maintained
until 1900, when women represented 45.3 percent of the labor force.
However, by that time, modifications were evident in the kinds of work
activities involving women: 52.6 percent were in domestic work, 24.6
percent in agriculture, 14.2 percent in handicraft, 4.2 percent in industry, and 4.4 percent in commerce and other activities.

Taking domestic activities as a reference, we can observe a strong
movement from 1872 to 1900 toward the expulsion of women from productive economic activities and even from commercial activities. In
agriculture, women constituted 21.1 percent of the total labor force,
and in industry, 91.3 percent. The extensive participation in industrial
activities can be explained by the structure of the sector, which

basically concentrated on textiles. The female labor force that left agricultural work settled in domestic activities and handicraft.

The situation of almost equal participation of men and women in the
national labor force was not maintained, however. By 1920, women represented only 15. 3 percent of the Brazilian labor force. In agriculture,
women's participation fell to 9. 4 percent; in industry, to 27. 9 percent;
and in commerce and related activities, to 22. 2 percent. The decrease
in female participation in industrial activities during the boom of World
War I, which produced a growth of almost 83. 3 percent in the industrial
work force (from 150, 841 workers in 1907 to 275, 512 in 1920), can be
explained by the fact that the new labor force was recruited solely from
the male population.

The 1940 Census shows a slight growth in women's participation
in the national labor force (from 15. 3 percent in 1920 to 15. 9 percent
in 1940). The tendency to reduced participation in industrial activities
continued, and in 1940 women represented only 25. 3 percent of the industrial work force. However, in both agriculture and commerce the
participation rose to 13. 3 percent and 22. 7 percent, respectively.

The 1950 Census also indicated the decreasing presence of women
in economic activities and, as a consequence, the growth of their
household role. In that year, women constituted 14. 7 percent of the
total labor force. In both the agricultural and industrial sectors, their
participation decreased: in agriculture, from 13. 3 percent in 1940 to
7. 3 percent in 1950; in industry, from 25. 3 percent in 1940 to 17. 4 percent in 1950. During the same period, women represented 32. 2 percent
in the commercial sector, an increase over the earlier Census.

According to the 1960 Census, women's participation in the Brazilian labor force increased to 17. 7 percent. This can be explained by
the industrial boom that occurred from 1955 to 1960. Nonetheless, the
increase in female labor in industry was not significant (from 17. 4 percent in 1950 to 17. 9 percent in 1960). The presence of women in commerce declined to 30. 7 percent, and in agriculture it increased to 10. 0
percent; this increase was made possible by the shift of the male labor
force from agriculture to industry during the industrial boom.

The 1970 Census revealed that women constituted 21. 0 percent of
the Brazilian labor force, an increase over 1960. They made up 9. 7 percent of the agricultural sector, 12. 2 percent of the industrial sector,
and 37. 8 percent of the commercial sector. According to a new Census
classification in terms of position, the 1970 Census indicated that wom-
en represented 27. 0 percent of employees, 10. 0 percent of autonomous
economic activities, 4.1 percent of employers, and 24.0 percent of workers without salary.

Even with the increase of women's participation in the Brazilian
labor forces during 1960-70, their overall involvement remains insignificant. Although women account for 50. 5 percent of the Brazilian population over ten years of age and 52. 8 percent of the population over
15, they constitute only 13. 0 percent of the first age group, and 15. 7

percent of the second, that are involved in some kind of economic activity. These data have even greater significance when compared with the 36.0 percent of males over ten years of age and the 43.0 percent of males over 15 years who are involved in economic activities.

The level of employment at various levels of capitalism is ruled by demands on labor that are related to the amount of capital expenditure (investment) and to the types of equipment that are part of fixed capital. Rises in capital affect labor productivity in such a way that the expansion of the system (its reproduction) can maintain or raise the demand on the labor forces. The capacity for its reproduction is the fundamental difference between the central and the peripheral areas of the capitalist system. In the central areas, this problem is solved through expansion, with the new areas incorporated into the system of the peripheral areas. This is why the disequilibrium between supply and demand of labor is greater in these peripheral areas. In peripheral societies, a high rate of growth in the population automatically produces a large labor supply that cannot be incorporated, because these areas operate with a low level of labor demand. This fact affects the capacity of peripheral capitalistic systems to increase their demands on the female labor forces. The relationship between economic development and increased demands on the female labor forces has validity only in the central areas of the capitalist system. At the same time, when compared with precapitalist modes of production, the capitalist system, even in its central areas, absorbs a relatively lower amount of the female labor forces.

In the capitalist system as a whole, full employment, or at least a very high level of employment, in the central areas is possible only with an increase in the rate of unemployment in the peripheral areas. This is why capitalism tends to create structural unemployment in its peripheral areas.

It is possible to talk about a Brazilian aspiration to hegemony in Latin America. Once it achieves this goal, the Brazilian capitalist system could have greater power over its internal unemployment rate. But this strategy depends on the ability of international capitalism to deal with its internal social tensions, and this possibility is becoming more and more remote. In these circumstances, it becomes very difficult for the capitalist system, in both its central and its peripheral areas, to solve the problem of incorporating women into the labor forces on the same level that it has incorporated men.

THE RESEARCH DESIGN

Very little research has been carried out on women in Brazil. What does exist has emphasized certain activities and explored such themes as the level of compatibility of women's performances as housewives and workers. The problems of lower-class women are almost totally ignored in the scientific literature.

The aim of this investigation is to explore, among a lower-class stratum of the population, the relationships between sex (which involves domination/subordination and cooperation relationships) and the level of compatibility between women's reproductive and productive functions.

Fieldwork was carried out in October and November 1973, among 393 family units in Ararquara, a medium-size city in the state of Sao Paulo. We interviewed 20 percent of the females in that sampling. It was not always possible to follow this objective, however. The sampling was carried out in different city areas, some of which were sparsely populated. It was necessary to omit houses located on streets with fewer than five houses or when interviews were refused. We interviewed housewives and widows (5. 2 percent). With the exception of a small group of unmarried women (21. 0 percent) in the mother's role, all others had some kind of relationship with a man: 91. 4 percent a legal relation and 3. 7 percent some other kind. Two percent were separated from their husbands.

THE SAMPLE POPULATION

This is a very poor population, with an illiteracy rate of 23. 0 percent, an average monthly income per family of Cr$ 212 (about U.S. $ 30) and an average monthly food expenditure of Cr$ 99 (about U. S. $14). In several cases, the amount spent on food is equal to the total family income. More than half of the families (53. 2 percent) spend less than Cr$100 (U. S. $14) per capita monthly on food, and a very significant number (21. 1 percent) spend less than Cr$15 (about U. S. $ 2) per capita monthly on food. As a consequence, the health situation is very poor: 41. 7 percent of the housewives, 27. 0 percent of the husbands, and 19. 0 percent of the children have health problems. In a scarcity condition, women always give up their own food to better feed their husbands and children. In several cases, the women declared that the family income was not sufficient for a satisfactory level of sustenance. By the end of the month some families have no food; begging then becomes frequent. The main diet staple is rice. Even beans, which are fairly inexpensive, do not appear in the diet of the majority of families. Animal protein is very unusual.

Compared with food, the housing situation of those interviewed is good. Three-fourths of the families own their homes. These houses are generally small and not always well-built, but in most cases they have water, electricity, and even sewage facilities. Only 25 percent of the families pay rent, with a monthly average of Cr$75 (about U. S. $11), but almost 20 percent of these pay less than Cr$ 30 (about U. S. $4).

The main source, and in most cases the sole source, of family income is the husband's work. Among the families interviewed, 16. 0 percent of the husbands were illiterate and 31. 3 percent had a rudimentary knowledge of reading and writing. Generally these men hold temporary jobs (23. 8 percent are self-employed and 76. 2 percent are employees), which is the major reason for the instability of the family. Approximately 15. 0 percent of the husbands work as masons, and approximately 5. 0 percent are agricultural workers, the latter living in the city and working on the orange and sugar plantations near Araraquara. On the whole, only 5. 3 percent of the husbands could be considered skilled workers (4. 4 percent among the employees and 8. 2 percent among the self-employed workers), while almost 94. 7 percent are unskilled workers earning very low wages.

It was found that 30. 0 percent of the wives of self-employed workers engaged in some kind of economic activity, while the same was true of only 15. 8 percent of the wives of employees. Perhaps this can be explained by the fact that the self-employed worker's working at home creates greater possibilities for women's economic activities. Thirty six and seven-tenths percent of married women who work are married to self-employed workers, while the rest are married to employees. In only one case was a married working woman solely responsible for the family income; in this case, her husband was unable to work because of poor health.

Income instability exists among both self-employed workers and employees. For various reasons, 23. 2 percent of the latter category do not have any kind of legal arrangement with the employer: because the employer refuses to legalize the situation, or the employee does not have the necessary working papers, or he was hired on a trial basis, or because the work is temporary. It appears that the temporary employment of the men pushes women into economic activities: 20.5 percent of employees with temporary jobs are married to women involved in economic activities, while 18. 6 percent of employees with permanent jobs have wives involved this way.

WOMEN'S ACTIVITY

According to the 1950 Census, women constituted 19. 5 percent of the Araraquara labor forces, a greater proportion than exists in the national pattern. At that time, women constituted 12. 5 percent of the agricultural labor force, 17. 2 percent of the industrial force, and 26. 4 percent of the commercial force. The participation of women in the industrial labor force is also higher locally than in the national pattern. This can be explained by the fact that the local industrial sector is concentrated in textiles, which traditionally has hired a large number of women. Women are also used in such small industries as soup, rope, and export bags. The local data from the 1960 and 1970 Census are not yet available, but we believe that the 1950 situation has been maintained. Among the women interviewed, 23. 0 percent engage in economic activities, with 15. 0 percent working outside the home and 8. 0 percent working at home.

TABLE 8. 1

Percentage Distribution of Women's Activities,
by Marital Status

Activity	Legally Separated	Single	Not Legally Separated	Widowed	Married
Worker outside home	50. 0	23. 0	67. 0	20. 0	12. 0
Worker at home	50. 0	12. 0	—	15. 0	7. 0
Household	—	25. 0	33. 0	65. 0	81. 0

Source: Compiled by the author.

The participation of women in economic activities varies according to their relations with men: 100 percent of the women who are legally separated from men are engaged in work, 75 percent of the single women, 35. 0 percent of the widows, and 19. 0 percent of the married women. These data are presented in Table 8. 1.

Among women who have or have had some relation with men (as married or separated women, or as widows), the existence of children and their ages have a bearing on their economic activity, as is shown in Table 8. 2. In any case women living without men are more active economically. All women appear to have some consciousness of this fact: 94. 0 percent of the women interviewed declared that it is easier to maintain a family and to educate children with the help of men; moreover, single women with young children go to work, while married wom-

TABLE 8. 2

Percent of Economically Active Women.
by Ages of Children

	No Children	Younger Than 7 Yrs.	7-13 Yrs.	14-20 Yrs.	Over 20 Yrs.
Married*	33. 3	16. 8	22. 0	24. 7	17. 4
Separated and widowed	—	21. 0	34. 1	34. 5	87. 5

*Five percent of the married women have no children.
Source: Compiled by the author.

en in the same situation stay home to care for their children. Even very
poor couples maintain this kind of traditional behavior.

For 91 percent of the working women interviewed, the main reason
to enter the job market is economic necessity (they must share the responsibility of family maintenance); only 9 percent do so because they
enjoy work. This "rationale" is a pattern in capitalist society, and is
particularly strong among lower-class women.

The large number of children per family is another element that must
be taken into account. The average number is four, but 5. 7 percent of
women have seven children, and 5. 2 percent have eight—and some have
ten, eleven, or twelve children. As an isolated element, child care is
not strong enough to keep women at home in a situation of economic
necessity. However, this situation can change when other factors are
present. Women with ten or twelve children do not work, and only 30
percent of those with eleven have some kind of job.

As can be seen in Table 8. 3 child care is the main reason for married women to stay at home. However, only 27. 7 percent of these wom-
en would like to have small families; 28. 2 percent would like to have
large ones; and 44. 1 percent are happy with their family size. Birth
control is or was used by 50 percent of the women interviewed. Among
those who are still using it, 60 percent have some kind of economic activity, and 44. 7 percent are housewives.

The patriarchal ideology predominant in the lower class decrees
that women are to be wives and mothers. In contrast with the middle-
class woman, who is educated toward social mobility, the lower-class
woman does not see work as a step in her social mobility. As a consequence, when she faces a situation in which there is no free child care
available and she herself is classified as an unskilled worker, she will
accept the guidance of the traditional patriarchal pattern. This situation
changes when the woman finds a good job: she will work even if she
has children to care for. Extended families (more than two generations
and aggregates), and relatives in general, which could provide a solution for the child care problem, are not part of the pattern in the area
under study. The families originally came from rural areas, and they
are isolated in relation to their community. Thus, when the woman goes
to work, the eldest son or daughter assumes the responsibilities of
child care.

Among women workers 43. 7 percent are employees and 56. 3 percent
are self-employed; only 33 percent of the total have some kind of legal
arrangement and are protected by labor legislation. In Brazil, legislation covering self-employed workers is not usual. Only those who receive high wages can afford the deductions prescribed by the labor legislation. In general this is not the case among women. When the woman
worker is married and her husband has legal protection, which includes
a retirement pension and social insurance for him and his family, she,
in order to avoid the deductions, accepts an unprotected situation. Besides the fact that labor claims by women are unusual, they work in

TABLE 8. 3

Reasons for Women's Economic Inactivity,
by Marital Status
(percent)

Reason	Married	Single	Widowed	Separated
It is not necessary to work	12. 7	0. 3	0. 7	0. 0
The husband does not want the wife to work	17. 3	0. 0	0. 0	0. 0
Child care	50. 1	0. 4	0. 0	0. 0
Health	10. 2	0. 0	2. 0	0. 7
Age	4. 6	0. 0	1. 0	0. 0
Total	94. 9	0. 7	3. 7	0. 7

Source: Compiled by the author.

sectors traditionally not covered by labor legislation. Among the women interviewed, 44. 8 percent do domestic service (as maids), which was just recently recognized by labor legislation, and 7 percent are temporary farm workers. Almost 67 percent of the women involved in some form of economic activity do not have any kind of protection under labor legislation. Of that percentage, 33. 1 percent results from the employer's refusal to legalize the situation and 29. 7 percent is due to the fact that as self-employed workers they cannot authorize the deductions prescribed by this legislation.

According to the answers received, 91. 1 percent of women employees have adjusted to a hierarchical structure in which they play an inferior role, although 44. 6 percent are dissatisfied with their wages. More than 50 percent would like not to work and to remain housewives. The same sentiment prevailed among women who were self-employed. It seems that the main aspiration among working women is to have a husband with a good job. In such a situation they could realize the ideal of a housewife in the way they were socialized.

In their roles as unskilled workers (49. 5 percent of them did not complete elementary school), responsible for the simplest and most monotonous tasks and receiving very low wages, they do not gain any satisfaction from their work. Going to work is a sacrifice, and they accept it because it is necessary.

When the general situation is poverty, any income helps; but women's contribution to the family budget is not significant. The main reason seems to be low wages. The minimum guaranteed wage at the time the research was done was Cr$312 (about U.S. $45) per month. But 23.9 percent of economically active women received less than Cr$100 per month (about U.S. $14), 52.8 percent received less than Cr$200 (about U.S. $28), and a total of 71.2 percent received less than the minimum guaranteed wage. It is true that for maids it is necessary to add to their wages the food supplied by the employers; but even with that, the highest wage among them is Cr$180 (about U.S. $27) per month. Only in a few cases, when they are employed as skilled workers, does the work of women contribute to the improvement of the family life style; for the others (93.3 percent) their work provides just enough to cover part of the family diet.

It is not just existing ideology that keeps the working class woman unidentified with economic activity. Her situation as housewife—which, of course, differs from class to class—acts against her maintaining any identification as a worker. While the middle-class woman has the maid to do the housekeeping, the lower-class woman does double work; she must go to her job to earn more money for the family and, at the same time, face the arduous duties of her own household. This double effort exhausts the woman, and eventually she will attempt to eliminate one of the two activities.

Constantly pursuing the ideal of housewife, the majority of these women never identify with their work, nor do they feel themselves to be effective members of the working class. This is the reason why, in this social class, paid work does not represent a source of liberation for women. Their direct participation in the class structure is always provisional, without commitment, and provoked by financial necessity. They behave much more like passive and dependent housewives than militant workers, which they are not. They succeed only in somewhat subduing the degree of male domination, and obtaining a little more freedom.

RELATIONSHIPS BETWEEN THE SEX CATEGORIES

The housewife is quite submissive to her husband. More than half of them (51.9 percent) do not even participate in the most difficult decisions, and do not have their husbands' permission to make any decisions. Only 26.6 percent have the freedom to make any decision on their own, when it is impossible to consult their husbands. The remaining 21.5 percent feel free only to make minor decisions which do not affect the family structure without prior agreement with their husbands. For women who work outside the home, the pattern is different:

- 40. 5 percent feel free to make decisions concerning the family, both major and minor.
- 26. 2 percent make decisions only on minor items.
- 33. 3 percent submit completely to their husband's decisions.

Considering all women engaged in economic activity, we have the following distribution:

- 38. 2 percent have the authority to make any decision (compared with 26. 6 percent for women who are not working).
- 25. 1 percent can decide only minor items (compared with 21. 5 percent of housewives).
- 36. 7 percent are completely subject to the husband's decisions (among housewives the percentage is 51. 9 percent).

It appears that while work by no means liberates the woman, the data show that for some of them it does promote more egalitarian relationships with the men of the household.

Control of the money in a poor home can be an index of the cooperative or the subordination-domination relationship between the sexes. This management is a painful task. Only 44. 8 percent of the women control the family budget. Women are given money only for specified expenses. Some husbands do all the family shopping and the wife has no access to the family income. Half of these men do not bring home their entire salary, holding part of it for personal expenses. Among women who are not engaged in economic activity, 41. 8 percent control the domestic budget. The other 58. 2 percent leave control to their husbands, of whom two-thirds keep part of their income for personal expenses. The percentage of family budgets under female control is higher among families of working women (56 percent). In the remaining families the husband controls the budget; and in one-third of these families, the husband takes out some money for personal expenses.

The majority of the married women declare they are treated well by their husbands, although a significant percentage (15. 9 percent) say they are badly treated. Some are often beaten by their husbands: 50 percent of the women who have ended their marriage say they have done so because of mistreatment. In these cases the children tend to support the mother. When the husband leaves the house, the children do not seem to take a position favoring either parent.

As Table 8. 4 shows, the presence of the mother seems to be more meaningful for the children than that of the father. The mother, either working or at home, always plays a vital role in the children's education. This is not true for the father, who has no role in their education without the mother's help. Women who work tend to be more involved in the children's education than those who do not. The man's role in this thus becomes even more weakened. When the mother is engaged in activities outside the home, she learns constantly and brings new things into the educational process of the family. The husband, instead of supporting the wife's work, generally retreats from the children's educational process altogether.

TABLE 8.4

Married Women's Responsibility for Children's Education,
by Place of Work
(percent)

Mainly Responsible for Children's Education	Place of Work		
	Outside Home	At Home	Housewife
Wife	54.7	30.7	28.3
Wife and husband	45.3	69.3	71.7

Source: Compiled by the author.

CONCLUSIONS

Poverty undermines all relations between the sexes. In a mass-consumption society, the marginal sectors have little freedom. Women are subject to male domination. They cannot criticize the ideology that supports domination. Freedom does not exist when we face misery and marginality. This can also be extended to men, who, in the same way as women, are caught in the ideology of male supremacy. This ideology is, to a great extent, responsible for the maintenance of the class system. The need to enforce the mythology of woman's place in the home prevents women from demanding free child care institutions and from supporting woman's claim for entry into the labor force. They perpetuate a structure unable to integrate the potential labor force. In so doing, man is maintaining a social system that oppresses not only the woman but himself as well.

WOMEN AND MODERNIZATION:
ACCESS TO TOOLS
Elsa M. Chaney
Marianne Schmink

What we wish to propose here is not simply the thesis that modernization fails to confer equal benefits on both sexes. Rather, we believe there is some evidence to support the view that women's situation actually worsens as the modernication process goes forward.

Several authors have addressed the question of whether the lot of women improves as the process of development proceeds. While no modern scholar could be described as overwhelmingly optimistic in this regard, the conclusions have been surprisingly divergent. The minority opinion, held primarily by those who have focused on increases in female labor force participation rates without noting exactly what women do, sees a positive link between economic development and female status (Bairoch and Limbor 1968; Johnstone 1968; Ramos 1970). But other evidence appears to call such optimism into question. Even crude economic activity rates for women (in contrast with those for men) do not seem clearly affected by degree of industrialization, as some have supposed (see United Nations 1962, p. 6 for a discussion).

Most authors describe a mixed situation (Bernard 1968; Hammond and Jablow 1973; Lanier 1968; Seward and Williamson 1970; Sullerot 1971). Collver and Langlois (1962, pp. 370-74), reporting on twenty countries around 1950, show that women's work participation rates vary greatly from country to country, regardless of the level of economic development. Others focus their attention on the exclusion of women from active participation in the development process, the net effect being a deterioration in the relative position of women (Boserup 1970; Bridenthal 1971; Hunt 1966; Knudsen 1969; Sinha 1965).

The authors wish to thank Gloria Gallotti of Fordham University for helpful research on women in the U. S. industrial labor force. They are also grateful to Carmen Diana Deere, University of California-Berkeley for many helpful comments. Errors of fact and interpretation, however, they acknowledge as their own.

Marxist analysts have related the decline of female status to the emergence of the nuclear family as the basic economic unit of society (Dalla Costa 1972; Leacock 1972, pp. 29-43; Madden 1972; Mitchell 1966, 1973) and to the advance of capitalistic industrialization, which placed women in the category of "secondary laborers" (Madden 1972, p. 25).

If we measure the elusive concept "status of women"* in terms of access to independent income in the economic sphere, participation in decision-making at policy levels in government and private spheres, and validation in the social sphere for child rearing and household tasks still largely performed by women, then it is not at all certain that women's lot improves as development goes forward. On several indexes suggested above, women's position not only does not improve, but deteriorates. Speaking particularly of the non-European areas of Asia and Africa (his remarks apply with some qualifications also to Latin America), Chester Hunt (1966, p. 20) comments:

> In most of these areas the process of development is seen as a male project in which women are given only token participation. Development represents an effort to bring the male part of the population into the world of the twentieth century while leaving most of the women in the restricted roles in which they were placed by the culture of a previous era.

Let us make clear at the beginning that our use of the terms "development" and "modernization" to stand for current attempts to transfer the effects of the industrial revolution to the less developed nations should not imply that we accept the development model as the ideal solution to the problems facing the Third World. The Western vision of modernization is not the only possible one; contemporary efforts of, for example, Fidel Castro and Julius Nyerere, stress the honoring of the traditional (especially the peasant tradition and form of social organization) within a more productive economy. In this model there is an emphasis on national autonomy and on cutting the ties of economic and cultural dependency with the industrialized nations, along with a

---

*Early definitions of status as a "legal" term explicitly note that women are exceptional cases (Mead 1930; Radin 1930; Stern 1930). Socioeconomic status, usually measured by income, occupation, and education, has been acknowledged to measure only one aspect of an individual's overall status (Brown 1965; Knudsen 1969; Radin 1930); a more complete definition requires some mention of the value or prestige society attaches to the characteristics and activities of the person (Brown 1965; Chinas 1973; Knudsen 1969; Lamphere 1973). We have thus included social validation of traditional female activities as one aspect of women's status (see Benston 1969, p. 19; Dalla Costa 1972).

skepticism about the desirability of large, formal institutions—including those of trade, communication, and education—associated with the West.

But the "development package" associated with Western efforts to extend individual competence and participation, increase economic productivity, and reform social structures has such wide acceptance that we find it useful to employ this framework precisely because we wish to point out its contradictions, particularly in relation to the position of women. Technological change may initially open up new job opportunities for women of middle and upper classes who have the necessary training for certain white-collar positions and in professions such as teaching, social work, and nursing. However, evidence across many cultures now demonstrates that opportunities decline for working-class women in both agrarian and industrial sectors.

WOMEN AND TOOLS

Marion Levy (1966, I, 11) has defined modernization in a way that is particularly apt for looking at what happens to women as the development process goes forward. Levy sees a society as more or less modernized "to the extent that its members use inanimate sources of power and/or tools to multiply the effects of their efforts." This definition is useful for our purposes because it does not equate development with factory production, and allows us to focus attention on agricultural modernization as well as on changes in manufacturing processes—an important consideration, since large numbers of women in the developing world still engage in both farming and market trading of agricultural commodities. A modern commercial farm resembles a factory more than it resembles a traditional hacienda or fundo, and modernization in the agricultural sector has implications for women's role and status analogous to modernization in the manufacturing sector.

To equate modernization with the development of ever more productive tools is, of course, only one of many definitions we might adopt. While the approach we have chosen is restrictive, we believe it may nevertheless illumine certain questions related to women's slow progress. Generally, access to improved technology represents one key element of the social power held by individuals or social groups. According to Richard Adams' formulation (1975, pp. 13-15), power relationships are based on control, defined as "making and carrying out decisions about the exercise of a technology" with respect to some energy form or flow. The concept of technology, while defined broadly to include knowledge, skills, and materials, clearly includes the specific tools associated with modern industrial development. Greater control, in this sense, rests on a "more efficient complex of tools, skills, and ideas, taken as a whole."

Although control over energy forms does not always imply social power, it is a necessary condition for its existence. Modern tools represent only one type of control, but one that is central to the industrial process and recent economic history. It is the power of modern tools to increase the fruits of human effort beyond the artisan's wildest dreams that makes the substitution of machines and technology for human effort a "revolution"; we believe it will be valuable to explore the access of women to modern tools, while acknowledging that our focus is narrow and partial.

Sex roles are differentiated to a greater or lesser extent in all cultures; it is our hypothesis that access to the tools and inanimate power upon which modernization depends also is differentiated on the basis of sex. As these tools become more sophisticated and the sources of inanimate power more complex and expensive, women are eased out of the most "modern" sectors. Since ever-increasing productivity confers prestige and rewards in modernized societies, women lose status. In this respect their situation is similar to the fate of other low-status groups in society; as Ivan Illich (1972, p. 30) has put it:

A society of very large tools must rely on multiple devices by which a majority can be excluded from claiming the most costly packages of privilege. These must be reserved to individuals to whom a high level of productivity can be imputed . . . people are imputed relatively lower productivity because they are born in the third world, because they are born black, and above all, because they are women.

In this essay we review the evidence bearing on women's access to increasingly complex technology in a modernizing world, with special attention to the Third World and to Latin America in particular. Technology, for our purposes, is defined to include skills and materials related to economic activities, as well as the organization of activities. Our thesis—that women become relatively "unproductive" as a group by virtue of their limited access to modern tools—is proposed as just one aspect of an extremely complex set of changes that accompany social and economic modernization. Neither do we propose it as a rule that holds in all situations; indeed, an understanding of the exceptions is clearly important. Rather, the focus on access to technology is appealing because it is broadly applicable in situations of change; it is a basic part of the analysis of women's relation to the production process as a whole.

WOMEN IN AGRICULTURE

For most societies, the advent of a cash nexus in a previously subsistence-oriented economy is the first step linking the traditional

economy to the mainstream of modern development. While many primitive economies utilize their own forms of "primitive" monies, modern
money provides a generalized medium that allows exchange outside the
local system through a common system of value. Mary Douglas (1967,
p. 120) has distinguished between primitive systems that function to
control exchange through rationing, and modern money, which "emerges
as a spontaneous solution to the need for easier trading conditions; it
represents the opening of opportunities." The transition from exchange
in kind to exchange for a generalized medium represents a technological
advance that facilitates trade and permits easy liquidation of commodities for profit accumulation and/or reinvestment.

In most traditional agricultural communities, the beginning stages
of commercial agriculture are combined with the continuation of basic
subsistence farming to meet most of the family's consumption needs.
The result is a division of production into subsistence (oriented to the
internal needs of the domestic unit) and cash crops (providing links with
larger economic systems), and it is often the female labor force that remains in charge of subsistence production in such cases.

Studies in Africa (Boserup 1970; Van Allen 1974) and in southern
India (Epstein 1962) have revealed how women's subsistence production
provided the basis for men's participation in the wider cash economy
through production of cash crops, processing and transport work, or migrant labor in mines and plantations. Where both sexes grow cash crops,
as in most West African countries, women typically grow only small
amounts for the internal market, while men take over the more lucrative,
large-scale growing of crops for export.

Even where trade is traditionally in the hands of women, men tend
to take over long-term and large-scale transactions when cash enters
the system (Bohannan 1955; Boserup 1970). Although in some communities a few women may become affluent and influential through trading,
as Sidney Mintz (1971, p. 265) has shown, women's activities hit an
"upper limit" when larger quantities requiring big investments are involved, since exporters and bankers often prefer to deal with men. Thus,
as export markets develop, the male has greater access to important
links that are denied to the female. (This aspect of the modernization
of agriculture and marketing is also related to the concept of proper
"domain" for women, discussed below.)

This division of productive tasks is often accompanied by the use
of distinct technologies. While women may cultivate with hoes, and
certainly these are implements that increase the productive capacity of
human effort, they generally do not use plows (White et al. 1974). Cash
cropping often requires the use of the plow, or more complex tools; but
in most cultures women are denied the opportunity to run earth-movers,
tractors, mechanized plows and cultivators, combines, and harvesters.
Several United Nations publications on the integration of women in development have underscored how agricultural modernization programs
systematically favor teaching males to work with new farm equipment,

"while women continue to use hand tools, increasing the productivity gap" (Germain 1974, p. 14). This happens even in countries where women traditionally have performed the major role in agriculture; technical assistance agents from the advanced countries, because of their image of the agricultural worker as male, simply ignore the real situation. As another United Nations publication (1973, p. 38) puts it:

> Although rural women do a large share of the agricultural work in most countries, very little is done to teach them modern methods of agriculture or the use of modern equipment so as to improve their contribution to agriculture. In nearly all countries, agricultural training at low, middle and high levels is given only to men, who in turn overlook the women farmers, . . . rather than to the women who are doing the work. Rural training of women is nearly always limited to training in home economics of one type or another.

Bernice Rosenthal (1973, pp. 23-30) demonstrates that in the Soviet Union, the early version of the enthusiastically toiling "new Soviet woman"—who had equal access to tools and could win recognition as a stakhanovite (a worker who markedly exceeds the production norm)— has been revised whenever the regime has had other priorities. * When capital was tight, she says, it was shifted from child care facilities and labor-saving devices for the home to direct investment in production. When the birth rate went down, motherhood was promoted even though women were still expected to work—but managers hesitated to invest in training women if they were often going to be absent on maternity leave. By 1940, Rosenthal (1973, pp. 29-30) concludes:

> Restricted opportunities to learn skills and primary responsibility for the home combined to relegate the majority of

---

*In the Soviet Union, for example, where prospects for entering and succeeding in a career probably are the best for women anywhere, Norton Dodge (1966, pp. 214-15) has found that women have not achieved full equality:

> . . . the proportion of women in the administrative and professional jobs . . . tends to decrease with each successive increase in rank, even in such fields as education and health, where the role of women is dominant. . . . There appears to be an undeniable tendency for female specialists in all fields to congregate in the lower and middle echelons. Perhaps the most striking instance of this is the small number of women among the [Communist] party professionals.

working women to the lowest skilled, most easily replaceable, job categories. Only at the university level was no serious effort made to discourage women; the number of women medical, engineering and science students continued to rise.

WOMEN AND INDUSTRIALIZATION

The modernization of textile production is an illustrative example of women workers' fate in the development process. When all thread is made by spinning with a primitive stick or simple spinning wheel, generally women manufacture thread with such relatively unproductive tools. All over the Andes, even today, one encounters women on the country roads, in the market, or even on buses, their hands occupied with their spinning. In most cultures, it is the women who work in the textile "industry" at home, spinning and weaving cloth for their families; women still dominate in the "putting out" stage of cottage industry.

As specialized economic enterprises take over the production of many goods once manufactured in the home (by both men and women, it should be noted), males move to the factories in far greater numbers than women. The women are left with only a residue of domestic tasks and are used as a reserve labor force at the lowest levels of industrial production. Ester Boserup (1970, pp. 110-12) finds this trend to be worldwide: summing up data from all the developing countries, she concludes (p. 112) that the evidence strongly suggests that

> . . . when larger industries gradually drive the home industries out of business, women lose their jobs, because the type of products they were making (home spun cloth, hand made cigars, hand made matches, etc.) are replaced by products factory made by a labour force composed of many more men than women. . . . in nearly all developing countries [Boserup excludes Hong Kong] women in industrial occupations account for less than one-fifth of all employees while they often account for one-third to one-half of own-account workers and family aids.

Industrialization typically begins in textiles, food processing, and leather goods, all at first requiring much handwork. Women, often considered more dextrous and patient than men (and willing to work for lower wages) may initially be preferred employees. But as techniques and machines improve, women hit an "upper limit" beyond which only the exceptional few ever pass. Most women remain in the low-paying, less-skilled jobs. Women sew in garment factories on power machines, typically performing one repetitive operation such as sewing up side seams;

but they seldom run cutting machines or supervise. Certainly there is irony in the fact that the inventions that gave North American factory production its start in the late 1800s were precisely those that theoretically "aided" women in their traditional labors: Hargreave's spinning jenny, Arkwright's throstle frame, and Cartwright's power loom.

A codicil therefore must be added to the hypothesis that access to tools is differentiated by sex: technological innovation can change the sex label of a job. The U. S. Census of 1905 demonstrates that men already had begun a slow, steady displacement of women in the cotton mills as the number of places in which women could profitably be employed in preference to or on an equal basis with men steadily declined. As the speed of the machinery increased, one "hand" could tend a greater and greater number of machines. Vallentin (1932, quoted in Bridenthal 1971) notes a similar drop in female employment in twelve of eighteen (mainly European) countries in the first two decades of the twentieth century.

Various rationales have been devised to explain why women appear to be particularly well suited to certain jobs and totally unfit for others. The "infinite patience" and dexterity arguments already have been noted. Jobs that require heavy lifting are thought to be harmful to women even today, when the automated forklift does the work. Everyone "knows" that women do not understand complicated machinery, and therefore are unable to cope with breakdowns; engineers must be men.

It is clear that from the early days of manufacturing in the United States, the jobs performed by women were different from those performed by men. Still another rationale was added in this case: women could not be permitted to operate the more complicated machines, especially as processes were speeded up, because it was feared their skirts would get caught in them! Humor has obscured the fact that Amelia Bloomer had a very practical goal in advocating the modest, skirtlike but safer garment that takes its name from her—she wanted to win access for women to society's productive tools. Because of women's tendency to cluster in less-skilled tasks, women's wages in the United States always have been less than men's (Abbott 1920, Chapter XII; Baker 1964, p. 81). As late as 1973, women were earning only 61 percent of men's salaries in the manufacturing sector (U. S. Dept. of Labor 1973, p. 6).* Evidence indicates that the gap between women's and men's salaries has widened in this country in recent years (Knudsen 1969).

Some cultures do not follow the Western pattern of involving women in the first phases of industrialization, either in manufacturing or mechanized farming. Sometimes women do not take the step because of social restrictions on their work outside the home; in other cases, advanced social legislation makes women more expensive to hire than men.

---

*The Council of Economic Advisers estimates that even when adjustments for differences in education and work experience are made, women still earn about 20 percent less than men in the same jobs.

Maternity leaves, child care provisions, and protective legislation (such as prohibition of overtime and night work for women) often enforced in the manufacturing sector ironically appear to work against incorporation of women in developing economies rather than in their favor. In Peru, for example, women are entitled by law to two month's maternity leave from the factory at 60 percent of their salaries. When the mothers return to work, they may leave their babies in the factory's day nursery. And they may take up to one hour each day to nurse their children. But such laws make women more expensive to hire than men, and more troublesome, since their jobs must be covered in their absence. David Chaplin, a sociologist who has studied the Peruvian textile industry, found that many factories had not hired any new woman workers since the "enlightened" legislation was put into effect in 1956. (See Chaplin 1971, pp. 226-27 for a discussion.)

Boserup is not inclined to accept this explanation at face value but, rather, to point to the fact that childbirth is a much more frequent occurrence in the underdeveloped world than in Europe or North America; hence the absence of women workers (and the necessity to fill in with temporary workers) might make women less desirable in the eyes of employers. As she notes (1970, pp. 113-14), the expenses of maternity leave and day care at places of employment can be (and sometimes have been) passed on to the government—through the taxing of all employers, for example, and not just those who hire women. Moreover, as Boserup and other analysts have observed, there is some evidence that male-dominated governments and labor unions may connive in demanding both equal pay for equal work and special benefits for women, knowing that this will influence employers to favor men for the best jobs in industry. Moreover, as Boserup has noted (1970, pp. 110-11), those countries now industrializing may invest in such advanced technology that women never leave the home for the factory. They may simply have no part in the process at all, since nations whose development is dominated and controlled by large corporations often skip the labor-intensive stages of industrialization where women formerly found opportunity. Even in societies where women enter the factories in large numbers as industrialization proceeds, the proportion of women employed in the secondary sector declines.

Joseph Ramos (1970, pp. 155-56) examines the process in more detail, describing the different subsectors of the manufacturing sector in Latin America, analyzing their particular dynamics of growth and showing how the increasing use of technology and more highly skilled labor has been responsible for the decreasing capacity of the manufacturing sector to absorb labor. According to our thesis, the demand for skilled labor to manage complicated machines is explicitly a "male-favored" demand. While we lack systematic data on female labor in relation to technological change in developing societies, we may draw some tentative conclusions from an examination of changes in labor force structure in these countries.

WOMEN IN THE TERTIARY SECTOR

The heterogeneous services sector has a much greater elasticity of labor absorption, particularly for women (Oppenheimer 1970; Ramos 1970, p. 143). In fact, it is largely because of the distinct pattern of female-dominated urban migration, a response to the employment opportunities in a service-dominated economy, that the structure of employment in Latin America assumes its peculiar characteristics (see Boserup 1970, pp. 186-88; Henderson 1968, p. 31; Schultz 1969, p. 52).

Only rarely does manufacturing absorb even one-quarter of the female labor force; in nearly all of Latin America, more than half the female labor force is employed in either the primary or the tertiary sector (ILO 1971, p. 7). Evidence on the relationship of these employment patterns to technology and modernization is lacking; however, it appears that women are favored for jobs in those sectors of the economy that are less "productive" than the industry sector. Victor Fuchs (1968, pp. 4-5) makes the following comment about the growth of tertiary-sector employment in the United States: "The major explanation for the shift of employment is that output per man grew much more slowly in the service sector than in the other sectors." He finds the most important explanation for lagging output in services in the relative upgrading of skill levels in industry; he also suggests that the secondary sector exhibits a more favorable trend in physical capital per worker.

Even if Fuchs has overestimated the productivity differential in the modern United States context, we would expect that it would be more striking in developing countries, where low-level personal service occupations dominate employment in the sector. O'Hagan (1968, p. 44) has described this trend:

> The only occupational choices for the large percentage of
> Latin American urban females who have not terminated ele-
> mentary school are self-employed marketing, production
> work in small workshops, and service work. The first two
> possibilities are progressively eliminated by mass produc-
> tion and distribution, leaving the services as the only sec-
> tor capable of absorbing lesser-educated urban females.
> Job possibilities exist in hairdressing, dry cleaning, laun-
> dering, etc., but the majority of females in the service
> sectors work in domestic services.

Nadia Youssef (1974, p. 28) describes the domestic service category in Latin America as "virtually an exclusive female domain." Thus, at least in Latin America, we find a large percentage of women workers employed in occupations characterized by low status and low productivity, and excluded from the benefits of labor union organization (ILO 1970; Schmink 1974; Smith 1971).

Because more sophisticated and productive tools are now used almost exclusively in specialized economic firms—whether these be commercial farms, manufacturing plants, or modern service "industries"—the productive tasks that women still perform in the home also tend to be denigrated. It is not accurate to picture the modern home as a unit completely stripped of all its productive functions by industry, agribusiness, and educational and recreative enterprises. Many crucial tasks have been removed, but much important residual productive work remains. Food must be given at least some final processing; children, at least in their early years, must be cared for; and clothes, personal belongings, and the living space must be made clean and comfortable. As Mariarosa Dalla Costa (1972, p. 26) underscores in her study, the home is where the reproduction and servicing of the worker take place; without the home, the modern industrial state could not function. In no society, however, are women's productive services or administrative functions in the household esteemed, paid for, or included in the national accounts. This is precisely because we "overlook" the real production that still goes on in the family.

Even in highly modernized societies, where women have access to power-driven tools, their productive activity revolves around the family unit, and their tools are not suited to any wider application. Women's household tools (they are, interestingly, called "consumer durables") are used mainly to produce more efficiently the family goods and services closely associated with women's traditional role: food, family, clothing, cleanliness, comfort, relaxation, and recreation (see Dalla Costa 1972, pp. 26-27; Larguia 1973, pp. 12-14). Women seldom have any say, as designers, technicians, operators, or supervisors, about mass-production machinery that makes goods for sale in the market, and particularly about tools that produce other machines. A household vacuum cleaner, for example, would soon break down if used to clean the halls of a large office building. Heavy-duty machines, typically run by male janitors, clean and wax the floors of business establishments (while maids continue to wield broom and dustmop for half the pay). A portable sewing machine will do very well for making the children's clothes and even for sewing for relatives, but it is not suited to mass production. Because their domain still is defined as the family unit, and because the kinds of tools they are allowed are severely limited in productive capacity, women, even in relatively modernized societies, find that this limited access to tools does not improve their status.

But what may be even more crucial for women's status is the fact that removal of "important" production to factories and commercial farms brings an increasing separation of the "production of family income" from the "consumption of family income," as Levy (1966, p. 209), among many other observers, has noted; there is also an overwhelming identification of earning with the male. Even though spending of family income gives women, in theory, tremendous potential power, Levy points out that women's role in family consumption reinforces the notion that the home is the sphere of woman's influence. Since training for and access to technological controls are more widely available outside the domestic unit, and given the low level of productivity associated with most domestic tools, the identification of women with home life limits their access to modern tools.

David Chaplin (1969) has suggested that women's participation patterns in industrial development go through two stages that may be correlated to their consumer role. In the first industrial revolutions in the West, when new occupations opened up that initially were "sexless" or unattractive to men, many women entered the labor force. Later, midway in the industrialization process, according to Chaplin, where relatively less labor was required and development brought prosperity, women "retreated" to specialized roles as homemakers and consumers. It must be emphasized, however, that this "retreat" becomes an option only in situations of prosperity, that is, among the middle and upper classes of both developing and developed countries. Lower-class women are often compelled to augment the family income through labor at low-paying and low-skilled jobs, in addition to performing activities related to home maintenance and consumption.

Similarly, the power available to women through home-based roles, particularly control of the family budget, clearly will be a function of household income level. Within those social sectors that benefit from the modernization process, including upper- and middle-class and socially mobile families, there is evidence to support Chaplin's contention that in a consumer-oriented economy "It takes time to spend money, more time than the average man can afford." Several observers have noted the same tendencies among middle classes in industrializing countries today. A prestige factor may also be involved; as Germain (1974, p. 15) notes, it frequently seems to be a mark of status if a woman is able to stay at home.

While some women exert a great deal of power through their domestic roles, the measurement of this power in relation to other kinds of power available in modern society remains a problem. This is largely a consequence of the often-noted dichotomy between man's and women's world/domain/place (Chinas 1973; Friedl 1967; Rosaldo 1974; Sachs 1974; Sanday 1974). Jessie Bernard (1973, pp. 20-21) contrasts the female "status world," where bonds are on a love-duty basis, and the achievement-oriented, competitive, and emotionally neutral "cash nexus" male world. The inhabitants of the female world are all but invisible to history and social science, Bernard says. "Men are furiously interacting with one another, but one hardly catches a glimpse of any woman." Margaret Benston (1969, p. 16), like Bernard, sees most women (along with serfs and peasants) as still inhabiting a pre-industrial world where domestic work has "use value" but not "exchange value"; thus their contribution is not esteemed. As Nancie Gonzalez (1973, p. 51) summed it up:

"Work" is defined as that which occurs outside the household
. . . only those who "work" may be accorded full status as
normal and honorable adult members of the society.

Curiously, this division appears to hold even though more and more
women may, in any given society, engage in productive work outside the
home. By and large, most societies view these women as outside their
proper sphere, working temporarily because of family emergency or un-
provided widowhood, and hence not serious about career or profession.
If most women are expected to go back to the home when the family difficulty has passed or when they remarry, then the fact that they are
present at only the lowest-paid and lowest-skilled levels is less up-
setting to ideals of equality and justice. Women often are regarded
(even when statistics clearly show that many are single and/or permanent heads of household) as an expandable-contractable reserve labor
force, to be called upon in times of national emergency and crisis (to
work, for example, in war production), and to be sent back afterward
to their proper domestic domain, especially if men need the jobs. (See
Chapter 8.)

WOMEN IN POLITICS

Professional and political life faithfully reflect the differential between those who control the tools of modernization and those allowed
only limited access. As societies become relatively modernized, a few
educated women do move out from the family sphere into professions
and politics; yet the boundaries and style of their participation continue
to be profoundly influenced by their classic roles as mothers and pre-
servers of the race. Most women go into fields analogous to the tasks
they perform in the home, especially the education and welfare of wom-
en and children. But women do not improve their inferior position very
much by turning professional. Feminine fields are neither prestigious
nor powerful because they are associated with the depreciated tasks of
birth and nurture; moreover, they involve access to society's powerful
new tools only in peripheral ways. Women in political life are no exception; they, too, tend to gravitate toward "feminine" tasks and to
define their political responsibilities in maternal terms. Many envision
their offices [to use descriptions originated by Talcott Parsons and
Robert F. Bales (1956, p. 47)] in terms of the nurturant, affectional, "expressive" tasks society assigns to women, rather than in terms of the
instrumental male role, which is more aggressive, authoritarian, and
achievement-oriented. A woman official sees herself often as a kind of
supermother, tending the needs of her big family in the larger home of
the municipality or even the nation. Thus, Eva Peron, perhaps the most
formidable female politician Latin America has ever produced, explained

her public role in terms of woman's eternal feminine tasks (1952, pp. 313-14; translation by Chaney and Schmink):

> In this great house of the Motherland, I am just like any other woman in any other of the innumerable houses of my people. Just like all of them I rise early thinking about my husband and about my children . . . and I go about all day thinking about them and a good part of the night. . . . When I go to bed, tired out, then instead of dreams, marvelous projects occur to me and I try to sleep before I burst. . . . It's just that I so truly feel myself the mother of my people.

In Latin America, women in politics are viewed as having a particular responsibility toward primary institutions, concerning themselves with the "domestic" affairs of the society and the nation: with the lot of the woman, the child, the old, the sick, the juvenile delinquent. Men, on the contrary, are thought to have their primary tasks in secondary institutions, the realm where tools intervene: industrialization, transport, communications, agricultural modernization, outer space. Nancie Gonzalez (1973, pp. 49-51) has noted these tendencies, seeing political activities as divided into two spheres: the "jural," or activities that relate one unit to another in the larger society, and the "domestic," or internal affairs of the unit. When women begin to break into the public realm, she says, they almost always concern themselves with domestic issues. Socialization of the young, she points out, includes school board politics, school taxes, busing. Welfare and health matters, once household concerns, now are public issues. Gonzalez suggests we need a new concept to fill in the gap between the familial-domestic world and the jural domain. She has used the term "supra-domestic" to cover those activities now at least partially controlled by the state. This concept is parallel to the idea of the supermother (Chaney 1973, pp. 103-39). As Gonzalez puts it (p. 53), "More and more are 'out there' [in the labor force and government], but a closer scrutiny shows that most are not doing the same things men do."

So far as taking on any leadership role in development planning and allied fields, very few women collaborate at this level. Recently the United Nations Commission on the Status of Women asked governmental and private organizations for their views on the role women might play in social and economic development. Replies from 77 countries and 36 nongovernmental associations showed that even where women are active professionally, their level of responsibility is low, except in certain sectors of the social field traditionally considered suitable for women. Their participation in higher planning bodies related to innovation and social change is "practically nonexistent." According to the survey, there is growing awareness all over the world that women's role is changing and should change, yet only a few countries have come fully to grips with the problem or are ready to embark upon new avenues (United Nations 1970, pp. 3-4).

SOME TENTATIVE CONCLUSIONS

The preceding description indicates many of the ways in which women's position deteriorates as development proceeds. These trends are not without their temporary exceptions; clearly, some aspects of the development process allow expanded female participation, especially in "transitional" activities—those that predominate for a time, then decline. Higher levels of economic activity by women during crisis periods (particularly wartime) thus typically decrease as the crisis passes. A shortage of preferred male workers has been noted as accounting for increased female labor force activity in both the United States and the Soviet Union (Dodge 1966; Oppenheimer 1970); this responsive secondary work force, however, is prone to return to the home when a more "favorable" demographic balance is struck.

More specific examples of temporarily expanding opportunities for women have also been mentioned; market trading, for instance, allows women to participate in the wider economy, but their possibilities for expansion are limited and their mobility from market into modern commercial activities is usually restricted. Similarly, the early history of industrial development in Britain and the United States reveals a greatly increased demand for female labor in factories; but this demand was based on the possibility of paying women lower wages than were paid to men doing identical work, and the positions held by women commonly were of low status and low mobility. Later advances in mechanization phased women out of the factory, especially as machines took over handwork (Monthly Labor Review 1936; Baker 1964). Highly mechanized production techniques that have characterized even the beginning phases of industrialization in later-developing areas, such as Latin America, have precluded the need for large numbers of female laborers.

Certain occupations that specifically favor female employment are highly correlated with early stages of development (O'Hagan 1968). Thus in Latin America domestic service clearly allows large numbers of women to find employment in urban areas, but such work is both very low in status and lacking in real possibilities for occupational mobility; patterns from the industrialized countries indicate that domestic service is a transitional occupation that declines and disappears with later stages of development and increased opportunities for employment in other sectors (Coser 1973). Other service occupations that expand in the early stages of development, especially in commerce, clerical work, and education, afford increased opportunities for female employment in most countries. Again, data from the more advanced nations suggest that in later stages of development, demand shifts to technical and scientific occupations—and these are fields in which women rarely have the opportunity for training and employment (Oppenheimer 1972; Seear 1966).

Most of the temporary benefits that development affords women thus tend to wash out eventually, leaving them relatively worse off than when

the process began. In this respect, women do not differ from other disadvantaged groups. In fact, women's activities seem to be almost by
definition low-status in societies at various socioeconomic levels. Thus,
traditional female chores such as housework and child care rarely bring
status benefits to women, and are neither paid nor counted as "work" in
Census enumerations or for purposes of calculating the gross national
product, except when such work is performed for persons outside the
family group (and, as we have seen, domestic service is an extremely
low-status occupation). Abundant evidence suggests, moreover, that
even occupations that are not initially low-status become low-status
as women enter the ranks (Knudsen 1969; Linton 1936, p. 118; Mead
1930).

     While the mechanisms determining female status cross-culturally
and through time are by no means clear, many authors have pointed out
that women in primitive hunting and gathering societies enjoyed a relatively high-status position in comparison with their modern counterparts
(Cooper 1932; Leacock 1972; Rohrlich-Leavitt et al. 1972). Some have
postulated that this higher status resulted from the importance of wom-
en's gleanings to community subsistence, and that the crucial indicator
of female status is the prominence of the contribution to the food supply.
More comprehensive examinations of societies across a variety of socioeconomic formations, however, have revealed that women's participation in production is not an adequate measure of their status position.
Significantly, however, contribution to subsistence appears to be a necessary, if not sufficient, factor in determining female status (Sanday
1973). The exclusion of women from production insures their low-status
position by removing their power base and control over resources.

     Given the process of modernization we have described, it is not
difficult to explain the almost universal worsening of women's status
that accompanies economic development. Terms like "development" and
"modernization" are widely considered to be scientific definitions of the
inexorable march of progress—marching, as it were, to its own drummer.
Sidney Mintz reminds us, as have many radical students of the development process, that these terms are in fact culture-bound; they describe
a process of economic expansion based on one dominant model, Western
capitalistic development. It is not widely recognized that the "technological imperative" carries with it a set of sex-role prescriptions, but
numerous examples exist of the operation of these norms in conjunction
with economic change. In particular, we have noted that women are considered incapable of handling or understanding complex machinery, and
thus often are deprived of access to useful tools.

     More generally, the Western patriarchal model prescribes the role
of breadwinner for the male, reserving the home for the woman. Thus we
find women traders limited to internal markets because the export com-
panies prefer to deal with men; technical advisers who introduce techniques for agricultural improvement exclude women from their educational programs; the exemption of women from productive work frequently is

among the "modern" ideals of prestige. The same image of proper domain systematically excludes women from the decision-making echelons of society, particularly from any participation in decisions about development and modernization. The more closely allied a society becomes to Western development models—and thus the more "successfully" developed—the more we can expect women to be excluded from the tools of the production process. And if we consider that the supposedly neutral term "development" refers to the Western development model, then our thesis holds across ideological boundaries.

The deterioration of women's status may thus be added to the array of unfavorable by-products of development. Expansion leads eventually not only to the degradation of the physical environment but also of the social environment, as various groups are systematically excluded from the tools of progress and their benefits. Women may enjoy more of the benefits of development than other minorities, but their participation and power in society as a group undoubtedly are more restricted.

REFERENCES

Abbott, Edith. 1920. Women in Industry. New York: D. Appleton and Co.

Adams, Richard N. 1975. Energy and Structure. Austin: University of Texas Press.

Bairoch, P. and J. M. Limbor. 1968. "Changes in the Industrial Distribution of the World Labor Force, by Region, 1880-1960." International Labour Review 98: 311-36.

Baker, Elizabeth Faulkner. 1964. Technology and Women's Work. New York: Columbia University Press.

Benston, Margaret. 1969. "The Political Economy of Women's Liberation." Monthly Review 21: 13-27.

Bernard, Jessie. 1968. "The Status of Women in Modern Patterns of Culture." Annals of the American Academy of Political and Social Science 375: 3-14.

_____. 1973. "My Four Revolutions: An Autobiographical History of the ASA." American Journal of Sociology 78: 11-29.

Bohannan, Paul. 1955. "Some Principles of Exchange and Investment Among the Twi." American Anthropologist 57: 60-70.

Boserup, Ester. 1970. Women's Role in Economic Development. New York: St. Martin's Press.

Bridenthal, Renate. 1971. "Beyond Kinder, Kuche, Kirche: Weimar Women at Work." Paper presented at the annual meeting of the American Historical Association, New York.

Brown, Roger. 1965. Social Psychology. New York: Free Press.

Chaney, Elsa M. 1973. "Women in Latin American Politics: The Case of Peru and Chile." In Female and Male in Latin America, ed. Ann Pescatello. Pittsburgh: University of Pittsburgh Press.

Chaplin, David. 1967. The Peruvian Industrial Labor Force. Princeton: Princeton University Press.

_____. 1969. "Feminism and Economic Development." Occasional paper. Typescript.

_____. 1971. "Some Institutional Determinants of Fertility in Peru." In Population Policies and Growth in Latin America, ed. David Chaplin. Lexington, Mass.: D. C. Heath.

Chinas, Beverly L. 1973. The Isthmus Zapotecs: Women's Roles in Cultural Context. New York: Holt, Rinehart & Winston.

Colliver, O. Andrew, and Eleanor Langlois. 1962. "The Female Labor Force in Metropolitan Areas: An International Comparison." Economic Development and Cultural Change 10: 367-85.

Cooper, John M. 1932. "The Position of Woman in Primitive Culture." Primitive Man 5: 2-3, 32-47.

Cornejo, Luz Elena, Olga Guarda, and Boris Chacon. 1971. "El balance de mano de obra, 1970." Nueva economia 1: 40-53.

Coser, Lewis A. 1973. "Servants: The Obsolesence of an Occupational Role." Social Forces 52: 31-40.

Dalla Costa, Mariarosa. 1972. The Power of Women and the Subversion of the Community. Bristol, England: Falling Wall Press.

Dodge, Norton T. 1966. Women in the Soviet Economy. Baltimore: Johns Hopkins Press.

_____, and Murray Feshbach. 1967. "The Role of Women in Soviet Agriculture." In Soviet and East European Agriculture, ed. Jerzy F.

Karez, pp. 265-302. Berkeley and Los Angeles: University of California Press.

Douglas, Mary. 1967. "Primitive Rationing: A Study in Controlled Exchange." In Themes in Economic Anthropology, ed. Raymond Firth, pp. 103-47. New York: Tavistock Publications.

Epstein, T. Scarlett. 1962. Economic Development and Social Change in South India. Manchester: Manchester University Press.

Friedl, Ernestine. 1967. "The Position of Women: Appearance and Reality." Anthropological Quarterly 40: 97-108.

Fuchs, Victor R. 1968. The Service Economy. New York: Columbia University Press.

Gendell, Murray, and Guillermo Rossel. 1967. The Economic Activity of Women in Latin America. Washington, D.C.: Pan American Union. DCAA/Doc. 21.

Germain, Adrienne. 1974. Some Aspects of the Roles of Women in Population and Development. New York: United Nations. ESA/SDHA/AC.5/3/Add. 1.

Gonzalez, Nancie L. 1973. "Women and the Jural Domain: An Evolutionary Perspective." In Center for Continuing Education of Women, A Sampler of Women's Studies. Ann Arbor: University of Michigan Press.

Hammond, Dorothy, and Alta Jablow. 1973. Women: Their Economic Role in Traditional Societies. Reading, Mass.: Addison-Wesley. Module in Anthropology no. 35.

Henderson, Julia J. 1968. "Impact of the World Social Situation on Women." Annals of the American Academy of Political and Social Science 375: 26-33.

Hunt, Chester L. 1966. Social Aspects of Economic Development. New York: McGraw-Hill.

Illich, Ivan. 1972. "Re-tooling Society: Draft." Cuernavaca, Mexico: Centro Intercultural de Documentacion. DOC A/E 72/369.

International Labor Office. 1970. The Employment and Conditions of Domestic Workers in Private Households. Geneva: International Labour Office. D/11.

_____. 1971. Statistical Information on Women's Participation in Eco-
nomic Activity in American Countries. Geneva: International Labour
Office. ILO/W.5/1971.

Johnstone, Elizabeth. 1968. "Women in Economic Life: Rights and Opportunities." Annals of the American Academy of Political and Social Science 375: 102-14.

Klein, Viola. 1965. Britain's Married Women Workers. London: Routledge & Kegan Paul.

Knudsen, Dean D. 1969. "The Declining Status of Women: Popular
Myths and the Failure of Functionalist Thought." Social Forces 48:
183-93.

Lamphere, Louise. 1973. "Women's Work, Alienation and Class Consciousness." Paper presented at the 72nd annual meeting of the
American Anthropological Association, New Orleans.

Lanier, Alison Raymond. 1968. "Women in the Rural Areas." Annals of
the American Academy of Political and Social Science 375: 115-23.

Larguia, Isabel. 1973. "The Economic Basis of Women's Status." Paper
presented at the IXth International Congress of Anthropological and
Ethnological Sciences, Oshkosh, Wis., and Chicago.

Leacock, Eleanor Burke. 1972. "Introduction." In Frederick Engels,
The Origin of the Family, Private Property and the State. New York:
International Publishers.

Levy, Marion J., Jr. 1966. Modernization and the Structure of Societies: A Setting for International Affairs. Princeton: Princeton University Press.

Linton, Ralph. 1936. The Study of Man. New York: D. Appleton-Cen-
tury.

Madden, Janice. 1972. "The Development of Economic Thought on the
'Woman Problem.'" Review of Radical Political Economics 4: 21-
39.

Mead, Margaret. 1930. "Women, Position in Society: Primitive." In
Encyclopedia of the Social Sciences XV, pp. 442-51. New York:
Macmillan.

Mintz, Sidney W. 1971. "Men, Women and Trade." Comparative
Studies in Society and History 13: 247-69.

Mitchell, Juliet. 1966. "Women: The Longest Revolution." New Left
    Review 40: 1-27.

_____. 1973. "Marxism and Women's Liberation." Social Praxis 1:
    23-33.

Monthly Labor Review. 1936. "Effect of Technological Changes in Em-
    ployment of Women." 42: 81-84.

O'Hagan, Maryann Joan. 1968. "The Distribution of Economically Ac-
    tive Females in Latin America According to Type of Industry and
    Occupation." Master's thesis, University of Texas at Austin.

Oppenheimer, Valerie Kincade. 1970. The Female Labor Force in the
    United States: Demographic and Economic Factors Governing Its
    Growth and Changing Composition. Berkeley: University of Cali-
    fornia Press. Population Monograph Series no. 5.

_____. 1972. "Rising Educational Attainment, Declining Fertility and
    the Inadequacies of the Female Labor Market." In Demographic and
    Social Aspects of Population Growth, ed. Charles F. Westoff and
    Robert Parke, Jr., pp. 305-28. Washington, D. C.: Commission
    on Population Growth and the American Future. Research Reports 1.

Organization of American States. 1971. America en cifras: 1970, situ-
    acion social. Washington, D. C.: Instituto Interamericano de Es-
    tadistica, Pan American Union.

Parsons, Talcott, and Robert F. Bales. 1956. Family, Socialization and
    Interaction Process. Glencoe, Ill.: Free Press.

Peron, Eva. 1952. La razon de mi vida. Buenos Aires: Ediciones Peuser.

Radin, Max. 1930. "Status." In Encyclopedia of the Social Sciences
    XIV, pp. 373-78. New York: Macmillan.

Ramos, Joseph R. 1970. Labor and Development in Latin America. New
    York: Columbia University Press.

Republica de Chile, Direccion de Estadistica y Censos. Muestra naci-
    onal de hogares. Santiago: Direccion de Estadistica y Censos.

Republica del Peru, Instituto Nacional de Planificacion (INP). 1966.
    Diagnostico del sector industrial. Lima: INP.

_____, Servicio de Empleo y Recursos Humanos (SERH). 1966. Diag-
    nostico de la situacion de los recursos humanos. Lima: SERH.

_____. 1971. Informe sobre la situacion ocupacional del Peru—1970. Lima: SERH.

Rohrlich-Leavitt, Ruby, with Barbara Sykes and Elizabeth Weatherford. 1972. "Aboriginal Woman: Male and Female Anthropological Perspectives." Revised version of a paper presented at the 71st annual meeting of the American Anthropological Association, Toronto.

Rosaldo, Michelle Z. 1974. "Woman, Culture and Society: A Theoretical Overview." In Woman, Culture and Society, ed. Michelle Z. Rosaldo and Louise Lamphere, pp. 17-42. Stanford: Stanford University Press.

Rosenthal, Bernice Glatzer. 1973. "The Role and Status of Women in the Soviet Union." Paper presented at the IX International Congress of Anthropological and Ethnological Sciences, Chicago.

Sachs, Karen. 1974. "Engels Revisited: Women, the Organization of Production, and Private Property." In Woman, Culture and Society, ed. Michelle Z. Rosaldo and Louise Lamphere, pp. 207-22. Stanford: Stanford University Press.

Sanday, Peggy R. 1973. "Toward a Theory of the Status of Women." American Anthropologist 75: 1682-1700.

_____. 1974. "Female Status in the Public Domain." In Woman, Culture and Society, ed. Michelle Z. Rosaldo and Louise Lamphere, pp. 189-206. Stanford: Stanford University Press.

Schmink, Marianne. 1974. "Dependent Development and the Division of Labor by Sex, Venezuela." Paper presented at the conference of the Latin American Studies Association, San Francisco.

Schultz, T. Paul. 1969. "Demographic Conditions of Economic Development in Latin America." In Latin America: Problems in Economic Development, ed. Charles T. Nisbet, pp. 41-72. New York: Free Press.

Seear, Nancy. 1966. "The Future Employment of Women." In Manpower Policy and Employment Trends, ed. B. C. Roberts and J. H. Smith, pp. 97-110. London: G. Bell & Sons.

Seward, Georgene H., and Robert C. Williamson, eds. 1970. Sex Roles in Changing Society. New York: Random House.

Sinha, J. N. 1965. "Dynamics of Female Participation in Economic Activity in a Developing Economy." In Papers Contributed by Indian

Authors to the World Population Conference, Belgrade, Yugoslavia, pp. 253-62. India: Office of the Registrar General.

Smith, Margo Lane. 1971. "Institutionalized Servitude: The Female Domestic Servant in Lima, Peru." Ph. D. dissertation, Indiana University.

Stern, Bernhard J. 1930. "Women, Position in Society: Historical." In Encyclopedia of the Social Sciences XV, pp. 442-51. New York: Macmillan.

Sullerot, Evelyne. 1971. Women, Society and Change. New York: McGraw-Hill.

United Nations. 1962. Demographic Aspects of Manpower: Report I, Sex and Age Patterns of Participation in Economic Activities. New York: Department of Economic and Social Affairs. Doc. ST/SOA/ Ser. A/33.

_____. 1970. Participation of Women in the Economic and Social Development of Their Countries. New York: Commission on the Status of Women. Doc. E/CN. 6/513/Rev. 1.

_____. 1973. Report of the Interregional Meeting of Experts on the Integration of Women in Development. New York: Department of Economic and Social Affairs. Doc. ST/SOA/120.

United States Department of Labor. 1969. 1969 Handbook of Women Workers. Washington, D. C.: Women's Bureau. Bulletin no. 294.

_____. 1973. Women Workers Today. Washington, D. C.: Women's Bureau. Revised.

Van Allen, Judith. 1974. "African Women—Modernization or Dependence?" Paper presented at the Conference on Social and Political Change: The Role of Women, Center for the Study of Democratic Institutions, Santa Barbara, California.

White, Douglas R., Michael L. Burton, Lilyan A. Brudner, and Joel D. Gunn. 1974. "Implicational Structures in the Sexual Division of Labor." Manuscript.

Youssef, Nadia H. 1974. Women and Work in Developing Societies. Berkeley: University of California Press. Institute of International Studies, Population Monograph no. 15.

10

PARTICIPATION
OF WOMEN IN THE
MEXICAN LABOR FORCE
Gloria Gonzalez Salazar

GENERAL CONSIDERATIONS

In the general context of women's backward position in the under-developed countries, their participation in economic activity is of great importance. Given the fact that work is the major source of income, and is related to access to education and culture as well as to the possibility of influencing, through union and other organizational activities, the mechanisms that determine the distribution of wealth and other important political decisions, women's limited participation in economic activities is responsible for their position of social inferiority and political backwardness in countries like contemporary Mexico.

In Mexico, however, as in other underdeveloped countries, the possibility of obtaining satisfactory employment is related to the capacity of the economy to employ people productively; and this, in turn, is related to all of the basic characteristics of the socioeconomic structure. For example, the possibility of obtaining satisfactory employment is conditioned by the insufficient development of productive forces, the imbalances between and within geographic sectors, the concentration of wealth and political power, the patterns of income distribution, and the scarcity of educational opportunities and other social services. From this perspective, many of the problems that affect women, affect the whole population.

This is not to say, however, that there are no problems specific to women. In view of distinctive traditional and cultural factors and the persistence of discriminatory practices, women's development is conditioned specifically by sex-defined roles as well as by the limitations imposed by the resource base and the extant opportunities (Spota 1968). Questions such as these should be examined, in a wider focus, from the perspective of the class structure, since discrimination against women, although a general phenomenon, stems from different sources and acquires different magnitudes in the different strata that form the social structure (Gonzalez Salazar 1972a).

While accepting the coexistence of occupational problems for the whole population along with those particular to women, we shall, in this essay, stress those that affect women, since a full consideration of the first would divert us from our theme to a consideration of the occupational structure resulting from the type of economic growth Mexico has undergone (Gonzalez Salazar 1972b).

We shall, therefore, not attempt an exhaustive comparison of the occupational structure according to sex, accepting the general problem of employment as given, although for illustrative purposes we include a few tables that sketch it. We shall, rather, focus our attention on the female economically active population (EAP), and resort to comparisons and other general references only when they are required for understanding the female EAP. The present essay, therefore, does not pretend to be an exhaustive study of the theme, but is only a very general examination of some national figures and other significant data to give a schematic view of the participation in the work force by Mexican women.

WOMEN IN PAID EMPLOYMENT

Mexico has practically achieved juridical equality for women. From the legal point of view, women's situation is satisfactory in terms of the fundamental aspects of civil, labor, economic, social, educational, and political rights. Mexican labor legislation covers two basic areas for the working woman: it espouses egalitarian principles between men and women as human beings, and it recognizes differences that call attention to women's essential role in procreation and other distinguishing characteristics of their sex, thus protecting and assisting them in their dual roles of mothers and workers (Gonzalez Salazar 1969).

However, legislation forbidding discrimination against women, which has been on the books for most of this century in Mexico, has not succeeded in abolishing it. Discrimination still persists in many of its traditional forms, especially in more backward areas. In addition, discrimination against women has been redefined in new alienating patterns, which to a great extent have been transmitted from the industrialized countries, with respect to the woman as an object within the culture of consumption.

Thus, in a context of the overwhelming poverty of most of the population—resulting from the uneven growth that Mexico has undergone in the last decades—false values act to deform the female image and to limit women's whole development as human beings. Women's confinement to the home and to repetitive jobs; their unconditional subordination to men; their passivity and lack of initiative in important questions; and their self-abnegation, understood as self-effacement before the interests of their husbands and children continue despite legislative advances, reducing the majority of Mexican women to a situation of inferiority and material and psychological dependence on the family and society. This varies, of course, according to urban and rural contacts, to regional variations, and to different social strata.

In this way the dominant socioeconomic factors, as well as traditionalist conceptions and modern redefinitions of women as "objects," have a decisive influence on the total number of women who work and study, and on the kinds of studies and professions they follow.

Nonetheless, the changes that have occurred in Mexico's economic development during the last decades have opened more diversified areas for many Mexican women; and their participation in the EAP has registered a continuous growth. The 4.6 percent of women who worked in 1930 became 7.4 percent in 1940, 13.6 percent in 1950, and 18.0 percent in 1960. From 1960 to 1969 the percentage increased only to 19.0 percent, but this is undoubtedly a result of the increase in unemployment, which discouraged many women from looking for work outside their homes.

In 1969, according to the last general census of the population, of 12,955,057 people constituting the EAP, 2,466,257—19.0 percent— were women. Of the 15,071,713 women over 12 years of age—the census criterion adopted for the measurement of the EAP—over 10.5 million women listed themselves as doing "household work" and only about 530,000 were students. In other words, of every 100 women, 18 worked and 10 studied. In contrast, of every 100 men, 70 worked and about 14 were students.

The highest rates of female participation in economic activity were found in the age groups 15 to 19 years, with a rate of 20.0 percent; 20 to 24 years, 24.1 percent; and 25 to 29 years, 17.4 percent. In the five-year age brackets between the ages of 30 and 59, the rate of participation varied between 15 percent and 16 percent, decreasing to 14.1 percent for those between 60 and 64 years of age. At the ends of the scale, 5.1 percent of girls from 12 to 15 years work, and 8-12 percent of women over 65 work.

As for the composition of the EAP by economic sectors, the most notable difference, in terms of sex, is the predominance of women in nonagricultural activity, which absorbs 89.2 percent of female workers, as well as in the large number of women—60.1 percent—in services. Only 53.9 percent of men work in nonagricultural activities, and 25.4 percent work in services. (See Table 10.1.)

At first glance this might lead one to believe that the occupational structure among women is more "modern" than among men, but the following observations are necessary. While only 10.8 percent of female workers are listed in agriculture and similar areas, in Mexico

TABLE 10.1

Economically Active Population of Mexico, by Economic Sector, 1969

Economic Sector	A Both Sexes No.	%	B Men No.	%	C Women No.	%	B/A %	C/A %
Total	12,955,057	100.00	10,499,800	100.00	2,466,257	100.00	81.00	19.00
Agriculture and related activities	5,103,519	39.4	4,836,865	46.1	266,654	10.8	94.8	5.2
Nonagricultural activities	7,851,538	60.6	5,651,935	53.9	2,199,603	89.2	72.0	28.0
Industry	2,920,255	22.5	2,441,412	23.3	478,843	19.4	83.6	16.4
Extractive	180,175	1.4	166,635	1.6	13,540	0.5	92.4	7.6
Manufacturing	2,169,074	16.7	1,721,548	16.4	447,526	18.2	79.4	20.6
Construction	517,006	4.4	553,229	5.3	17,777	0.7	96.9	3.1
Services	4,183,758	32.3	2,665,115	25.4	1,482,643	60.1	64.0	36.0
Electrical generation, transformation, and distribution	53,285	0.4	48,575	0.5	4,710	0.2	91.2	8.8
Transportation	368,813	2.9	315,424	3.0	17,389	0.7	95.3	4.7
Commerce	1,196,878	9.2	862,937	8.2	333,941	13.5	72.1	27.9
Other services	2,158,175	16.7	1,100,475	10.5	1,057,700	42.9	51.0	49.0
Government	406,607	3.1	337,704	3.2	68,903	2.8	83.1	16.9
Insufficiently specified activities	747,525	5.8	509,408	4.9	238,117	9.7	68.1	31.9

Source: IX Censo general de la poblacion, resumen general abreviado. Mexico City: SIC, 1972.

186

the various types of unpaid work performed by women in rural areas, especially in the most backward areas, tends not to be included in the Census because of the unwillingness to give information, as well as because of other difficulties in collecting information. It is also significant that such a high percentage of women work in "services"; 42. 9 percent work in "other services, " a rubric that includes numerous traditional services requiring few qualifications, and others that are superfluous. Women working as domestic servants in private houses number, according to Census figures, over 488, 344—19. 8 percent of the total of working women. Furthermore, 161, 243—6. 6 percent—do ordering and cleaning in commercial establishments and in hotels and other lodging houses, and prepare and sell foodstuffs. Another 68, 903— 2. 8 percent—are in government, so one might estimate that at least one-third of the economically active women are concentrated in tradi- tional activities connected to services conventionally called "appro- priate to women's sex. "*

Now if we add to these figures the "insufficiently specified activi- ties" (activities of very low productivity and income), which absorb 238, 117 workers (9. 7 percent of the total), one can roughly estimate that about 40 percent of working women are not satisfactorily placed in the labor market. Moreover, this does not take into account that modern and traditional activities coexist in all economic sectors, and that there is visible and latent underemployment in all productive areas. For example, commerce is significant for the female EAP, in that it employs 333, 941 female workers, or 13. 5 percent of working women. However, underemployment of women in this area is shown by the large numbers of door-to-door peddlers; the assumption that commercial occu- pations imply high salaries and substantial qualifications does not apply to this group. †

---

*The data on the subcategories within major economic sectors of activity correspond to the specifications of the IX General Census of the Population. They are not included in Tables 10. 1-10. 3 for reasons of space. In general, the data referring to the Census information can be found in the corresponding official sources.

†According to a statement by Concepcion Rivera, Secretary of Accion Femenil of the Federacion de Trabajadores del Distrito Federal de la Confederacion de Trabajadores de Mexico (CTM), the federal law is violated in about 95 percent of the commercial establishments of Mexico City. Most of the employees, predominantly women, receive neither the minimum salary nor overtime, and they are not registered with social security. Few unions include these workers; and in the large establishments, the unions act as enterprises that favor the owners. In other cases the unions are nonexistent or exist only on paper. El Dia, March 25, 1973.

Although the number of female industrial workers has increased, the industrial sector does not provide broad job opportunities for women of the popular classes. This is a result of the general level of unemployment, but also it follows from some of the labor and social security laws protecting women: the additional restrictions imposed on the owners of industry and the definitions governing activities "appropriate" to women limit job opportunities. Thus, while the percentages of women in industry—a total of 19.4 percent (0.5 percent, 18.2 percent, and 0.7 percent for extractive, manufacturing, and construction industries, respectively)—are satisfactory for a country like Mexico, these percentages do not imply the direct participation of all these women in the production of goods. Many pursue administrative or other kinds of work.

It may be roughly estimated, on the basis of our understanding of the field, on some of our estimates, and on cross-correlation of the data in Tables 10.1, 10.2 and 10.3, that less than 600,000 of the female nonagricultural wage workers are really workers, less than 400,000 are administrative personnel, and the rest are domestic servants in private houses and manual workers. Naturally, this does not take into account the higher occupational categories, the administrative, technical, and professional occupations.

In accordance with the prevalent general model, and excluding the more favored strata, it appears that most Mexican women are concentrated in occupations of low or medium remuneration that demand very few qualifications. The inferior character of the jobs requires minimal levels of responsibility and initiative on the part of the women who fill them, and provide scant possibilities of promotion, even among secretarial and administrative personnel.

The dominant value system operates to discriminate against women in various ways. For example, the narrow definition of women's natural roles and characteristics contributes to shaping the demand for female labor, limiting them to occupations that in some way have to do with, or are related to, their traditional activities. Among these occupations are many of the worst-paid jobs and those promising least advancement. Although some jobs do not have these negative traits, in one way or another they limit vocations and aptitudes that are found in traditional male areas of economic activity.

This is underscored by women of the popular classes, who besides working in domestic service and related activities, are found in the food industry, in clothing and shoe factories, and in home artisan work, and perform jobs in other people's homes and various traditional personal services, all under the classification of "laborer." In the intermediate and even higher strata, much of the demand for female labor is for administrative work in areas abandoned by men, or areas in which women have displaced men to fill the demands of the enterprises for "decoration" or "display." In these cases women tend to accept working conditions and salaries below standards acceptable to

TABLE 10.2

Economically Active Population of Mexico, by Occupation, 1969

Occupations	A Both Sexes No.	%	B Men No.	%	C Women No.	%	B/A %	C/A %
Total	12,955,057	100.00	10,488,800	100.00	2,466,257	100.00	80.98	19.04
Professionals and technicians	733,209	5.7	485,268	4.6	247,941	10.1	66.2	33.8
Higher administrative personnel in the public and private sectors	319,828	2.5	267,777	2.6	52,051	2.1	83.7	16.3
Administrative personnel	977,179	7.5	579,347	5.5	397,832	16.1	59.3	40.7
Entrepreneurs, sales personnel	967,267	7.5	698,258	6.7	269,009	10.9	72.2	27.8
Various service personnel and vehicle drivers	1,560,614	12.0	876,173	8.3	684,441	27.8	56.1	43.9
Agriculture and cattleraising workers	4,952,200	38.2	4,724,803	45.1	227,397	9.2	95.4	4.6
Nonagricultural workers	2,768,780	21.4	2,415,701	23.0	353,079	14.3	87.2	12.8
Insufficiently specified occupations	675,980	5.2	441,473	4.2	234,507	9.5	65.3	34.7

Source: IX Censo general de la poblacion, resumen general abreviado. Mexico City: SIC, 1972.

men. In the teaching profession, where women are most highly represented, the highest percentage of women is found at the preschool or primary level. In other professions they concentrate in areas of social welfare: medicine, nursing, social work, and the humanities. *

Cultural values exclude many women from many occupations—for example, from those requiring prolonged contact with men, especially in technical work, be it manual or professional. This is because of the presumed or real dangers that this work implies to their virtue and the social image of femininity, in addition to the more or less direct rejection of women by the men. Naturally the rejection is more direct if a woman occupies a position of command or of supervision; then obstacles are placed in her path not only by men but also by other women. This is the case even in areas in which men are not predominant, since the other women clearly express the society's dominant values. Thus, it is not simply a matter of the law permitting women to enter any occupation or legal profession, but of women actually being able to do so. Neither is it a question of equal pay for equal work, because even when the law is obeyed, the problem is being able to reach the more lucrative occupations and to achieve promotion within them.

In this context, Mexican women's opportunities and possibilities of developing their vocations and capacities are very limited and very conditioned, both by the socioeconomic and cultural framework and by their own internalization of the values of masculine domination, which lead them to accept what happens as natural facts of life. By adapting their self-realization to those values, they establish a norm for defining their attitudes toward other women (Castellanos 1973).

Thus the great mass of female workers are easier objects of exploitation than are male workers, because of the kinds of occupations they have, because of their low qualifications, and because they frequently act as a supplementary or marginal labor force. Contributing to their exploitation are their own personalities, which are socially molded for self-abnegation, subordination, and sacrifice, largely because women alone combine economic activity with family obligations in a situation in which complementary services, especially day care centers, are lacking.

---

*If we compare men's and women's participation in the EAP by field of activity, it is appropriate to point out that in manufacturing, the only area in which women predominate is in the manufacture of clothing, where they provide 63. 1 percent of the labor force. Women are also significantly represented in various areas of textile production, in food production, in the manufacture of small basketry items, and in pottery, in which women are 27. 1 percent, 23. 3 percent, 46. 3 percent, and 24. 1 percent, respectively, of the labor force. Among primary school and kindergarden teachers, 61. 0 percent are women; in medical services and social assistance, 67. 9 percent are women.

TABLE 10.3

Economically Active Population of Mexico, by Source of Income, 1969

Source of Income	A Both Sexes No.	%	B Men No.	%	C Women No.	%	B/A %	C/A %
Total	12,955,057	100.00	10,488,800	100.00	2,466,257	100.00	81.0	19.0
Salary	8,054,822	62.2	6,411,327	61.1	1,643,495	66.6	79.5	20.5
Worker/employee	5,395,766	41.7	3,895,595	37.1	1,500,171	60.8	72.0	28.0
Day laborer/rural worker	2,659,056	20.5	2,515,732	24.0	143,324	5.8	95.0	5.0
Entrepreneur/employer	797,452	6.2	630,229	6.0	167,223	6.8	79.0	21.0
Independent worker	3,256,616	25.1	2,777,333	26.5	479,283	19.5	85.3	14.7
Ejidatario	815,560	6.3	784,101	7.5	31,459	1.3	96.0	4.0
Other	2,441,056	18.8	1,993,232	19.0	447,824	18.2	82.0	18.0
Unpaid family worker	846,167	6.5	669,911	6.4	176,256	7.1	79.0	21.0

Source: IX Censo general de la poblacion, resumen general abreviado. Mexico City: SIC, 1972.

Among the more favored classes, there are female entrepreneurs, or heads of enterprises that manufacture automobile and electrical parts, or managers of auto transportation concerns, expensive hotels, vegetable export firms, or other industrial businesses. There are a number of female lawyers, journalists, economists, sociologists, highly trained technicians, and university professors and researchers. There are also many female deputies, magistrates, ministers in the cabinets of the states, judges, and administrators in various public and private offices (see Navarrete 1969, pp. 119-20).

In addition, according to the Census, women were highly represented in "professional services," where they constituted 33.6 percent of the labor force. In research and scientific institutions, women made up 30.6 percent of the professional staff. However, the absolute figures are low and do not take account of the actual labor done under those rubrics.

However one looks at it, the analysis of data on principal occupations shows, in support of what we have been saying, the highest representation of economically active women in administrative personnel (40.7 percent), in service (43.9 percent), in nonspecified activities (34.7 percent), and in commerce (27.8 percent).

Nonetheless, data on principal occupational groups shows that of the total of female workers in 1960, 7.6 percent were technicians and professionals, and 0.6 percent were administrative personnel. In 1969 those percentages had increased to 10.1 percent and 2.1 percent, respectively, which seems to indicate a favorable evolution, although very disparate levels of employment are included in these occupational brackets.

The Census figures on earned income confirms our argument. Of the 2,171,789 working women who declared their income, 47.7 percent had monthly incomes up to 499 pesos; 26.0 percent had incomes between 500 and 999 pesos; 21.4 percent had incomes of between 1,000 and 2,499 pesos; 3.5 percent had incomes between 3,500 and 4,999 pesos; and only 1.4 percent had incomes of 5,000 pesos or more (see Table 10.4).

If at first sight the figures for the men are almost as depressing, it is worth noting that the male EAP figures in Table 10.4 are depressed by the large numbers of men who work in agriculture and connected fields, as well as in areas in which the unpaid work of women is not included. Thus, independently of the fact that the small proportion of women in the same sector have incomes that are similarly depressed, such figures are not strictly comparable, because the female EAP is not preponderantly agricultural. We have seen that 89.2 percent of women work in nonagricultural fields.

The analysis of the data on the nonagricultural EAP (see Table 10.5) confirms our observations on the inferior position of most women in the labor market. This is clear from the large numbers of women in the lower income brackets, for most women receive far lower incomes

TABLE 10.4

Economically Active Population of Mexico, by Monthly Income, 1969

Income (Mexican pesos)	A Both Sexes No.	%	B Men No.	%	C Women No.	%	B/A %	C/A %
Total	11,620,469	100.00	9,448,680	100.00	2,171,789	100.00	81.3	18.7
0 to 499 pesos	5,199,096	44.7	4,162,733	44.1	1,036,363	47.7	80.1	19.9
500 to 999 pesos	3,134,301	27.0	2,569,225	27.2	565,076	26.0	82.0	18.0
1,000 to 1,499 pesos	1,473,323	12.7	1,189,716	12.6	283,607	13.1	80.8	19.2
1,500 to 2,499 pesos	951,003	8.2	770,920	8.1	180,083	8.3	81.1	18.9
2,500 to 4,999 pesos	555,368	4.8	478,870	5.1	76,498	3.5	86.2	13.8
5,000 to 9,999 pesos	200,092	1.7	182,022	1.9	18,070	0.8	91.0	9.0
Over 10,000 pesos	107,286	0.9	95,194	1.0	12,092	0.6	88.7	11.3

Note: The totals are different from those in the preceding tables because not all workers declare their earned incomes. 89.7 percent of the total EAP (90.1 percent of the men and 88.1 percent of the women) declared their earned incomes.

Source: IX Censo general de la poblacion. Mexico City: SIC, 1972.

TABLE 10.5

Nonagricultural Economically Active Population of Mexico, by Monthly Income, 1969

Income (Mexican pesos)	A Both Sexes No.	%	B Men No.	%	C Women No.	%	B/A %	C/A %
Total	7,349,574	100.00	5,357,498	100.00	1,992,076	100.00	72.9	27.1
0 to 499 pesos	1,909,451	26.0	1,011,655	18.9	897,796	45.1	53.0	47.0
500 to 999 pesos	2,413,177	32.8	1,873,250	35.0	539,927	27.1	77.6	22.4
1,000 to 1,499 pesos	1,366,188	18.6	1,088,009	20.3	278,179	14.0	79.6	20.4
1,500 to 2,499 pesos	883,711	12.0	707,703	13.2	176,008	8.8	80.1	19.9
2,500 to 4,999 pesos	506,841	6.9	433,505	8.1	73,336	3.7	85.5	14.5
5,000 to 9,999 pesos	182,931	2.5	165,928	3.1	17,003	0.8	90.7	9.3
Over 10,000 pesos	87,275	1.2	77,448	1.4	9,827	0.5	88.7	11.3

Note: Data from the economically active population that declared earned income, from which the incomes from agricultural and related fields have been subtracted.

Source: IX Censo general de la poblacion. Mexico City: SIC, 1972.

than do men. Thus, while only 18. 9 percent of men had earned monthly incomes of up to 499 pesos, 45. 1 percent of economically active women were in that position. And considering this and the next income brackets together, where only 53. 9 percent of men received up to 999 pesos, 72. 2 percent of the women received this abysmal income.

Table 10. 4 also shows that in the higher income brackets, men's positions are always more favorable than are women's. Thus, while 20. 7 percent of male workers received between 1, 000 and 2, 499 pesos, only 21. 4 percent of women appear in those brackets. 5. 1 percent of the men and 3. 5 percent of the women appear in the monthly income bracket of 2, 500 to 4, 999 pesos. Moreover, in the groups receiving 4, 000 pesos or more, men reach 4. 5 percent and only 1. 3 percent of women receive this income.

In all subcategories of the service sector, which includes 60. 1 percent of the female EAP, the numbers of women who received incomes of up to 999 pesos are higher than those among men. This is especially the case in "commerce" and "other services, " in which 59. 7 percent and 48. 5 percent of the male workers, and 74. 5 percent and 72. 9 percent of the female workers, had this income. The situation is particularly grave in "other services, " which absorbs 42. 9 percent of Mexican working women. * In manufacturing, 52. 9 percent of men received up to 999 pesos per month, while 72. 9 percent of women were in this income bracket. This category, which includes a number of traditional occupations and in which large numbers of women are employed, adds further to the considerable number of underpaid women.

In short, since the female EAP is predominantly nonagricultural, the kind of work women do is revealed by the incomes that most women receive. In Table 10. 5, 72. 2 percent of working women receive less than 999 pesos per month. The still-modest bracket of monthly incomes between 1, 000 and 1, 499 pesos contains 14. 0 percent of female workers. Only 12. 5 percent of women are in relatively satisfactory intermediary positions; the 1. 3 percent of women in the 4, 000 pesos bracket are in truly exceptional positions.

---

*A large part of the female EAP is concentrated in areas where by definition the pay is generally low, and women in more traditional employ are in an even worse situation. A curious example is found in the category of domestic service in private homes. Here 48. 0 percent of the men who do this work receive incomes of up to 499 pesos per month, while 87. 0 percent of female domestic servants receive that amount. 32. 5 percent of men in domestic service receive between 500 and 999 pesos, but only 9. 5 percent of women are in the same situation. Practically all women are in the lowest income brackets, and only an infinitesimal proportion manages to achieve the second income bracket. Men's incomes increase significantly, at least until the bracket receiving up to 3, 499 pesos per month.

In addition to the lack of educational preparation, one of the factors that conditions many women's precarious situation is the low level of unionization; there is great difficulty in organizing the independent laborer, especially the female. We do not have data according to sex, but we do know that only 22.5 percent of all workers are unionized (7.6 percent of agricultural and cattle-raising workers, 33.0 percent of those in commerce and services, and 59.0 percent of industrial workers). The occupational placement of the great majority of the female labor force leads us to believe that unionization among women is infinitesimal (Anuario Estadistico de los Estados Unidos Mexicanos 1969).

Thus, sometimes for lack of unionization, and sometimes for lack of aggressive organizations that really represent the interests of the workers, especially the problems specific to women, many women continue to be exploited while laws intended to protect them often worsen rather than improve their situation. * This has been the case with the law requiring day care centers in establishments employing a specified number of female workers. It resulted in owners' reducing the demand

---

*The employees of short-order restaurants, taco shops, and coffee shops, who are mostly women, do not receive minimum wages, are not enrolled in social security, and do not have recourse to the most elemental legal protections to which female workers have rights. In the case of strikes, given the small capital of such establishments, the owners' reaction is frequently to close the source of employment. Statement by Consuelo Maldonado, General Secretary to the Syndical Union of Female Workers of Coffee Bars, Restaurants, Bakeries and Similar Establishments in the Federal District, El Dia, January 22, 1973.

Seamstresses are traditionally exploited in Mexico, where they practically never receive a minimum salary, although they are made to work ten to twelve hours daily. Statement by Concepcion Rivera, Secretary General of the Organization of Female Workers, El Dia, February 21, 1973.

In the sewing profession, in which millions of women and children are exploited, and over which there is no control, since most work in their homes, workers are paid fifteen to twenty cents to sew collars onto shirts and five to seven pesos to sew pants, which are then sold at high prices in shops. Statement by Rafael Elizante, representative of workers of Section 9 of the CTM, El Dia, January 27, 1973.

When many women who work at night leave their jobs, be they in hotels, hospitals, factories, or restaurants, they are subjected to extortion by members of the uniformed police, under the threat of being taken to the stations and being charged with "infamous activities." Concepcion Rivera, Secretary General of the Organization of Female Workers, El Dia, February 13 and 21, 1973. See also Gonzalez Salazar 1972a.

for female labor below the level already established. The law, which
prohibited certain kinds of employment for women for reasons of health,
and excluded them from work after 10 P. M. , has caused those who need
work under such conditions to become even more exploited, accepting
abysmally low pay just in order to have an income.

Nonetheless, recent modifications have been introduced into labor
and social security legislation that benefit women. A promising development is the consolidation, under more promising conditions, of day
care centers as a branch of social security. The new law, which has
been in effect since April 1973, permits, through a withholding tax of
1 percent on salaries, the institution of what has been called "a system of solidarity between bosses and laborers" that was to be initiated
in the first trimester of 1974. Through a contribution of 0. 3 percent of
salaries, 506 day care centers, to which 165, 000 children will be
admitted, were to be in operation by 1976; 115 units serving 50, 000
children were expected to operate during the first trimester of 1974. *

Recent reforms of the federal labor law regulate domestic work and
establish better working conditions and pay scales. Domestic service
will be covered by social security (Diario Oficial 1973), although only
on a voluntary basis for the present.

FINAL OBSERVATIONS

It is not an exaggeration to state that education is of major importance for all the important aspects of individual and social life, for it
provides possibilities for fuller human development and has an intimate
relation to occupational perspectives, income levels, and opportunities
for upward social mobility and conscious political participation. This
does not, however, imply a direct causal relationship; structural
parameters remain dominant both quantitatively and qualitatively. Given
this emphasis, the raising of educational standards among women is of
singular importance for the achievement of higher status. This process
of upgrading permits the restatement of the contradictions at a higher
level with each advance made.

In view of the importance that education has in determining the
flexibility of female occupations and woman's incorporation into the
labor market, some general data on the educational characteristics of
adult women over 25 years of age are worth considering. From the same
perspective, but with an eye to the future, data on school aid are

---

*Statements by public servants of the Mexican Social Security
Institute, published in various newspapers on July 10, 1973, October
21, 1973.

equally important. According to Census data on years of schooling, among all women over 25 years of age, 42 percent had no primary instruction, 27. 7 percent had only the first three years of primary instruction, and 24. 1 percent had from four to six years of primary studies. Only a bit more than 7 percent had some form of postprimary instruction. If we separate the data on postprimary schooling, it may be observed that among men of these ages, 4. 1 percent and about 2 percent had one or two years of secondary or preparatory school, respectively, while only 2. 6 percent and 0. 7 percent of women had had such instruction. On the higher educational levels, 1. 5 percent of men had completed between one and six years of study, whereas this was the case for only 0. 6 percent of the women.

We have the following information on financial assistance to various educational levels:* among the primary school age groups of 6-14 years, 60. 1 percent of boys and 58. 2 percent of girls received some form of assistance. At the secondary or prevocational level among children 11 to 18 years of age, 13 percent of the boys and 9 percent of the girls received aid. At the preparatory or vocational level (14-20 years), 5. 6 percent of the boys and 2. 2 percent of the girls received aid.

At the middle professional level, after the completion of secondary or prevocational school, the percentages for aid to both sexes are about 1 percent in the age groups of 14 to 29 years. However, assistance for higher professional learning for the population over 16 years of age is 1. 5 percent for the men and only 0. 5 percent for the women.

However, the participation of women in higher education and in academic and scientific activities is increasing. For example, at

---

*We are dealing only with broad illustrative indicators that refer to the significance of education for occupational flexibility. Labor demand is not for the age groups that correspond to any given educational level, but for the graduates of the preceding level, or graduates of trades within each level. In all cases referring to educational data, the percentages have been obtained from the data on the total population in the age groups discussed. IX General Census of the Population, Mexico, 1970.

The internal composition of school enrollment from the secondary to the superior level is available for 1970: of a total of 1, 820, 863 students, 1, 129, 933—72 percent—were men and 690, 930—38 percent— were women. The latter were enrolled at the various levels in the following proportions: secondary and prevocational, 28. 1 percent; professional with only secondary previous studies, 64. 1 percent; professional with previous preparatory studies, 37. 0 percent; professional, in the higher levels, 26. 4 percent. Guadalupe Rivera Marin, unpublished studies on economic aspects of female labor in Mexico.

the National University of Mexico, whose students are representative of the whole country, the female student population at the higher professional level has risen from 16. 0 percent in 1959 to 20. 8 percent in 1965 to 22. 4 percent in 1969. The number of female teachers increased from 7. 8 percent in 1959 to 11. 9 percent in 1965 to 12. 5 percent in 1969. Similar increases are also perceptible among the number of female researchers at the various centers for scientific research at the University (Anuario Estadistico de la Universidad Nacional Autonoma de Mexico).

Nonetheless, in view of socioeconomic conditions and cultural factors, it is deplorable that female preferences in careers are not very diversified; women still orient themselves basically toward the humanistic and social professions, such as medical assistants. Obviously this is meant not to criticize those occupations, which are authentic vocations; but it is frequently the case that in such "choices" there are socioeconomic and cultural factors that result in a waste of talent that could be applied with great success in the professions reserved for men. These professions are lucrative to those who practice them and are of great importance for economic development. For example, in 1971, over 20 percent of the total female population was enrolled in the College of Philosophy and Letters, over 17 percent in the Medical School, 9. 2 percent in the Dentistry School, and over 13 percent and 12 percent, respectively, in the Department of Commerce and Administration and in the Law School, while just over 2 percent were in the Architecture School and only 0. 4 percent were in the Engineering School. The uniformity of choices is underscored even more if individual careers rather than institutions are considered.

A brief examination of the data on career enrollment at the national level for 1969 shows that of 35, 916 female students, 5, 371 became public accountants; 5, 168 worked in medicine; 3, 014 in law; 2, 058 in dentistry; 1, 868 in psychology; 1, 831 in pharmaceutical chemistry; 1, 149 in biology; and 1, 083 in business administration. Taken together, these account for 65 percent of the total female student population; the first two careers mentioned, at over 14 percent each, are the most representative. In decreasing order of importance, other careers that have fairly significant numbers of women in them are plastic arts, economics, history, teaching, and social work, in addition to a group of special areas in chemistry besides pharmacy. These add up to another 15 percent of female students. While we need not examine in great detail the way in which the final 20 percent breaks down, it is worth pointing out that it duplicates the general tendency of the majority—toward choices ranging between medical assistance and related professions, on the one hand, and commercial administrative careers, socioeconomic sciences, and humanities, on the other. The absence or minimal participation of women in technical and similar careers is pointed out in engineering, in which, except for those connected with administration, chemistry, and biology, the percentages of female participation vary from virtually zero to two percent (Annuario de la Asociacion Nacional de Universidades e Institutos de Ensenanza Superior en Mexico 1970).

Finally, it is worth pointing out that while women's opportunities are limited as a function of their sex in all social strata, there is a painful contrast between the minority that has achieved a substantial educational base, and has been able to incorporate itself into the labor market in satisfactory and even privileged roles, and the masses of women, especially in the more backward and rural areas. In this respect, the first group—especially those who have achieved public positions—has a responsibility to struggle (as it often fails to do) for the development of the huge human potential represented by women, which does not exhaust its possibilities in procreation and the care of offspring.

This is not to say that work should be considered a panacea for the evils afflicting women, or as the sole means for them to realize their potential as human beings. From the present perspective, in which all extant social models deserve questioning, women's participation implies much more than their passive entry into the status quo. Both the forces that affect women specifically and those that affect the whole population must be questioned.

From this point of view it is worth hoping that women, in a not too distant future, will be capable of participating actively in the critique of our societies and of fighting to realize the structural changes necessary for growth and social progress. Part of this is the struggle for scientific and technological advance applied to social interests. World interdependence demands, as a characteristic of responsible maternity, not only control of and decision concerning procreation, nor only the careful raising of children in the family or the small community, but also concern with the type of societies in which they are growing and with international concerns.

Proposals such as this do not imply a modernized universal conception of maternity or feminine problems but, rather, woman's involvement in a process in which she struggles beside the man for a more rational and egalitarian society that permits the realization of all human potential, including her unique characteristics.

Such hopes may seem distant, especially for the underdeveloped countries, since before they can be realized, women must resolve many specific problems in order to achieve greater social participation. However, there can be no doubt that the efforts of women in social sciences can help greatly; there, from a critical, objective, and impartial perspective, they may be able to transcend traditional perspectives on social problems and thus contribute to the understanding of those problems that view the female population of mothers, workers, and citizens as part of the total social problem.

REFERENCES

Anuario Estadistico de la Universidad Nacional Autonoma de Mexico .

Anuario estadistico de los Estados Unidos Mexicanos. 1969. Mexico
    City: SIC.

Anuario de la Asociacion nacional de universidades e institutos de
    ensenanza superior en Mexico. 1970.

Castellanos, Rosario. 1973. Mujer que sabe latin. Mexico City:
    SepSetentas. Especially pp. 7-41.

Diario Oficial. 1973. No. 42, August 29.

Gonzalez Salazar, Gloria. 1969. "Situacion juridica de la mujer en
    Mexico." In La mujer y los derechos sociales, ed. Ifigenia M.
    de Navarrete, pp. 105-23. Mexico City: Ed. Oasis.

_____. 1972a. "La mujer: Condiciones estructurales y educacion."
    In Reforma educativa y apertura democratica, pp. 106-24.
    Mexico City: Ed. Nuestro Tiempo.

_____. 1972b. Problemas de la mano de obra en Mexico. 2nd ed.
    Mexico City: Universidad Nacional Autonoma de México.

Navarrete, Ifigenia M. de. 1969. La mujer y los derechos sociales.
    Mexico City: Ed. Oasis.

Rivera Marin, Guadalupe. n. d. Unpublished studies on economic
    aspects of female labor in Mexico.

Spota, Alma. 1968. Igualdad juridica y social de los sexos. Mexico
    City: Ed. Porrua.

11

**THE HISTORY OF
WOMEN'S STRUGGLE
FOR EQUALITY
IN PUERTO RICO**
Isabel Pico Vidal

In Puerto Rico, women's history has been directly related to the intensity of organized women's movements. Not since 1930, when the suffrage movement ended, has there been the interest found today. Women are again asking historical questions in a search for their collective identity and for an analysis of their condition. However, the Puerto Rican woman trying to understand herself in a historical perspective has few facts to rely on. We still know very little about how women lived at different times; how they interacted with their children, husbands and parents; and how they began to develop a consciousness of their distinct role in society.

In my academic work on Puerto Rican women I have done some research on the social and economic forces that shaped and changed women's lives in the twentieth century and on the nature of the development of feminist consciousness on the island. I would like to present in this brief essay some preliminary notes for the study of Puerto Rican women and their participation in the social conflicts of the early twentieth century.

Most of the nineteenth century was marked by the lack of both a feminist movement and a strong feminist consciousness. This is understandable because of the precarious educational and employment situation of women on the island. In 1899 there were 5,045 inhabitants in Puerto Rico with more than primary education; 72 percent of these were men. Of the 1,387 women with some education beyond primary schooling, 82 percent remained at home, outside the labor force (U. S. Department of War 1900). Under these circumstances it was not possible for a true feminist movement to develop in the nineteenth century, as it did in

This article is part of a broader study on Puerto Rican women and the political process.

England, France, the United States, and other countries that had greater economic and social complexity. *

The development of industrial capitalism in Puerto Rico at the turn of the twentieth century started a slow transformation in the economic function of women from unpaid production for home consumption to gainful employment in the manufacture of articles for sale. In the nineteenth century only a few women (47, 701) were employed outside the home in gainful occupations and, according to the 1899 Census, the great majority were employed as domestic servants (18, 453), laundresses (16, 855) and seamstresses and embroiderers (5, 785). Only 3, 910 were classified as laborers. Women's rate of participation in the labor force increased substantially during the first three decades of the twentieth century. From the rather low rate of 9. 9 percent in 1899, women's rate of participation reached 26. 1 percent in 1930, the highest experienced in our history (see Table 11. 1). This dramatic increase in a predominantly agrarian economy was due primarily to the growth of manufacturing industries, such as tobacco processing and home needlework (McBride 1917, p. 717; Weller 1968, p. 62). The development of new commercial enterprises and the influx of foreign capital searching for cheap labor accelerated women's participation in the labor force. In 1930, 52. 3 percent of all women in paying jobs were working in the manufacturing sector, 29. 7 percent were in domestic and personal services, and only 9. 4 percent were in agriculture. While the percentage of women in domestic and personal services declined from 78. 4 percent to 29. 7 percent, that sector remained the second most important area for women's work. † (See Table 11. 2.)

---

*Only a few women from the upper classes fought, in a limited way, for the right to education; at the same time they enriched our cultural heritage, particularly in the arts and sciences. For biographical sketches of prominent women of the seventeenth, eighteenth, and nineteenth centuries, see Angelis (1910); Benitez de Gautier (1856); Ferrer (1881); Labra (1869); Rodriguez de Tio (1971); and Tapia y Rivera (1870).

†Before 1930 the largest number of women were employed in the manufacture of tobacco, and the sugar and molasses industry gave employment to the largest number of children. In 1909, of the 1, 654 female wage earners in all industries combined, 81. 1 percent were employed in the manufacture of tobacco; and of the 758 wage earners in all industries under 16 years of age, 79. 3 percent were in the sugar and molasses industry (U. S. Department of Commerce and Labor 1912). In 1920, the number of women working in cigar and tobacco factories increased to 8, 573 and in 1930 to 9, 290. In both years, women outnumbered men working in these jobs. Apparently men were gradually displaced from their jobs or promoted to skilled jobs within the industry (U. S. Dept. of Labor 1920, 1930). Almost all the hand- stemming in the tobacco leaf industry was done by females (U. S. Dept. of Labor 1941).

TABLE 11.1

Participation in the Puerto Rican Labor Force, by Sex, 1899–1970
(14 years or older)

Year	Females		Males	
	Number	Percentage of Female Population	Number	Percentage of Male Population
1899	47,701	9.9	268,664	59.9
1910	73,596	21.7	303,993	93.1
1920	84,094	21.6	319,201	84.1
1930	122,488	26.1	374,958	81.0
1940	144,360	25.0	457,630	79.4
1950	138,517	21.3	458,950	70.7
1960	144,260	20.0	449,840	65.7
1970	212,421	22.9	471,369	54.7

Source: U.S. Department of Commerce, Census of Population 1899–1970.

TABLE 11.2

Female Participation in Puerto Rican Labor Force, by Economic Sector, 1899-1930

	1899		1910		1920		1930	
	Number	Percent	Number	Percent	Number	Percent	Number	Percent
All sectors	47,701	100.00	76,892	100.00	86,462	100.00	125,777	100.00
Agriculture, fishing, mining	1,868	3.90	10,779	14.00	17,719	20.30	11,948	9.40
Commerce, transportation	1,729	3.60	1,037	1.00	1,199	1.30	2,349	1.80
Manufacturing, mechanical industries	6,389	13.30	18,194	20.30	30,809	22.80	65,846	52.30
Professional services	311	0.60	1,487	1.80	3,253	3.60	5,661	4.50
Domestic, personal services	37,407	78.40	45,149	58.00	32,482	27.10	37,424	29.70
Clerical occupations	—	—	189	.20	937	.90	2,500	1.90
Public service, other	—	—	47	.06	63	.07	49	.03

Sources: U.S. War Department, Census of Population, 1899; U.S. Department of Commerce, Census of Population, 1910-1930.

On the other hand, needlework attained the status of an industry of commercial importance in the late 1920s (U.S. Dept. of Labor 1950). While some fine needlework was done before that date, production was small. It was not until World War I interfered with the supply of embroidery from Europe that needlework extended throughout rural communities, small towns, and cities in Puerto Rico. With this gain in production there was an increase in employment. The Census of 1920 showed roughly 16, 000 persons in the cotton garment industry; the Census of 1930 showed 40, 000. Over a fourth of these were employed in factory work, but the great majority were home workers. The needlework industry in Puerto Rico was predominantly a woman's industry. In the 1935 Census of Puerto Rico, 99 percent of the persons who gave their gainful occupation as "home needlework and embroidery workers" were female. During the 1930s, home work in the needle trades involved not only the greatest numbers of women but also the greatest numbers of abuses (U.S. Dept. of Labor 1934).

Over 50, 000 women who did home needlework received a wage of one, two, or three cents an hour. Most of the abuses, such as late payments, payment in merchandise instead of cash, and the withholding of pay increases by unscrupulous middlemen, were perpetrated against women working at home. Nonetheless, salaries below subsistence level and long working hours were common in all factories and workshops. According to this study, working women in canning factories were not even provided with seats; from early morning they stood in front of their worktables, peeling grapefruit and pineapples so close to each other that their elbows touched. Those who worked six or seven days a week received an average salary of $3.59. On the other hand, women worked an average of 36.9 hours a week stripping tobacco and earned an average salary of $7.57 a week (U.S. Dept. of Labor 1934).

Women's participation in professional services and clerical occupations also increased substantially during the first three decades of the twentieth century. With the expansion of the public school system under U.S. domination, teaching became one of the main occupations of upper- and middle-class women. Gradually, teaching became, for all practical purposes, a "female" occupation. In 1899, there were 246 female teachers in Puerto Rico, constituting 30 percent of all persons in the teaching profession. By 1930, 74.5 percent of all teachers were women. The same thing happened in nursing and clerical occupations. Women constituted 50 percent of all persons engaged in these two fields in 1910. In 1930, 66 percent of all clerical workers and 94 percent of the nurses were women.

This fundamental change in women's economic function had profound repercussions in the social order of the Puerto Rican community. The new relationship of women to production brought about changes in social and sexual patterns expressed by different classes. For the first time, women recognized a collective experience for members of their sex and defined that experience as a position of subjugation. This new

TABLE 11.3

Women and Men in the Teaching Profession in Puerto Rico, 1899-1930

Year	Total	Women	Percent	Men	Percent
1899	809	246	30.0	563	69.9
1910	2,239	1,172	52.3	1,067	47.6
1920	3,742	2,636	70.4	1,106	29.5
1930	5,730	4,254	74.5	1,456	25.4

Source: U.S. War Department, Census of Population, 1899; U.S. Department of Commerce, Census of Population, 1910, 1920, 1930.

TABLE 11.4

Puerto Rican Women Typists and Secretaries, 1910-30

Year	Total	Males	Females	Percent of Women
1910	225	112	113	50.0
1920	839	333	506	60.0
1930	2,309	776	1,533	66.0

Source: Compiled by the author.

TABLE 11.5

Puerto Rican Women's Employment in Nursing, 1899-1930

Year	Total	Males	Females	Percent of Women
1899	127	63	64	50.0
1910	252	63	189	75.0
1920	393	31	362	92.0
1930	976	55	921	94.0

Source: Compiled by the author.

consciousness was based on the new role of women as producer, introduced by industrialization.

For those women who entered the labor force at the beginning of the
twentieth century, oppression was part of their new collective experience. But oppression meant different things to different groups and
classes of women. The growing work force of women had developed an
internal hierarchy. While the unskilled industrial workers showed life
styles and attitudes characteristic of the proletariat, women in such
professions as teaching and nursing set themselves apart from their
sisters. Moreover, the dichotomy between women who worked and those
who remained at home was further accentuated by the culturally defined
"proper sphere" of women.

Working-class women at the beginning of the century felt their oppression in class terms and organized around their work. In his work
on the development of the Puerto Rican working-class movement, Angel
Quintero Rivera describes how women's participation in the growing tobacco industry gradually broke the traditional patterns of their employment as mere collaborators of men in agricultural tasks. It raised wom-
en to a relatively equal position with men in the productive process
within similar conditions of exploitation (Quintero Rivera n. d.). Economic exploitation by employers under the new system of production
was inhumane. The Employment of Women in Puerto Rico, a report drawn
up in 1933 under the joint auspices of the federal and insular Departments of Labor, showed that substandard wages in sweatshops, long
hours, and poor sanitary conditions prevailed in canneries, tobacco
processing, cigar factories, and home needlework (U. S. Dept. of Labor 1934). Gradually these conditions generated a spirit of solidarity
and a common struggle among workers against employers that to a great
extent blurred the traditional differentiation between the sexes.

By and large, women tended to join men in the ranks of organized
labor and experienced their own sense of strength and power in trade
unions. As early as 1904, working-class women had organized female
associations within trade unions: Union de Damas de Puerta de Tierra,
Union Federada de Patillas, Union de Escogedoras de Cafe de Arecibo,
Union de Damas Obreras de Guayama, Union Protectora de Damas de
Mayaguez, and Union de Obreras Domesticas de Ponce. Later, many
women participated in the creation of the Free Labor Federation. Josefa
Perez, a worker from Puerta de Tierra, in 1904 wrote a letter to Romero
Rosa, a member of the Propaganda Commission of the Free Labor Feder-
ation, demanding that women workers be organized within the union
(Pagan 1973, p. 324).

During 1910-20, some outstanding working-class women became
symbols of militant trade unionism. Among them were Concha Torres,
a leader from Puerta de Tierra who was the first woman in Puerto Rico
to speak at a political rally; Paca Escabi de Pena, a union leader from
Mayaguez; Francisca Andujar; and Juana Colon, from Comerio, who was
very active organizing tobacco strippers at the big factory of La Colec-

tiva and became one of the most militant women in the Socialist Party
founded by Santiago Iglesias in 1916 (Azzize 1974).

Naturally, most women workers directed their attention to wages
and hours. They realized their wages were three to four times lower
than those of men working in comparable jobs because of the inferiority
ascribed to their positions. As working women they fought against the
notion of the ideal woman that prevented their full participation and remuneration in industry. They rejected notions of feminine frailty, weakness, social purity, moral superiority, and passivity.

The best exponent of the new ideology was Luisa Capetillo, in her
writings Ensayos libertarios (1904-07), Influencias modernas (1916),
and Mi opinion sobre las libertades, derechos, de la mujer como com-
panera, madre y ser independiente.* This last book, written in 1911,
is a collection of essays that could well be considered the first "wom-
en's lib" manifesto in Puerto Rico. Capetillo was an exceptional woman
who participated in the formation of the first artisan groups that the
Free Federation of Labor organized in urban centers. Later she participated in a crusade on sugar plantations, raising class consciousness
among workers. She was also a reporter for the newspaper Union obrera
and established the journal La mujer, devoted to women's issues. In
her writings Capetillo defended libertarian socialism, rationalism, in-
ternationalism, and women's liberation. She condemned religious fanat-
icism, the double standard, women's slavery in marriage, and economic
exploitation in the factory. Capetillo also challenged the social con-
ventions of her time. She was the first woman to wear slacks in public
in Puerto Rico, and she had children outside of marriage.

Women's active participation in working-class struggles engendered
a different conception of women as "comrade." The new conception, of
which Capetillo was the most radical expression, was a denial of the
patriarchal ideology typical of the hacienda social system. To a certain
extent the struggle for woman's equality had its origins in the artisans'
tradition of dissent from the Puerto Rican landowners and employers
(Quintero Rivera 1973).

Long before women were granted the right to vote, the Socialist
Party had a requirement in its party bylaws that no committee could be
organized unless one-third of the members were females. In its 1919
political platform, the Socialist Party defended universal suffrage for
men and women.† But in general the ballot, legal rights, and other

---

*Norma Valle is preparing a biography and a collection of the writ-
ings of Luisa Capetillo. For a preview of her preliminary research, see
her "La primera en liberarse" (1974).

†See the Socialist Party program of 1919, in Quintero Rivera (n. d.,
pp. 89-94). Another important document that contains the Socialist
Party's defense of women's suffrage is a memorandum of the Territorial
Executive Committee dated December 29, 1923 (Pagan 1924).

social reform issues seemed irrelevant or secondary compared with the
more pressing problems of daily life. Trade unionism absorbed their
attention and energy. At the same time, working-class women viewed
the women's suffrage movement as designed for those of the privileged
class. They feared what actually happened in 1928: that the right to
vote was granted only to literate women, thus increasing the power of
the political parties that represented the propertied class. Naturally,
the Socialist Party opposed the legislative bills that granted the ballot
exclusively to women who could read and write.

The seedbed of the suffragette movement that developed in Puerto
Rico was the increase in respectable jobs open to women of the upper
and middle classes. With the transformation of the social system of
haciendas to a system of sugar plantations controlled by U. S. corporations, Puerto Rican upper classes suffered structural changes that
directly affected women's condition. Many small and medium landowners lost their property, moved to town, and gave their children an
education in the traditional professions. Within this process there
emerged a growing number of women for whom work was not only a form
of self-fulfillment and personal independence but also an economic necessity. This social phenomenon occurred at a time when the new colonial administrators had decided to expand the educational system, to
make it coed and available to females on relatively equal basis. * These
reforms, well received by women from the petite bourgeoisie and the
traditional landowning class, probably explain why women from these
classes were more tolerant of the colonial power than were their male
counterparts. To a great extent, the first generation of professional
women were rather insecure regarding their individual fates, wanted to
be accepted, and frequently assimilated the values of the prevailing
political system to achieve their individual aims.

On the other hand, women's professionalization and all other
changes in this direction were viewed by men of the upper classes as
part of the process of "Americanization" that had to be avoided. This
defensive cultural conservatism was part of a reaction against the imposition of a foreign culture and way of life that characterized the anticolonial struggle in Puerto Rico. As a result, the feminist movement
emerged and developed apart from anticolonial protest. On some occasions, it was in conflict with them. †

---

*The University of Puerto Rico, established in 1903 on the guide-
lines of North American Teacher's Colleges, became a predominantly
female institution in terms of the student body. During 1903-23 approximately 2, 791 students graduated, with women constituting 74 percent
(Hernandez 1974).

†In 1909, when a bill for the legal emancipation of women was presented by Nemesio Canales in the House of Delegates, Jose de Diego,
the most important leader of the independence movement at that time,

However, the goal of the electoral franchise acquired a special meaning for the growing sector of professional women who were deprived of the most fundamental civil and political rights. The new study and work experiences raised women's consciousness in relation to their position of inequality vis-a-vis their male counterparts. In 1909, female schoolteachers demanded eligibility to be appointed to local school boards. In 1917, the first feminist organization—the Liga Femenina Puertorriquena—was established; and in 1925, the Puerto Rican Association of Suffragist Women demanded the ballot for women from the U.S. Congress and from the local legislature. * After more than ten years of struggle, literate Puerto Rican women acquired the right to vote in general elections. The bill was approved in 1929, but they were not able to vote until 1932. It was not until 1936 that the literacy requirement was abolished.

Even though the suffrage movement eliminated the most obvious forms of discrimination against women in the legal superstructure and promoted reforms in education and labor, it did not fundamentally alter the patriarchal society. Unfortunately, the revolutionary promise of radically changing the quality of life for women never materialized for the great majority of Puerto Rican women.

The feminist movement's single-minded emphasis on obtaining the vote helps to explain not only the movement's failure to reach working-class women but also its increasing inability to move beyond its immediate goal of the franchise. By the time the bill was passed, the vote was no longer a means to an end. It was the only end most suffragists envisioned. In the years after 1930, feminism as a movement and as a consciousness became increasingly isolated.

REFERENCES

Aguilar, Isabel Andreu de. 1935. "Resena historica del movimiento sufragista en Puerto Rico." Revista Puerto Rico (June).

Alvarado, Carmen Rivera. 1972. "La contribucion de la mujer al desarrollo de la nacionalidad puertorriquena." In La mujer en la lucha hoy, ed. Juan Angel Silen and Nancy Zayas. Rio Piedras, Puerto Rico: Ediciones Kikiriki.

---

opposed the bill, arguing that women needed no additional rights (Canales 1967, pp. 175-77). During the 1930s Pedro Albizu Campos, president of the Nationalist Party, confronted the suffragists on several occasions and urged them to give priority to the fight against colonialism.

*For a brief but good summary of the development of the suffragist movement in Puerto Rico, consult Isabel Andreu de Aguilar (1935) and Mercedes Sola (1922).

Angelis, Maria Luisa A. 1910. Mujeres puertorriquenas. San Juan: Tipografia Real Hermanos.

Azzize, Vamila. 1974. "Luchas de la mujer obrera, 1910-1920." B. A. thesis, General Studies Faculty, University of Puerto Rico.

Benitez de Gautier, Alejandrina. 1856. "Sobre la educacion de las mujeres." Guirnalda puertorriquena 1: 1-3.

Canales, Nemesio R. 1967. Paliques. San Juan: Ediciones Isla.

Ferrer, Gabriel. 1881. La mujer en Puerto Rico. San Juan: Imprenta El Agente.

Hernandez, Isabel Pico de. 1974. "Los estudiantes universitarios y el proceso politico puertorriqueno (1903-1948)." Ph. D. dissertation, Government Department, Harvard University.

Labra, Rafael Maria de. 1869. Conferencias dominicales sobre la educacion de la mujer. Madrid: Imprenta Rivadeneyra.

McBride, N. W. 1917. "Women Workers of Puerto Rico." International Socialist Review 18 (June).

Pagan, Bolivar. 1924. El sufragio femenino. San Juan.

Pagan, Igualdad Iglesias de. 1973. El obrerismo en Puerto Rico. Ediciones Juan Ponce de Leon.

Quintero Rivera, Angel. 1973. Lucha obrera en Puerto Rico. Rio Piedras: Centro de Estudios de la Realidad Puertorriquena.

_____. n. d. "De artesano a proletario: Los tabaqueros y la tradicion radical." In Gervasio Garcia, Ricardo Campos, and Angel Quintero Rivera, Socialista tabaquero: Origenes de la lucha obrera en Puerto Rico. Rio Piedras: Centro de Estudios de la Realidad Puertorriquena.

Rodriguez de Tio, Lola. 1971. Obras completas, four vols. San Juan: Instituto de Cultura Puertorriquena.

Sola, Mercedes. 1922. Feminismo. San Juan: Cantero Fernandez y Cia.

Tapia y Rivera, Alejandro. 1870. "El aprecio de la mujer. Azucena 1 (November 30).

United States Department of Commerce and Labor, Bureau of the Census. 1912. Thirteenth Census of the United States. Manufactures. 1909. Washington, D. C.: U. S. Government Printing Office.

United States Department of Labor, Bureau of the Census. 1920. Census of the United States. Washington, D. C.: U. S. Government Printing Office.

_____. 1930. Census of the United States. Washington, D. C.: U. S. Government Printing Office.

_____. 1941. Puerto Rico: The Leaf Tobacco Industry. Washington, D. C.: U. S. Government Printing Office.

_____, Wages and Hours Division. 1934. The Employment of Women in Puerto Rico. Washington, D. C.: U. S. Government Printing Office.

_____. 1950. Report on Puerto Rico: The Needlework Industry. Washington, D. C.: U. S. Government Printing Office.

Valle, Norma. 1974. "La primera en librarse." La hora (April 25-May 1): 12-43.

Weller, Robert H. 1968. "A Historical Analysis of Female Labor Participation in Puerto Rico." Socio-Economic Studies 17, no. 1 (March).

The partial commitment of women in productive spheres of the economy is paralleled in political life. The putative "passivity" of women and their identification with domestic roles is sustained by ideological stereotypes contained in the mass media and in the literature of the social sciences. Television programs and radio serials in Latin America dramatize a stereotyped model of women as domesticated, home-bound martyrs that contains and limits aspirations for self-determination. Whatever mobility they aspire to is through men, as depicted in Simplemente Maria and other radio and t. v. serials, as well as photonovelas. The church maintains an image of the passive Virgin, responding to the will of others, as the ideal of womenhood. The magazines and sections of the newspapers catering to women cultivate consumer appetites that spin a web of conformity to the desires of men and the class mobility they promise.

Papers by Morris Blachman, Jane Jaquette, Michele Mattelart and Vivian Mota reveal the techniques by which this stereotyped image of women is manipulated by the dominant male hierarchy to contain and distort political actions by women. A paper by Ximena Bunster provides a case study of a woman who escapes such control mechanisms in her political leadership of the Mapuche Indians to acquire land rights legislated by the Popular Unity Party.

Blachman criticizes North American and Latin American social scientists for their lack of concern with and data about women's political activities, as well as for the deficiencies in their models. Focusing on "interest group therapy," he asserts the pernicious effect of this type of liberal bourgeois ideology on the social sciences. This formulation, based on a model of society inherited from Locke and Hobbes, rejects any understanding of a power structure, whether defined by race or by class. By means of a functional equilibrium model, changes in society are explained as a response to particular events with no historical antecedents. The impact of this kind of theory, Blachman points out, is to interpret the rise of groups as a response to external manipulation, as in the case of the Brazilian feminist movement. Although the study of class structures is more generally accepted in Latin America than in North America, the study of sexism is relatively new; and Blachman calls for an analysis of its functioning within class-defined parameters as a priority for research.

Jane Jaquette's critique of North American political scientists points to the limited perspective on political behavior that focuses on participation by voting and, lacking a class analysis, assumes that the more participation, the better the political process. With their emphasis on formal channels of political participation, they ignore the considerable area of influence that women exert in informal settings. As a result

of limited and distorting perspectives, certain stereotypes of women
have persisted. The persistent notion of the "conservative female" survives despite a long tradition of radical activity in peasant revolts, mining strikes, and urban and rural guerilla movements. Jaquette suggests
that it is probably not that women are inherently more conservative; they
may just be less attracted to radical causes because of the failure of
radicals to recruit women and because of the threat to the family that
women feel is implied by the left in the attack on traditional values.
Like Blachman, she advocates that North American social scientists revise their notions of participation in terms of the class and cultural variables.

One of the basic conflicts between North American and Latin American women is that freedom is defined by the former as the ability to act
like men and to gain their rights and perquisites, while latter link female power to sex-role differentiation. Pointing to this difference in
outlook, Jaquette shows how these culturally differentiated spheres
give rise to different motivations and goals in the women's movements.

When women do emerge in political activities in Latin America, they
most frequently enter arenas that are extensions of domestic affairs,
while men predominate in affairs relating to industrialization, transport,
communications, and even outer space. Vivian Mota indicates how this
specialized role of women operates in the political life of the Dominican
Republic. Participation in public life is generally limited to women of the
elite classes, who tend to support the status quo. The alienation and
conservatism of the masses of women stem in part, she states, from
domination by males in the left-wing parties. The "Trujillista feminists"
achieved the vote through the patronage of the dictator, who saw in
them the possibility of broadening his support. By cultivating intragroup
rivalries among the women, he was able to contain and control their
movement. The women, consequently, were able to achieve limited
goals such as the right to vote, because they did not challenge the system.

The ability of right-wing political leaders to take advantage of the
political reserves of feminine support is seen in the case of Chile.
Mattelart shows how the opposition to Allende was able to manipulate
the discontent based on consumer shortages in a feminine movement
that threatened the Popular Unity government. Although the pots-and-
pans demonstration appeared to be organized by women, it served the
interests of all the bourgeiosie, who were desperate to attack the mobilized sectors of the working class and poblaciones. Mattelart shows the
prestige enjoyed by women in a kind of apolitical martriarchy in Chile
under Frei's Christian Democratic government as well as in the Allende
period. She documents how the ideologues of the Chilean opposition to
Allende contained the political emancipation of women by seeing to it
that protests were carried out in such a way as to preserve the myth of
their eternal feminine qualities. The politicization of women in the resistance to Allende was thus turned into an anti-liberation activity that
preserved middle- and upper-class privilege. This is demonstrated in

their role as mourners for the loss of democracy in Spetember 1970, and later confirmed in the march of the empty pots and the support that the wives of truckers and miners gave to the strike that crippled the government in its final months in power. The threat to feminine stereotypes in this emergence into public roles was overcome by stressing the traditionally feminine components of their demands as consumers and housewives.

Mattelart's analysis of the manipulative strategies used by the bourgeoisie to mobilize women, in times of crisis, to defend the traditional order, along with that of Mota, provide a model for understanding the co-optation of women's political participation. Conservative leaders, by masking class interests as the eternal feminine mystique, are able to direct and contain women's movements for liberation within parameters set by the dominant male hierarchy. Thus far there has been no comparable attempt by left-wing leaders either to win over or to direct feminist movements. Women working within left-wing political movements tend to do so in the context that men define, with feminist issues subordinate to class interest. Some of the reasons for this failure are the priority given to class-based over sex-based inequality in their programs, and the centering of their activity in public arenas, such as unions, political parties, and other places where women's participation is limited if not excluded. Another unstated factor might be that men of the left are less certain of their ability to control and contain an autonomous women's movement, since they neither influence nor control the army, the Church, the police force, private industrial firms, or other aspects of the coporate domain.

Ximena Bunster's paper, based on the autobiography of a Mapuche Indian woman who became a leader in the land seizures during the Popular Unity government, exposes the limited view of those who contain their understandings of liberation in a mold defined by a single class and cosmopolitan stratum. Llanquitray, a Mapuche woman who had worked as a servant, became a leader of her people when the tribe began to seek the land that Allende's government promised to distribute in the land reform. Because of the deep traditions of respect for women, she did not have to overcome the negative aspects both of an external and internal nature that women of the domain non-Indian culture are socialized to accept. She used her position as the daughter of a respected family in the tribe and as a woman in charge of preparing the feasts on the occasion of the meetings concerning the land issues to gain entry into the councils of tribal leaders and to organize a cohort of supporters. The collective basis of the Indian society mitigated both class and sexual distinctions, and as a consequence she was able to devote herself to collective goals in her political role.

The range of case materials indicates the need for a multi-faceted approach in the study of women's political activities set up to account for the class, ethnic, and regional variations that influence the kind and degree of mobilization. The rigid definition of the political sphere breaks down immediately when we concern ourselves with women as

well as men for we include informal and formal interaction, and "private"
or domestic arenas as well as public in the scope of our analytical
models.

12

FEMALE POLITICAL
PARTICIPATION IN
LATIN AMERICA
Jane Jaquette

It is no longer necessary to justify an essay that focuses on female participation nor to argue that the political participation of women is fundamental to the promotion and implementation of policies of development and resource management. The more interesting question, however, is whether this focus can tell us not only about women, though that itself is a worthy goal, but also about the concepts we use and the prescriptive biases that color our interpretations. Thus the purpose of this essay is to examine the data that exist on women and political participation in Latin America and, in doing so, to look at the limitations of some easily identifiable perspectives: the conventional North American political scientists' view of participation and the North American feminist view of sex-role stereotyping.

The standard view of participation, developed in the North American and European contexts, is that individuals "participate" by voting and/or by working for political parties and campaigns, by joining interest groups, and by trying to affect policy. Levels of participation are sometimes measured by the level of knowledge an individual has of how the system works or who holds public office. Feelings of personal "efficacy" are also taken as a measure of political participation. In all cases except the last-mentioned, these indexes depend on the existence of formal organizations and regularized procedures for choosing leaders and transferring power. For this reason they are able to give us only a partial picture of participation in Latin American politics, where elections are only one factor among many in the process whereby elites are closen and policy choices made, and where informal "clientele" networks rather than functional interest groups are the major actors in the political system.

Further, the conventional prescription for participation, in the North American view, is "more is better," providing participation remains within the established procedural boundaries. The assumption that all participation is good rests on the American experience (or myth) of a classless society; it does not allow for the possibility that the encouragement of participation by all may in fact result in the dominance

of a few, just as the theory of the market does not allow for the growth
of monopolies. In short, the North American view of participation does
not recognize the variable of class. Similarly, North American feminism
tends to regard the participation of upper-class women as good, without
dwelling on the question of whether it may oppress, or be used to co-
opt, lower-class women.

Finally the feminist sensitivity to sex-role differentiation and the
tendency to measure liberation by the degree to which women adopt male
roles may skew our perceptions of the real issue: female power. North
American experience to the contrary, it may be possible to maximize female power by retaining sex-role differences. The alternative seems
to have been to view Latin American women as backward or passive or
weak; and that image seems to me to be strongly contradicted by the
data we have on the personality traits of the Latin American woman.

A final caveat: this essay almost inevitably talks of the "Latin
American woman," which is incorrect. There is no such person. The
differences between women in Buenos Aires, Cuzco, and Santa Domingo
are as great as the similiarities that unite them; and even within national
borders there are rural/urban, ethnic, and class differences that defy
easy generalization. What makes this effort possible is that useful
generalizations have been made about Latin American political systems,
political culture, and attitudes toward women. These similarities are
basic to the discussion that follows.

THE CONTEXT OF FEMALE PARTICIPATION

We begin with the assumption that political participation in general
is one element of a complex of modernization variables, and that we will
find a relationship between suffrage, and levels of economic development and female literacy. We find that women are eligible to vote in
all the American republics. However, for the majority of Latin American
women, suffrage is a recently attained political right: the majority did
not gain that right until after World War II.

It is interesting to note that, of the countries with the highest per
capita GNP in 1958 (Venezuela, Argentina, and Chile), none granted
women the right to vote before World War II. Ecuador, with one of the
lowest levels of economic development by this measure, was the first
to grant women the vote; and Columbia, with a literacy rate for women
of over 70 percent, was one of the last to do so. The obvious lack of
a simple positive correlation among these factors would seem to indicate
the importance of historical experience within each nation. In this regard it should also be observed that the countries with the strongest
democratic traditions are not necessarily the first to grant female suffrage. Traditionally (prior to the coup in Chile), Uraguay, Costa Rica,
and Chile have been considered the most democratic of the Latin

American nations. Of those, only Uraguay granted women early suffrage; women in Costa Rica and Chile were denied the right to vote in presidential elections until 1949.

TABLE 12.1

Women's Suffrage, Per Capita GNP,
and Female Literacy in Latin America

Country	Year Suffrage Granted	1958 Per Capita GNP	Percent Female Literacy
Ecuador	1929	185	63.09
Brazil	1932	232	44.06
Uruguay	1932	493	91.49
Cuba	1934	—	80.03
El Salvador	1939	238	44.50
Dominican Republic	1942	251	62.43
Guatemala	1945	268	31.78
Panama	1945	370	94.20
Argentina	1947	552	89.75
Venezuela	1947	775	58.42
Chile	1949	391	82.40
Costa Rica	1949	353	83.96
Haiti	1950	251	8.45
Bolivia	1952	102	22.78
Mexico	1953	302	60.74
Honduras	1955	196	41.47
Nicaragua	1955	255	50.99
Peru	1955	183	68.53
Columbia	1957	233	71.13
Paraguay	1961	139	68.53

Sources: Chaney (1971), p. 509; Statistical Abstract of Latin America 1968, table 83 (at market prices); compiled by the author.

Literacy is not only a hypothetical factor that can be correlated with women's suffrage; it is, in many nations, a legal requirement to vote. Since the male literacy rate exceeds that of females in every country but Cuba and Uraguay, the literacy requirement works to the disadvantage of women. Yet even when they are eligible to vote, women tend to register at a lower rate than men. (Chaney 1973, p. 110).

The most detailed study of female political participation in Latin America that has been done thus far is Elsa Chaney's (1971; also see

Meneses 1934; Morton 1962). She argues that the traditional values
regulating female behavior, particularly the institution of the family,
are significant barriers to participation. One indicator of the degree to
which women escape the purely domestic sphere is the level of female
participation in the labor force. Only 13. 6 percent of the women in Latin
America are economically active, compared with 56. 9 percent of the
men. The world average is 27. 2 percent, with 21. 3 percent in the U. S.
and Canada, 28. 1 percent in Asia, and 41. 4 percent in the Soviet Union
(Chaney 1973, p. 131).

The fundamental argument behind these figures is that lower female
participation in the work force, as well as women's very limited visi-
bility in politics and other public spheres, is the result of the persistence of traditional values about the proper role of the female and the
continued strength of the family as an enforcer of sex-role stereotypes.
The issue is machismo:

> In the main, politics remains a "man's world" and male val-
> ues are regarded as appropriate. Role expectations in poli-
> tics, as in other spheres of action, require that a man must
> get his own way; he may brook no opposition nor share his
> power with anyone else. To do so would be to show traits
> of femininity, of submissiveness and of passivity (Stevens
> quoted in Chaney 1971, p. 74).

Nadia Youssef (1971) employs a different measure of economic activity of women—the percentage of women involved in non agricultural econc
economic activity—and argues that the relatively high percentages of
women engaged in such work in Latin America, in all sectors of the
economy from domestic work to trade, factory work, and professional
employment, indicates that Latin American women are relatively emancipated, that they are allowed to assume nontraditional, public roles.
The fact that many Latin American and Middle Eastern countries are at
the same level of economic development, yet female employment in the
nonagricultural sectors in Latin America is much higher in Latin America
than in the Middle East (see Table 12. 2), suggests that "female differences in participation cannot be attributed to variations in labor market
demands" (Chaney 1971, p. 433) but, rather, to the "cultural definition
within a society regarding the type of work deemed appropriate for
women" (Chaney 1971, p. 431). By that definition, Latin American
women are only slightly more "culturally oppressed" than their North
American and European counterparts, and are much more emancipated
than Middle Eastern women, with Asian women somewhere between.

Conclusions about cultural limitations on labor force participation
of course have implications for political participation as well. There
is more information available concerning attitudes of Latin American
women toward work than toward political participation. In general it
shows that women are surprisingly supportive of work outside the home,

as indicated in studies by Nora Kinzer (1973), Shirley Harkess (1973), Margo Smith (1973), and Armand and Michele Mattelart (1968). Attitudes toward female political participation seem much more ambivalent.

TABLE 12.2

Female Participation in Nonagricultural Economic Activities
in Selected Countries, Circa 1960

Country	Female Activity Rate (percent of female population 15 and older)
United Kingdom	40.4
United States	32.0
Sweden	31.4
Japan	28.8
Israel	22.0
Hungary	25.7
France	29.3
Argentina	22.4
Chile	21.8
Costa Rica	16.3
Jamaica	35.7
Peru	15.3
Panama	23.3
Ecuador	21.8
Mexico	12.0
Nicaragua	19.0
Indonesia	10.9
Thailand	11.8
India	8.8
Iraq	2.6
Egypt	3.5
Pakistan	2.3
Turkey	2.7

Source: Youssef (1971): table 1, 428-29.

Ninety percent of Harkess' sample (working-class and migrant barrios in Bogota) approve of a married woman with children working outside the home if she has a "responsible person" to care for them; and over 50 percent of the recent arrivals and 70 percent of the long-term residents approve even when child care provisions are not specified (Harkess 1973, p. 244). This would indicate that a key cultural barrier to female work force participation in the United States—the middle-class view that the mother should stay home with young children—is not a significant factor in Latin American cultural values, and that a woman's "freedom to work" increases with urban residence. * Urban/rural differences are a recurring pattern in the attitudinal data reviewed, with urban respondents significantly more favorable toward choices for women. It is possible to argue, however, that the rural/urban differential is better explained by class differences and by cultural lag. On the one hand, rural areas do not have strong upper and middle classes that can compete in size and self-confidence with their urban counterparts. Given that there has been a long tradition of female participation in agricultural labor, perhaps rural disapproval of women working is a result of rural, lower-class women reflecting what they believe to be urban middle-class values. Perhaps it also represents the desire of rural, lower-class women to escape poor working conditions and low-status labor. The fact that class and rural/urban residence are not independent variables should make us wary of the simplistic view that women in cities are more "feminist" because they are more "modern."

In another study that supports the view that Latin American urban attitudes favor women working, Cornelia Flora (1973, p. 74) examined women's magazine fiction and found that middle-class Latin American women were portrayed as jobholders (64 percent) with "meaningful" jobs more often than North American middle- or working-class women. The Mattelarts found 50-80 percent approval of a woman working outside the home in their urban sample of women, with least approval among the lowest class (MacLachan 1972, p. 69). Only 20 percent of rural women approved of such work. In all cases for which we have data, however, husbands disapprove of women working outside the home at significantly higher rates than do their wives (Mattelart 1968; Harkess 1973; Steinmann and Fox 1969).

The Mattelarts' study, which found such strong support for women working in the urban areas, also found a recognition in all classes in both rural and urban areas that the "situation of women in society has changed" (Mattelart 1968, p. 114). Yet 62 percent of their rural sample thought women should leave politics to men; 56 percent of their lower-class urban sample, but only 12 percent of the women in the

---

*Harkess found that class mobility—the striving for middle-class status—reduced the women's desire to work and approval of women working. Both the Mattelarts and Harkess found the strongest approval for work in their middle groups—for Harkess, the group intermediate between recent arrivals and long-term working-class women; for the Mattelarts, their clase media superior.

urban upper and middle classes, agreed (Mattelart 1968, p. 161). * Their survey also emphasized participation in organizations. Over 67 percent of rural women and 68 percent of urban lower-class women belong to no organizations (mothers' groups, neighborhood organizations, cooperatives), and an astounding 84 percent of the urban middle-class women declared no organizational memberships. Upper-class urban women were the most active of all groups, yet only 10 percent belonged to political parties (compared with 4 percent for the middle class) and 15 percent to religious groups (versus 6 percent for the middle class). The reasons most frequently given for lack of organizational activity were lack of time and unavailability of groups, even by women in the urban areas.

Perhaps it should be noted here that a bias toward group membership is not solely the property of the North American social scientist. It might also be expected from a "corporatist" view of Latin American politics, although North American experience focuses on the functional interest group, while corporatism emphasizes institutional groups and informal networks (see Newton 1970). The Latin American left also promotes organizational membership, particularly union membership, to represent the economic interests of the masses. The Mattelarts, in probing this issue, found that the majority of urban and rural women of all classes in Chile believed they should organize at the neighborhood level, and 40-90 percent of the women interviewed believed they should organize themselves "at the level of their work" (Mattelart 1968, pp. 149, 153), indicating more than token response to this ideal, although they were often unable to provide any reasons for doing so. They conclude that even the favored urban women "lacks consciousness of her political role" (Mattelart 1968, p. 158) and that, for many, politics is seen as a "waste of time."

In a more conventional survey done in Mexico, William Blough (1972, p. 206) found that 25 percent of the women in his sample, compared with 55 percent of the men, "talked about politics at least occasionally." Twenty-three percent of the men, but only 8 percent of the women, were or had been members of a political party. Only 4 percent of the women had tried to "influence a law." The comparable figure for men was 16 percent.

Similarly, Steffan Schmidt's (1973, p. 17) examination of Colombian survey data found that women were less informed that men about political leaders and were less interested in becoming active in local politics (males, 19.2 percent; females, 13.7 percent). In Bogota, Harkess (1973, p. 240) found that only 16 percent of her female sample would vote for a woman as head of the barrio junta when she was

---

*On the whole, however, the change was interpreted in terms of freedoms and opportunities by urban middle- and upper-class women and in terms of material comforts by rural and urban lower-class women.

described as "equally qualified" as her male opponent. But the figure
jumped to 78 percent when the woman was presented as "better educated" than the man.

From this very scarce data it seems that Latin women are less restricted by culture in choosing to work outside the home than North
American women, if attitudes are measured, but that female political
participation is less clearly favored. Rural/urban, and especially class,
differences are significant in determining attitudes toward work and,
more generally, toward participation.

VOTING AND FEMALE POLITICAL BELIEFS

Figures on the level of female voting participation vary, but almost
all indicate that women vote less often than men. In Schmidt's data
(1973, p. 15), women's votes average about 40 percent of the total vote
in Colombia from 1957 to 1968; Chaney's figures for Peru and Chile
(1971, p. 281) show that only 33 percent of the women in Peru are registered to vote, compared with 57 percent of the men. In Chile the
figures are 61 percent and 78 percent respectively. Blough's study of
Mexican women finds that although 82 percent of the males sampled
had voted in the 1958 presidential election (the first in which women
could vote), only 48 percent of the women had done so.

There is some data to indicate that, as in the United States, female
voting rates increase over time and in response to urbanization. In Argentina, for example, Paul H. Lewis (1971, p. 428) found that 83.7
percent of the women voted in the 1965 Congressional elections, compared with 82.7 percent of the for men. Thus there is some evidence
that the female voting rate may be amenable to change within a relatively short period and that, as Evelyne Sullerot (1971, p. 226) has
observed, the issue of female representation and not voting will be the
major problem for Latin American as well as for other Third World women.

Data on women's political attitudes and evidence concerning the
impact of female voting are very rare, although there is much impressionistic material. The most commonly held view of women as political participants is that they are more conservative than men. Alleged dependence of women on the Church was used to deny them the franchise in
Mexico and Chile (Morton 1962; Chaney 1971). It is significant that
the vote was given to women in Colombia under the conservative Frente
Nacional; class restrictions on voting and women's "natural" conservatism may have played a role in Colombia comparable with that suggested
by the suffragists' "Southern strategy" in the United States (Kraditor
1971). In Peru and Argentina, the franchise was extended to women by
"populist" leaders whose regimes were based on increasing participation within the traditional social framework rather than on radical struc-
tual and institutional change. More recently, female conservatism has
received considerable attention because of the role played by women in

bringing down the radical government of Salvador Allende in Chile. An
earlier precedent may be found in the women's marches that accompanied
the fall of Joao Goulart and the establishment of a repressive military
regime in Brazil in 1964.

The conservative female stereotype is countered by a long tradition
of radical political activity on the part of women, including participation
in peasant revolts (Neira 1968), in mining strikes (Nash 1973), and in
rural and urban guerrilla movements. (Jaquette 1973b). These contrasts
may only serve to illustrate the impossibility of generalizing about
women in Latin America, even when the classic sociological variables
of class and rural/urban differences are taken into account.

Survey and voting data, while extremely sketchy, tend to give only
marginal support to the impressionistic view of female conservatism.
In Mexico, where a series of revolutionary governments denied women
the vote, first on the basis of religious ties and then for fear they would
support the conservative opposition party (PAN), Blough (1972, p. 217)
found that church attendance had little effect on attitudes of men and
women, and that only a slightly higher percentage of women (16 percent,
versus 13 percent of the men) identified with the PAN, while 84 percent
of the men and 80 percent of the women identified with the official party
of the Revolution, the PRI. The equation of PRI support with radicalism
and support for PAN with conservatism is difficult to sustain, however,
since a vote for the PAN represents an opposition vote to Mexico's
"single party," the PRI, and thus may be interpreted as a "radical" alternative. Support for PAN is greater in urban areas and among individuals with a higher education, regardless of sex.

In Argentina, Lewis' study of female voting (1971) shows women
more likely to vote for conservative parties and less likely to vote for
radical parties at every class level, with markedly disproportionate
female support for the "confessional" Christian Democrats. Yet any
evaluation of female conservatism depends on the position assigned
to the UCRP, which accounted for three-fourths of the female "status
quo" vote and for the 3 percent difference between males and females
in that category (see Table 12.3). The case can probably be made that
women are less radical than men rather than more conservative, a fact
that seems ironic, given the efforts made by radical parties in Argentina
and elsewhere to recruit women and develop feminist programs (see
Meneses 1934; Chaney 1974; Jaquette 1973b).

One factor that may affect female resistance to "radical structural
change" may be the attachment of women to the institution of the family.
The argument can be made that the family reinforces female "passivity"
and curbs the activity of women outside the home. It is less often noted
that women themselves have a stake in the family as a strong institution
in which they have power (socialization of children, the enforcement of
social sanctions against women and men who deviate from accepted behavior patterns, and the preservation of moral and spiritual values that
are still a part of the Latin American cultural heritage.)

TABLE 12.3

Male and Female Voting, in Argentina, by Party Category, 1965

Parties	Male	Female
Revolutionary parties (Orthodox Peronists, neo-Peronists, Socialists)	43.5	38.9
Reformist parties (UCRI/MID, Christian Democrats)	12.6	13.9
Status quo parties (UCRP, Progressive Democrats, UDELPA, Conservatives)	37.3	40.7

Source: Lewis (1971), Table 3, p. 432.

The importance of the Latin American family as an effective agent of social control makes it the perennial subject of attack by radical political movements promoting change. Yet by opposing the family, these movements shift the focus of power and activity from the private, informal sphere, where women have maintained considerable influence, to the public, formal sphere, where males dominate. It is not surprising, then, that so many female respondents, both political and economic leaders and "followers" (survey respondents) have stated that their roles as wives and mothers are of primary importance to them (Kinzer 1973; MacLachlan 1972). What is lamentable, perhaps, is the linkage between support for the family and support for other conservative values.

Again, class is a factor. The institution of the family is stronger in the upper and middle classes, where the framed wedding picture is a necessary part of the furniture, a sign to distinguish the legally married women from those with lower status, who are more likely to be in common-law unions. Thus defense of the family can become defense of a class position. This produces both conflicts and paradoxes. The "rational" defense of the family may be consistent with a rational defense of class for the upper-class woman, but this is less so the farther down the social scale you go. For women in the lower classes, acquisition of middle-class status often depends on broad institutional changes that threaten upper-class interest. There is also the anomaly of the lower-class women who is more "liberated" than her middle-class counterpart, who has more options and more independence from men (as Oscar Lewis' Five Families inadvertently illustrates). Yet this "liberation" is rarely desired by the individual, who wants nothing more than to attain the middle-class status of respectable marriage. Then,

too, there is the tragedy of the almost inverse relationship (except at
the very top) between class position and the satisfaction of sexual needs.

In one of the few surveys to deal with the changing roles of
women, the Mattelarts found that although over 40 percent of their rural
sample and over 80 percent of their urban respondents recognized the
positive effects of the change in the status of women in Chile, which
they in terms of greater physical and psychological freedom—"Now I go
out more" and "Now I go where I want to go"—an average of 16 percent
of the rural sample and 24 percent of the urban sample (excluding upper-
class women) saw negative effects. Their complaints focused on male/
female relations, with comments like "Men are no longer respectful,"
the observation that men are more often drunk and that they "keep women
and no longer get married" (Mattelart 1968, p. 169). The Mattelarts'
data show that women are less likely than men to favor the liberalization
of divorce laws and to view the increasing incidence of divorce as a sign
of "moral disintegration." This attitude was specifically characteristic
of women in the urban lower class, those most affected by middle-class
aspirations (Mattelart 1968, p. 105). In a similar vein, Julio Mafud
(1966, p. 75) has observed that the "sexual revolution" in Argentina
leaves women "deeply ambivalent," caught in the conflict between the
desire for independence and the claims of the traditional family structure.

The effects of the female orientation toward the family may be viewed from yet another standpoint—the way in which women socialize their
children toward politics. Kenneth Langton (1969, p. 75) found that in
Jamaican families, as in American ones, women tend to be the transmitters of political identification (contrary to the conventional view of
women as submissive within the family in political matters), but that
in families headed by women, "males are not as politically interested
and efficacious, and are less likely to engage in political activity.
. . ." Thus, in the absence of a father figure, the woman appears to
impose depoliticization on male children; however, the presence of the
father does not have a positive effect on the politicization of daughters.
(See also Aviel 1974.)

Female alienation is a factor touched upon in a number of surveys,
but its implications for participation and "conservatism" are rarely explored. Schmidt (1973, p. 16) reports that women have less trust in
others than do men. The Mattelarts found rural and lower-class urban
men were much more likely than women in the same groups to agree
with the observation that "women are happier today than they used to
be," although the results were reversed for urban middle- and upper-
class respondents. Class differences in responses may indicate that
although general values may have changed, conditions of life remain
unchanged for lower-class women or are perceived as poor relative to
expectations of change. It might also be argued that a gap between
ideals and reality may have a politically radicalizing effect on lower-
class women if there were any suitable political movement to crystallize those feelings. It is equally clear that new views of women's

role have been absorbed into upper- and middle-class attitudes without bringing about any changes in the class structure itself.

It might be assumed that urbanization and education would reduce female alienation, but this is not fully borne out by the data. Although feminist attitudes may be more prevalent as one moves up the class ladder, greater female pessimism survives. Blough (1972, p. 215) found that Mexican women remain more pessimistic than men and are more likely to vote against the regime as education increases. A study done in 1969 in Colombia found that women with more education were less likely to be satisfied about prospects for the future than were women at lower educational levels (Schmidt 1973, p. 22).

Finally, it should be asked whether women participate less, not because they are "lesser men," but because they simply find politics irrelevant to their needs. The Mattelarts (1968, p. 198) found that at all class levels in Chile, the most important problem for women was their economic situation: lack of money, the high cost of living, or (in the case of rural women) poor working conditions. The second most important problem was marriage. Given the salience of economic and family-related problems to most women, it is not clear what the political system in its current form has to offer them. It is interesting that the Mattelarts' attempt to translate immediate concerns into ideological issues (asking women to respond to questions about the "social integration of women" and "awareness of class barriers") did not in general provoke a positive response, although urban upper- and middle-class women did see these issues as important more often than rural and lower-class women did.

CLASS AS A VARIABLE

The preceding discussion indicates that class, a realtively unimportant variable to most North American researchers, who tend to focus more heavily on family and education as determinants of political attitudes, * may be extremely significant in the Latin American context, while sex is a secondary variable. Almost all of the Mattelart data show a strong dichotomy between the attitudes of rural and urban lower-class women, on the one hand, and urban middle- and upper-class women, on the other. The Harkess data on women in Bogota indicate that class mobility may also be significant: contrary to the expectation that residency in the urban area would have a modernizing effect on

---

*Sidney Verba and Norman H. Nie (1972, p. 340), however, argue that "social status has a closer relationship to political participation in the United States than all but one of the nine other countries for which it was possible to obtain data . . . ."

attitudes, Harkess found more similarity between long-term residents and recent arrivals than among the intermediate group. She concludes (1973, p. 250):

> Whether the issue is politics, education, work or family power, the two groups are more similar than they are dissimilar. Their expressed attitudes may be similar because the goals and patterns of their lives are alike. The very poor recent arrivals feel economically insecure while the long-term resident lower middle class feels socially insecure. Both groups experience a relative deprivation that full fledged working class or middle class families do not. [The latter] seek status within a world that they know.

While class can have either a conservatizing or a radicalizing influence, radicalization seems to require special conditions, particularly interaction with a homogeneous group in which class consciousness is already present. The mobile world of the urban migrant, and the exposure of women in particular to middle- and upper-class standards of consumption and behavior through employment in the domestic and service sectors, may have a strong co-optive effect, as Vania Bambirra has observed with regard to the "women's press" (1972, p. 79):

> The basic characteristic of the women's press is that it is directed towards the concerns of bourgeois and petty bourgeois women—the latest fashions, culinary recipes, wallpaper, and the routine, mediocre dramas of those who have time to live them. But this women's press also reaches working class women. It reaches them and serves to alienate them from their real world, the world of their class. It imposes upon them the values of the dominant classes, makes them aspire to the bourgeois way of life.

If we extend this view, we see that the question of participation is not simply one of quantity, to be gauged by measures of voting and participation in organizations that in turn correlate with other measures of "modernization." Political acts such as voting, party membership, or even marching in the streets may serve the purpose of ratifying or achieving a certain class membership or status, rather like owning a television set or driving a car. In some cases, even nonparticipation can become (or can be interpreted as) a political act, a refusal to participate in the existing system that is characterized by extreme class differences and the exploitation of one class by another. * The North American view that all participation is good must be reinterpreted in the light of class conflict.

---

*In his "Message to Women" Camillo Torres argued: "The vote is a new form of exploitation which the oligarchy invented. . ." (cited in

Once the problem is defined in this way—and the fact that upper- and middle-class Latin American women are "freer" to participate in public life than North American women because of the availability of domestic help is an irony that draws attention to possible class conflicts inherent in the North American feminist movement—there is a limited range of possible approaches. On the one hand there is the radical solution of organizing women and men into a revolutionary movement to overthrow the system of class domination and perhaps bring into question the material basis of status. On the other hand there is the liberal "good deeds" approach of exhorting upper- and middle-class women to be aware of the class basis of their privileges and freedoms, an attempt that, if successful, will result in either charity or reformism.

An alternative to the above might center on the organization of women based on a conscious principle, either feminist (as has been the North American experience) or at the workplace. The Latin American left's critique of U. S. feminism centers on its individualism and its "lack of social objective." As the Mattelarts write (1968, p. 211; emphasis added):

> The liberal ideology of emancipation does not imply
> directly any social objective. In a revolutionary society,
> by contrast, emancipation becomes an instrument of con-
> sciousness (concientizacion). It is the principle of mobil-
> ization itself which implies solidarity and a cohesion
> which opposes the individualism of the liberal movement.
> Revolutionary emancipation will not isolate the mass of
> women from the rest of society, but will make them a pres-
> sure group in the transformation of structures and attitudes
> of the old society. For this reason it will not produce a
> degeneration of the movement into feminism.

Thus any tendency on the part of North American feminists to view their movement as truly and uniquely revolutionary because it attacks male domination, which is at the root of all domination (as Kate Millet and Shulamith Firestone have argued), will be resisted by Latin American radicals. It is not clear whether these differences arise from a different set of priorities (economic rather than social issues) or a desire to avoid a movement that, however radical it may be on its own terms, has been defined as "white, middle class" and "North American," or whether they are basic and lasting differences that will persist because the economic conditions that give rise to class exploitation are

---

Schmidt 1973, p. 17). Latin America has a long tradition of casting blank ballots as a protest. Apathy is hard to measure, since voting and valid electoral registration cards are identification documents that must be shown for the holder to receive social security and other benefits, and are used as identification for the police.

more intense than sexual domination. Nor is it clear that North American women can ignore those economic conditions, any more than they can ignore the economic situation of black women in the United States. The Cuban revolutionary example only serves to illustrate how essential the resolution of class issues is to the focus on women's issues. In that context it is significant that many of the issues of sex stereotyping, which are at the heart of North American feminism, have been raised (see Cuba Review 1974).

THE INSTITUTIONAL BIAS OF NORTH AMERICAN POLITICAL ANALYSIS

The most obvious problem in the attempt to measure female political participation by studying voting and organizational membership is the fact that much of Latin American politics occurs outside conventional political institutions. While female suffrage in many of the countries for which we have data has coincided with recent periods of relatively open, "democratic" politics, the military coups in the 1960s serve to remind us that democratic government is not a permanent pattern. Indeed, many political scientists have taken the position that electoral politics when they occur, are only one element of a much broader spectrum of more or less legitimate political activity, including strikes, coups, demonstrations, and behind-the-scenes bargaining between the government, however constituted, and key groups.

Thus any attempt to gauge female participation and/or political influence that concentrates on conventional institutions is doomed to superficiality. What makes it necessary to rely on this kind of data, however, is the nearly total lack of measures or indicators of participation in these extra-institutional spheres, a lack that limits our ability to analyze all groups in the polity, not only women. To do full justice to this expanded notion of the political, we would need indexes of female participation in the groups or classes that "count," their role in informal networks of communication and influence, their participation in clientele linkages, and their role in strike activities, urban land seizures, and barrio politics.

Preliminary attempts to judge the probable level of female participation in these areas yield contradictory interpretations. On the one hand, if organizational membership (in unions, barrio associations, and occupational pressure groups) is in some sense a surrogate measure for extra-institutional or nonconventional participation by women, then it would seem that women are at least as disadvantaged here as they are in more formal political institutions, although conclusions to this effect must surely depend on future study. If, on the other hand, access to informal communication networks is central to power, then there is some reason to believe that women may play a major role and be recipients of "value allocations" as often as, or perhaps more often than,

men. I know of no research on "clientelism" or "corporatism" in Latin
America that has been directed to the question of female participation,
although data already gathered on women in labor unions might be reex-
amined and new questions might be asked about the relevance of data
on women in the family.

Another significant bias of the institutional participation research
is its tendency to assume that as modernization occurs, female participation will automatically increase. Bernard Rosen and Anita La Raia's
study of modernization of women in Brazil offers a rather classic example
of this type of reasoning (1972, pp. 353-54):

> The position that industrialization encourages new atti-
> tudes and behavior stresses the experiences women have in
> industrial society which enhance their competence and feel-
> ings of self respect, and alter their relationships with
> others—particularly other family members. It is said that the
> omnipresent mass media which seem to penetrate every nook
> and cranny of industrial society inform as well as entertain
> women, thus broadening their horizons. Everyday experiences
> on city streets and in stores and shops sharpen their faculties
> and sensitize them to the importance of competence and
> achievement. The opportunities for employment outside of
> the home . . . enrich them intellectually as well as finan-
> cially. Women in industrial societies, then, have the chance
> to acquire personal resources. . . .

It does not take the consciousness of a Vania Bambirra to note the
equation of modernization with capitalist values, nor should the bias
against the family as the carrier of traditional values go unobserved.
Nonetheless, the major criticism of this approach is the equation of
modernization with expanded freedoms and resources for women. There
is a growing body of literature that indicates that women lose power
as urbanization and industrialization proceed; and studies of African
women (Van Allen 1974; Boserup 1970) and of Latin American peasant
women suggest that women may have more political and economic power
in the traditional sector than in the modern, as indicated by female control of marketplaces in Ghana and Bolivia.

The absorption of women into urban life, where males dominate
both economic and political activity, may provide yet another case of
"the development of underdevelopment," exacerbated by the adoption
of North American and Western European technology and entrepreneurial
styles that are male-dominated. As Heleieth Saffioti has written in reference to Brazil, under a capitalist system where it is necessary to restrict the number of workers, sex becomes "a prior and concomitant
filter to the process of competition, with the objective of restricting
the number of persons who may, legitimately, participate." The desig-
nation "female" justifies the marginalization of enormous numbers of
women from the structure of classes on the basis of her role in

reproduction and socialization and by virtue of the "immaturity" that society traditionally attributes to them (Saffioti 1969, p. 387). In effect, it is not the feminine qualities of women that make it possible to exclude them; rather, like blacks in the United States, they are "stigmatized"—readily identifiable and thus readily barred from access (see Rogowski and Wasserspring 1971).

Finally, the impact of the "modernization of the family" on female participation may have effects different from those conventionally hypothesized. On the one hand, the tendency to develop a nuclear family structure as a result of geographical mobility, and perhaps of imitation of the North American pattern, increases the Latin American women's ability to make certain kinds of choices; but this may occur at the price of power in other spheres. She can, if "modernized," take a job, increase her education, expand her contacts with men—but at the potential cost of sources of informal power available to her in the extended family. This is surely one of the reasons for the "ambivalence" noted by the Mattelarts and Mafud. On the opposite end of the social scale, the imitation of middle-class values, such as the favoring of marriage over consensual unions, may actually reduce female leverage and options vis-a-vis males and the outside world.

REPRESENTATION AND THE ISSUE OF SEX-ROLE DIFFERENTIATION

As Maurice Duverger noted in his 1953 study of women in politics, women have increasingly achieved more equal participation as voters, but they have yet to make real progress in being elected or appointed to office. This is true not only in Latin America, where women are less than 2 percent of the total membership of legislatures (Chaney 1971, p. 102), but also in the United States and most of Europe where less than 5 percent of the national legislative offices are held by women. This compares with around 15 percent in the Scandinavian countries and between 15 and 20 percent in the Socialist countries, which have an ideological commitment to female representation.

Elsa Chaney's study of women in politics in Chile and Peru looks at a national sample of women in bureaucratic posts and a second group of women elected officials at the municipal level in the capital cities of Lima and Santiago. (In Chile, women were 7.9 percent of the regidores in 1968; in Peru 4.7 percent of the concejales were women.) A "demographic profile" of women political leaders in both countries found many similarities: women leaders came from the middle or upper classes; had had university training, often in the "masculine" professions of law and engineering; and usually were natives of the capital (that is, neither migrants nor from the provincial upper class). They tended to be older than their female colleagues in other professions and and were more likely to be married (Chaney 1973, pp. 121-22) and to have smaller families (Chaney 1971, p. 372).

One of the conclusions of Chaney's study is that upper- and middle-class women are freer to enter politics for the same reasons that they are freer to enter the professions in general. The availability of servants means that the Latin American woman can choose to have both a career and a family. The fact that the capital city is usually the largest and most economically advanced city means that it is less likely that women will have to force husbands and family to leave their jobs and personal ties to "go to Washington." Further, among these classes, as both Kinzer's (1973) and Youssef's (1973) data show, there is no stigma attached to a professional career for the woman, rather, there may be considerable reward in terms of family expectations (of the father, not the husband), status, and even a sense of social duty or noblesse oblige.

In analyzing the attitudes and political style of female leaders, Chaney concluded that these women carry their domestic roles over into politics. They work in the "feminine" fields of education, health, and social welfare rather than in finance, labor relations, or the foreign ministry; and they tend to legitimize their participation as an extension of their duties as amas or dueñas de casa (terms for which the English word "housewife" is a weak translation). Thus the female politician becomes the supermother, and her approach to politics is both idealistic and centered on immediate social concerns. "If I were President," a female Chilean party leader said (Chaney 1973, p. 105):

> I would . . . do my best to budget so that everything
> essential would be covered. The housewife must feed her
> family and house them, she has to see to their education
> and to their health. These things are, to my mind, the most
> urgent problems facing Chile at the present moment.

To the North American mind, the notion of the housewife-President calls up a rather horrifying image of misplaced female energies, of a woman with dustmop in hand, reducing major policy decisions to the mundane level of what to have for dinner. It flies in the face of our basic feminist tenet that the perpetuation of sex-role stereotypes is the cause of female oppression in the male-dominated worlds of politics and employment. Chaney (1971, p. 18) levels a more serious charge: that the women politicians lack long-range, sophisticated political vision:

> Their prescriptions for development very often do not
> go beyond what Chileans call "mejoras"—little improve-
> ments to relieve the most pressing and immediate problems
> . . . suggested without any interest or preoccupation about
> the structures of the economy and society which cause such
> conditions. Women in the survey consistently revealed a
> lack of ability to conceptualize on a macro-societal level.

This interpretation is parallel to the description of women voters in Campbell et al. (1960): that women seem unable to "conceptualize" about politics and that they respond to the (less sophisticated) personality factors rather than to issues in a campaign. Without comparable data on male politicians in Chile, we have no way of knowing whether men take "macro-societal" views of political problems or whether such views, if taken, are associated with effective responses to those problems—as the criticism of women implies they are. Can we distinguish "macro-societal" reasoning from sterile ideological positions? In favor of women leaders, it might be noted that the kinds of issues that concern them are exactly those issues of major importance in developing countries and that are becoming key issues in industrialized nations as well, as resource scarcity is recognized as a limit to growth. Whether you take the functionalist or the neo-Marxist view, the "quality of life" issues such as health care, child care, and land use planning are critical issues, even if less prestigious than foreign affairs and labor relations. This is even more the case in countries where the government, rather than the "free market." must take the responsibility for allocating these benefits.

If we continue to pursue the possible benefits of sex-role differentiation, it may also be possible to justify the supermother approach to politics within Latin American cultural and institutional parameters. As noted earlier, the fact that the woman plays a much more powerful role in the family, which is itself a more powerful institution than the family in the U.S., means that women have a stake in maintaining the family and that the rejection of standards of "femininity" and "masculinity" may mean real loss of power (Jaquette 1973). The carry-over of sex roles into the public sphere is noted more positively by Chilean anthropologist Ximena Bunster (quoted in Chaney 1973, p. 104):

> What happens is that we extend matrimonial roles to work. . . . [W]e tend to treat the man as a mother would and not as if he were the husband, the lover or the colleague. The Chilean is a mama who approves, sanctions, corrects, quite different from the North American environment where professional relations are marked by the sense of competition.

In the Latin American cultural milieu, "mother power" is accepted as legitimate by males and females alike. By contrast, in the North American "competitive" milieu, such resources are depreciated by being dismissed by males and females as sentimental, emotional, and inappropriate. In the male world, to be called "feminine" is to be dismissed as a real contender for power.

An interesting ramification of the notion of supermother that has not yet been explored is the hypothesis that men, too, may be extending their family-designated roles into the political sphere, a modern adaptation of Jean Bodin's view that the polity is the family writ large. But in

contrast with Bodin, societal legitimacy and social norms would be enforced by the mother, backed by the religious power of the Virgin. If
that is the case, the North American view of Latin American politics
as not quite believable may be correct and not merely ethnocentric.
Public politics are only "cockfights," for show (this hypothesis might
reason); the real issues of power are being decided elsewhere. At this
point the neo-Marxists would agree: "elsewhere" is New York and Washington. Perhaps we should look as well to the female sphere.

The legitimacy of "feminine" resources in the political arena may
provide an explanation for the spectacular success of certain female
politicians in Latin America who have gained national and even international prominence. Eva Peron of Argentina is the most obvious example, but Maria Eugenia Rojas de Morena of Colombia and Maria Delgado
de Odria of Peru also come to mind. While all three of these women
gained access to politics through marriage or kinship ties with male
politicians, each was successful in her own right. All share a similar
style, that of the populist patrona parlaying personal charisma and
patronage to create bases of support among the urban poor. All three
are women of power: the standard biography of Eva Peron in English is
subtitled The Lady with the Whip; and in Colombia, Maria Eugenia is
referred to as "muy macha" (Schmidt 1973, p. 10). From Betsy Ross to
Margaret Chase Smith, women leaders have scrupulously avoided an
image of masculine power in U.S. politics. Women who failed to do
so—Eleanor Roosevelt, perhaps, and Shirley Chisholm—have been pun-
ished rather than rewarded for their audacity.

Finally, it can be argued that in a political system or a society
organized around corporatist principles—that is, based on the representation of recognized groups rather than individuals—sex differentiation
may be quite consistent with the rational pursuit of power. * Political
parties commonly have "women's sectors" that do more than supervise
campaign mailings, and women are commonly considered one of the
groups toward which government policy and group-specific outputs may
be directed. The fact that corporatism begins by positing differences
among individuals rather than by assuming "equality" among them may
enhance the possibilities of social justice and representativeness rather
than subjecting sets of individuals who do not fit the standard norm
to the limbo of what Robert Paul Wolff and others (1969) have described
as "pure tolerance."

The preceding discussion has been guided by the assumption that
female power, rather than the elimination of sex-role differences,
should be the criterion for judging the degree of oppression of women
and for measuring the female "good." This is not to deny that, at least
in the North American context, female power and the elimination of

---

*I am indebted to Jamie Fellner (History Department, Stanford
University) for reminding me of the linkage between corporatism and
the integration of women as a group.

sex-role differences are inextricably linked. To many women in the United States, freedom has come to mean the freedom to act like men and to gain the rights and perquisites that male status brings. Such a demand is no less a demand for structural change than the demand made by Latin Americans that the class structure be overthrown. Both are revolutionary.

However, if, in her own culture, the Latin American woman denies the relevance of this formulation to her situation, we should not be quick to take this as further evidence of the degree to which Latin American women are backward and oppressed. The liberation of the Latin American woman cannot come out of a wholesale adoption of foreign models and alien goals. Nor can we forget that the encouragement of women as political participants may have a result different from the one we expect: it may further class differences and more firmly fix upper- and middle-class values. In a game where some of the players win all of the time, not all participation is progress.

In the end, I do not think this is an appeal for moral relativism. It is, rather, a warning that legitimate goals, such as the increase of female power and freedom, may take different institutional forms and be subject to restraints different from those of the North American experience. Consciousness and participation are worthy goals, but true consciousness can be created only out of each individual's understanding of her own situation.

REFERENCES

Aviel, Jo Ann. 1974. "Changing the Political Role of Women." In Women in Politics, ed. Jane Jaquette. New York: John Wiley.

Bambirra, Vania. 1972. "Women's Liberation and Class Struggle." Punto Final (Chile), February 15. Translation in Review of Radical Political Economy 4.

Blough, William S. "Political Attitudes of Mexican Women."

Boserup, Ester. 1970, Woman's Role in Economic Development. London: St. Martin's Press.

Campbell, Angus, et al. 1960. The American Voter. New York: John Wiley.

Chaney, Elsa M. 1971. "Women in Latin American Politics: The Case of Peru and Chile." Ph.D. dissertation, University of Wisconsin.

_____. 1973. "Women in Latin American Politics: The Case of Peru and Chile." In Female and Male in Latin America, ed. Ann Pescatello. Pittsburgh: University of Pittsburgh Press.

_____. 1974. "Women in Allende's Chile." In Women in Politics, ed. Jane Jaquette. New York: John Wiley.

Cuba Review. 1974. "Women in Transition." 4.

Flora, Cornelia Butler. 1973. "The Passive Female and Social Change: A Cross-Cultural Comparison of Women's Magazine Fiction." In Female and Male in Latin America, ed. Ann Pescatello. Pittsburgh: University of Pittsburgh Press.

Harkess, Shirley J. 1973. "The Pursuit of an Ideal: Migration, Social Class, and Women's Roles in Bogota, Colombia." In Female and Male in Latin America, ed. Ann Pescatello, pp. 231-54. Pittsburgh: University of Pittsburgh Press.

Jaquette, Jane S. 1973a. "Literary Archetypes and Female Role Alternatives: The Woman and the Novel in Latin America." In Female and Male in Latin America, ed. Ann Pescatello, pp. 3-28. Pittsburgh: University of Pittsburgh Press.

_____. 1973b. "Women in Revolutionary Movements in Latin America." Journal of Marriage and the Family 35 (May).

_____, ed. 1974. Women in Politics. New York: John Wiley.

Kinzer, Nora Scott. 1973. "Women Professionals in Buenos Aires." In Female and Male in Latin America, ed. Ann Pescatello, pp. 159-90. Pittsburgh, University of Pittsburgh Press.

Kraditor, Aileen S. 1971. The Ideas of the Woman Suffrage Movement, 1890-1920. Garden City, N.Y.: Doubleday-Anchor Books.

Langton, Kenneth P. 1969. Political Socialization. New York: Oxford University Press.

Lewis, Paul H. 1971. "The Female Vote in Argentina, 1958-1965." Comparative Political Studies (January).

MacLachan, Colin. 1972. "The Feminine Mystique in Brazil." Proceedings of the Pacific Coast Council on Latin American Studies. Report of a conference held in Monterey, California, October 26-28, 1972.

Mafud, Julio. 1966. La revolucion sexual argentina. Buenos Aires: Editorial Americalee.

Mattelart, Armand, and Michele Mattelart. 1968. La mujer chilena en una nueva sociedad. Santiago: Editorial del Pacifico.

Meneses, Romulo. 1934. Aprismo femenino peruano. Lima: Ediciones Atahualpa.

Morton, Ward M. 1962. Woman Suffrage in Mexico. Gainesville: University of Florida Press.

Nash, June. 1973. "Women in the Mining Communities of Bolivia." Paper presented for the IX International Congress of Anthropological and Ethnological Sciences, Chicago, August 28-30, 1973.

Neira, Hugo. 1968. Cuzco: Tierra o muerte.

Newton, Ronald C. 1970. "On 'Functional Groups,' 'Fragmentation,' and 'Pluralism' in Spanish American Political Society." Hispanic American Historical Review 50: 1-29.

Pescatello, Ann, ed. 1973. Female and Male in Latin America. Pittsburgh: University of Pittsburgh Press.

Rogowski, Ronald, and Lois Wasserspring. 1971. "Does Political Development Exist? Corporatism in Old and New Societies." Sage Professional Paper II (24).

Rosen, Bernard C., and Anita La Raia. 1972. "Modernity in Women: An Index of Social Change in Brazil." Journal of Marriage and the Family 34 (May).

Saffioti, Heleieth Iara Bongiovani. 1969. A mulher na sociedada de classes. Sao Paulo: Ed. 4 Artes.

Schmidt, Steffan. 1973. "Woman in Colombia: Attitudes and Future Perspectives in the Political System." Paper presented at the annual meeting of the Society of Applied Anthropology, Tucson, Arizona, April 1973.

Smith, Margo L. 1973. "Domestic Service as a Channel of Upward Mobility for the Lower Class Woman: The Lima Case." In Female and Male in Latin America, ed. Ann Pescatello, pp. 191-208. Pittsburgh: University of Pittsburgh Press.

Steinmann, Anne, and David J. Fox. 1969. "Specific Areas of Agreement and Conflict in Women's Self-Perception and Their Perception of

Men's Ideal Woman in South American Urban Communities and Urban Communities in the United States." Journal of Marriage and the Family 31:281-89.

Sullerot, Evelyne. 1971. Woman, Society and Change. World University Library.

Van Allen, Judith. 1974. "Memsahib, Militante and Femme Libre: Political and Apolitical Styles of Modern African Women." In Women in Politics, ed. Jane Jaquette, New York: John Wiley.

Verba, Sidney, and Norman H. Nie. 1972. Participation in America. New York: Harper and Row.

Wolff, Robert Paul, et al. 1969. The Critique of Pure Tolerance. Boston: Beacon Press.

Youssef, Nadia. 1971. "Social Structure and the Female Labor Force: The Case of Women Workers in Muslim Middle Eastern Countries." Demography 8: 427-39.

_____. 1973. "Cultural Ideals, Feminine Behavior and Family Control." Comparative Studies in Society and History 15: 326-47.

13

SELECTIVE OMISSION AND
THEORETICAL DISTORTION
IN STUDYING THE
POLITICAL ACTIVITY
OF WOMEN IN BRAZIL
Morris J. Blachman

Certain patterns of analysis seem to recur in the literature which could be taken as evidence of a "male" perspective, regardless of whether the authors are male or female .
. . . the male perspective views women as needing to come
up to male standards of "participation," "independence,"
or "political realism" to achieve equality. This approach
does not acknowledge the fact that women may be prevented
from assuming male roles by the application of sanctions
nor does it question the legitimacy or the necessity of doing things the way male politicians have always done them
(Jaquette 1973).

A new perspective in the social sciences is needed if
we are to find out what women are really thinking and feeling, if we are to come to grips with women's social and political situation and if we are going to try to change it (Eisenstein 1973).

The purpose of this paper is to contribute to the general discussion
concerning the contribution of the social sciences, particularly political science, in helping us understand the relationship between women
and politics. My own interest in studying this relationship has stemmed from both personal and professional concerns. I believe that the
subordinate position of women in society—like that of other oppressed
groupings—is intolerable. Professionally, I am concerned with understanding the ways in which power is created, distributed, and utilized.
I was able to combine my interests by studying the political activity of
women in Brazil.

I set two initial research tasks for myself. One was to compile a
bibliography on the subject, to see what kinds of materials were available and to begin a preliminary examination of them. The second task
was to review the appropriate theoretical works that relate to the issues
of the creation, distribution, and application of power by groups in

general and of the specific factors that affect the ability of women to act politically (what prevents, inhibits, contributes to, or facilitates organized political activity by women. The pursuit of these two tasks and subsequent research efforts have led me to question the utility of "mainstream" contemporary social science as the basis for formulating significant theoretical questions and for developing a better understanding of these phenomena. *

There are two principal criticisms I would like to raise. First, scholarship on Brazil, and I suspect on the rest of Latin America, has been woefully inadequate, in that the works produced generally have failed to portray, much less explain, the political activity of women—selective omission. Second, the mainstream theoretical orientation used to explain the political activity of groups at best is not conducive to, and at worst precludes, the formulation of adequate research questions for studying the issues mentioned above—theoretical distortion.

SELECTIVE OMISSION: A CASE STUDY

A good example of the selective omission of women's political activity is the suffragette movement in Brazil. Let us examine some of the highlights of that campaign. While studying and traveling in Europe, Bertha Lutz had been impressed by the efforts of the suffragettes, particularly those in England, to gain equal rights. When she returned to Brazil, she began her public campaign to organize women with a letter to Revista da semana in 1918 (Federacao Brasileira 1918). In April 1922, Ms. Lutz attended the Pan American Conference of Women in Baltimore, Maryland. She had been chosen to represent the League for the Intellectual Emancipation of Women, of which she was founder—in 1921—and President (Bulletin of the Pan American Union 1922, p. 350). The League was the first woman's organization in Brazil that was not oriented primarily toward religious or charitable ends. It was replaced August 9, 1922, when the Federacao Brasileira pelo Progresso Feminino was formally established, an occasion marked by the visit of Carrie Chapman Catt, President of the International Woman's Suffrage Alliance and of the Pan-American Association of Women (Federacao . . . 1962, p. 1). The goals of the Federation were clearly stated in the organization's statutes (Federacao Brasileira pelo Progresso Feminino 1922):

1. To promote the education of women and elevate the level of their instruction;
2. To protect mothers and children;

---

*In this paper, I am limiting my comments to the dominant approaches in North American social science. I realize that there are social scientists in the United States who do not utilize these mainstream approaches.

3. To obtain legislative guarantees and practices for women's labor;
4. To assist the initiatives of women and help orient them in the choice of a profession;
5. To stimulate the spirit of sociability and cooperation among women and interest them in social questions and public issues;
6. To assure women the political rights that our Constitution confers on them and to prepare them for the intelligent exercise of those rights;
7. To bolster the ties of friendship with the other American countries in order to guarantee the perpetual maintenance of peace and justice in the Western Hemisphere.

Four months later the Federation held its first major conference, and once again Ms. Catt attended. The Federation had begun its campaign. The significance of its organizational effort can be seen in the degree of involvement its members were able to engender. * In relatively short order, there were affiliated leagues in thirteen states.

On December 12, 1927, the Federal Senate began its second discussion of legislation that would grant women their political rights. The Federation urged the Senate to grant women their political rights (Federacao . . . 1927):

The Brazilian Federation for the Progress of Women has the high honor to direct to the Senate of the Republic this petition containing 2,000 signatures, and comes to solicit the Senate's support for the recognition of the political rights of women.

The collection of 2,000 signatures is an indication of the extensive effort put forth. The total estimated population of literate women in 1927, computed from the 1920 and 1940 Censuses, was about 2.5 million.

Convinced of the justice of their cause, the leadership of the movement believed that with publicity and through the responsibility of their own actions they would be able to make a sufficient number of male politicians realize that women deserved to be granted their political rights. Their heavy reliance on influencing public opinion led the members of the Federation to make extensive use of the newspapers, telegrams, and letters (interview with Dona Bertha Lutz, 1971).

---

*This discussion about participation must be understood within the following context: the movement appealed to and involved middle-class and lower-upper-class women, primarily in the major urban centers. Many of the demands of the movement, such as the vote, were, in an immediate sense, totally irrelevant to the majority of Brazilian women, who were illiterate and therefore not eligible to vote anyway.

In 1931, the Commission on the Reform of Electoral Law and Processes reported to the provisional government, recommending that some women should be permitted to register to vote, but only under limited and specified conditions. The feminist leadership decided the time had come to meet directly with Getulio Vargas to resolve the situation. Near the end of the discussion one of the women present, Carmen Portinho, reportedly was angered by what had occurred. She put her view forcefully to President Vargas: "Half of the revolution wants to give half of the vote to the Brazilian women. We want all or nothing." Vargas responded, "Well, then, I will give it all to you" (Rodrigues 1962, p. 79; interview by Blachman with Zeia Pinho Rezende, 1971). As a result of the efforts of the Federation, the second article of the electoral code of 1932 was reformulated to state, "A legal voter is any citizen over 21 years of age, regardless of sex, who is registered in accordance with this code" (Tabak 1971, p. 182).

During the next two years, the Federation continued to lead the fight to guarantee that the new constitution would include the key provisions it believed to be necessary. In addition to the assistance of its various state branches, the Federation was joined by several other national feminine associations—Liga Electoral, Uniao Universitaria Feminina, Uniao Profissional Feminina, Uniao de Funccionarias Publicas, Syndicato de Dactylographas, and Associacao Nacional de Enfermeiras Diplomadas.

Once the constitution was adopted in July 1934, the women turned their energies from winning the vote to identifying and electing women candidates, as well as those men who had supported or would support key feminist issues. The following was excerpted from a letter addressed to the Second National Feminist Convention on Political Parties and Personalities (Neves and Tavares 1934):

> The Second National Feminist Convention in Bahia, through the initiative of the Brazilian Federation for the Progress of Women, orientor of organized national feminine opinion, with the presence of delegates from all the national associations and confederate states, launched a new program of legislative, administrative and social claims destined for the defense of women, that is, of half the population of the country.
>
> This program, in which is concentrated the most just human aspirations of civilization and progress inspired by the profound necessities of the modern world, ought to serve as a paradigm for public action by all those who desire the support of the feminine associations that have been confederated from among the electorate that they represent.
>
> Consequently, the Convention has decided:
> a. To launch feminine candidates for federal representation;

    b. To support and indicate, in the future, the names
of women, to occupy administrative and judicial positions, who merit the support of organized feminine
opinion;

    c. To recommend other competent male or female can-
didates and to parties who have given effective support
to the legitimate claims of the "Brazilian women" and
who commit themselves to defend their interests, by
means of consultation and previous agreements, and
to support the feminine names indicated by the convention.

    As far as feminine candidates are concerned, the Se-
cond National Feminist Convention resolved to put forth the
most prestigious names, according to national feminine
opinion, as well as those who might be indicated by the
various State Chapters affiliated with the Federation.

The women's groups were active and hopeful. Then in 1937 Vargas
declared the "New State," which ended the organized political activity
of women, as well as that of other groupings. By the time the Vargas
regime had been toppled in 1945, the momentum and support of the
women's movement was dissipated. The Federation, though it continues
to meet today, has been unable to regain its former strength.

    The frustration felt by members of the Federation as they tried to
rebuild a woman's movement after World War II was expressed in a report of the organization (Federacao . . . 1962):

    The present position of woman is less happy than it ap-
pears. Brazilian women remain apathetic, seeming to conform completely with that which others might obtain for them.
They have a complete lack of interest in group work, engag-
ing in activity only for . . . personal advantages and not
for the best of the collectivity, except in their charity work,
which alleviates individual suffering. Woman's difficulty
in gaining access to high positions continues. Few are those
elected to Congress, as women have still not become conscious of their power. The progress during the last twenty
years has been minuscule.

    In the meantime, the Brazilian Federation for the Pro-
gress of Women has not lost interest in pursuing the fight.
But, evidently, it necessitates a strict collaboration with
other women, and in large numbers, in order to move forward. Group work is essential. And a campaign of clarifi-
cation is imposed on us. It is necessary that today's women
know how difficult it was to achieve that which today they
so tranquilly enjoy. And they also ought to know that nothing more could be achieved if it had not been for that. We
appeal, then, to women of good faith that they work with us.

The Brazilian Federation for the Progress of Women, which
has not stinted in its efforts for 40 years, will continue to
be firm: women of Brazil, give us your hand and we will go
forward!

The point of this brief account of the women's movement in Brazil,
highlighting its period of greatest activity, is only to establish that such
a movement did take place. Many middle- and upper-middle-class
women in the major urban centers of Brazil took part. Unlike the rapid
entrance and exit of massive numbers of women into the political institution in 1964, the movement of the 1920s and 1930s was a sustained
political act. The effect of the movement was almost to double the
size of the electorate*—a factor that has significance only to the degree
that the elections mattered. It also helped open the door for more active
participation by women in education and the economy.[†] Finally, the
activities of the movement were well-documented in the press—though
clearly some newspapers were more sympathetic than others.

SELECTIVE OMISSION: SOME CONSEQUENCES

What is known about this movement? The answer is "Surprisingly
little." If we examine the works in English that treat the period in question, we find a form of selective omission operating in which the various
authors give us no hint that such a movement existed. The maximum
amount of attention is usually limited to a passing reference to the ex-
tention of the vote to women. (The books examined were Burns 1970;
Dulles 1967, 1973; Loewenstein 1942; Poppino 1968; Skidmore 1967;
Young 1967). Even Brazil Election Factbook (Schneider et al. 1965),
a work directly concernd with the vote, has no mention of the movement
in the section where a brief political history is presented. The books
mentioned above appeared in English, but a similar phenomenon can be
noted in works published in Brazil (Fausto, 1971; Rodrigues, 1965;
Sodre, 1967; see also Bello 1966; Lambert 1971). Nestor Duarte (1966)
does an excellent job showing the historical relationship between the
family and the polity. One might expect that he would have been particularly interested in examining the implications of the movement on that
relationship, yet he does not examine the women's movement at all.
Another example is Glaucio Ary Dillon Soares' work, A democracia
que passon (1972), in which he analyzes the transformation of the

---

*I am speaking here only of potential. By 1940 women made up 43
percent of those eligible to register (Blachman 1973a, p. 12).

[†]The movement was of course an important factor in this process,
but it was not the only one.

Brazilian electorate. In seeking to explain the expansion of the electorate, the one factor he omits is the impact of the granting of suffrage to
women.

There have been some publications that have looked seriously at
the political activity of Brazilian women, but they are few. The most
complete treatment is that of Joao Batista Cascudo Rodrigues, A mulher
brasileira: Direitos politicos e civis. His principal concern is to relate
the history of the attainment of the vote by women. Unfortunately, the
book was printed in a limited edition and copies are extremely hard to
obtain, especially outside the Northeast of Brazil. The only other major
work that deals in part with the movement is Heleieth Saffioti's pioneer-
ing theoretical study, A mulher na sociedade de classes: Mito e realidade (1969a). Aside from these two efforts there are only a very few
articles and pieces in books that discuss women's political activity
(Matias 1964; Moraes 1971; Morais 1968; Muraro 1969; Studart 1969;
Tabak 1971; Thome, 1968).

The paucity of items on Brazil would seem to be representative of
much, if not all, of Latin America. Martin Sable's two-volume bibliography A Guide to Latin American Studies (1967), contains 5,024 cita-
tions. There are no entries under the heading of "Feminism," and only
ten under the heading "Women." Of the ten, the first and eighth are the
same monograph; two others are general works on Latin America that
contain sections on women; one is a U.S. Department of Labor publication listing protective labor legislation for women in 91 countries; one
is the annual report of the Inter-American Conference of Women; two
are related to non-Latin parts of the Caribbean; and one is the diary of
a Brazilian favela dweller. Only three of the 5,024 entries—including
the diary—could be considered serious studies of women in Latin
America.

The blindness (or exclusive selectivity) extends beyond the world
of overt political activity. One of the keys to maintaining the traditional
division of labor between men and women in Brazil was the Civil Code. *
Prior to August 27, 1962, the Brazilian Civil Code declared that the
husband was the head of the family. He had nearly complete power over
his wife and children. She needed his permission to work, to travel, to
open a bank account, to run for political office, or to receive an inheritance. In addition, he had the authority to determine where they would
live. The wife had no recourse. The change in 1962 made the wife a
collaborator in family decisions; removed the restrictions on her right
to travel or work; and gave her the right to go to court if she believed
that her husband's decisions were not in the best interests of the family (see Bueno 1970; Farhat 1971). Although the Brazilian wife was not

---

*Prior to 1962 the Civil Code maintained the division of labor, and
also gave legal status to the lack of differentiation between the family
and the polity. The authority of the state was used to guarantee the
continued subordination of Brazilian women (see Blachman 1973a).

yet accorded equal status with her husband, the change was substantial. Nevertheless, in "The Political and Legal Framework of Brazilian Life," Anyda Marchant does not even mention the change, though she does refer to other modifications in the Civil Code that she considers to be important (Marchant 1971, pp. 124-27).

The systematic bias that often results in the omission of historical materials relating to women can have a pernicious effect. When I was conducting my research in Brazil, I was often asked what was the subject of my work. When I answered that I was examining the political role of women, invariably I was met with the same response. "Oh! I didn't know they had one." Usually this was followed by a snicker or two, and then a remark like, "When you do your personal interviewing let me know, I'll do some of it for you." My first reaction was to attribute the response to some form of male chauvinism. After a while, however, it occurred to me that their response was more profound than I had realized. When they said, "I didn't know they had one," they were being quite truthful. Once I became aware of this, I began to question people in an attempt to learn just how much they did know about the movement. Almost without exception, there was no awareness that Brazilian women had been so involved in politics.

When analysts ignore or exclude such phenomena from their work, for whatever reason, they contribute to building a distorted and deficient collective historical memory. I am not suggesting that the oft-quoted maxim of George Santayana is necessarily true: "Those who do not remember the past are condemned to repeat its mistakes" (quoted in Loewenheim 1967, p. vii). However, it is clear that one can not learn from historical occurrences if one knows little or nothing about them.

The omission of historical materials concerning the organized political activity of women also creates a problem for the researcher, in that secondary sources are limited and, as time passes, fewer and fewer of those who possess firsthand knowledge and, perhaps, who also have access to relevant materials, are alive. Not only does the research task become more difficult, but significant portions of the experience may never be reconstructed.

THEORETICAL DISTORTION

The paucity of historical material poses a serious problem for the researcher, but perhaps even more serious is the inadequacy of contemporary North American "mainstream" theoretical orientations. We all know that no scholar can describe or explain the full complexity of social reality. The choice of what is emphasized and what is excluded is based on the particular philosophical and theoretical orientation of the researcher. Consequently, we need to know what we are selecting in and what we are selecting out when we choose one approach over another.

When we examine the literature on the political participation of societal groupings, we find that the dominant theoretical construct is interest group theory. Ostensibly, interest group theorists want to know
how groups generate and use power. They argue that the behavior of
groups is key to understanding politics (Bentley 1908, pp. 208-09; Rothman 1964, p. 72; Truman 1951, pp. 21-23). They see society as "conceived of simply as a plurality of groups interacting with each other,
and . . . the political process . . . [as] essentially a process of group
competition for power over the allocation of resources" (Latham 1964,
p. 40; Rothman 1964, p. 75). The groups are seen as being in a "state
of constant motion, and it is through this motion and its interactions
that these groups generate the rules by which public policy is formulated
. . ." (Latham 1964, p. 43; Truman 1951, p. 65). These motions are
due to a disturbance of the previous patterns of interaction. In other
words, the equilibrium, which is assumed to be an underlying basis of
society, is destroyed. The groups then seek either to restore the old
balance or to create a new one. "This activity will disrupt the patterns
of other individuals and groups in a wave-like effect [thereby bringing
more groups into play] until a new balance on all three levels [indivi-
dual, group, and society] develops" (Rothman 1964, p. 77; also see
Truman 1951, pp. 26-33).

The interest groupers recognize that "all interest groups are not
equally powerful" (Redford et al. 1965, p. 212). Or, as David Truman
put it (1951, p. 36):

> The fact that one interest group is highly organized
> whereas another is not or is merely a potential group—
> whether the interest involved is that of affording more pro-
> tection to consumers, greater privileges for brunettes, or
> more vigorous enactment of civil rights—is a matter of
> great significance at any particular moment. It does not
> mean, however, that the momentarily weaker group, or in-
> terest, will inevitably remain so. Events may easily pro-
> duce an increased rate of interaction among the affected
> individuals to the point where formal organization or a sig-
> nificant interest group will emerge and greater influence
> will ensue.

The disparities in power are accounted for on the basis of differences
in organizational characteristics, group efforts, and external intrusions.
The identification of social groupings in this theoretical approach,
grounded in liberal ideology, recognizes no long-lasting structures—
such as class—that would prevent some groups from forming or from
having access to the political arena. Truman is quite explicit in pointing out his belief that most categories of groups are not useful, because
any particular group that arises and seeks claims in the political arena
does so only in response to the new issues created by the breaking of
the old, patterned equilibrium. The process is continuous, so that

today's equilibrium will be broken in the near future and a new one will be established. The new equilibrium will include new social groupings, and will likely involve the reordering of the old groups that still exist.

What, might we ask, is wrong with interest group theory? Paraphrasing Stanley Rothman's critique of Truman, we can say that the basic weaknesses of the theory lie not in the relations among the propositions put forth, but "in the conceptual framework itself" (Rothman 1964, p. 91). There are two basic arguments I wish to make. First, the theory may lead us away from recognizing factors that inhibit access to politics and contribute to a kind of political activity that is extremely limited in scope. Second, the theory, along with its ideological base, may lead women, as well as others, to formulate political strategies based on the distorted explanation of social reality.

The conception of social groupings accepted by interest group theorists takes no account of structured inequality in society. The fluidity of movement proposed by the interest groupers leads one to believe that all groups face essentially the same basic problems. No one group or set of groups is seen as having problems specific to them in organizing and, eventually, in effectively exercising power. The inability to recognize structured obstacles that some groups face and others do not face is compounded by the narrowness of the overall model (Rothman 1964, p. 91).

> An analysis of political behavior in terms of groups gives little information as to the pattern of group politics in a given society.
> . . . the study of politics must not only involve the study of groups . . . . [In addition] changing conceptions of reality, the ideas of political theorists, changes in socioeconomic structure may all be found to play a role . . . if one examines a society historically.

I would suggest that these two facets of interest group theory—pluralist fluidity and a narrow conceptual framework—would preclude an analyst from fully understanding or explaining organized women's political activity in Brazil. For example, I believe, based on my research in Brazil, than an evaluation of the potential for organized political activity by Brazilian women must include an assessment of the relationship between the institutions of the family and the polity. I would argue that the social meaning of being a woman in contemporary capitalist society is based on the position of the woman in the family, particularly in her roles as wife and mother (Zaretsky, 1973, p. 73). The division of labor in the family has resulted in the privatization of the woman's position, reinforced by a set of values through which men and women are seen differentially. The lack of differentiation between the family and the polity means that the woman occupies a similar subordinate position in the division of tasks, as well as in the values that reinforce it, in the political institution (see Blachman 1973a). The problems faced by women, if they wish to act politically, are qualitatively different from those of other groups. Both the expectations of their behavior, by them as well as by men, and the positions they occupy in the polity greatly reduce their ability to have a significant, continuing impact in noncrisis situations. To assume that there is no structured difference among groups is to misread social reality. In addition, I believe it is well-established that the class composition of a particular group of women would affect their ability to exercise political power. Such class distinctions are not easily grafted onto the theoretical context of interest group theory.

Interest group theory permits the analyst to examine those groups that are readily identifiable. But what about the phenomena that Peter Bachrach and Morton Baratz (1970) have called "the other face of power?" As political analysts, I believe we want to know not only which social groupings are politically active, but also which have been unable to be so because the "mobilization of bias" in the society has prevented them from acting (Schattschneider 1960). Again, theoretically speaking, interest groupers have not been able to deal satisfactorily with this category of phenomena.

What are the implications of this theoretical construct? Susan C. Bourque and Jean Grossholtz, in their paper "Politics as an Unnatural Practice: Political Science Looks at Female Participation" (1973, p. 1) point out that the explanations of the disparities in political participation of "women, blacks, minorities, [and] those of low income and status" offered by political scientists have

> . . . provided a justification for those disparities and
> freed the discipline from the need to seek alternate explana-
> tions which would question the distribution of roles, status
> and power as well as the very definition of politics. The
> conclusion reached by this sort of orientation is that the
> fault lies with the excluded group who simply won't get or-
> ganized and participate in the ways open to them.

Interest groupers' failure to recognize the effects of general societal conditions on the political activity of women (groups) leads them and others to assess the "success" or "failure" of a group on the basis of factors primarily internal to the group. Failure to "make it" is attributed to a lack of competence or innate inability. The locus of the problem is left squarely with the group, and is seen as only tangentially subject to control by the society. This phenomenon of "blaming the victim" has received considerable attention in recent months. Zillah R. Eisenstein comments directly on this problem in her paper, "Connections Between Class and Sex: Moving Towards a Theory of Liberation." Although she refers specifically to the situation in the United States, I believe her argument holds, in large measure, for Brazil as well (Eisenstein 1973, p. 7):

The American feminists appear to work from the belief
that the society is organized in terms of a pluralist arena
of power. They saw women as a group, which once enfran-
chised, would take its place in the competition for power
and influence on an equal footing with other groups, either
as a group or as a part of preexisting groups. Given their
conception of where power is located and from what it derives, the inequalities arising from class and sexual oppression stood outside their [conception of the] political arena.

WHERE DO WE GO FROM HERE?

A number of people are attempting to develop theoretical approaches
that, at least, avoid the kinds of omissions and distortions discussed
above. * Among the more fruitful efforts have been those aimed at understanding and elucidating the relationship between sex and class (Saffioti 1969a; Dreitzel 1972; Firestone 1972; Millett 1971; Reiche 1971;
Eisenstein 1973; Zaretsky 1973; Jaquette, 1973; Bourque and Grossholtz
1973; Bambirra 1972; CEREN 1972; Costa 1972). I believe the spate of
works of the last few years seeking to rectify our distorted lenses is
already having an impact. We are at the beginning of a less myopic,
more penetrating social science. Perhaps we can now look forward to
the development of more discerning theoretical constructs that will lead
us to see and register the kinds of social phenomena that in the past
have so often been omitted, and will help us to define, understand, and
explain those phenomena more fully.

---

*I would offer as a tentative suggestion that the lack of attention
to women in the works of many Latin American scholars is also related
to the theoretical constructs used. These constructs fall in a category
we might call "post-Marxist." The concept of class is key for identifying social groupings. Ironically, looking at society primarily in terms
of class tends to reduce the possibility for examing women as a legitimate category of analysis. Often the class position of a woman is defined in terms of her father or husband, depending on whether or not she
is married.

REFERENCES

Azevedo, Thales. 1961. "Familia, casamento e divorcio no Brasil."
Journal of Interamerican Studies 7 (April): 213-37.

Bachrach, Peter, and Morton S. Baratz. 1970. Power and Poverty: Theory and Practice. New York: Oxford University Press.

Bambirra, Vania. 1972. "Liberacion de la mujer y lucha de clases."
Planteamientos 6 (February 15): 10-15.

Beauvoir, Simone de. 1968. The Second Sex. New York: Random House.

Bello, Jose Maria. 1966. A History of Modern Brazil 1889-1964. Stanford: Stanford University Press.

Bentley, Arthur F. 1908. The Process of Government. Chicago: University of Chicago Press.

Blachman, Morris J. 1973a. Eve in an Adamocracy: Women and Politics
in Brazil. "Occasional Papers," no. 5. New York: Ibero-American
Language and Area Center, New York University.

_____. 1973b. "Women and Politics: The Brazilian Mixture." Cadernas,
Centro de estudos rurais e urbanos no. 6: 147-73.

Bourque, Susan C., and Jean Grossholtz. 1973. "Politics as an Unna-
tural Practice: Political Science Looks at Female Participation."
Paper delivered at the 1973 annual meeting of the American Political
Science Association, New Orleans.

Buarque de Holanda, Sergio. 1969. Raizes do Brasil. 5th rev. ed.
Rio de Janeiro: Livraria Jose Olympio Editora.

Bueno, Ruth. 1970. Regime juridico da mulher casada. Rio de Janeiro:
Forense.

_____. 1971. "A mulher na decada de 70." Juridico.

Burns, E. Bradford. 1970. A History of Brazil. New York: Columbia
University Press.

Centro de Estudios de la Realidad Nacional (CEREN). 1972. "Sexualidad, autoritarismo y lucha de clases." Cuadernos de la realidad
nacional 12 (April).

Chaney, Elsa. 1971. "Women in Latin American Politics." Ph.D. dissertation, University of Wisconsin.

Costa, Mariarosa Dalla. 1972. "Women and the Subversion of the Community." In The Power of Women and the Subversion of the Community. Bristol, England: Falling Wall Press.

Cruz, Levy. 1967. "Brazil." In Women in the Modern World, ed. Raphael Patai. New York: Free Press.

Daugherty, Charles, James Rowe, and Ronald Schneider, eds. Brazil Election Factbook. Washington, D.C.: Institute for the Comparative Study of Political Systems.

Diegues Junior, Manuel. 1972. "Estrutura social brasileira: Aspectos de passado e trans-formacoes presente." Revista brasileira do Estudos politicos 33 (January): 31-61.

Dreitzel, Hans Peter, ed. 1972. Family, Marriage, and the Struggle of the Sexes. New York: Macmillan.

Duarte, Nestor. 1966. A ordem privada e a organizacao politica nacional: Contribuicao a sociologia politica brasileira. 2nd ed. Sao Paulo: Companhia Editora Nacional.

Dulles, John W. F. 1967. Vargas in Brazil. Austin: University of Texas Press.

_____. 1973. Anarchists and Communists in Brazil, 1900-1935. Austin: University of Texas Press.

Eisenstein, Zillah R. 1973. "Connections Between Class and Sex: Moving Towards a Theory of Liberation." Paper delivered at the 1973 annual meeting of the American Political Science Association, New Orleans.

Engels, Frederick. 1971. The Origin of the Family, Private Property and the State. New York: International Publishers.

Expilly, Charles. 1936. Mulheres e costumes do Brasil. Sao Paulo: Companhia Editora Nacional.

Farhat, Alfredo. 1971. A mulher perante o direto: Doutrina legislacao, jurisprudencia e formulario. Sao Paulo: Edicao Universitario de Direito.

Fausto, Boris. 1971. "A Revolucao de 1930." In Brasil em perspectiva, 3rd ed., ed. Carlos Guilherme Mota. Sao Paulo: Difusao Europeia do Livro.

Firestone, Shulamith. 1972. The Dialectic of Sex: The Case for Feminist Revolution. New York: Bantam Books.

Freyre, Gilberto. 1963. The Mansions and the Shanties. New York: Knopf.

_____. 1964. The Masters and the Slaves: A Study in the Development of Brazilian Civilization. New York: Knopf.

Gans, Marjorie, Jose Pastore, and Eugene A. Wilkening. 1970. "A mulher e a modernizacao da familia brasileira." Pesquisa o planejamento 12 (October): 97-139.

Golembiewski, Robert T. 1964. "The Group Basis of Politics." In Readings in Political Parties and Pressure Groups, ed. Frank Munger and Douglas Price. New York: Thomas Y. Crowell.

Greer, Germaine. 1971. The Female Eunuch. New York: Bantam Books.

Jaquette, Jane S. 1973. "Studies of Female Political Participation Review and a Discussion of the 'Male Perspective.'" Paper delivered at the annual meeting of the American Political Science Association, New Orleans.

Jesus, Carolina Maria de. 1962. Child of the Dark. New York: E. P. Dutton.

Lambert, Jacques. 1971. Os dois brasis. 7th ed. Sao Paulo: Companhia Editora Nacional.

Latham, Earl. 1964. "The Group Basis of Politics: Notes for a Theory." In Readings in Political Parties and Pressure Groups, ed. Frank Munger and Douglas Price. New York: Thomas Y. Crowell.

Loewenheim, Francis L., ed. 1967. The Historian and the Diplomat: The Role of History and Historians in American Foreign Policy. New York: Harper and Row.

Loewenstein, Karl. 1942. Brazil Under Vargas. New York: MacMillan.

Marchant, Anyda. 1971. "The Political and Legal Framework of Brazilian Life." In Modern Brazil: New Patterns and Development, ed. John Saunders. Gainesville: University of Florida Press.

Matias, Rodrigues. 1964. Marcha da familia com Deus pela liberdade. Sao Paulo: Empresa Grafica "Tiete."

Millett, Kate. 1971. Sexual Politics. New York: Avon Books.

Mitchell, Juliet. 1971. Woman's Estate. New York: Pantheon Books.

Moraes, Tancredo. 1971. Pela emancipacao integral da mulher. Rio de Janeiro: Ed. Pongetti.

Morais, Vamberto. 1968. A emancipacao da mulher: As raizes do preconceito antifeminino e sue declinio. Grafica e Editora CITAL.

A mulher no servico publico. 1957. Servico de Documentacao, DASP. Rio de Janeiro: Departmento de Imprensa Nacional.

Mulheres do brasil (pensamento e acao). 1971. 2 vols. Fortaleza: Ed. Henriqueta Galeno.

Muraro, Rose Marie. 1969. A mulher na construcao do mundo futuro. Petropolis: Vozes.

_____. 1970. Libertacao sexual da mulher. Petropolis: Vozes.

Nazario, Diva Nolf. 1923. Voto feminino e feminismo. Sao Paulo.

Neves, Maria de Carmo Vidigal Pereira das, and Laurentina Pugas Tavares. 1934. "A II. Convencao nacional feminista aos partidos e personalidades politicas." Bahia, August 30. Mimeographed.

Noqueira, Oracy. 1962. Familia e comunidade: Um estudo sociologico de itapetininga. Rio de Janeiro: Centro Brasileiro de Pesquisas Educacionais. Series VI, "Sociedade e Educacao."

Ortner, Sherry B. 1972. "Is Female to Male as Nature Is to Culture?" Feminist Studies 1 (Fall): 5-31.

Pescatello, Ann, ed. 1973. Female and Male in Latin America. Pittsburgh: University of Pittsburgh Press.

Poppino, Rollie E. 1968. Brazil: The Land and People. New York: Oxford University Press.

Rabello, Sylvio et al. 1969. A participacao da mulher no mercado de trabalho. Recife: Instituto Joaquim Nabuco de Pesquisas Sociais.

Redford, Emmette S., et al. 1965. Politics and Government in the United States: National, State and Local Edition. New York: Harcourt, Brace and World.

Reed, Evelyn. 1971. Problems of Women's Liberation: A Marxist Approach. New York: Pathfinder Press.

Reiche, Reimut. 1971. Sexuality and Class Struggle. New York: Praeger.

Rezende, Zeia Pinho. 1970. "O trabalho e a mulher." Separata de Jurisdica.

Rodrigues, Joao Batista Cascudo. 1962. A mulher brasileira: Direitos politicos e civis. Fortaleza: Imprensa Universitaria do Ceara. "Colecao Mossoroense," XI, ser. C.

Rodrigues, Jose Honorio. 1965. Conciliacao e reforma no Brasil: Um desafio historico-cultural. Rio de Janeiro: Ed. Civilizacao Brasileira.

Rosen, Bernard C. 1962. "Socialization and Achievement Motivation in Brazil." American Sociological Review 27 (October): 612-24.

_____. 1964. "The Achievement Syndrome and Economic Growth in Brazil." Social Forces 42 (March): 341-53.

_____, and Manoel T. Berlinck. 1968. "Modernization and Family Structure in the Region of Sao Paulo, Brazil." America Latina 2 (July/September): 353-60.

_____, and Anita L. LaRaia. 1972. "Modernity in Women: An Index of Social Change in Brazil." Journal of Marriage and the Family 34 (May): 353-60.

Rothman, Stanley. 1964. "Systematic Political Theory: Observations on the Group Approach." In Readings in Political Parties and Pressure Groups, ed. Frank Munger and Douglas Price. New York: Thomas Y. Crowell.

Sable, Martin H. 1967. A Guide to Latin American Studies. 2 vols. Los Angeles: Latin American Center, University of California at Los Angeles.

Saffioti, Heleieth Iara B. 1969a. A mulher na sociedade de classes: Mito e realidade. Sao Paulo: Quatro Artes.

_____. 1969b. "Profissionalizacao feminina: Professoras primarias e operarias." Araraquara: Faculdade de Filosofia, Ciencias e Letras. Mimeographed.

_____. 1969c. "Mulher: Questao de ciencia." Boletim da cadeira de sociologia e fundamentos sociologicos de educacao (Araraquara) 4 (September): 45-63.

Schattschneider, E. E. 1960. The Semi-Sovereign People. New York:
     Holt, Rinehart and Winston.

Schmitter, Philippe C. 1971. Interest, Conflict and Political Change
     in Brazil. Stanford: Stanford University Press.

Schneider, Ronald M., James W. Rowe, and Charles Dougherty. 1965.
     Brazil Election Factbook. Washington, D.C.: Institute for the Com-
     parative Study of Political Systems.

Silvert, Kalman H. 1970. Man's Power: A Biased Guide to Political
     Thought and Action. New York: Viking Press.

Skidmore, Thomas E. 1967. Politics in Brazil, 1930-1964: An Experiment
     in Democracy. New York: Oxford University Press.

Soares, Glaucio Ary Dillon. 1972. A democracia que passon (desenvol-
     vimento, classe e politica durante e segunda republica). Brasilia.

Sodre, Nelson Werneck. 1967. Historia da burguesia brasileira. 2nd
     ed. Rio de Janeiro: Ed. Civilizacao Brasileira.

Souza, Antonio Candido de Mello. 1954. "The Brazilian Family."
     Brazil: Portrait of Half a Continent, ed. T. Lynn Smith and Alexan-
     der Marchant. New York: Dryden Press.

Studart, Heloneida. 1969. A mulher, brinquedo do homen? Petropolis:
     Vozes.

Tabak, Fanny. 1968. "A declaracao universal e os diretos da mulher."
     Revista de ciencia politica 2 (October/December): 115-43.

_____. 1971. "O status da mulher no Brasil—vitorias e preconceitos."
     Cademos da PUC-RJ (August): 165-201.

Tavares de Sa, Irene. 1963. Eva e seus autores. Rio de Janeiro: Agir.

_____. 1966. A condicao da mulher. Rio de Janeiro: Agir.

Thome, Yolanda Bettencourt. 1968. A mulher no mundo de hoje. Petro-
     polis: Vozes.

Torres, Joao Camillo de Oliveira. 1965. Estratificacao social no Brasil.
     Sao Paulo: Difusao Europeia do Livro.

Truman, David B. 1951. The Governmental Process: Political Interests
     and Public Opinion. New York: Knopf.

Tudor, Talitha do Carmo. 1970. "Trabalho da mulher com encargos de familia." Separata de Juridica.

Vinhas, M. 1970. Estudos sobre o proletariado brasileiro. Rio de Janeiro: Civilizacao Brasileira.

Wagley, Chalres. 1963. An Introduction to Brazil. New York: Columbia University Press.

Weber, Max. 1949. The Methodology of the Social Sciences. New York: Free Press.

Werneck, Olga. 1965. "O subdesenvolvimento e a situacao da mulher." Revista civilizacao brasileira 1 (September): 331-41.

Willems, Emilio. 1953. "The Structure of the Brazilian Family." Social Forces 31 (May): 339-45.

Young, Jordan M. 1967. The Brazilian Revolution of 1930 and the Aftermath. New Brunswick, N. J.: Rutgers University Press.

Zaretsky, Eli. 1973. "Capitalism, the Family, and Personal Life." Socialist Revolution 3 (January-April): 69-125.

Organization or Organization-Related Works

Bulletin of the Pan American Union. 1922. 54 (April): 350-52.

Federacao Brasileira pelo Progresso Feminino. 1918. Letter from Bertha Lutz. Revista de semana, December 23.

_____. 1922. Estatutos da Federacao Brasileira pelo Progresso Feminino.

_____. 1927. "Desde que uma so exista nao ha motivo para que nao sejam eleitoras todas as mulheres habilitadas no Brasil." Pamphlet.

_____. 1928. "Manifesto feminista." Educacao diretoria geral da instrucao publica e sociedade de educacao de Sao Paulo 3 (May).

_____. 1929a. O voto feminino perante a justica (alguns julgados). No. 9.

_____. 1929b. Os direitos politicos da mulher: Jurisprudencia. No. 10.

_____. 1929c. Os direitos politicos da mulher: Opinioes e pareceres. no. 11.

_____. 1932. Cruzada nacional de educacao politica e convencao bien-nale e quinzena de estudos da constituicao.

_____. 1933a. 13 principios basicos: sugestoes as anteprojeto da con-stituicao, by Bertha Lutz. Rio de Janeiro: Ed. da FBPF.

_____. 1933b. A nacionalidade da mulher casada, by Bertha Lutz. Rio de Janeiro: Irmao Pongetti.

_____. 1937a. "Mulher: Opiniao feminina organizada." Boletim da FBPF. 3, 1, 2 (January, February).

_____. 1937b. O trabalho feminino: A mulher na ordem economica e social. Rio de Janeiro: Imprensa Nacional.

_____. 1962. "Atividades da Federacao brasileira pelo progresso femini-no," by Maria Sabina Albuquerque e Zeia Pinho Rezende. Mimeo-graphed.

14

POLITICS AND FEMINISM
IN THE DOMINICAN REPUBLIC:
1931-45 AND 1966-74
Vivian M. Mota

The political evolution of Dominican women has been congruent
with the various socioeconomic systems and ideologies that have under-
lain the history of the Dominican Republic.

First, this evolution has not been complete, and nor has it included
all Dominican women. Just as there are inequalities between social
classes, there is political inequality among Dominican women. A small
group has a high level of political development, but most women do not.
Although we do not have enough data to demonstrate it conclusively, we
can suggest that historically the participation of Dominican women in
politics is positively correlated with a high level of education, which
is related to a generally high socio-economic status.

The second characteristic of women's political evolution in the
Dominican Republic is that it has been sporadic, with periods of no
activity except voting.

Finally—and this listing does not claim to be exhaustive—the third
characteristic is that in periods of high political participation among
Dominican women, the activity has occurred predominantly among women
belonging to the dominant class, or women with strong interests in the
permanence and strengthening of that class. Therefore women's political participation has been in close collaboration with the system and has
posed no threat to it. On the other hand, the political efforts of working-class women, or of women of the left, have failed because of the
following factors: First, what I call the "despotism of the left," which
is basically masculine. Second, the lack of a genuine theory of feminine
oppression, which should include and coherently relate the aspirations
of women as an oppressed group—specifically oppressed because of
their sex—to the aspirations of exploited classes in general. The lack
of such a theory has frustrated the task of politically conscious women
of the left. Third, the alienation and conservatism of the masses of
women, which not only makes it difficult to raise their consciousnesses
and change their passivity, but also prevents a sustained organizational
effort. Fourth, the tremendously repressive character of the system,

which, in the light of the above-mentioned factors, especially the third, also has impeded consciousness-raising and popular mobilization among women.

The third characteristic, the lack of political consciousness among lower-class women and the absence of radical feminism in the left, must be the subject of further study and analyses. In the present essay, we will attempt to demonstrate how the lack of a feminist movement imbued with a revolutionary ideology has led to elitist feminism in the service of reaction.

Two specific groups will be the subject of our study. The Trujillista feminists were those women who formed a feminist movement in the early years of the Trujillo era. The second group, the Reformist feminists, does not exist as a formal group in the political life of the Dominican Republic. Nevertheless, the political behavior and activities of certain women and women's groups since 1966 do have common characteristics. The adjective "Reformist" refers to their support of President Joaquin Balaguer's policies and ideological leadership, rather than to formal party affiliation.

We shall attempt to show a historical continuity between these two groups, as expressed in their willful collaboration with the Trujillo and Balaguer regimes, respectively.

TRUJILLISTA FEMINISTS

In 1931 a group of women formed an organization called Accion Feminista Dominicana, which was to shape the course of feminism in the Dominican Republic for many years to come. In its charter, the group stated its basic membership requirements: "good conduct, literacy, and being over 18 years of age." With such membership the movement hoped to become "a true feminist union formed by Ladies and Young Women who live, some off their income, others teaching, others from industry, work and study" (Lara Fernandez 1946, pp. 10-11).

Given those specifications, the movement was generally composed of "ladies" of a certain social standing and educational level. According to the Second National Population Census (1935), illiteracy was rampant—about 70 percent of the population—and predominant among the lower classes. Thus, women of low economic and educational status were automatically excluded from the feminist movement of the 1930s.

Accion Feminista lacked a program of clear and concrete ideas with respect to Dominican women. Its documents display moralistic and familistic concerns: lack of education for women, the destruction of the family, prostitution and the abandonment of children, alcoholism, drugs.

The movement was also preoccupied with the need for training women who would not spend money on unnecessary luxuries, and who would be prepared to "earn their families' living with dignity. Should the need arise, Accion Feminista wants women, even those possessed of great fortunes, to receive training which will permit them to administer their wealth, and make them capable of sustaining the moral and material equilibrium of the home, because one must not forget that the equilibrium of the home means the equilibrium of the nations" (Lara Fernandez 1946, p. 11).

Nevertheless, Accion Feminista did play a part in the political arena. But its political demands were couched in the sugary speeches and general style of the period—and of the class to which its leaders belonged. Above all, these women aspired to secure their rights as full citizens: "If we have good rulers, she [the woman without rights] will be unable to lend them support; if we have bad rulers, she will be unable to prevent their emergence, nor persuade them to mend their ways with soft meditations" (Mejia de Fernandez, in Lara Fernandez 1946, p. 25).

The leaders of Accion Feminista had a very specific concept of politics and of what female intervention would entail. Politics was seen as a depressing and savage spectacle, a bloody struggle that the soothing and charitable hand of women could help to civilize. Thus, women could apply to politics, to the public sphere, what they had traditionally done in the home. * Trujillo, of course, encouraged this unthreatening concept (Lara Fernandez 1946, p. 22):

> I sympathize with this movement for social justice for women. I believe that we can consider the need for granting women the rights of citizenship. Dominican society will benefit when our women take their delicate sentiments to the civic arena. The electoral process will gain in constructive efficiency. Our women will put to the service of the people ideas and feelings of social conservation that are not now present. . . .

The significance of feminism in this period must be understood within the specific context of trujillismo. By 1933, "the Great Benefactor" had been in power for three years, and had consolidated his position as the indisputable boss of political life. His power and personal ambition, as well as a tyrannical style of government, had been felt throughout the Dominican Republic. Given this monopoly of power, the dictator represented the only immediate possibility for women to win their civil and political rights. The feminist movement therefore became a political counterpart to male-dominated organizations that asked, with patriotic fervor, that the tyrant continue in power.

------

*This concept of politics and the extension of the maternal role to public life are examined more extensively by Chaney (1973). I am grateful to her for having called my attention to this point.

TRUJILLO AND ACCION FEMINISTA

Some writers believe that feminism in the Dominican Republic had no autonomous origins or development, and that "it is possible that Trujillo began this movement . . . in the years of 1940-1941 to put himself abreast of modern currents of equality between the sexes" (Galindez 1956, pp. 333-34). Leaving aside the historical error made by Galindez, * it would be very debatable to consider Accion Feminista as a mere creation of Trujillo. Such a unilateral viewpoint ignores the objective conditions of oppression that characterized the lives of Dominican women, and which fostered a true feminist consciousness. This is not to deny the use Trujillo made of the movement—which would be tantamount to affirming that Accion Feminista escaped the organizational norms universally imposed by the dictatorship.

The women of Accion Feminista showed in their writings a feeling of inequality, expressed at times with blind rage, although sweetened by the style (Lara Fernandez 1946, passim):

> Women, so sadly abandoned by the law, which only
> grants rights to men. . . . Feminism will lead to women's
> happiness, preparing them to always marry for love and not
> of necessity or haste to the first man who arrives, for fear
> of facing life alone. . . . Women's inferiority complex was
> nothing else but the offspring of the old traditions, which
> are changing. . . .

The objective conditions for this change, mentioned by one of the founders of the movement, began to appear years before the creation of Accion Feminista. Of the fifteen women who composed the first Board of Directors, eight were women with university education or with advanced training, although in areas related to teaching. Some of these professionals had also acquired postgraduate degrees in other countries, which was rare at the time.†

---

*It is possible that Galindez's error, like his general treatment of the feminist movement, follows from the lack of importance that he, as well as other authors, attribute to the movement, especially when it comes to denying its own intrinsic motives. Other writers, all male, who studied the dictatorship, ignore or barely mention these women. See Bosch (1965), Crassweller (1966), Martin (1966), Rodman (1964), Wiarda (1968).

†'Dr. Sofia Oliva, who graduated from the University in Santo Domingo as a dentist has returned to her home from Cuba, where she obtained the degree of Doctor in the University of Havana. " Bulletin of the Pan American Union 57, no. 5 (May 1924): 532. Notices such as these are current in the Bulletin. Lara Fernandez also offers a list (1946, pp. 106-15) of professional women.

The educational background of the movement's founders is a partial explanation of its emergence, since generally access to higher education serves to awaken men and women politically. The birth of Accion Feminista can also be explained, as can the birth of other similar movements in Latin America, by a favorable international climate. The Fifth International American Conference held in Chile in 1923, and the Sixth, which took place in Havana five years later, * touched on the problem of the lack of civil and political rights among Latin American women, and were the seedbed for what later became the Interamerican Commission of Women (Portela, 1968, p. 124). Dominican delegates related to women in Accion Feminista attended both conferences.

The first meeting of the Interamerican Commission of Women took place in Havana in 1930; and Gloria Moya de Jimenes, a member of the Club Nosotras (literally Our Club), which was the parent organization to Accion Feminista, attended (Scott 1931, p. 502). There was a feminist effervescence throughout the continent at that time that, although long limited to the juridical sphere, doubtless acted as a catalyst for groups and organizations of women who had previously limited themselves to salon and literary circles.

Dominican women got the vote relatively early. North American women won the vote in 1920, and Ecuadorians in 1929; but the Chileans won it in 1949; the Peruvians in 1955; Columbians in 1957; and Paraguayans in 1961 (Newhall 1936, p. 424; Chaney 1973, p. 110). Dominican women voted constitutionally for the first time in the 1942 elections, and had already voted "symbolically" in 1934 and 1938.[†] Married women achieved recognition of their civil status in 1942, with the passage of Law 390.[‡] At the same time, a series of laws was passed to reinforce the maternal role of Dominican women, and thereby soften

---

*"Incidentally, the Sixth PanAmerican Conference will long be remembered by the women of the Continent as that which first gave its floor in an informal session to a group of representative women headed by Miss Doris Stevens, Chairman of the Committee on International Action, Mrs. Jane Norman Smith, President of the National Council, both of the National Women's Party of the United States, and Mrs. Mona Lee de Munoz Marin, of the Porto Rican branch of this party . . . ." Bulletin of the Pan American Union 62, no. 4 (April 1928): 339-40. Both Miss Stevens and Mrs. Munoz Marin were well-known in Dominican feminist circles.

†The symbolic votes of 1934 and 1938 were decreed on November 22, 1933, by Presidential Decree no. 858. It conditioned granting the vote to women on their turnout for the vote of 1934. See Bulletin of the Pan American Union 68 no. 11 (November 1934): 842.

‡Promulgated on December 14, 1942. See Gaceta oficial, no. 5535; Codigo civil de la Republica Dominicana.

the potential consequences of a strong feminist movement. Perhaps the most blatant of these laws (no. 279) established an award—a medal and the "people's eternal gratitude"—for women who gave birth to eleven or more children. * This law still exists but is not enforced.

It must be remembered, however, that eleven years passed between the creation of Accion Feminista in 1931 and the Twenty-Fourth Constitutional Reform promulgated on January 10, 1942 (Galindez 1956, p. 108), granting women the right to vote. This delay can be understood only in terms of the improved bargaining position of women, its relation to the changing needs of the Trujillo regime, and the increased mobilization of women.

The uniqueness of the feminists' political position lay in their bargaining power, in their capacity to mobilize new sectors of the population—women formerly distant from political partisanship—in favor of the regime. In return, upper-class women could expect concrete concessions, while the female masses would gain the "right" to vote for Trujillo. The significance and political weight of the feminist movement increased over time, as a function of internal and external forces confronting the Trujillo regime.

By the early 1940s, internal and external factors had converged to make "democratic liberalism," on a very superificial level, a political imperative for Trujillo. On the one hand, the industrialization process in the Dominican Republic was rapidly gaining momentum, accelerating rural-urban migration and the general proletarization of the masses. A potentially volatile social situation was emerging in the cities, and the politically shrewd dictator recognized the need to increase his control over vast sectors of the population.

In the international arena, the extreme brutality of Trujillismo was known throughout the world. The war-time situation had deepened economic ties between the Dominican Republic and the United States, and Trujillo's "negative image" represented a political liability to Roosevelt's New Deal and "Good Neighbor" policies. Thus, the pressure was on to lend the tyrant's rule a more democratic facade. Concessions to feminist demands in this period represented a convenient mechanism. Trujillo could demonstrate his new-found liberalism and show a wider base of popular support.

The "try-out" feminine votes of 1934 and 1938 are a clear example of Trujillo's caution in dealing with the feminist movement. [†] In the 1934

---

*Other measures included schools of home economics, free milk for poor women, and the National Junta for the Protection of Motherhood and Infants.

†One theory has attributed the symbolic votes of 1934 and 1938 to Trujillo's fear that feminism would get out of hand. See Sanchez Lustrino (1938), p. 210. Given the brutal character of Trujillo's dictatorship, it is difficult to believe that he "feared" the delicate demands of feminist organizations, except within the context of international public opinion.

election, only 96, 427 women out of an adult female population of about
280, 000 went to the polls. In 1938, however, 344, 909 women voted. *
While the total count of female votes seems much too high, there is no
doubt that between the two elections, Accion Feminista at the national
level, and local feminist clubs in the provinces, carried out an intensive campaign to increase the number of women voters. Thus, by 1942,
the Trujillista feminists had effectively demonstrated their capacity to
mobilize support for the dictatorship. Trujillo could magnanimously
grant the vote to women, without running any major political risk.

Trujillo did much more than grant women the vote. At the same time,
he managed to create an intragroup rivalry between the feminists' leaders, thus assuring the death of the movement.†

Accion Feminista, as a movement unto itself, gradually disappeared
from the political scene in the Dominican Republic, although some of
its leaders continued to be politically active at the national and provincial level on a personal basis. By 1942, there was a "Feminist Section"
in the Trujillista Party, registered with the Dominican Party, founded
and controlled by Trujillo. Three years leter the Trujillista Party disappeared, and the women's section became the "Feminist Branch" of the
Dominican Party. The National Council of Women, which emerged from
within this party, is today affiliated with the Inter-American Commission
on Women.

The feminist movement of the 1930s and 1940s did achieve its basic
objectives. Its demands presented no real threat to the system and, on
the contrary, directly contributed to the stability of that system. The
rigid structure of Dominican society made liberal reforms of any sort
thoroughly irrelevant for the overwhelming majority of Dominican women.

It is this characteristic—the class origins of the Trujillista feminists—that limited a priori the fundamental objectives of the movement.
Their demands were necessarily undynamic, since the system could not
withstand profound changes, only subtle modifications. The undynamic
nature of feminism in this period predetermined its disappearance, and
its achievement meant very little for the great majority of Dominican
women.

---

*According to the Census of 1935, there were 314, 461 women be-
tween the ages of 20 and 85 or over in the country. In spite of the increase in the 15-19 year-old age group that occurred between 1935 and
1938, it would be difficult to get 344, 909 women of voting age in 1938,
in view of deaths and emigrations, not to mention the percentage of
women who wouldn't vote. See United Nations Demographic Yearbook
(1948) p. 111. Galindez (1956), p. 85, describes the election: "319, 680
electors voted out of the 348, 010 registered voters." This indicates
that not even 100 percent of the males voted.

†Chaney (1973), p. 111, cites cases of rivalry in Chile; Galindez
(1956), p. 333, cites rivalry in the Dominican feminist movement.

REFORMIST FEMINISTS

In 1966, Joaquin Balaguer, the newly elected President, appointed women to the governorships of all twenty-six provinces. This executive decision was without precedent in the history of Dominican politics. Since that year, the country has had women as Secretaries of State, Undersecretaries of State, Ambassadors, Senators, Representatives, and members of the National Development Council.

This conspicuous presence of women in the workings of government has been interpreted, both at home and abroad, as a sign of political progress for women under the Balaguer regime. * Given the historical precedent of Trujillista feminism, however, such affirmations must be met with extreme skepticism. We must again examine the ideological and class basis of feminism, and its relation to the Dominican political process in general, in order to evaluate its social and political significance for the contemporary period.

The concept of political activity that guides the Reformist feminists is not substantially different from that of their Trujillista predecessors. Basically, they maintain that women's contribution to politics consists of a serene and balanced personality, tact, and skill (see Baez Berg 1974, p. 3). The woman in politics is the mother who soothes in difficult moments, who tranquilizes a tumltuous world, and, above all, who serves as "a permanent example of the moral principles which are the basis of our Christian traditions" (see also Licelott Marte de Barrios, "El por qué de una mujer en la vicepresidencia de la Republica," Listin diario, February 18, 1974, p. 3). Women see themselves, then, in the role of "supermother"[†] in a larger home—the political arena. Their private role is not fundamentally altered, but simply widened to include the public sphere.

The phenomena described by Chaney (1973, p. 105), that "the majority of women who obtain elective or public positions carry out stereotyped female jobs in ministries and agencies which, on many occasions, have nothing to do with development and social change," is not predominant in the Dominican Republic; but current female feminist activity has centered on two aspects—education and legal reforms—as a panacea to discrimination and the oppression of women.

The following statements by feminist spokeswomen are indicative of this tendency:

---

[*]Balaguer, who was the "President" when Trujillo was assassinated in 1961, was elected in 1966 and reelected in 1970 and 1974.

[†]In a paper I was writing when Chaney's article was published, I said with reference to the "supermother," although in another context: "The use of Mary as the model Catholic woman has served to also mystify the earthly woman, that of flesh and bone, who in our country has been converted not only into a forced mother, but a supermother" (Mota 1973, p. 125).

The working woman of the country, as an integral part
of a whole, and of a traditionally exploited class, is the
appropriate victim of her own deficiencies and ignorance
(Pelaez 1973, p. 9; emphasis added).

Liberation is the fight for capacity and excellence and
we must struggle so that the State and all the large businesses provide opportunities for women to become capable, and
to be able to collaborate with men (Carmen Mendoza de Cor-
niella, "Cree liberacion un asunto de preparacion intelec-
tual," El Caribe, May 5, 1973, p. 3-A).

The goal of women's training schools is to achieve a
higher level of education, so that women may improve their
knowledge and understanding of matters concerning the home
(see Manuel A. Quiroz, "Afirma mujer dominicana avanza a
conquista metas," El Caribe, April 7, 1973, p. 3-B; emphasis added).

An entire book could be compiled of such quotations, while references to the need for creating more jobs and industrial schools to train
male and female workers are almost nonexistent. *

Equal emphasis has been placed on the need to enact legal reforms,
primarily in the Labor and Civil Codes. Reformist feminists view their
fight for equality with men as largely dependent on the revisions made
in these codes and on the Dominican woman's awareness of her rights
under the law. On June 15, 1973, through Balaguer's Decree no. 3587,
a special commission composed of six women was given responsibility
for revising legislation to ensure "complete legal equality, both civil
and political, for women" (Listin diario, June 19, 1973, p. 2). As of
September 1, 1975, this commission had not come up with any results.

Thus, the problems of Dominican women are viewed as "specific
deficiencies" whose remedies are entirely compatible with the political
and social system in existence. (See Carmenchu Brusiloff, "Mujer RD
se enfrenta discimen legal," El Caribe, July 5, 1973, pp. 1, 12. "Re-
caba incorporar mujer a labor desarrollo del Pais," ibid., August 3,
1973, p. 6). Moreover, women's personal development and their participation in the development of the country can be achieved within the
system, given that their problems can be corrected, without recourse
to drastic measures. There can be no doubt that this attitude serves

---

*An an indication of the educational level of Dominican women, in
the age group 15-49; 25 percent had no education; 26.4 percent completed one-three years of primary education; 22.7 percent completed
four-six years of primary education; 8.6 percent completed intermediate
education; 7.2 percent completed secondary education; 1.4 percent
completed university education. Encuesta demografica nacional (Santo
Domingo: 1973), p. 30. Data from the 1970 Census.

those groups that "would not be benefited by a radical social change" (Corten and Corten 1968, p. 5). This attitude also, and in a broader context, corresponds to Balaguer's own "ideology of change."

In the electoral campaign of 1966, Balaguer was presented as the candidate of the "bloodless revolution," while his opponent, ex-President Bosch, was linked to the sector that had "initiated" the bloody civil war of 1965. The motto of "bloodless revolution" meant in 1966—and still means today—that necessary changes can and should be achieved through gradual, nonviolent reforms, with respect for the rights of the individual and private property (see Balaguer 1966, passim). The bankruptcy of this ideology has been proved not only in the Dominican Republic but throughout Latin America and the world, yet the class composition of the Dominican feminists—petite bourgeois and upper-class women—created the logical basis for embracing Balaguer's policies and collaborating with his government.

Balaguer's victory in 1966 was, in part, won by the women's vote. In his electoral campaign, he appealed to the Dominican woman for support, to her enormous "reserves of maternal sentiment." He also sought and was granted that women of twenty-five or more were allowed to vote without the cedula personal de identidad (El Caribe, December 30, 1966, p. 14). This way he could count on the support of many mothers who had suffered during the civil war.

The reward for feminine support was rapid integration into the benefits of political partisanship. The distribution of twenty six appointive governorships and a variety of other posts was a foretaste of what women can expect from working within and for the system.

Thus, the benefits are enticing for both sides. Reformist feminists can contribute toward preserving their class position while finding outlets for personal ambition in posts newly opened to female "occupancy." At the same time, Balaguer plays on feminism in much the same manner as Trujillo did, using it to bolster the stability of his regime.

Nevertheless, there is a qualitative difference in the political tactics employed by Trujillo and Balaguer with respect to feminism. The Dominican bourgeoisie has become more sophisticated, more practiced in manipulating the political activity of women to serve its own ends. In the present period of official reformism, feminist participation in government is being used as an effective tool in the political struggle.

> The traditional way of attracting the masses through personal gifts, distributions of food, sewing machines or wedding trousseaus, which was cultivated during the Trujillo years is still in force today. This method of working with the masses in a paternalist and reactionary way has yielded magnificent results for the Reformist party, principally in its efforts at proselytizing among women of the lower strata of the population. . . . Female Secretaries and Subsecretaries of State, 26 female Governors, the Crusade of Love, and the constantly increasing activities

of the wives of military men, validate their promises of
greater feminine participation and guarantee effective penetration in this sector (Tejada 1973, p. 11).

This type of activity, primarily carried out by an organization called
"Crusade of Love," headed by Balaguer's sister Emma, and other women
from the ranks of the bourgeoisie, is undeniably effective. "Conditioned
throughout their lives to be practical (they only spin dreams about their
love-lives, and these are well channeled by the system using the radio
and television soap-operas) women easily fall prey to such vote-buying
politics" (Tejada 1973, p. 11). In some cases, personal favors take
on an "entrepreneurial" dimension; vending booths are apportioned in
the market place, and Mothers' Centers are established in which women's
handicraft work is sold at ridiculously low prices to "tourist" shops and
exhibited at regional fairs (see Licelott Marte de Barrios, "La mujer
deberia participar mas en el desarrollo de la comunidad." El Caribe,
December 2, 1972, p. 7-A. Francisco Alvarez Castellanos, "Atribuye a
mujer funcion en desarrollo." Listin diario, June 20, 1972, p. 13).
Thus, the Reformist feminists appear before the masses as fairy god-
mothers who feed and clothe the poor. "Maternalism" has become a key
element of demogogic politics.
Other parties along the political spectrum have "seen the light"
and are in strong competition for the favors of Dominican women. The
Movement for National Reconciliation, for example, if victorious in the
May 1974 elections, promised to enact far-reaching reforms in favor
of feminism:

Women are called upon to accomplish beautiful, significant work in the fields of education and social work and
the National Conciliation Movement counts on them as a
magnificent reserve for the realization of the plans made by
the future Secretary of Social Matters and other government
departments, which will provide propitious fields of activity
for the delicate feminine sensibility ("Afirma MCN aspira un
regimen democratico." Listin diario, July 31, 1973, p. 13;
emphasis added).

The support given to the candidacy of a woman, Altagracia Bautista
de Suarez, for Vice-President of the Republic/in the May 1974 elections
is the most recent example of upper-class feminism in the service of
bourgeois politics. For these women, this candidacy "would turn large
sectors of the population toward reformism, not only among women, who
would feel honorably 'represented', but also among other groups representative of Dominican society." (Baez Berg 1974). Bautista de Suarez,
representative of a Reformist feminist, conceives women's liberation
as the result of "women's ability to achieve perfectly, at the side of
their companions, the anguish and sublime mission that is allocated to
[us] women: to be mothers, if only of a minuscule part of humanity"

(Listin diario, December 28, 1972, p. 9). Unfortunately for these women, Balaguer chose to run with his same Vice-President, Goico Morales.

All this rhetoric is in the name of women, of all women of the country, without their having expressed the desire for such mouthpieces. They do not have a radical feminist movement that could fight their oppression and marginality. This allows the Reformist sector to take advantage of the alienation and passivity of masses of women for its own benefit.

CONCLUSION

The extension of women's traditional role in the home to the political sphere implies no qualitative changes in the situation of women as a whole, nor in the political and economic system that perpetrates their positions. It means, simply, that more women occupy positions of power and can, in turn, be used by the existing power structure to further its objectives. Radical feminism, in the sense of fundamental changes in the hierarchy of male-female relations, has never existed in the Dominican Republic.

The Reformist feminists, like their predecessors of the Trujillo era, can never achieve fundamental improvements for the masses of Dominican women, much less "liberate" them from oppression. For what characterizes the traditional feminism of both periods is its compatibility with the existing social, political, and economic system— and its interests in protecting the capitalist system. It is this very system that prevents the possibility of liberation for the masses of Dominican men and women. In the end, the task of creating a revolutionary political consciousness rests on the shoulders of a feminist movement among the popular classes, and not among the "conservative" classes.

Unfortunately, such a movement does not exist in the Dominican Republic for the reasons I proposed very tentatively in the introduction. It has been launched on two occasions, but never was able to develop.

REFERENCES

Baez Berg, Olga. 1974. "Una candidatura aglutinante. " El nacional de i Ahora!. February 21, 1974.

Balaguer, Joaquin. 1966. El reformismo. Filosofia politica de la revolucion sin sangre. Santo Domingo: Publicaciones Reformas.

Bosch, Juan. 1965. The Unfinished Experiment: Democracy in the Dominican Republic. New York: Praeger.

Chaney, Elsa. 1973. "Women in Latin American Politics: The Case of Peru and Chile." In Female and Male in Latin America, ed. Ann Pescatello. Pittsburgh: University of Pittsburgh Press.

Corten, Andre, and Andree Corten. 1968. Cambio social en Santo Domingo. Special Study no. 5. Rio Piedras, Puerto Rico: Instituto de Estudios del Caribe.

Crasweller, Robert. 1966. Trujillo: The Life and Times of a Caribbean Dictator. New York: MacMillan.

Galindez, Jesus de. 1956. "La era de Trujillo." Un estudio casuistico de dictadura hispanoamericana. 4th ed. Santiago: Editorial del Pacifico.

Lara Fernandez, Carmen. 1946. Historia del feminismo en la Republica Dominicana. Ciudad Trujillo: Imp. Arte y Cine.

Martin, John Bartlow. 1966. Overtaken by Events: The Dominican Crisis from the Fall of Trujillo to the Civil War. Garden City, N.Y.: Doubleday.

Mota, Vivian M. 1972. "La mujer en la historia dominicana." Unpublished.

_____. 1973. "Algunas consideraciones sobre la Iglesia Catolica, la mujer y la planificacion familiar." Estudios sociales 7 (July-September).

Newhall, Beatrice. 1936. "Woman Suffrage in the Americas." Bulletin of the Pan American Union 70 (May).

Pelaez, Casilda. 1973. "La oficina nacional de la mujer." Ultima hora, July 20, 1973.

Portela, Maria Concepcion. 1968. "America y las organizaciones femeninas." EIDOS (Spain) no. 29 (December):

Rodman, Selden. 1964. Quisqueya: A History of the Dominican Republic, Seattle: University of Washington Press.

Sanchez Lustrino, Gilberto. 1938. Trujillo: El constructor de una nacionalidad. Havana: Cultural.

Scott, James Brown. 1931. The International Conferences of American States, 1889-1928. New York: Oxford University Press.

Tejada, Leonor (pseudonym). 1973. "La mujer y el continuismo."
    Ultima Hora, October 24.

Wiarda, Howard. 1968. Dictatorship and Development: The Changing
    Methods of Control in Trujillo's Dominican Republic. Latin Ameri-
    can Monographs, Second Series, no. 5. Gainesville: University
    of Florida Press.

15

CHILE: THE FEMININE
VERSION OF
THE COUP D'ETAT
Michele Mattelart

"Once we saw the Chilean women were marching, we knew that Allende's days were numbered." A Brazilian engineer (who freely admitted to pursuing a number of interests outside his profession) made this statement to a journalist from the Washington <u>Post</u> in January 1974. During the interview he claimed that the responsibility for this enterprise of women's mobilization could be laid at the doorstep of extreme right-wing organizations and Brazilian businessmen who taught the Chileans how to use their women against the "Marxists." Such arrogance, such self-assurance would not dare to display itself at any but the present moment, when the sedition apparently has been crowned with success. But this spokesman for the Brazilian reactionaries was not the sort of man to ignore the possibility that similar experiences might occur elsewhere. A lesson was to be learned here, having to do with the active part women could play in the counterrevolutionary struggle, as the engineer announced when he said, "Women are the most effective weapon you have in politics. They have a great capacity to display emotion and to mobilize quickly. For example, if you want to spread a rumor like 'The President has a drinking problem,' or 'He had a slight heart attack,' you use the women. The next day it is around the country. . . . The women's most crucial role is to prove to the military that they have wide civilian support."

The last sentence shows us that, in the logic of sedition, mass demonstrations of the right wing and mass women's demonstrations, especially, are nothing but new and improved versions of these campaigns aimed at swaying public opinion that, in the last analysis, have but one objective: setting in motion the armed faction of the conspiracy. "They supplied us for three years," Pinochet said the day after the coup, as he expressed his gratitude for the action of "democratic" broadcasting and laid stress on the effectiveness of the women's unceasing clamor. Evidently, the psychopolitical struggle has undergone a new type of programming. Moreover, the Brazilian engineer confirmed a continuity between the women's demonstrations and the public opinion

campaigns when he revealed that Brazil had assisted the Chilean right
with two specific kinds of paramilitary support: the planning of the
women's mobilization and the creation of institutes for the study of
public opinion. The ideological struggle waged by the right against
the Popular Unity, the "conquest of minds," as they put it, was no
longer just a matter of a few slogans distributed in cheap pamphlets:
it had become incarnated in the streets. The offensive no longer relied
exclusively on a limited number of human brains to generate propaganda
pictures: it threw into the melee the counterrevolutionary potential of
its feminine clientele, converting it into an army of activists recruited
from the masses. The woman served as a democratic pretext for brutal
intervention; indeed, her cause came to be equated with that of the
business and professional organizations.

In public speeches the pretext became the alibi of a bad conscience:
"The woman has taught us men a real lesson. She has shown herself
indomitable, ready to defend that which was just. She has demonstrated
a resistance capable of withstanding every test. We want women to
participate in the administration of the country. We want them to play
a role as important as that of the corporations, the armed forces, and
the political parties." (El mercurio 1974). Remarks such as these made
by General Leigh on the day following the coup may seem a rather unusual addition to the annals of global fascism; as a token of recognition
for services well-perfomed, the Chilean woman would see herself re-
paid with the right to direct representation in a future "parliament",
alongside the corporations, the armed forces, and youth. Nowadays,
however, there seems to be a great deal of bashfulness, of reticence,
indeed, on the part of the junta when it comes to raising this issue, *
while the generals—who seem to always be postponing the transfer of
power to their civilian accomplices in the coup—never tire of "feminist"
rhetoric. For them, the woman is one of the pillars in the "national reconstruction."

One important question remains to be answered. What has happened
with respect to the woman's self-image within the dominant ideology?
It is necessary to gauge accurately the overall significance of this
question, because of the bankruptcy of the traditional image of the
woman, one that the Chilean bourgeoisie had fostered as much as or
more than any other, was well on the way toward being declared at the
time of the coup. On the one hand, a stock of traits had been sanctified by the dominant ideology: respect for privacy, nonparticipation
in politics, feminine bias in perceiving and understanding the world at

---

*In General Pinochet's last declaration of principles, delivered in
the Gabriela Mistral building on March 11, 1974, there is no longer
any question of a "parliament." Moreover, General Leigh today cen-
sures a program (made by the women who actively participated in the
resistance against Allende) that appeared on Chilean television and
accused Chilean men of being somewhat stay-at-home.

large, confinement to the realm of house chores. On the other hand, the
bourgeoisie, as if overnight, suggested to its women that they acquire
characteristics that lent credence to "another" feminine reality: women
in politics, women on streets filled with violence, streets that had
ceased to be synonymous with window-shopping. The woman was to
be a mass-production "pasionaria" for enticing men to combat, a woman
who was not content with merely caring for the soldiers—her son, her
husband, her father—returned from war. But she was no longer the individual heroine, in the manner of Ines de Suarez, the lover of Pedro
de Valdivia, who alone defended the fort of Santiago against the "sav-
ages." She could no longer be held up for adoration because such unique
and exceptional women, after all, do nothing except better sanctify the
normality the lives that other women lead outside the combat zone. We
propose to examine the ideological mechanisms to which the Chilean
right had recourse in its efforts to prevent the mass mobilization of its
female contingent from being interpreted as a definitive break with the
woman's traditional self-image.
        Events that occurred during the three years Chile spent under the
Popular regime can give us an appreciation of the profoundly anti-liber-
tarian spirit of the women's emancipation movement, a movement sponsored by a bourgeoisie threatened in its class intersts. While those
three years reveal the elasticity of what the bourgeoisie saw as its
conception of "femininity," they also demonstrate the boundaries within
which the movement for "emancipation" was forced to evolve, a movement that the bourgeois theoreticians publicy extolled. Moreover, the
Chilean affair gives us direct exposure to what amounts to a paradigm
for the utilization of women, in both an ideological and a political context, which could be applied not only to other countries in Latin America but also to other countries where the forces of the left, by playing
according to the rules the democratic game, have a historic opportunity
of acceding to government control. It is certainly appropriate to stress
both the aspects unique to the Chilean affair and those peculiar to the
situation of the Chilean woman. But we should not forget the methods
and strategies that the instincts and will to survive of the international
reaction are capable of fomenting.

ON FOOT, BY HORSE, BY CAR

        In the course of the Popular regime's three-year rule, several epi-
sodes demonstrate the constant presence of women at key moments of
the class confrontation. On September 4, 1970, Allende was elected
with 36. 2 percent of the votes cast. The majority of the female electorate showed its preference for right-wing candidates: 68. 3 percent
of the women voted for Allesandri (38. 4 percent) or for Tomic (29. 9

percent)—candidates, respectively, of the National Party and the
Christian Democrats. Allende received only 30.5 percent of the women's
vote. *

During the period between the elections and the accession of the
Popular forces to government control, a group of women from the oligarchy, like birds of ill omen dressed entirely in black, surrounded the
Palace of the Moneda and started a funeral procession to show that they
were in mourning for the death of democracy in Chile.

A year and a half later, another woman from the oligarchy stationed
her horse in front of the same Moneda, in order to protest against the
threats of expropriation made against her and her large estate. She had
travelled the immense distance between her fundo in the South and the
capital entirely on horseback, receiving the approbation of the right
wing throughout the journey. The conservative press saluted her as
the Amazon of liberty. She could be seen threading her way through the
streets of Santiago, atop her horse, dressed in only a bathing suit, no
doubt to symbolize the state of undress to which she had been reduced
by the Popular Unity.

Women participated in the first mass demonstration staged by the
right. The last, before the putsch, was a women's demonstration as
well. This first demonstration, known as the "march of the empty pots,"
which took place on December 1, 1971, constituted one of the indexes
that gave Fidel Castro, then visiting Chile, cause to declare: "During
this first year the reactionaries have learned more and have learned
it better than the revolutionaries." Organized by the Democratic
Women's Front, which united the female members of the National Party
and the Christian Democrats, it was the first occasion that the right
had, since it was still unsure as to the strategy it should adopt, to
measure the effectiveness of its street protests. In March 1972, the
right wing decided to rely on support from its "masses" and to relegate
the traditional vehicles for exerting pressure (the parliament, the
courts, the parties, the "contraloria"—a kind of audit office that had
become a veritable state within a state) to a secondary role. These
demonstrations were repeated at regular intervals. They all had as their
common thematic symbol and noisy showpiece a pot, which the women
would beat with a lid or spoon. Commencing on the evening of December
1, 1971, the echo of these pots was soon heard in the residential districts of every Chilean city. A month or fortnight did not go by without
our hearing this metallic rallying cry on every street corner between
the hours of 8 and 10 P.M.

The women's demonstrations always followed the same pattern.
Assembled around a central group of bourgeois women of all ages, who
arrived in automobiles and were often accompanied by their maids, were

---

*In 1964, women subscribed to the candidacy of Frei by a large
majority (63 percent). At this time, Allende received only 32 percent of
the women's vote, as against 45 percent of the men's.

women from the petite bourgeoisie (always in the majority), together with a lesser number of women from the "poblaciones" (shantytowns) and the Lumpenproletariat. All of these were encircled by the militants, helmeted and armed with chains, who were recruited from the paramilitary faction of the extreme right wing known as "Fatherland and Liberty," which had an active women's branch especially trained for purposes of sedition. This was "Poder Feminino," or "Woman's Power," a group that later came to control all the dynamic energies of the women's front in the final months of the Popular regime.

Bourgeois women were again present when the opposition parties began openly to court the armed forces. On numerous occasions, the women provoked the army by exciting the soldiers' "macho" reflexes and arousing their ambitions for power. Many times women went to the Military Academy to throw grain at the Chilean soldiers, thereby treating them like hens, chiding them for what they supposed to be weakness and lack of virility. When the Popular Unity took charge of food distribution and committees for food distribution and control of prices, the women of the right supported the merchants when they created and organized a systematic sabotage effort directed against this egalitarian form of food distribution. Their success or lack of it depended, of course, on the neighborhood. Women repeated the same form of open aggression against the policemen who were posted in the community offices by hurling insults and pieces of money at them in order to demonstrate their disdain for these "mercenaries" of the Popular order.

Finally, General Prat, accused of maintaining the constitutionalist tradition within the army, was harassed by one woman from the oligarchy. Her individual demonstration took on a collective dimension after the frustrated coup d'etat of June 29, 1973, when a group of officers' wives (the same ones who offered their jewels and wedding rings to the Junta to refloat the treasury and begin the "national reconstruction") organized meetings under the windows of General Prat in order to make his position even more untenable and further damage his morale. The Brazilian engineer mentioned earlier took note of the day-to-day influence a woman is capable of exerting upon her immediate circle of acquaintances and emphasized that the military men, most of whom have a wife and home, could not escape their influence. The force of the women's demonstrations burst out again eight days before the coup d'etat of September 11, during the largest march ever organized by the Chilean right, one in which women chanted slogans aimed at forcing Allende to resign.

In retrospect, one commentator compared this demonstration with the Sao Paulo women's march of 1964, which preceded the fall of Joao Goulart by two weeks. Nonetheless, we should qualify this oft-repeated analogy by taking note of one major difference: in Brazil, the demonstrators marched while reciting the rosary, whereas in Chile the right made no such appeal to the piety of its women (piety having passed somewhat out of fashion as a possible source of motivation for the urban masses in Chile). The only exception to this seclarism was during the period in which the chief theme of the mobilization against the Popular regime was the project for the reform of popular education, where a clerical bias crept into the classic antagonism between public and private schools. Once the putsch was a fait accompli, however, the clerical bias took on the proportions of an invasion and became one of the steps by which order was to be restored in the family as each of its members, and the woman in particular, was reassigned to the role dictated by tradition.

But the women's opposition movement did not restrict itself to the high and middle bourgeoisie, as the above examples, illustrating the active participation by women in the civil resistance movement against Allende, would tend to suggest. The right also counted upon the support of women in the working classes and petite bourgeoisie. Participation in this regard was of two kinds. First, women were able to work with community organizations that had been set up under the previous government and that continued, in a number of cases, under the control of the Christian Democrats and the National Party during the Allende period. I am speaking here of the centros de madres (a kind of charity workshop set up in the slums) and the juntas de vecinos, organs of joint local administration in which women actively participated. The right organized several demonstrations with these groups of pobladoras (shantytown dwellers) during the period in which the Christian Democrats still seemed to be the principal opposition force (that is, until October 1972, at the latest).

The second kind of participation open to the women from the lower classes and the petite bourgeoisie was less autonomous, since it depended on whether the women's demonstrations were organized as expressions of solidarity with the strikers' movement to which their husbands, sons, or brothers belonged. Episodes included the demonstration staged by the wives of the men who struck the El Teniente copper mine*—the "heroic wives of the miners," as they were described by the

---

*In order to commemorate this event, the junta has decided to make June 26 the "Day of the Working Woman." One remark seems necessary here: we must guard against ascribing to the movement of working-class women in the employers' strike, and therefore to the resistance organized by the right, a numerical importance it never had. The number of workers who responded to the strike call at the El Teniente copper mine, a strike ordered by the opposition, is estimated at approximately 4,000, against a total of 12,750 workers employed at the mine. The number of miners' wives, daughters, and sisters who marched on Santiago on June 26, 1973, was not greater than the number of strikers. Though our purpose in this article is not to analyze the mobilization of the women of the Popular Unity, a few words on it are needed here. Since they were of a defensive nature and without precise political import as a response to the demonstrations of the opposition, they attracted fewer demonstrators and were less spectacular. We should also note that the women of the Popular Unity and of the left in general were mobilized with a great deal of enthusiasm for all the general demonstrations, which reunited a

right-wing press. The newspapers took special delight in being able to
chalk up to the opposition the kind of women's solidarity movement that
until then had been the exclusive property of traditional struggles for
liberation in Latin America: one need only think of the marches organized
by the wives of miners in Bolivia. The wives of transportation workers
prepared "public soup kitchens" on the street corners of Santiago in
order to gain public sympathy and make the passerby feel sorry for their
husbands, who, at that very moment, were receiving more from the hands
of capitalism to continue their strike than they could by working.

The text of one of the announcements for the last women's demonstration includes all the sectors of the female population that the opposition purported to represent. It also illustrates the extreme lengths
to which the subversion went:

Chilean Women!
Mr. Allende does not deserve to be President of the Republic.
Mr. Allende has led the country into a catastrophe.
We don't have bread for our children!
We don't have medicine for those who are sick!
We don't have clothes to wear!
We don't have a roof to put over our heads!

We have been violated, humiliated, and hounded because
we have defended our sons, because we have shown solidarity with our striking husbands, because we have gone
into the streets to arouse the sleeping consciences of so
many men!

We summon all women to an affair of honor!
Wednesday, September 5, at 8 P.M.

Give the cry: wives of transport workers, women employed
in the paper factory, peasant women, "pobladoras," students, businesswomen, secretaries, nurses, social workers,
women in liberal professions, and the Women of the Chilean Gremios!*

---

considerable number of militants and sympathizers of both sexes roughly
equal in numbers. But it is above all in the context of their life in the
neighborhoods that women of the popular classes are mobilized daily
and have participated actively in the changes in the community where
they live. Thus they give proof of a great militancy that has not always
been recognized by the left, which fails to take into sufficient consideration the specific problems of the women's struggle.

*The best translation of "gremialist" is "corporative." The women
usurped the name from their husbands who participated in the general
strike launched by the corporations, transport workers, doctors, and
similar groups.

Note the proletarian content of the demands of the bourgeois women. What has gone into operation here is a hoax, for if women from many diverse social strata do coexist within the rank and file of the right wing, they do so in vastly different proportions, which the slogans have no interest in revealing. Putting its few women of the people into the forefront, the bourgeoisie waves the banner of the proletariat. Its collective action usurps the motivation of the poor consumer, for whom it is the price of bread that counts (the Popular government did all in its power to protect the price and availability of bread). Consumption, the ritual need of the bourgeois woman, oriented toward sumptuary goods, becomes survival, reduced to the needs of bare subsistence.

Moreover, there are limits to the solidarity shown by the bourgeois. One should not believe that the right-wing woman, who has, by and large, descended from the possessor class, has abandoned her class stereotypes and divested herself of a sense of superiority when it comes to making one tentative step toward the other sectors. The only change that occurs when she goes to war is that this prevalent attitude no longer manifests itself explicitly, except vis-a-vis those women of the people who refuse to go along with her class project. Then her vituperations show us the distance remaining between social sectors, a distance that cannot be bridged unless the bourgeoisie so desires. "Look at those plebeians! Who do they think they are?," the bourgeois women exclaimed when they saw women (their sisters?) of the revolutionary populace trying to organize community food distribution by themselves.

Such was the more spectacular side of the women's resistance movement vis-a-vis the Popular Unity. But the resistance had, above all, a day-to-day quality that penetrated the home, the family, and the network of neighborhood relationships, where it became associated with the incessant comings and goings of the rumor mongers. If the principal topic of feminine complaint was poverty in the kitchen, then the center of her interest was hoarding. Both would seem to follow from a similar definition of what a woman is. You take to the streets to shout for "bread," but in the meantime you stock up as if there were no tomorrow. Or, in the words of a song intoned over and over again from the podium during Popular demonstrations: "The right has two pots, one very small and one very large; on the first it drums in the streets; in the second it hoards and heaps. . . ."*

"There is no meat, there are no eggs in this new Chile," the women of the right would chant in the vicinity of the Moneda, while, like ants, they voluntarily participated in the deterioration of the national economy by accumulating commodities within their larders, whose size varied according to social position (since "penury" had not made budgets equal), and by organizing and supplying the black market.

---

*A song by the folklore group Quilapayun: "La derecha tiene dos ollitas."

Defense of the children against the "Marxist yoke" was another powerful motivating factor, though it was proclaimed at more infrequent intervals and always within the framework of the Centros de Apoderados (centers for the parents of schoolchildren), united under the National Federations. These centers received decisive aid from the mothers of the dominant classes and the petite bourgeoisie.

IN SPITE OF EVERYTHING, GALLANTRY IS DEMANDED

Many examples in El Mercurio, the oldest daily paper of the Chilean bourgeoisie, attest to the fact that the right decided to give the women, or organizations in which women participated, a role in the strategy it adopted to overthrow the Popular Unity government. This strategy was founded on the mobilization of a mass front. The new civic duties were clearly spelled out: "No lady of the house," it was announced on November 9, 1971, "no citizen, no one today prepared to express himself or take action has the right to expect that others will defend the liberty of the country. The organizations formed in the urban districts, the schools, and the factories must win the cooperation of these democratic masses."

Thus, the same bourgeoisie that waited until 1949 ungraciously to accord its women the right to vote (they had been petitioning for it since 1898) and that never favored their requests in the matter of civil rights, suddenly hurried to expand the woman's traditional role. Obviously, the bourgeoisie could no longer sit by and allow the female to limit herself to an existence as the passive mother, spouse, and the lady of the house who traditionally assured the reproduction of the key values of the system. The bourgeoisie now required that she become active, that she organize, that she mobilize herself for the defense of "democracy," of which she was about to become the living symbol.

The element upon which the right was counting, and which it intended to use with impunity, was a throwback, paradoxically, to the distance between women and politics that the dominant ideology sanctified, a distance that, once insinuated into the individual subconscious, permitted the right to offer, and make the woman accept, the new mode of female behavior as if it were devoid of all political content. The right was able to rely for support upon the traditional stock of images and values that fixed the form, manner, and style of women's behavior, and thus legitimated these demonstrations and identified them as the spontaneous responses of the most apolitical sector of public opinion, gathered together and mobilized by the survival instinct. The women became a "democratic" sector of society, having been "naturally" inspired to defend that universe of traditions, those values of "justice" and "liberty," that serve to mask the oppressive fatality of the bourgeois order.

The wording of yet another rallying cry, prepared for the final right-wing demonstration, indicates how the bourgeoisie, using the image of woman as mother, appropriates the task of representing working-class people and how, by virtue of this unexpected "popular" majority, the bourgeoisie went about giving its most violent appeals for insurrection a democratic tinge:

Chilean Women!

Mr. Allende has said he would resign if working-class people demanded it.
We are the people! Every child of this land has come from our womb!
Today, Wednesday, 5 A. M. to 5 P. M. in front of the Catholic University and in all the cities throughout the land, we women will take Mr. Allende at his word (El Mercurio 1973).

The right was able to camouflage the defense of its class interests behind the protests of women, behind demands that, since they have to do with subjects traditionally of marginal political interest (home, familial organization, care and education of children), and thus, apparently, not connected with a class strategy. Moreover, within the group of demands that served as the focus of the demonstrations, the right attempted to overstep—with less prudence as time passed—the domain of agitation whose scope was specifically feminine, in order to give vent to grievances that were clearly political in nature and that were shared by the other opposition fronts.
    Accounts of marches such as that of the "empty pots," as given in the conservative press, reveal the value that the bourgeoisie attaches to the activity of the women's front and do much to show the ideological and political benefits that the conservatives expected to gain. Such accounts actually aided the right in its efforts to legitimize, to "naturalize"—one might almost say to "sanctify"—its opposition to the Popular regime. In the calendar of violence that El Mercurio published on January 6, 1972, under the title "1971-1972: Under the Popular Unity, a Year of Violence," the entry for December 1 says:

The largest women's demonstration in recent memory ended with acts of criminal aggression against women, acts which were undertaken by the counter-demonstration brigades of the Popular Unity. . . . Police agents threw teargas canisters, thereby arousing the indignation both of the women demonstrating and of the spectators.

On the day after the march, comments of some of the demonstrators were transformed by the same paper into the following sensationalistic headline: "We got beaten up despite our being women!" Women now devoted their time and effort to this new kind of activity as if it were a matter of life and death, even though marching, for many, took the place of the "canasta tea." "Certainly, I demonstrate," they said. But even though the demonstrations may not have been foreseen in the code of feminine behavior, certain parties demanded that the code remain in effect and that it guarantee the woman both a privileged status and the right to be seated first at table.

The objective pursued by the writers of such accounts and commentaries was of course to project the image of a Marxist government as generator of violence, chaos, and aggression, against both women and the community as a whole. The downfall of the code of gallantry, even if the woman first transgressed against it, was seen as the precursor of the destruction of civilization. The culprit is supposedly Mr. Allende, the man obstinately pursuing a disastrous course of action. The would-be aggression and the would-be Marxist repression were made to justify the "democratic" defense.

The same symbolic idea—this time under the guise of a "court of miracles"—appeared in the newspaper account of another incident included in the calendar of violence:

> On March 22, a march was conducted by a group of
> cripples protesting the delays to which they had been sub-
> jected by a law forbidding the importation of prosthetic
> devices. The demonstration was brought to a shameful
> conclusion when the police, who were only obeying higher
> authority, intervened with excessive force.

Weakness. Innocence. A state of defenselessness (woman equals cripple). The bourgeoisie—which, in the absence of a "responsible" father, arrogated to itself the right to represent and defend all the weak and oppressed—reactivated all the components of the female stereotype (softness, sensibility, natural sympathy for peace and order), in order to hide under a veil of innocence, to insinuate or reinforce the idea that the order approved and defended by women was the order best for the country.

THE CORPORATIVENESS OF WOMEN

The constitution that the military junta promised on the day following the coup d'etat was to have assured women representation in the "parliament," at the side of the corporations, the armed forces, youth, and the political parties. During the entire period of its opposition to the Popular regime, the bourgeoisie continued to foster the idea of the natural corporativeness of women, an idea already implicit in the presentation of the women's movement as democratic. At the outset, the women's front signified a vehicle for action against the Popular Unity government; because the front took on this meaning, the right was able to mobilize women by using such arguments as food scarcity. Through the woman, the right also was successful in mobilizing the consumer, that anonymous representative of the middle classes, against the measures of the Popular Unity. But there was a cluster of ideas already implicit within the constituency of this front, dovetailing with the corporative ideology taking shape among the various alternatives of the struggle, ideas which crystallized in a conceptual and practical response to Marxism: a project for the reform of society whose fundamental axis was corporative power (see Mattelart 1974).

In defining the woman according to attributes which have their origin more in nature than in history, the dominant ideology prepared the way for the idea of female corporativeness that became manifest in the speeches of the junta. The concept of woman that the bourgeois ideology fostered really served the purpose of bypassing the direct effect of the class on the individual, of sidestepping the antagonism of the classes, and of denying that it was an essential contradiction to begin with. By virtue of the universalizing "sign" of nature, the female condition would guarantee a fundamental continuity of interests among women. And it was in this sense that the image of the woman—holding now to the dominant mythology—could traverse all the social sectors and act as the connecting link in a tangible unity. "Women's power" took refuge behind the same "democratic" alibi that the power of the corporations used, a power that groups and assembles individuals according to their specialty. There is a female function and specialty, just as there is a specialty behind every trade group.

The bourgeoisie tended to enclose its women within the quite limited specialty and function rapidly and rigidly, lest they acquire bad habits from their street experiences, such as the taste for political power. One can't help seeing a parallelism here between the destiny of the women and that of the corporations, which returned to their technical functions once the right had regained power over the state. The same process occurred where women were concerned; the woman was told to mind her own business once the political work had been done. Sra. Pinochet exhorted her peers, even as the smoke was still rising from the palace of the Moneda and the Mapocho River had begun to carry the first corpses (La tercera de la hova 1973):

> Mothers, do not allow the children whom you have
> cradled and whose tears you have dried with tenderness
> and self-sacrifice to be torn from you by hatred, which
> turns people into ferocious beasts and causes them to de-
> stroy their brothers. . . . She who is addressing this mes-
> sage to you is a mother like other women, and she knows
> that you can do much for peace and mutual understanding
> among Chileans. . . . The tears of your heart will be the
> redemption of all. . . .

The directors of Women's Power said (El Mecurio 1973):

> The Chilean woman, through her sufferings, her humil-
> iation, and her heroism, has safeguarded the libertarian

> hopes of Chile . . . understands that the reconstruction
> of Chile will be an undertaking worthy of a disciplined and
> patriotic people. It is for this that Women's Power calls
> upon all Chilean women to demonstrate once more their
> unflagging spirit of sacrifice.

Abnegation. Spirit of sacrifice. Love. We had come a long way from
that hatred aimed at Allende long before he was struck down by bullets!

The "power of the woman" had become nothing other than her natural disposition to passivity. The traditional feminine image, all of
whose retrogressive meaning the junta's rhetoric exalted, had come
away healthy and whole from its confrontation with history, so that the
woman may be restored to her pedestal as the tutelary angel of the
Family, of the Fatherland, and of Property. It is no accident that these
three words, each capitalized, were the ones that crowned the program of
"Fatherland and Liberty," which today serves to inspire all of the putsch
generals.

DISCOVERING SEVERAL ANTECEDENTS

Out of all the factors contributing to an explanation of how the
Chilean right was able to mobilize a woman's front of such importance
and effectiveness, as soon as it had need of one, we shall consider
three: the presence of certain traits within the personality of Chilean
women, the existence of mechanisms for the participation and organization, and the circumstances through which women are introduced into
the processes of production.

"Tell me, Cazota, in your land, is everything as beautiful as your
women? In that case, my felicitations." We are told by the chronicler
who records the conversation that these were the words spoken by Louis
Phillipe to a Chilean ambassador in France. The chronicler, writing
at the turn of the century, goes even further: "In all the periods of this
country's history, the woman has occupied a position of honor within
the society, no matter what the circumstances were under which the
loving influence of her superior spirit has had occasion to make itself
felt" (Poirier 1901). These remarks could just as well have been
uttered today. Each crisis, however, reveals traits that are not
the exclusive property of the Chilean woman.

And if women's political activity has been able to develop so
quickly over the past three years, it is undoubtedly due, in large measure, to the condition of women in this land. If the dominant culture
has integrated—as it does in all capitalist settings, even given the
unique characteristics of Latin America—the values that sanctify the
subordinated status of the woman, then, in practice, the woman occupies a central position from the point of view of economy and family organization. Within the proletariat, this situation can be verified with

what is, perhaps, an uncommon degree of precision. Since "free" marriages are common, and the man of the house often deserts it, the woman becomes the pillar of family unity and acts as such. The Popular Unity government voted into law a bill giving these unmarried women the family assistance allotments they had been denied in the past. Women in the well-to-do districts, in addition to exercising uncontested authority within the domestic sphere, made their presence felt in the public domain as well, even if it was always under the discriminatory but little-argued egis of the women's cause: in the social services, teaching, interior design, secretarial work, and paramedical services.

Even though it is not quite correct to speak of a feminist movement in Chile, a small group of women from the dominant class distinguished itself in the first decades of the century by its struggle to obtain guarantees in the exercise of civil and political rights. * They did not take to the streets on that occasion, but on January 8, 1948, about forty of them staged a demonstration inside the Chamber of Deputies. This was the day on which they secured the right to vote from the men of their own social class. Nevertheless, the leaders of the women's movement, in their struggle against the Popular Unity regime, appear to be more the heirs of what was known during the period as the "senora's club" than of the handful of young suffragettes or the women's Civic Party. The Civic Party came into existence at the time of the creation of the Federation of Students and lost all its popularity by leading a losing campaign for the legalization of divorce, after it had fought, as early as 1920, for the right to vote. The "senora's club," composed of aristocrats often in the public eye, cried scandal and was able to dissolve the Civic Party, which was accused of undermining morals and family stability. The movement for the "Emancipation of Women," which took the place of the Civic Party, met opposition for its "Communistic leanings," even though it did not have a single thing in common with any leftist ideology. It too was destined to lead a brief life.

---

*The "emancipation" of the Chilean woman of the privileged classes of course rests upon the exploitation of the women of the people, those who have immigrated from rural areas. In 1968, 100 percent of the well-to-do women who had a job also had a housemaid and at least 30 percent had two. Even when those women do not have a job, they have maids. During the same period, 85 percent of the married women without a job had at least one maid. In the petite bourgeoisie, 88 percent of the women who worked were assisted in their domestic chores; but among those who did not work, only 40 percent received such help. For more information on the situation of the woman in Chile before the Popular Unity, see Armand and Michele Mattelart (1968). Some aspects of the question in the days since then have been treated by Vania Bambirra (1971; 1972).

It was not until 1970 that the struggle for women's participation, having allied itself with the bourgeoisie, ceased to be the creation of a few individuals and took on real significance. It was then that the "interest she takes in her household and family forces her to abandon the tranquillity of the home and evokes those she-wolf instincts within her which are brought to life at the sight of her children being attacked by the Popular Unity." We quote: "By an 'historic 'crusade of the empty pots, ' woman found a way of demonstrating to the government that . . . if it should prove necessary, she would leave her cozy kitchen in order to devote her energies to warfare" (Eva 1974). Actually, until then, the Chilean woman of the dominant classes had always known how to establish a compromise with the norms prescibed by masculine authority. The "light" weight of her servitude had seemed to her to be compensated for by the advantages she received in return: order and affluence within the home, relative freedom of movement on the outside, and the "veneration" of the stronger sex. The activities in which she engaged did nothing in the long run but make her discover the value she had been attaching to this system.

The rallying of a "popular front" for women no doubt was aided in the achievement of its ends by the existence of mechanisms (instituted by the preceding administration) for the integration of women into the political process. The right finally capitalized on the "social incorporation" of the population, which had been permitted under the participationist regime of Frei, by setting up a network of grass-roots organizations, such as the "district committees," cultural centers, and especially the mothers' centers. At the same time, we must recognize that the latter, as well as the other grass-roots organizations, were later converted into battlegrounds. The outcome of these battles was often decided in favor of the forces seeking change. Because of the cooperation of many of the women's centers, women of the middle classes were able to function within the poblaciones and in the committees set up to handle food distribution and prices mentioned earlier. * Generally speaking, however, these women's centers were established at the district level (especially within the peripheral social sectors). In conformity with the principles of assistance to the "marginals," they were based upon norms of participation and ideological schemes that, given the circumstances of class confrontation, soon proved to be better suited for orienting women toward the maintenance of the traditional system. These centros de madres served as meeting places for a clientele of mamitas who tended to confirm and confine one another in their roles as mothers and wives. The women were organized around specifically feminine tasks and were placed under the tutelage of middle-class or

---

*In offering the woman an opportunity to exercise real popular power, the food distribution centers mark, albeit prematurely, the starting point of a movement for the emancipation and participation of women.

upper-middle-class women who received electoral support for their candidates in exchange. Conceived with the intention of integrating women into a "communal" society, these centers reinforced a conservative ideology and, under the cover of participation, removed women from any action or political allegiance contrary to the system. They created the illusion of neutralizing the signs of "marginality" of lower-class women and in the same way, deprived those signs of their explosive charge. By once more learning obedience, many lower-class women found themselves effectively demobilized.

Moreover, these centers were instrumental in developing norms of mutual association and habits of coexistence among women of the possessor class and those of the proletariat by cultivating in the latter a traditional mode of attachment to the "patroness." One phenomenon in particular came into widespread usage under the Popular regime and could be considered to be directly affiliated with the kind of relationship I am speaking of here. When the problem of food distribution became the day-to-day focus of everyone's concern, the women of the populace frequently had a madrina (godmother) in the residential district who would buy from them—at a good price, but one lower than that of the black market—products that the women had been able to acquire in the stores, at the official prices, by waiting in the long lines.

When we consider the circumstances surrounding the introduction of women into the production process, we can easily see that the Chilean woman from the proletarian districts or from the petite bourgeoisie could scarcely have been affected except by the mechanisms of socialization and participation that existed at the residential level. Of course, the largest percentage of the female population was of marginal importance to economic productivity. According to the census of 1970, little more than 19 percent of the women over the age of twelve had paying jobs outside the home, as opposed to nearly 69 percent of the men. Taking only adult women into consideration, we find that this percentage is reduced to 11 percent; marital and familial responsibilities served to steer a great many away from being wage earners. (Contrary to the situation in more developed countries, Chilean women do not rejoin the work force later in marriage). Moreover, the limited sectors of employment toward which women are oriented, through tradition and lack of true choice, reduce the chances of their becoming aware of influences different from those predominant in the forms of organization just described.

Almost 40 percent of the working women in the 1970 Census were employed as maids, washerwomen, or ironing ladies in individual homes. Less than 45 percent of these domestics were enrolled by their employees in the social security program. Twenty percent of the Chilean women who had paying jobs were factory workers, a small fraction of whom were unionized. The remainder were distributed among those who practiced a profession or technical specialty (16 percent) and those who were employed in the public service administration or private enterprise (25 percent), as secretaries and saleswomen, for example. The

lack of professional qualifications among the women of the petite bourgeoisie, since it added to their fear of change, made them more suscep-
tible to the litanies of the right. * If things had been different, it is
still possible to wonder whether the movement sponsored by the professional corporations might not also have caught the women, instead of
being satisfied to utilize and appeal to her as mistress of the house.
Of course, the few professional associations (or "colleges") with female
majorities in their membership all participated in the United Confederation of Chilean Professional Organizations, chartered in 1971 in order
to form the first corporate front against the Popular Unity. They included
the college of nurses, the college of social workers, the college of
midwives, and the college of librarians.

It is obvious that all the factors that facilitated and explain the
formation of a women's front on the right can be traced to one major
source: the rapport between the women and the state in a capitalist
society. Within the period during which the class struggle intensified
in Chile (1970-73), the woman, who was dependent upon and the accom-
plice of bourgeois ideology, faced with what she mistakenly interpreted
as the overthrow of institutions, behaved in a manner similar to that
prescibed for her vis-a-vis the male sex. During time of peace, the
dominating class carefully refrains from equating the identification of
the power of the state with the power of the male, so as to give women
the impression that they have a democratic relationship with the state,
just the same as any citizen is entitled to by law. When the state
changes hands and threatens to escape the control of the bourgeoisie,
however, the woman tends to resent this conflict, just as if the institutions were being deserted by the virile element that normally protects
her.

In order to fight against "Marxist authority," the woman calls the
state to task for its failure to assert authority, the synonym of order.
For militant women of the bourgeois order, the state is a man's affair.
They no longer have any fear of infringing upon the code of "feminine

---

*The right-wing women's organizations and the parties pursued
these women as their proselytes. One might often hear these women, in
their forties and usually jobless, comment among themselves: "Such
and such called me up" or "Such and such invited me to a meeting."
One can see a demonstrable parallelism between the tactics used in the
Dominican Republic by the Balaguer regime and those of the Chilean
right. It is not accidental that the tactics of the former functioned on
the basis of m chanisms of participation similar to those instituted in
Chile by the Christian Democrats and also had the same conception of
the role to be played by the woman in society. The doctrinaire members
of the Chilean Christian Democrats also participated in the planning of
that "Cruzada del Amor," undertaken in order to organize the women
after the North American invasion (see NACLA 1974).

reserve and modesty"; the preferred list of insults against the police
and armed forces faithful to the government and popular masses is drawn
from "macho" semantics.

THE FEMININE PRESS WHEN IT'S TIME FOR KARATE

Statements made by two men who worked in the same Santiago factory (Mattelart and Piccini 1974) can teach us something about the
awareness that the most enlightened sector of the working class had of
the role of broadcasting, controlled by the bourgeoisie, in its offensive.
They also show us that within this sector of society the peculiar vulnerability of women with respect to daily manipulation was appreciated to
the fullest. Moreover, the comments quite fairly delineate the real
causes of this difference in receptivity between male and female:

> Through the news, the headlines of their newspapers
> or radio programs, the "momios" everywhere gave preferen-
> tial treatment to women. The latter, who do not always
> understand what is going on, let themselves be convinced
> by the lies and start making allegations against the govern-
> ment.
> We others, we are affected less, because we don't
> listen to the radio all day; in the factory this sort of thing
> doesn't happen. Because we have meetings there is more
> awareness and they [the "momios"] can't fool us. But when
> we go home at night we find ourselves in a different situa-
> tion and we don't always know how to go about convincing
> the wives.

We forget too often that the confinement of the woman to the home constitutes a permanent reference point for the programming of radio and
television broadcasts. The radio, above all, literally accompanies the
woman on her domestic rounds. It makes her "exile" more gentle, more
gratifying, in order better to reproduce that exile and more effectively
generate the conditions of her confusion. How many hours of radio
and television programming have as their principal object the stimula-
tion and satisfaction of the woman's need to combat her own alienation?
What holds true in time of peace becomes doubly valid in time of war.
In wartime you can tune to the same station and find that direct appeals
for action have taken the place of melodrama and sentimentality.

In order to understand the total scope of this phenomenon, we
needn't consider only the qualitative break with the past that occurred
in the newspapers and other media under right-wing control in the days
of the Popular Unity regime. We must also take into account a purely
quantitative element. The bourgeoisie preserved intact all of its various
communications facilities. It even expanded newspapers like the

Tribuna, which every day spat the most insulting headlines at the President. It was only in television that the right lost a part of its former power, for there it soon became clear that the state channel (the only one whose broadcast range covered the entire land) would pass automatically into the hands of the new government. The Popular Unity went out of its way to ensure that all sectors of national life shared in the pluralistic use of the state-owned broadcasting media. Thus, the airing of contrasting opinions was guaranteed. Yet, with the complicity of imperialism, the forces of reaction attempted by all available methods to regain this lost portion of their former power—trying to confiscate the "worker's channel" and to extend the range of Channel 13 (operated by the Catholic University of Santiago), which unconditionally supported the sedition movement, over the entire country. Its former director, Hasbun, today deposed from his position by the junta, also provided the services of spiritual adviser to the board the magazine Eva.

The broadcasting networks constituted the favorite platform of the bourgeoisie for the launching of its offensives. In order to accomplish its new mission, the communications apparatus had to undergo an important transformation. Abandoning its earlier concept of public opinion, the bourgeoisie now defined its clienteles according to the concrete place which each occupied in the resistance and the particular interests that could motivate it. In order to contribute to the agitation and organization of its potential clienteles, the right-wing programs were directed to particular fronts, such as management, the professional corps (journalists, doctors, lawyers, engineers), youth, and women, the latter being not the least in importance. Between November 1970 and June 1972, El Mercurio devoted 120 editorials to the women's front alone. Here we shall present only one excerpt, which purports to discredit the social organization of Socialist countries in the eyes of the female public. Under the title "The Brutal Work Done by Women," this editorial was directed to "those employees and those female workers who, joyous to the point of euphoria, are on their way to a political propaganda meeting" (El Mercurio, November 10, 1971):

> Only some of them will obtain supervisory positions or
> posts within the regular bureaucracy. Only some of them
> will be granted the privilege of receiving extra food stamps
> or a few additional square feet to live in, and rare will
> be they who can work honestly, with all the consideration
> due to the weakness of their sex, but who will dispose of
> their time by carrying out their domestic and family func-
> tions.

The lines of impact after each terror campaign converge preferentially upon women. The menaces of "Marxist totalitarianism" to the homefront, to the survival of family ties, and to the education of the children have been, and remain, the arguments that anti-Communism always brings to bear. Such menaces threaten, above all, to paralyze the women and to emphasize the conservative traits of the dominant female culture. Starting in 1964, the Christian Democrats, campaigning for Frei against Allende, brought Juana Castro, half sister of Fidel, to the podium in order to persuade the Chileans to fight against Communism. In 1970, the same theme was repeated, this time with stepped-up violence and a few other variations. "Your children will be sent to Moscow," the tracts said. "They will make them denounce their parents." By utilizing arguments and images centered upon the mother and the child, the right even suggested legitimizing the overthrow of the Popular Unity government by any means available. "His mother is about to wait in line. . . . This child cannot wait until 1976! The Chilean children need a solution NOW." So reads the caption to a photo that shows a child alone, his pants badly fastened, crying in front of his house in one of the poor quarters.

In order to stimulate active resistance among women, the bourgeoisie also broke with the norms that usually govern the organization of the women's press (Mattelart 1970; 1973). Aside from the numerous photo romances and weekly rotogravures, the Chilean bourgeoisie controlled three magazines, two with a national circulation (Eva and Paula) and a third, Vanidades, conceived in Miami but printed in Santiago. Under the Popular Unity, these journals continued to represent 80 percent of the total circulation of the woman's press, with about 200,000 copies printed every two weeks. The most spectacular change in the women's press, however, took place in the pages of Eva, which originally belonged to a group representing the Christian Democratic press. In an interview with foreign journalists, its director avowed her explicit intention of making the magazine into an instrument of agitation: "I have declared war on the Popular Unity. Women must fight; we must help them, stimulate them, mould them." The uninformed observer needed only to read the editorials, a few articles in the various sections, and the many items scattered throughout its pages to be convinced of the new identity, unusual in a review of this genre, that the periodical had assumed.

This conversion was realized in two ways: through the improvised adoption of an entire set of "intellectual" references, and through the politicization of all areas of daily life. The nomenclature used for each theme remained more or less constant, with one exception: renouncing its rigorous isolation within the spheres of sentiment, modernity, material preoccupations, and household maintenance, the revue inaugurated several sections designed to "inform" the women about the national political scene and to "open their eyes" to the antagonism of the two systems of life currently engaged in conflict. This information was usually filtered through the prism of femininity, which meant that the cult of "femininity" imposed its own mechanisms of selection and approach when it came to choosing significant aspects in the material treated. As a result of the new informational function of the journal, politicians in the government or in the opposition found themselves discredited or esteemed (depending, of course, on their political

allegiance) more as a result of their physique and private conduct than
of the political program they applied or espoused.

The formulas used by the magazine to adapt the thought of Marx,
Lenin, and Mao, so that its readers might understand their intellectual
adversaries, made a great deal of the misfortunes that befell their wives,
daughters, or companions. Sometimes, the review preferred to present
them as great thinkers whose relevance had dwindled in the light of
current events. Lastly, the actors on the national scene who had special authorization to appear in the pages of Eva, and who were always
depicted in a favorable, affable, domestic, even "reassuring" light,
were the representatives of the armed forces.

One section of the journal, in particular, contributed in the most
obvious manner to mobilizing its female leadership. Introduced after
the defeat of the reactionary forces in the employers' strike of October
1972, it continued to appear, quite regularly, though it later ran under
the heading "Plan of Female Action." The editors here encouraged women
to redouble their belligerence and gave them precise instructions as to
how they might do so. For instance, in the number for November 23,
1972, it said:

> All the warlike forces of the world are preparing their
> men. The soldiers are trained by doing gymnastics, exer-
> cises, and by going to theoretical courses which aid them
> in combat. The Chilean woman must imitate this method,
> which gives such good results throughout the world.
> Gymnastics: Some articles of Eva recommend certain exer-
> cises for reducing or correcting faults in one's figure. But
> gymnastics fulfills a more important function. When a per-
> son is healthy, one is agile, and this quality permits one
> to carry out more demanding activities, to mobilize oneself
> without fatigue and take better advantage of one's time.
> Training: Given that the physical alone will not suffice,
> one must also develop the mind. For this, it is enough to
> read the newspaper at least two or three times a week. By
> knowing what is going on and what the Communist, the
> MIRist, the National, and the Christian Democrat is think-
> ing, the woman can accomplish her task all the more effec-
> tively. We can't live on the moon. . . . the books of John
> LeCarre, Vicki Baum, and Leon Uris furnish examples of
> totalitarian ideology. . . . This source of sustenance
> will enable us to remember the object of our struggle.
> Moral strength: We must not forget that sacrifice is the
> forge of the will. It is not logical to squander one's money
> on the gaming tables when that money is needed for the
> Cause in order to finance the opposition radio or prevent
> Channel 13 from accepting the conditions imposed upon it
> by the Government. Wars cannot be waged only a few hours

each day. One must remain in the trenches throughout
the day so as to serve as an example of sacrifice and
action. A woman who still thinks it necessary to have a
minimum of five pairs of shoes, more than ten dresses,
etc. . . has not lived this conflict. Nor is she any better
than those who have not mobilized themselves as yet in
order to collect funds and support for workers' groups,
whether it be those for social action (like the Red Cross,
Drop of Milk, My House, or Christ's Home) or for political action. . . .

The article ends with an exhortation to the woman to choose a training
post within the "regular armies" (political parties), the "fifth column"
(infiltration into the ranks of the enemy), or the guerrillas (groups for
direct action against Marxism).

There is a more diffuse presentation in the rest of the review, distributed through all the articles that concern the daily preoccupations
of the housewife. Complementary to the more radical, it is perhaps
more in harmony with what the less radical currents within the right-
wing coalition view as the proper course of opposition to the popular
regime. All the recipes, all the fashion columns, all the advice on
interior design, the horoscopes, the pleasantries, the humor, the
opinion polls, the reflections serve to further distill the image of famine
and scarcity and to mobilize every reflex against the "popular regime,"
by cultivating a nostalgia for the good old days, by painting the future
black, by depicting the government as incompetent and the present
situation as untenable. In the issue of November 23 (we return to the
same issue in order to observe the vehemence and day-to-day appeal
of the magazine's contribution to resistance on the woman's front),
twenty pages are devoted to eating. They are divided into two main
parts: on the one hand, recipes and menus "in time of war" which are
based on "available products;" and, on the other, recipes and menus
of the "good old days." The first part is punctuated with remarks such
as the following: "Before, the merchandise bought itself; now one acquires it with the sweat of the waiting line" (sic). . . "everyday it is
getting harder to distinguish oneself as lady of the house . . . ." The
second section is devoted to fabulous dishes of the past and is charged
with the task of stressing, by way of contrast, the poverty of the present and parading the unbelievable repasts of the oligarchy and land
proprietors.

When the right wing threw all stockpiled products onto the open
market the day after the coup d'etat, its newspapers and reviews described the tears of joy which the spectacle of regained abundance
brought to the eyes of the housewife. "The second independence of
Chile" went on all fours with the "liberation of the housewife." As soon
as the stocks were depleted, inflation galloped in to attend to the task
of pulverizing the rhetoric of the right.

REFERENCES

Bambirra, Vania. 1971. "La mujer chilena en la transicion al socialismo." Punto Final (Santiago de Chile), June 22.

_____. 1972. "La liberacion de la mujer y lucha de clases." Punto Final (Santiago de Chile), February.

El Mercurio (Santiago de Chile). 1973a. September 4.

_____. 1973b. September 14.

_____. 1974. September 23.

Eva (Santiago de Chile). 1974. January.

La tercera de la hora (Santiago de Chile). 1973. September 23.

Mattelart, Armand. 1974. Mass Media, Ideologies, et mouvement revolutionnaire. Paris: Anthropos.

Mattelart, Armand, and Michele Mattelart. 1968. La mujer chilena en una nueva sociedad. Santiago de Chile: Editorial del Pacific.

_____. 1970. "El nivel mitico de la prensa seudo-amorosa." Cuadernos de la realidad nacional (Santiago de Chile) 3 (March).

_____. 1973. "Apuntes sobre lo moderno: Una manera de leer el magazine." Casa de las Americas (Havana), March-April.

Mattelart, Michele, and Mabel Piccini. 1974. "La television y los sectores populares." Comunicacion y cultura (Buenos Aires) 2: 3-75.

NACLA. 1974. "Feminismo Balaguerista: A Strategy of the Right." NACLA's Latin American and Empire Report 8, no. 4.

Poirier, Emile. 1901. Chile and the Panamerican Exposition. Buffalo, N.Y.:

Washington Post. 1974. "The Brazilian Connection." January 6.

16

**THE EMERGENCE OF A
MAPUCHE LEADER: CHILE**

Ximena Bunster

This study is presented with the hope of raising interest in new lines of investigation of women's behavior and political participation in cross-cultural contexts. The traditional approach assumes that political preoccupation and political activity are mainly male concerns in which women have participated only tangentially. It is not surprising, then, that we have little information on the rates of female political participation, and on the historical and social conditions that encourage or limit the processes of consciousness-raising and political involvement among women in given structural situations. Even less surprising is the total absence of systematic concern with the description and evaluation of women's political activity in developing countries—in this case, in Latin America. We know little or nothing about the working-class woman, the peasant woman, and the Indian woman of the Third World. *

Nash (1974) says that this fact should not surprise us, since the ethnographic and theoretical study of Latin American social reality is defined almost totally by men. Recently female social scientists have begun to criticize the models presented, and to contribute their own perspectives to the study of Latin American social reality, as well as to the choice of research topics.

Nash also presents data from recent investigations that show that the female is omitted from most historical and social studies of Latin America. In historical and political studies there is almost a total absence of commentary on women's political activities. In contrast, in

---

*Jane Jaquette has edited a very original book of articles written by American women political analysts, <u>Women in Politics</u> (1974). Nonetheless, because it is a pioneer work in the field, it centers its attention on the North American context. The comparative examples are interesting, but scarcely representative of the political and social reality of Latin America.

literature and in studies on the family and analyses of popular culture,
females have leading roles. However, these literary and cultural roles
include distortions that adjust female roles to male stereotypes. When
social scientists accept these stereotypes, they are unable from the
outset to understand the changing reality of women's participation in
the economic, political, and social life of Latin American societies.
Nash, in her lucid and critical evaluation of this state of affairs in the
social sciences, emphasizes the absolute necessity of including female
perspectives in all analyses of social reality.

This essay analyzes the public role of a young Mapuche agriculturalist. She created both the ideology and the strategy to reclaim Indian
lands during the government of Popular Unity in Chile. Through the
anthropological and autobiographical study of Llanquitray—her name
for the purposes of this presentation*—we may understand the motives
behind her behavior. A sketch of Llanquitray's life cycle, placed in the
structure of contemporary Mapuche society and in the context of the
values of a culture in transition, facilitates understanding of her successful political activism.

The description of a life cycle is a classical methodological exercise of anthropology. It can also become a heuristic tool, indispensable
for the investigation of the processes of change that marked the life of
this woman who was able to move out of the private social arena and
into the public arena, thus obtaining access to the power structure.
The same methodological resource helps us to understand the political
socialization of a leader, her qualities of command, and the reasons
for the recognition of her prestige by the men who accepted her orders.
No less important is the explanation obtained, through the same medium,
of the Mapuche Indians' interpretation of the agrarian reform of the Popular Unity government, and the historical context in which these events
took place.

In the following pages, Llanquitray's life cycle is briefly described.
The most important stages in it permit an evaluation of her behavior and
a sociological explanation for her innovative role.

Llanquitray is at present a Mapuche agriculturalist who lives on
the land that belongs to her family on one of the many Indian reservations of the Cautin Province.[†] She is single, thirty eight years old,

---

*This paper is a short part of the book Llanquitray, Autobiografia de
una mujer Araucana, which will soon be published.

[†]The Mapuche, or Araucanian Indians, represent a large and important tribe of South America. They have a population of 700,000 of which
450,000 live in the countryside in the provinces of Arauco, Bio Bio,
Malleco, Cautin, Valdivia, Osorno, and Llanquihue. These provinces
are in south-central Chile. These 450,000 Mapuche live on more than
3,000 reservations or small Indian communities.

The principal activities of the Mapuche are agriculture, cattle-raising, truck farming, horticulture, and the growing of fruit. Their

and the oldest sister to four male siblings. When her father died, she
was left in charge of cultivating the family property. He died proud
of his daughter's achievements: through "invasion" she had returned
the lands stolen from his ancestors. As the strategist of the invasion,
Llanquitray was supported at all times by her father, as well as by the
men and women of five other reservations. She lives in the country, but
travels to the city on certain occasions. Although she is single, she
wears a wedding ring, since her fiance, also Mapuche, died of a heart
attack while she was caring for her people's interests. She directs the
agricultural tasks with the help of her younger brothers. Her affections
are divided among her widowed mother, the children of those who surround her, and her constant preoccupation for the Mapuche cause. Llanquitray says:

> It is believed and commented on among the Mapuche that
> a good seed is never lost. This means that no matter
> how badly off a person may be at a given moment in his
> life, no matter how sad and anguished a person may be in
> a desperate situation, in the long run the person will prevail,
> if he or she has had a good ancestry. Such a person does
> not die defeated.

Llanquitray sees herself as the logical result of a succession of
generations of Mapuche of good family who have transmitted from fathers
to children the fundamental values of the cultural and social indentities
of the Chilean Indian. She feels a profound respect for what she calls
her "race" (ethnic group) and great pride in its ancestors. In her political activity she believes that she has interpreted and achieved the ambitions and dreams of many Mapuche. She maintains that the violent
reclaiming of the ancestral lands of her people, usurped largely during
this century by unscrupulous oligarchies to further enlarge their latifundia, was her reply, and the reply of the Indian people, to the agrarian reform of the Popular Unity government.

Llanquitray was the oldest daughter of her father's second marriage.
He had been a childless widower, and her birth was received with expectation and joy by both families. Her maternal grandmother was her

---

lands are not suitable for other kinds of cultivation.

The Mapuche population constitutes a true Chilean subculture,
with distinctive ethnic characteristics and a separate language, mapu-
dungun; their political system, the administration of reservations, was
imposed by the Chilean government during the past century.

Besides these basic differences from the rest of the Chilean population, it is appropriate to note other characteristics, such as the practice of shamanism, the celebration of collective tribal ceremonies, and
the belief in nature gods and spirits as well as the practice of witch-
craft.

most important socializing agent, the one who introduced her to the
Mapuche world view, to Mapuche myths and beliefs. Her childhood was
a gay exploration of Mapuche culture. This grandmother was always
present; she taught her the language, which she learned to speak perfectly, with all the rhetorical flourishes appropriate to the great speakers
and caciques of yesteryear, from whom she was descended. When Llanquitray was ten years old, she thought, felt, and believed as a Mapuche.

Her father was as decisive an influence on her as was her maternal grandmother. He molded the mental image that she gradually built
of herself, her family, and the rest of the Mapuche population. With
earnestness and passion he told her the history of his valiant and war-
like people: of the glorious battles and the unparalleled strategies used
by the great loncos who fought against the Spaniards. Llanquitray absorbed the lives of these great warriors, their courage and streadfast-
ness in the defense of Indian territory as it was inexorably occupied by
the Spanish enemy and later administered by the Chilean government
through a system of reservations. She heard from her father, first with
surprise and then with growing indignation, about how her grandfather,
like so many other caciques and commoners on the reservations, was
the victim of fraud perpetrated by one Jose Miguel Sanfuentes, a wealthy
landowner. The Sanfuentes lands adjoined the Indian lands of their
ancestor and those of four other reservations. Her father described in
detail how her grandfather fell into the trap laid by the landowner and
the sophistries he used to take over this land and other Indian lands.
He told her how the grandfather lived, became poor, and died enmeshed
in useless litigation against the landowner. Llanquitray was overwhelmed with pain at her grandfather's impotence against Chilean institutions
and his inability to obtain justice. She was also overwhelmed with an
almost physical anger against the landowner. The grandfather's disadvantage was enormous because he did not speak Spanish, and he did
not know how to read and write.

Llanquitray's grandfather's obession with justice led him to ignore
the cultivation of the land. He spent his time and money on useless
complaints before the Indian Tribunal, presenting demands that only
gathered dust in the archives of dishonest judges and lawyers. The
judicial lack of interest and inefficacy in helping the dispossessed
Mapuche originated with the shrewd landowner. He knew that money
bought silence. Llanquitray felt her grandfather's desperation, which
was increased by a chain of frustrations and humiliations following
his demand, in order to obtain justice, to have an interview with the
President of the Republic. The old man was aware of his inability to
express himself in Spanish to the President, and contracted the services
of a lenguaraz, or interpreter, who was a primary-school teacher. The
grandfather traveled 800 kilometers by train, from Temuco to Santiago,
with the interpreter. In the capital, the teacher led him to a mansion
in Ejercito Street (where the oligarchs resided), and both were received
by the Commander in Chief. The grandfather explained his problem. The
President, in a conciliatory tone, told him to return to his Indian lands

with confidence, because they would be returned after a peremptory
Presidential order to that effect, to the <u>hacendado</u>, Jose Miguel Sanfuentes. The grandfather's joy was short-lived. When he returned to Temuco, he discovered that Sanfuentes had bribed the schoolteacher and
had contrived the miserable scheme. The alleged interview was no more
than a cruel farce in the residence of one of Sanfuentes' brothers, who
had pretended to be the President.

In Llanquitray's socialization, little or nothing was left to chance.
She was sent to a boarding school, where her grandfather's memory and
the suffering he underwent because of the lack of the language and literacy with which to defend himself against the unscrupulous Chilean was
reinforced. His memory led Llanquitray to follow her family's tradition
of education and probity.

The Catholic mission's boarding school was in the heart of Arau-
cania, the land of the Mapuche. There Llanquitray was in contact with
other Mapuche girls and was happy. Soon she abandoned the purely
Indian world of the reservation and the Mapuche mission to enter the
sixth preparatory year in a public school in Temuco, an institution for
indigent young women. She met Chilean girls, many of them orphans,
who lamented the loss of their parents.

At the end of her preparatory years, Llanquitray entered the Young
Women of Temuco's Lyceum, where for three years she studied humanities. At that time she began to attend and participate in Mapuche student meetings. Some of her Chilean companions called her "Indian"
and "Mapuche" and "native." She began to learn about discrimination.
Her father made a great effort to have her board at the Baptist College,
founded by a North American congregation. She studied there for one
year. Llanquitray felt even more discriminated against by the foreign
teachers. Nonetheless, the Baptist College offered one advantage: it
was coeducational and, according to Llanquitray, "It was there that I
began to learn to treat men as friends and no more." This was her last
year of school. She returned to reservation life to help with the agricultural labor and to give her younger brothers an opportunity to go to
school.

Her desire to know other worlds took Llanquitray to the resort town
of Vina del Mar, close to the port of Valparaiso and Santiago. This was
the first time she left the province of Cautin. She found a job in a private house, where she was companion and nurse to a sick woman. The
woman and her husband, both elderly, treated her as a member of their
family and included her in their outings and social activities. The
woman belonged to an association of Catholic women who were active
in paternalistic social work that provided spiritual and material aid to
the poor. Llanquitray accompanied the woman on her Sunday visits to
the poor inhabitants of the hills of Valparaiso. The tremendous poverty
and the sordidness of the lives of these families profoundly depressed
her. She questioned her own motives for helping these poor Chileans,
rather than helping her own Mapuche. She began to compare the style
of urban poverty with that of the Indians and decided that the latter had

more opportunities to improve their situations than did the urban poor.
At this point she decided to return to the Mapuche world, and to dedicate herself to the understanding of Mapuche problems and to contribute
to their solution.

When Llanquitray returned to the countryside, she was not yet
twenty years old. Upon her return to the reservation, she learned that
her eldest brother had gone to work in Argentina. As the oldest daughter,
she then became her father's assistant and began to organize agricultural labor, to take produce to the markets at Temuco, and to obtain loans
for seeds and fertilizer.

As a result of her trips to Temuco, Llanquitray began to participate
in a great Mapuche movement called the Araucanian Corporation, which
lasted for many years. The movement was led by Venancio Conuepan,
a Mapuche of distinguished ancestry who had occupied high public positions during the government of President Carlos Ibanez. In this period
Conuepan stimulated and appointed many Mapuche aldermen, governors,
and parliamentarians, and placed others as public servants in the Ministries of Land and Colonization. After his public life, he became the head
of the Auraucanian Corporation in the province of Cautin.

Llanquitray admired this man whose efforts had been dedicated to
the integration of the Mapuche—without loss of their identity—into the
whole society. Her understanding of the basic problems of Mapuche
society deepened. She learned from Conuepan that the Mapuche should
not permit the imposition of laws allowing division of the reservations.
Such laws would entail the atomization of the communities, because
they would permit the sale of Indian lands to private individuals. As a
consequence, the Mapuche community would lose its territorial base
and the internal cohesion of its cultural norms.

When Conuepan died, the Araucanian Corporation weakened. According to Llanquitray, it weakened because the leaders who followed
him were too authoritarian enough to their followers and "were not able
to interpret the needs of their followers" to reach the masses.

During President Frei's government, Llanquitray took yet another
step in her training as a future leader. On her periodical trips to town
to sell her family's agricultural produce, she became familiar with the
results of the First Mapuche Congress, which took place in the province
of Malleco. Many Mapuche from the seven Chilean provinces in which
the native population is concentrated, attended this conference. The
Mapuche participants, many of whom slept in a field underneath the
stars for four days, explored and discovered their common problems.
They decided to work on a legislative bill to create a National Confederation of Mapuche Associations. Each association was to be a minimal
basic unit of interaction, including the representatives of three to five
reservations. Such units would permit democratic discussion of problems and rapid communication among the network of associations. In
order to belong to one of these associations, it was only necessary
to be Mapuche and to be interested in solving common problems. Thus

a strong political unit based on shared perceptions was created. Llanquitray, enthusiastic and applauding the initiative, said:

> This National Confederation of Mapuche Associations will
> have its own organization, and will not be susceptible
> to political manipulation. This is a great thing. Because
> the Mapuche have only served as instruments, as pedestals
> for the huincas [thieving Chileans] to climb upon. The
> huincas, the politician, goes ahead and develops his
> career, while the Mapuche always lives his life in misery.

During the government of Popular Unity in Chile, the historical
and political setting necessary for Llanquitray's achievement of full
maturity as a Mapuche leader appeared. The sociopolitical context,
with the radical reforms and the massive, complex politicization that
characterized it, stimulated and facilitated Mapuche participation in
the process of change.

For President Salvador Allende, the implementation of the government's agrarian reform was as important as the nationalization of copper.
In order to transform Chilean society from a capitalist underdeveloped
economy to a socialist economy, the following agrarian objectives were
listed (Barriaclough et al. 1973, p. 18):

> 1) A rapid change in the system of landholding, through
> the elimination of latifundia and stimulating the growth of
> cooperatives and other socialist forms of agricultural pro-
> duction. 2) a change in the relations between agriculture
> and the rest of the economy, by increasing production and
> productivity, intensifying production and eliminating rural
> unemployment, while improving agricultural incomes in re-
> lation to the other sectors. 3) to stimulate the democratic
> participation of the peasantry at all levels of decision mak-
> ing, through peasant councils and other peasant organiza-
> tions. 4) to plan and reorient agricultural production to
> better use the natural and economic advantages of the prin-
> cipal geographic regions of the country and 5) to eliminate
> the backwardness and isolation of the poorer rural groups
> such as the Mapuche and the peasants of the Norte Chico.

The advances achieved in the agrarian field during the almost three
years of the Popular Unity government are impressive, especially if we
recall that they were achieved in such a short time. A great number of
latifundia were expropriated, including the largest sheep-raising establishment in the world, the Sociedad Explotadora de Tierra del Fuego,
which included more than 3.5 million acres. Peasant councils were
also formed; these were to increase peasant political participation,
and functioned to oversee regional planning and to acquire the credits
necessary for the land to be cultivated for the benefits of its workers.

While these policies were being implemented, peasant pressure took the form of land invasions, in an effort to accelerate the objectives of the agrarian reform. During 1971, for example, 1,278 land invasions took place in four provinces of south-central Chile. In the decade prior to Salvador Allende's government, peasants had invaded land as a way of pressuring the government to grant them better salaries and benefits. The Mapuche had reclaimed latifundia by invading lands usurped from their ancestors by unscrupulous landowners. In contrast, during the first year of the Popular Unity government, both the peasants and the Mapuche had invaded latinfundia, in order for the land to belong to them. Generally the invasions were settled by government mediation, or expropriation.

In order to understand the revolutionary choice made by many Mapuche Indians in southern Chile—among them Llanquitray and her followers—we must understand the difference in attitude between the Chilean peasant and the Mapuche Indian over land ownership. The Mapuche agriculturalist owned his land and had felt tied to it from ancestral times, through inheritance. This attitude differed from that of the non-native Chilean peasants, who had never owned the land on which they worked. The agrarian reform presented them with the possibility of owning the land they worked, because of the fundamental changes in the agrarian structure and the power structure.

The non-Indian peasantry saw the agrarian reform as an opportunity to obtain social justice; its fighting cry was "The land for those who till it." The Mapuche agriculturalist, who always owned land—although little of it—interpreted the agrarian reform of the Popular Unity government as an opportunity to reclaim usurped ancestral lands. These were very extensive: at least 25 percent of the lands that the government originally gave the Indians when it moved them to the seven southern provinces was, in 1971, in the hands of non-Mapuche agriculturalists. The battle cry of the Mapuche was "Restitution of usurped lands."

Llanquitray was profoundly taken by the political situation in which she found herself. She evaluated the ultra-left revolutionaries and synthesized Mapuche feelings on "invasions of restitution" when she said:

> Many people claim to be revolutionaries, but they are
> so only on the surface, like those of the MIR. * Many young
> men from the city think that if they pick up a gun and be-
> come involved with us, the Mapuche, they will be following

---

*MIR, or the Movement of the Revolutionary Left, is a political party that advocated radical structural changes through violence. One week after the election of Salvador Allende, the MIR formally created the MCR, the Peasant Revolutionary Movement, whose members assisted many peasants in the invasion of fundos. There were a great number of ex-students of the secondary and university level in both MIR and MCR.

the example of Fidel Castro, or Che Guevara. Nonetheless, we Mapuche, those of us who think about all this, know that to make a revolution one must feel it deep inside, and then obey this terrible necessity. Anything else is not right, and to my way of thinking is a kind of theatre, a farce. Because the MIR people are young university men with long hair, the sons of rich fathers. They have had all comfort, wealthy, almost regal lives, the education and money with which to satisfy their whims.

Good revolutionaries are those who feel deeply inside themselves the need to fix the situations in which they find themselves. Chile, at this moment, is in a kind of revolution, because we are all in a revolution of changes.

Many Mapuche feel the need to make a pichi revolution [pichi means "small" in Mapuche]. They do it through the land invasions. When the Mapuche doesn't have enough land to work, he feels marginalized and poor. Then he decides to invade an establishment. It is organized between relatives and neighbors and the seizure is made. If there is a lack of land, there is no way to work and harvest, or to increase the number of domestic animals raised. Nor are there means to feed ourselves, to clothe ourselves, and much less to educate our children. If the Mapuche come to these serious decisions, it is because there is no law which favors us at this time. Because the celebrated law which presently rules the country serves us not at all. And why doesn't it serve us? Because it was made by the rich, the same rich who took away our land. That is the truth.

Now that we have a legislative bill which was written and analyzed by us, the Mapuche, the peasants who live on the land and work in the countryside, now this bill is being attacked in the Senate. And it is being attacked by the same rich, the same powerful ones, who imposed their laws on us. *

How can the rich, the parliamentarians of Congress accept our new law? How can they approve it if they know it was made by the people, by Mapuche agriculturalists? Naturally it is not a good law for them, because they know that they will be prejudiced by it.

So, what does the Mapuche do? What does he think? If he makes a juridical claim for a piece of land usurped by a rich man twenty or thirty years ago, it can take fifteen, twenty or thirty years to reclaim it through the Court.†

---

*Llanquitray alludes to the legislative bill proposed by the Popular Unity government to annul discriminatory earlier legislation.

†She refers to the Indian courts. These were created in a paternalist spirit by the Chilean government, with the intention that they would

He can sell everything he owns and be out on the streets,
and he will never win his claim. Why? Because a poor
person cannot put himself before a rich one. Impossible!
Not even worth dreaming of. He realizes that the laws
which exist are useless to him: they protect the powerful,
because they were made by them to protect themselves.
The Mapuche knows through the <u>kuifiche</u> [the elders of the
community] the size of the lands which belonged to him,
and the pieces which were usurped. But that is of no use,
because in the law presently being discussed in Congress,
restitution can only be done through the law. And these
are very rare cases, because to be able to prove an usur-
pation of Indian territory, it is necessary to show the
titles of Merced, and in numerous cases, these are accepted.

Nonetheless, the Mapuche continues insisting that
the lands of his ancestors were much greater than those
on which he is presently working and living. He alleges
that it can be demonstrated that his land was usurped,
that there are proofs in his community, the ancient people
of the community who know the old boundaries. The old
ones can explain how the land was taken from the Mapuche
and subdivided. But the declarations of the elders are not
accepted by the Chilean authorities, nor are the claims.
So, what does the Mapuche do? He resorts to violence.
It is necessary to resort to violence!

Peasant agitation intensified during the first year of Salvador Allende's government. Some landholders feared the expropriation of their
haciendas and spontaneously ceded bits of land on the edges of their
great properties to the government, with the secret hope that the high
officials of CORA (Agrarian Reform Corporation) would annul the documents or forget to intervene in their properties.

The grandson of Jose Miguel Sanfuentes, the unscrupulous landowner who had robbed Llanquitray's grandfather and Mapuches from five
other reservations of more than 500 hectares of land, was the heir and
proprietor of his grandfather's haciendas.

The young politician and lawyer's name was the same as his hated
grandfather's. He was the Christian Democrat deputy for the province,
in opposition to the government. Jose Miguel Sanfuentes was well aware

------

administer the Indian law to protect the Mapuche. In practice, Indian
legislation has been inoperative and prejudicial to the group of people
it was supposed to benefit. It served to weaken the Mapuche people
and to stimulate the growth of special courts, which decided against
Mapuche complaints and assisted in the theft of their lands through
legislation.

of the land disputes between his grandfather and the Mapuche. Nonetheless, as Christmas approached in 1970, he decided to make himself agreeable to his tenants and to the government by giving them a small part of his extensive property. Naturally, what he planned to give them as a gift was part of the land that his grandfather stole from the Mapuche.

This news traveled through the countryside and the city of Temuco. It reached Llanquitray, who desperately sought means to frustrate Sanfuentes' plans. Mapuches on reservations adjacent to Sanfuentes' latifundium, whose land had also been stolen at the beginning of the century, became worried. They went to Llanquitray for help, since she embodied all the conditions of leadership among the Mapuche. She was descended from a good family, was an excellent agriculturalist, and knew as much as (if not more than) most agriculturalists about the cultivation of land. Moreover, she knew both the Mapuche and the Chilean worlds; her experience in native society and in the national society allowed her to "counsel her own," a highly valued function among the Mapuche and one that the caciques of yesteryear always performed.

Upon her return from one of her visits to Temuco, Llanquitray found a large group of Mapuche waiting for her at her house. They asked her to find a solution to their common problem. She decided that the 500 hectares usurped by Sanfuentes' grandfather must be retaken. Otherwise, they would never be recovered: there was no other solution. That same night, they planned the invasion. Llanquitray asked for the opinion of each of the affected villagers. One of them, Marileo, was frightened by the possibility of an armed confrontation between the landholders and themselves. Llanquitray, to convince him, said:

> Look, Marileo, if we are frightened that they will come
> and get us and throw us out of our invasion, we will achieve
> nothing here. However much we have a government of the
> people, President Allende is not going to come right here to
> ask about our different problems. That's impossible. We
> have to try and resolve them ourselves.

With these words, she convinced the fearful, and the invasion was set for the following day. She explained that it could not be two days later, because it would coincide with the closing of the Mapuche Congress in Temuco, which she was attending. She synchronized both events magnificently.

Llanquitray organized the group; and the next day, very early, she led twelve men and another woman, her cousin, on the invasion. The two women went ahead to show the way. They broke the fence of the Sanfuentes fundo (Chilean contradiction for "latifundo"), went in, armed a little hut, and put up a Chilean flag as a sign of an "invasion of restitution." At dawn the population of the five participating reservations —more than 200 people—joined them.

Meanwhile, the Second Mapuche Congress was taking place in Temuco. It was attended by more than 300 delegates from the provinces

of Arauco, Bio Bio, Malleco, Cautin, Valvidia, and Osorno. The delegates, organized in Mapuche Associations structured like syndicates,
were meeting to discuss problems related to agriculture, health, education, and the restitution of lands, as well as the need for new Indian
legislation. The conclusions of the Congress were later passed on as
recommendations to the government.

Llanquitray, at a congress with exclusively male delegates, presented herself as a "volunteer" to administer the kitchen and care for
the feeding of the delegates. Her great organizational capacity led her,
moreover, to organize the reception committee for the Chilean authorities who attended the congress. Among these were ministers of the
regime, newspaper men, and important politicians.

After directing the invasion, she left instructions with her followers
and proceeded to Temuco to attend the closing of the Mapuche Congress.
It was the December 19, and she knew there would be an open assembly at which the delegates would present their recommendations to the
Popular Unity government.

In the gymnasium of the school where this massive meeting was
being held, she arranged to speak with the director of the committee
analyzing land tenure. He was an old primary-school teacher, who had
known her since she was a child. She asked him to give her time to
speak to the delegates during the general assembly. He agreed, and
warned her that the President of the Confederation of the Mapuche Association, who belonged to the Christian Left Party, did not approve of
"invasions" because he felt violence was not productive.

Once on the podium, Llanquitray took the microphone and spoke
in Mapuche to her people and in Spanish to the press and government
officials. She explained the reasons that led her and her companions
to plan and execute the invasion, referring to the court cases between
her grandfather and Sanfuentes. She explained that this was the way
she and her companions understood the agrarian reform of the Popular
Unity government. As they heard her words, the delegates and all those
present broke out into a long ovation. A great tumult ensued. The Mapuche leaped from their seats, stood up, applauded, shouted, and
stamped their feet in jubilation.

After her speech to the congress, Llanquitray was no longer anonymous; she became a respected and well-known figure among all Mapuche.
She was the unquestioned Mapuche leader and was visited by the Director of Indian Affairs from Santiago and various other personages of
the Popular Unity government. She was the adviser to government officers who submitted a series of situations, problems, and conflicts related to maladjustments between native institutions and the national
society to her judgment. And she gave her verdicts.

The Minister of Agriculture and promoter of the agrarian reform,
Jacques Chonchol, met her during the summer of 1971, when the Ministry of Agriculture was working in the province of Cautin. Impressed by th
the intelligence and courage of the Chilean Indian, he promised that the
Sanfuentes fundo would head the list of the list of the sites to be

expropriated in the province. Llanquitray requested an audience to ask
him to expedite the measure. She described her impression of the conversation with the Minister in these words:

> Minister Chonchol received me very well. He was very
> pleasant and very sensible. At all times he showed his ap-
> proval of what we had done, and he even said to me: "Tell
> the rest of your companions for me, that I am in complete
> agreement with what you have done." And he added, "You
> know, comrade, the Mapuche problem is the hardest prob-
> lem, and if the Mapuche don't face it and take it into their
> own hands they won't be much better off. No matter how
> much this government wants to do for the people, it will
> never know exactly what the different problems are, because
> they are all so varied. You are the ones who must unite and
> act and help yourselves."
> If at this time, and this is very secret, Minister Chon-
> chol said to me, "the government, through its representa-
> tives, could go out to the country and say in everyone's ear:
> You, unite yourselves, reunite yourselves, and take the
> land, we would do it. And you know why," he said to me.
> "Because the law doesn't favor you in any way. Do not wait
> for the law to help you. The law is made by the rich to pro-
> tect themsleves."
> In other words, Minister Chonchol's instructions were
> precisely what I had been thinking. I answered him proudly:
> "Well, that's why we made the invasion, because to us,
> the Mapuche, what we are interested in is land. With land,
> in some way we will work it, because land is the only thing
> that lasts: we will all come to an end, we will all die, and
> the land will remain. The Mapuche, after the neglect to
> which they have been submitted, have a clear ideology to
> follow: it is of the Left, but they will not permit changes
> to be imposed on them. The Mapuche will be happy to be
> included and incorporated in the changes, as long as their
> point of view is respected. The Mapuche are united by
> their own particular problems, and in their efforts to solve
> them they pay heed to their grass roots."

Llanquitray's capacity to direct and collaborate in the organization
of land recovery movements for the Mapuche people was clearly shown
by the respect she achieved among Mapuche students in secondary
schools and university in Temuco. During 1971, when the scholarship
money for the Mapuche students did not reach Cautin because of a delay in the offices of the Directory of Indian Affairs in the capital, she
did not hesitate to support the student cause. She came to town from
the country, urged the students to act, "invaded the street" by forming

barricades to block the traffic to the Office of Indian Affairs and sought
the support of the students at the Regional University of Temuco. She
explained her participation in these words:

> The Mapuche agriculturalists completely supported the
> protest invasion which native students led in the city of
> Temuco. All of them, not only the fathers who had struggled
> to be able to board their sons in the city, were concerned
> with the threat that their children would be thrown out of
> their lodgings into the streets by their landlords because
> of their inability to pay the rent. The students' scholarships
> were taking forever to arrive from the main office in Santiago.
> The fathers of the students and I decided that this was a
> grave injustice on the part of the Government, as was the
> fact that there was in Temuco, the capital of the province
> of Cautin, where there are most Mapuche, no special resi-
> dence for Mapuche students.
>
> One day a young Mapuche student arrived in the coun-
> try while we were in the fields. We blew a horn to call a
> reunion. Our Mapuche companions came from the surrounding
> areas and convened to hear him. The young man asked the
> peasant fathers to support their sons. That same night
> twelve people were left to help do guard duty at the invaded
> institution.
>
> We already had an organized movement since the inva-
> sion of the Sanfuente fundo, so Mapuche agriculturalists
> were used to contributing 5 escudos towards spending emer-
> gencies. After hearing the young student, we agreed to give
> him 100 escudos from our funds, so he and his companions
> would not lack food. This was for a common fund to which
> all contributed so that all could eat. And the men who tra-
> veled from the country to guard the invaded building also
> took potatoes, tortillas, eggs, cooked chickens and apples.
> They already knew how to contribute to the common cause.
>
> I went to the city with the second group. There I saw
> what a tremendous struggle it was for everyone, to help the
> young people in their protest, in full winter. Although we
> took turns in groups of six to eight people, it was very hard.
> It rained all the time. We had a meeting and decided to in-
> vade the street. We made barricades with some wood we
> found, which was being used to make a prefabricated house
> by the Office of Indian Affairs.
>
> Very soon the policemen arrived, but they couldn't
> arrest us. It was raining torrentially, and I was up to my
> knees in water. The policemen patiently redirected traffic
> onto another street. The personnel at the office of Indian
> Affairs couldn't get into their offices to work: the students

would tell them "This office has been invaded, gentlemen, return to your houses to rest."

One of the officers of the Bureau got desperate and took the president and secretary of the student group to Santiago in his station wagon. They went to have an interview with the Minister. The Minister promised to send the scholarship money and to allocate funds for a residence for Mapuche students. There! The strike was solved and the invaded building was returned!

We, the agriculturalists, support the students. We knew that their problem was almost the same as that of their peasant fathers. For if their fathers didn't have enough money to educate their children, it was because they hadn't enough land to cultivate. So, they needed the return of the lands which had been stolen from them by the rich latifundistas years ago, or else, they need the Government of Popular Unity to give them other lands.

We have recounted some of the relevant aspects of the life cycle of a Mapuche agriculturalist who became the leader of her group. Although we cannot present here all the necessary background for an exhaustive analysis of the reasons for the success of her innovative leadership, we will attempt an approximate diagnosis.

Llanquitray's structural position in Mapuche society facilitated her political role. First, she was the eldest daughter in her family, and she was single. Thus, she had as many rights as did her father in the family structure. When her next brother emigrated to Argentina, she and her father made decisions jointly about cultivating the family lands. She also was familiar with the procedures to obtain credits, tools, and fertilizers from the pertinent institutions of the national society, and thus became an intermediary who was knowledgeable about both Indian and Chilean society.

Her family, on both paternal and maternal sides, enjoyed prominent positions in Mapuche society. She was a descendant of ulmenes and loncos, a decisive factor contributing to the support she received from her followers during the processes of change they shared with her.

Leadership, as it is culturally defined among the Mapuche today, requires that the leader exhibit a group of attributes which originated far back in Araucanian history. Araucanian society never centralized Mapuche-Huilliche authority in a single individual or in an administrative body. Authority was divided among local units of government, headed by an <u>ulmen</u>, known in Spanish as a <u>cacique.</u> The <u>ulmen</u> was generally advised by a confidant, known as a <u>lonco.</u> The status of <u>ulmen</u> was hereditary through the paternal line. A respected <u>cacique</u> had the obligation of economic, religious, and social life of the community; and to serve as adviser and judge in the personal matters of given individuals.

Llanquitray's paternal ancestors were very influential (in modern Mapuche, all rich or influential people are called ulmen, whether or not they are lonco). and her grandfather's valor was well-known. On the maternal side, Llanquitray exhibited an impressive gallery of relatives active in regional politics or primary-level teaching.

Other important agents in Llanquitray's evolution as a leader were those who socialized her. Her maternal grandmother taught her love and concern for her language and culture. Her father contributed to her development by insisting on keeping alive the memory of her grandfather's exploits and his death while attempting to recover his usurped lands.

However, it is interesting to note that Mapuche society has always had two traditional types of leadership roles reserved to the female sex. The machi, or Mapuche shaman, was a woman in most cases; and the Mapuche perceived "doctor" as a feminine role. When a machi died, her prestige required the same kind of funeral as that of a publicly prominent man, whether or not he had been an ulmen or a lonco. The hue-pufe was also, until some 100 years ago, another leadership role traditionally reserved for women. She was the public orator who spoke at great tribal ceremonies and who, because of the wisdom she manifested, was permitted to give her opinions publicly.

As important as Llanquitray's structural position—together with her agents of socialization, and certain cultural elements—was the political framework that gave her the opportunity to express herself. Only within that framework was she able to participate in representing a great sector of the Mapuche, to mature as a strategist of change, and to thus crystallize her thinking as a leader.

> I believe that a good leader measures himself by the way he behaves before his group. There the leader must put himself at the service of the people who believe in him and support what the people think by satisfying their needs. A leader must not feel important, but must speak to the people, must analyze their most urgent problems, and try to solve them, whether they be great or small. A leader must also attempt to reconcile those who fight among themselves. What is important is to maintain the unity of the group, and take the problems up at the meeting, that is, to put them on the table, so that they may be discussed among all, and resolved among all.

> One must always let people know when one is aware of a problem. That is, the grass roots of the leader's support must be informed of everything.

> I believe that unity occurs in the face of the most urgent needs of the people. I am always ready to help when we speak of a topic that bothers us all, and that affects us all equally.

> It is very difficult to work with groups who wish to remain separate from others. Or those who don't want to act

because of fear. In spite of this, since there is never a
lack of problems or needs which affect everyone, one must
speak and dialogue with the people of such a group, until
their interests and needs are elicited. Only then can they
be urged on to action. All this without forcing, or imposing
upon them, one's own opinions or decisions. They must be
led to the point that they themselves can see how they can
benefit, or solve their problem better. The leader's decisions
must be those of the majority, so that all feel that they have
participated in them. Only in this way will a group of people
feel understood and represented by a leader. This way they
feel that the decision taken is everybody's and that it has
been analyzed and studied. When all have spoken, then one
can go ahead with a group. That's why I think that a person
with the capacity to lead cannot feel superior to the others,
but quite the contrary, a leader must feel that she is just
one more person in the group. For example, a leader should
never speak of having done this or that, or that he or she
is capable of many things, because then the people won't
accept it. That it why I am always talking about all of our
work, that we have all taken part in, and that we have all
benefited from.

Only in this way can people remain in agreement, and
this is the reason I appeared as a leader before the others.
I feel that I am only a woman, who has lived and suffered
and felt in her own flesh the problems of her marginalized
people. I was obliged through the pressure of all the Mapuche companions who believed in me to behave in the way
that I have, directing the invasion of a fundo. As the president of the invasion and of its organization, I have participated as an "important woman," but important only as long
as she is able to concern herself with interest and abnegation with the people's needs.

A woman with a sensible, human and spontaneous character has no problems in expounding her ideas and in making
plans: it is done in a more human way, with this feeling of
love for all. Every time that she feels understood, her ideas
become more profound, and her valor stronger before any ob-
stacle. Because she has a group in front of her who supports
her in her ideas, in a way that she becomes the voice of a
people. When she speaks, she feels she is not alone, but
that all are speaking, because she is expressing the thoughts
of others. This I have found very important: because when one
speaks and transmits ideas, one expounds the problems of
others. For this reason, one must take account of the opinions of the people, and moreover, accept their ideas.

Here a woman's patience is important; because I think
it is much harder among men, because men are authoritarian.

So there is a given moment in which his patience comes
to an end, and he becomes a director. He tries to im-
plant his ideas, and practically begins to give them out
as rules for the rest of the people. He tells them they
must do this, do that, and that's it. In contrast, the
woman says: "Well, we could do this . . . and you, what
do you think? Do you think it would work out better this
way?" The people then feel secure, and sure that they
are participating.

REFERENCES

Barraclough, Solon, et al. 1973. Chile reforma agraria y gobierno Popular. Buenos Aires: Ediciones Periferia.

Bunster, Ximena. 1964. "Una experiencia de antropologia aplicada entre
los Araucanos." Anales de la Universidad de Chile No. 130.

_____. 1968. "Adaptation in Mapuche Life: Natural and Directed." Doc-
toral dissertation, Columbia University.

_____. 1970. "Algunas consideraciones en torno a la dependencia cul-
tural y al cambio entre los Mapuches." In Segunda semana indi-
genista. Temuco: Ediciones Universitarias de la Frontera.

Greenberg, Edward S., ed. 1970. Political Socialization. New York:
Atherton Press.

Jaquette, Jane S., ed. 1974. Women in Politics, New York: John Wiley.

Nash, June. 1974. "A Critique of Social Science Models of Contemporary
Latin American Reality." Paper read at the Congress on Feminine
Perspectives in the Social Sciences, Buenos Aires.

Stuchlik, Milan. 1974. Rasgos de la sociedad Mapuche contemporanea.
Santiago: Ediciones Nueva Universidad.

Zimbalist Rosaldo, Michelle, and Louise Lamphere, eds. 1974. Woman,
Culture and Society. Stanford: Stanford University Press.

drugs: abuse, 266; hallucinogenic, 91, 97
Dubois, W. E. B., 3
dyadic relations, 90, 91

ecology, 11
economy: agrarian, 105; capacity of, 183;
    change of, 13, 105, 166, 175, 206; de-
    pendency of, 161; development of, 71,
    129, 151, 184, 199, 222, 224; and
    divorce, 77-78; and dominance, 236; and
    family, 291; growth of, 184; household,
    131, 132, 140-42; indexes of, 1, 3, 7,
    224; industrial, 105; instability of, 77-
    78; international integration of, 147;
    leaders of, 230; organization of, 291;
    peasant, 130; potency of, 37; and pro-
    fessions, 199; rural, 71; service, 169;
    specialized production in, 166, 169;
    subsistence, 52; underdeveloped, 308;
    urban, 134-36; and women in, 203, 224
Ecuador, 222, 269
education, 13-14, 26, 40, 43, 49, 74, 120,
    140, 162, 169-70, 174, 175, 183, 196,
    197-98, 199, 200, 202, 206, 210, 232,
    237, 238, 250, 265, 266, 268-69, 272,
    273, 288, 297, 313; coeducation, 306;
    reform of, 283-84; university, 40; and
    women, 65
egalitarian: food distribution, 283; prin-
    ciples in labor legislation, 184; society,
    200
El Mercurio, 287-97
El Teniente, Chile, 284
electoral politics, 235
elite, 5, 26, 74, 87, 218, 221
employment, 105-08, 131-32, 139-40, 151,
    153, 169, 174, 183, 184-97, 199, 202,
    206, 208, 209, 233, 294
energy, 162
engineering, 199, 237, 297
Enlightenment, 49
entrepreneurs, 192
equality, 39, 171, 190, 202-11, 246, 273
equilibrium, 217, 253-56, 267
ethnic: group, 304; variation, 219
ethnocentrism, 87
Europe, 167
Eva, 298-300
evolution, 112, 192, 265
exchange, 95, 96, 164; control of, 163;
    value, 69; of women, 92
exploitation, 9, 196-97, 208, 233
expropriation, 309, 311

fascism, 280
factory, 188, 206, 294
family: and abortion, 43; and alienation, 80-
    81; and authority, 25-26, 33, 251; Better
    Family Living Projects, 10; and change,

28, 53, 80, 229-30; and children, 43,
    154-55, 200; and class, 25-26, 230-31;
    communal, 81; consumption unit, 28; con-
    trol, 118; defense of, 230-31; dependence
    on, 185; egalitarian, 12; extended, 8,
    237; and fertility, 63-64; and ideology,
    25-29, 115, 171-72; income, 7, 152, 170;
    land, 303; and machismo, 26; nuclear, 8,
    12, 81, 106, 112, 237; obligations, 190,
    294; planning, 61, 63-64; and polity, 250,
    254; and privacy, 80; roles, 70, 76, 115,
    239; size, 43, 118; and social control,
    229-30; and socialization, 32, 231; struc-
    ture, 25, 55, 63, 110, 291, 316; threats
    to, 218, 266, 297; urban, 139; and women,
    63-64, 148, 238
Federal and Insular Departments of Labor,
    Puerto Rico, 208
federal labor law, Mexico, 197
federations: Federacao Brasileira Pelo Pro-
    gresso Feminino, Brazil, 246; Federation
    of Students, Chile, 292; Free Labor Fed-
    eration, Puerto Rico, 208; National Fed-
    erations, Chile, 287
female: ambivalence, 148; base of household,
    75; behavior, 289, 295-96; bias in per-
    ception, 280; consciousness, 202; con-
    servatism, 229; discrimination, 184;
    entrepreneurs, 192; femininity, 190, 281,
    298; function, 290; labor market, 192;
    magazine readership, 299; mystique, 219;
    oppression, 238; participation, 148, 221-
    41; personality, 148; perspective, 83,
    302, 303; pessimism, 232; power, 222;
    production, 139; researchers, 199; re-
    sources, 240; roles, 228, 239; socializa-
    tion, 148; stereotypes, 9-11, 219, 289;
    tasks, 293; version of coup d'etat, Chile,
    279-300
feminism: Acción Feminista Dominica, Domin-
    ican Republic, 266-71; in Chile, 292; and
    class, 272; and education, 272; priorities
    in movement, 234; Reformist Feminists,
    Dominican Republic, 276; rhetoric, 280
food: committees for food distribution and
    price control, Chile, 283, 293; distribution,
    81, 286; Food and Agricultural Organization,
    10; industry, 188; scarcity, 289
France, 37, 49, 203
freedom: and class, 234; and domination, 159;
    to participate, 233; physical, 231; to work,
    226
Frente Nacional, Colombia, 228
fronts: corporate, 295; Democratic Women's
    Front, Chile, 282; popular front for women,
    Chile, 293; of women, 291
function: differential quality of, 170; eco-
    nomic, 206; and family, 28; functional
    equilibrium, 217; functional groups, 227;

NEUMA AGUIAR is with the Instituto Universitario de Pedquisas of Rio de Janeiro and has a Ph. D. from Washington University in Saint Louis.

MORRIS J. BLACHMAN is a professor in the Department of Government and International Studies, University of South Carolina.

XIMENA BUNSTER currently visiting Fulbright scholar in anthropology at Rutgers University and was formerly Professor of Anthropology, National University of Chile. Her Ph. D. in anthropology is from Columbia University.

JORGE GISSI BUSTOS is Professor of Psychology at the School of Social Work, Catholic University of Chile, and the author of several articles on male-female relationships in Latin America.

ELSA M. CHANEY is a professor at Fordham University and holds a Ph. D. from the University of Wisconsin. MARIANNE SCHMINK, a graduate student at the University of Texas at Austin, is doing research in South America on women in the labor force.

MARIA DEL CARMEN ELU DE LENERO is with the Instituto Mexicano de Estudios Sociales and is the author of La mujer que habla and A donde va la mujer.

GLORIA GONZALEZ SALAZAR is Professor of Economics at the Universidad Nacional Autonoma de Mexico and the author of numerous articles on the labor force in Mexico.

JANE JAQUETTE, Assistant Professor of Political Science at Occidental College in California, is editor of Women in Politics and numerous articles on women in Latin America. Her Ph. D. is from Cornell.

ELIZABETH JELIN is currently affiliated with the Centro de Estudios de Estado y Sociedad in Buenos Aires. She is a native of Argentina and has also worked in Mexico and Brazil, where research for this article was conducted.

MICHELE MATTELART now lives in Paris and was formerly with the Centro de Estidios de la Realidad Nacional in Santiago. She is the author, with Armand Mattelart, of La mujer chilena en una neuva sociedad and numerous articles on the mass media in Latin America.

VIVIAN M. MOTA is a graduate student at Cornell University and Professor of Sociology, Universidad Autonoma of Santo Domingo.

JUNE NASH is Professor of Anthropology at City College of New York and City University of New York, and has written In the Eyes of the Ancestors: Belief and Behavior in a Maya Community and, with Juan Corradi, Ideology and Social Change in Latin America.

ISABEL PICO VIDAL is Assistant Professor of Political Science at the University of Puerto Rico. She holds a Ph.D. from Harvard and has done extensive research on women and student movements in Puerto Rico.

HELEN ICKEN SAFA is Graduate Director and Professor of Anthropology at Rutgers and the author of The Urban Poor of Puerto Rico.

HELEIETH SAFFIOTI is Professor of Sociology at the Universidada de Araraquara and the author of La mujer na sociedate da clase, to be published in English as Women in Capitalist Society (Monthly Review Press).

JUDITH SHAPIRO is with the Department of Anthropology at the University of Chicago.

J.F. Bergin PAPERBACK TEXTS

* **PEOPLE IN CULTURE:** A Survey of Cultural Anthropology
Ino Rossi and contributors
ISBN 0-03-051021-X   1980

* **WOMEN AND COLONIZATION:** Anthropological Perspectives
Mona Etienne and Eleanor Leacock, editors
ISBN 0-03-052581-0   1980

* **A WORLD OF WOMEN:** Anthropological Studies
of Women in the Societies of the World
Erika Bourguignon and contributors
ISBN 0-03-051226-3   1980

AGING IN CULTURE AND SOCIETY: Comparative
Viewpoints and Strategies
Christine L. Fry and contributors
ISBN 0-089789-001-9   1980

and in Cloth

* **DIMENSIONS OF AN ANTHROPOLOGY OF AGING**
Christine L. Fry and contributors
ISBN 0-03-052971-9   1980

* **WHEN NOMADS SETTLE**
Philip C. Salzman and contributors
ISBN 0-03-052501-2   1980

* **THE ENTREPRENEUR AS CULTURE HERO:**
Preadaptations for Nigerian Economic Development
Bernard Belasco
ISBN 0-03-052096-9   1980

*Distributed by Praeger Publishers